A HIGH COUNTRY NEWS READER

A People's History of Wilderness

EDITED BY

MATT JENKINS

HIGH COUNTRY NEWS BOOKS
PAONIA, COLORADO

A People's History of Wilderness
Edited by Matt Jenkins

Publisher's Note: Many of the articles and essays published in *A People's History
of Wilderness* have been previously published in *High Country News*.

Cover design: Cindy Wehling
Interior design: Patty Holden Productions

This book is published on recycled stock.
High Country News Books is a signatory to the Green Press Initiative.

High Country News Books
PO Box 1090
Paonia, CO 81428

Library of Congress Cataloging-in-Publication Data

A people's history of wilderness / edited by Matt Jenkins.— 1st
American pbk. ed.
    p. cm.
 Previously published in *High Country News*.
 Includes index.
 ISBN 0-9744485-1-6 (pbk.)
 1. Wilderness areas—United States—History. I. Jenkins, Matt. II.
High Country News.
 QH76.P46 2005
  333.78'216'0973—dc22

                                                        2004020392

International Standard Book Number (ISBN): 0-9744485-1-6

Table of Contents

SECTION 3: Tapping the Wild

Preface

This book's intellectual home is not, as I once imagined it would be, the realms of classic wilderness like the High Sierra or Wyoming's Wind River Mountains, but a muddy oil and gas patch in northeast Utah that looked as if a battalion of panzer tanks had just plowed through it.

On a cold and clear day in December 2003, I met Uintah Mountain Club members Nancy Bostick-Ebbert, Paul Ebbert and Tom Elder in Vernal, Utah, and we set out in search of the White River proposed wilderness. For hours, we ground away in four-wheel drive through axle-deep mud, lost in the maze of oil and gas service roads, blindly turning down various forks, trying to find a way to the White River. Finally, we abandoned our vehicle at a well pad and walked down a rock-threaded dry wash.

Winding down into the depths of the river canyon, we entered a different world. Sphinx-like sandstone spires rose over a fringe of cottonwoods. The languid, ice-dappled glide of the White River's water, under a blanket of early winter light, mesmerized us as it flowed toward the Green River. There was no need to explain why this small piece of the vast federal estate deserved formal protection.

But the White River's journey toward wilderness protection, like that of many other areas in the American West, has been as tortured as the oil and gas well-perforated moonscape that surrounds it. In 1985, a local doctor named Will Durant, an oil and gas driller named Doug Hatch and a machinist named Clay Johnson gathered around Hatch's kitchen table to work out a proposal to add the White River to the National Wilderness Preservation System. The three wrote out a plan that covered 9,700 acres of spectacular river canyon that the landlord, the federal Bureau of Land Management, had never leased for oil and gas development.

But local politics had always been a tough game for environmentalists in the area. By the 1990s, with Utah politicians becoming increasingly anti-wilderness, the local Uintah Mountain Club turned for help to the Southern Utah Wilderness Alliance, a Salt Lake City-based environmental heavyweight.

SUWA expanded the White River proposal to about 19,000 acres and inserted it deep into the 9.1-million-acre statewide wilderness proposal that it, along with numerous smaller groups under the umbrella of the Utah Wilderness Coalition, was trying to sell to a national constituency over the heads of the Utah delegation.

The strategy, Bostick-Ebbert told me, was this: "If your reasonable requests are not met with any type of civility, ask for a lot more, and then you'll be able to negotiate back to a reasonable middle."

The proposal never got far in Congress, and although various members of Utah's congressional delegation proposed several wilderness bills of their own, SUWA fought them, insisting that anything less than 9.1 million acres was a sham.

For a few years, the stalemate held. Under the Clinton administration, the Department of the Interior gave interim protection to millions of acres of citizen-proposed wilderness, including the expanded White River proposal, where much of the newly added land had already been leased by a consortium of oil and gas companies. Though most of the citizen-proposed lands got no closer to formal protection as wilderness, they were, by and large, off-limits to development.

But holding the line with administrative "de facto" wilderness protection was a world away from convincing Congress to provide permanent wilderness protection. After Republican George W. Bush took office as president in 2001, he began a series of sweeping changes to federal policy that prioritized energy development and reduced protections for public lands. And in March 2003, the state of Utah resurrected a six-year old lawsuit challenging the federal government's authority to protect citizen-proposed wilderness lands. Just two weeks later, Bush's Interior secretary, Gale Norton, and then-Utah Gov. Mike Leavitt, R, settled the case. Suddenly, millions of acres of proposed wilderness lands—not just in Utah, but across the entire West—were open for drilling and other development.

It was a stunning concession on the part of the federal government, but it also showed how vulnerable those lands had always been. One wilderness organizer I spoke with after the settlement said, "That was always the risk with the all-or-nothing strategy— everything you were holding could disappear in a heartbeat."

The stalemate over wilderness had suddenly turned into an outright crisis, and the White River proposed wilderness symbolized what was at stake. The settlement opened the door for the oil and gas consortium to begin the permitting process to drill 15 wells in the area. Within months, the Bureau of Land Management began auctioning off leases in 18 citizen-proposed wilderness areas in Utah, and seven citizen-proposed wilderness areas in New Mexico, Wyoming and Colorado. A second round of leases was auctioned off during the summer of 2004.

With the 40th anniversary of the Wilderness Act at hand, the time seemed ripe for a re-examination of the wilderness movement.

President Lyndon Johnson signed the Wilderness Act into law on Sept. 3, 1964. The act defined wilderness as an area "affected primarily by the forces of nature, with the imprint of man's work substantially unnoticeable," that "has outstanding opportunities for solitude or a primitive and unconfined type of recreation." The Wilderness Act immediately created 9.1 million acres of wilderness on land managed by the U.S. Forest Service, National Park Service and the U.S. Fish and Wildlife Service (the Wilderness Act was extended to the Bureau of Land Management in 1976).

In the years after 1964, Congress added nearly 10 times more land to the National Wilderness Preservation System, which today includes 662 wilderness areas totaling some 106 million acres. By delegating the authority to create wilderness to Congress, the Wilderness Act democratized the wilderness movement, allowing citizens to develop their own proposals and take them to their congressional representatives. That tradition was established with the 1965 Lincoln-Scapegoat Wilderness proposal in Montana, described in Section 1. Over the years, it has led to the creation of numerous statewide citizens' coalitions and a wide array of individual groups, including the Southern Utah Wilderness Alliance, Colorado Environmental Coalition, Nevada Wilderness Project, Friends of Nevada Wilderness, New Mexico Wilderness Alliance, Arizona Wilderness Coalition, Montana Wilderness Association, Wyoming Outdoor Council, Idaho Conservation League, Oregon Natural Desert Association and Oregon Natural Resources Council, the Washington Wilderness Coalition, the California Wilderness Coalition and smaller organizations such as the Uintah Mountain Club.

It is these citizens' groups and their grassroots proposals—precisely the land stripped of protection with the 2003 Utah wilderness settlement—that now stand at the center of debates about the future of wilderness.

High Country News arrived on the scene in 1970, just as the movement began to hit its stride. Based first in Lander, Wyo., and then in Paonia, Colo., *HCN* was, and still is, the only newspaper to cover Western environmental and community issues on a regional level. (The paper covers Colorado, Utah, Montana, Wyoming, Idaho, New Mexico, Arizona, Nevada, California, Oregon and Washington—the area that, consequently, is the focus of this book.)

HCN was established by a wildlife biologist and rancher named Tom Bell, who, as his successor Ed Marston later wrote, "was most shaped by his love of nature and by his reaction to the collapse of the West's natural world brought on by man's bludgeoning of it. One of his several responses was to found *High Country News* as his pulpit." That sermonizing spirit set the early tone for *HCN*, which was an incubator—and occasional halfway house—for some of the West's rising environmentalist stars.

In later years, under Ed and his wife, Betsy, who became editor, *HCN* kept alive Tom Bell's passion for the land. At the same time, it took on a more critical, journalistic role—occasionally provoking the ire of the environmental community that it covers.

This book draws on the best of the nearly 500 stories about wilderness that *High Country News* has run over 34 years. It brings many stories back into the light after a long layover in the paper's archives, and offers an inside look at how wilderness is made—from the pivotal people behind the Wilderness Act, to the creation of citizens' wilderness proposals and the arduous process of building political support for them, to the intense and ongoing doctrinal debates within the movement.

If you spend even a little time with working wilderness activists, you quickly appreciate the tremendous powers of imagination it can take to see past the parts of the job that don't show up in the photographs on The Wilderness Society's calendars—the bad maps, the burned-out clutches in four-wheel drives, the cactus spines in the knees, the drill rig that suddenly shows up in the middle of a proposed wilderness area.

It can be supremely unglamorous work. John Wallin, a Nevada wilderness organizer, once told me: "We ask volunteers, 'What do you want to do?' and they'll say, 'Whatever you want.' So we're like, 'Great! Then help us lick a thousand envelopes.'"

But it's real work, and important work, and it takes a lot of it just to keep the idea of wilderness alive. Forty years after the Wilderness Act was passed, the wilderness movement is facing serious challenges. But as the stories in this book show, the movement has a rich heritage to draw from—one which can offer genuine solutions for places like the White River.

—Matt Jenkins

Acknowledgments

Heartfelt acknowledgment is due to Tom Bell, who created *High Country News* and turned it into one of the West's real icons, and to Ed and Betsy Marston, whose thoughtful journalism became the standard that the paper's next generation is striving to uphold. *High Country News* — along with the entire West — owes an immense debt to all of the staff writers and editors, and especially the freelancers, who have tried to make sense of the region for 34 years.

This book would not have come together without the interest, encouragement and challenges from the current editorial team at *High Country News*. Publisher Paul Larmer, who has always had a keen sense of the role wilderness plays in debates about the future of the West, provided valuable suggestions for the introduction. Editor Greg Hanscom, who first suggested doing the book when I was still hosing the mud off my truck after the White River trip, helped untangle the latter sections. Greg has always insisted that his staff never call a spade anything other than a spade, and both the paper and its readers are better off for that. Assistant editor Laura Paskus read and provided valuable comments on innumerable drafts, and repeatedly convinced me, in moments of doubt, that wilderness really *is* important. Contributing editor Michelle Nijhuis, who worked her magic on many of these stories when they first appeared in *HCN*, returned to help edit several sections of the book. Thanks also go to Cindy Wehling, *HCN*'s tireless art director, for making this the book we wanted it to be. Diane Sylvain helped sand the burrs off the stories and commentary contained herein.

Thanks are due as well to Doug Scott, the wilderness movement's in-house historian and the policy director of Campaign for America's Wilderness, and Tim Mahoney, a longtime wilderness champion who is now a consultant to the Campaign. Both men have been unstintingly generous with their time and knowledge.

This book is for Laura, who is rootin', tootin', reporter's-note-book-wielding proof that being a great journalist does not mean having to be dispassionate. Thank you.

The Minds
Behind Wilderness

Aldo Leopold, the primary force behind the creation of
the Gila Wilderness in New Mexico in 1924.

—PHOTO COURTESY UNIVERSITY OF WISCONSIN-MADISON ARCHIVES

A t first glance, wilderness doesn't seem to have much to do with people. The authors of the Wilderness Act, for instance, took great care to write "man" out of the picture:

"A wilderness, in contrast with those areas where man and his own works dominate the landscape, is hereby recognized as an area where the earth and its community of life are untrammeled by man, where man himself is a visitor who does not remain."

Yet in reality, the story of the Wilderness Act—and of wilderness—is as much about people as about land.

This section opens with competing accounts of who was the "father" of America's wilderness system. On the one hand is forester and naturalist Aldo Leopold, who argued for the creation of the Gila Wilderness in New Mexico in 1924, 40 years before the Wilderness Act. On the other is Forest Service recreational engineer Arthur Carhart, the man whom writer Peter Wild says was responsible for "the first official act of wilderness preservation," at Trappers Lake, Colo., in 1919.

Regardless of who was first, their actions set into motion an evolving system of wilderness protection. In 1929, the Forest Service began to designate "primitive areas." Then, in 1939, at the urging of Forest Service lands and recreation chief Bob Marshall, the agency issued a regulation that allowed it to designate "wilderness" areas.

The next big leap forward was the call for congressionally protected wilderness, an idea that was honed over the next decade and a half by numerous luminaries. In 1956, Howard Zahniser, the executive director of The Wilderness Society, wrote the first draft of the Wilderness Act, and Minnesota Sen. Hubert Humphrey and Pennsylvania Rep. John Saylor introduced it to Congress. Despite growing public sentiment for wilderness, it would still take eight hard years—and more than sixty drafts of the Wilderness Act—before it finally passed.

In the years following 1964, members of Congress, such as

Sen. Lee Metcalf, D-Mont., have helped usher numerous important wilderness bills to the floor of Congress. But the effort was by no means limited to high-profile congressmen. Other pieces in this section tell the stories of the movement's local foot soldiers, including Montana hardware store owner Cecil Garland, who crusaded to create the country's first citizen-proposed wilderness, the Lincoln-Scapegoat. They also chronicle the rise of a new generation of professional wilderness activists, whose work spanned the country from the marbled halls of Congress to long days on the road, traveling between wilderness field hearings in the West.

SEPTEMBER 11, 1989

The Gila Turns 65: Our First Wilderness

BY BECKY RUMSEY

In that country which lies around the headwaters of the Gila River I was reared. This range was our fatherland; among these mountains our wigwams were hidden; the scattered valleys contained our fields; the boundless prairies, stretching away on every side, were our pastures; the rocky caverns were our burying places...

— Geronimo, Apache chieftain, *Autobiography* (1905)

In 1924, quietly, and with very little fanfare, the U.S. Forest Service created the first federal wilderness reserve. It was the Gila Wilderness of New Mexico, born out of the urgings of a young and eloquent forester named Aldo Leopold. It would take another 40 years and 6,000 pages of testimony before Congress passed a national wilderness bill. In contrast, the document creating the Gila Wilderness was a mere eight-page inter-office memo setting aside nearly 800,000 acres.

Today, the Gila contains 558,000 acres—the 1964 Wilderness Act split off the adjacent 202,000-acre Aldo Leopold Wilderness. The Gila ranges in altitude from 5,000 feet to nearly 11,000 feet. Known for its rich riparian habitats, it is home to varied and numerous wildlife in the West.

"There are seven different life zones in the United States," says Andrew Gulliford, director of Western New Mexico University's museum, "and five of them are represented in the Gila."

Both recreational and species diversity make the Gila special to New Mexico author Dutch Salmon. He says it combines elements of the Rocky Mountains and the Sierra Madre of Mexico.

"Within a hundred miles of Silver City you can go from the Lower Sonoran Zone, which is Chihuahuan grassland full of cholla and mesquite, to an alpine zone that gets 40 inches of rain or snowfall a year and is full of blue spruce."

"Take the Gila River as another example," says Salmon, who canoed 200 miles down the river and wrote a book about it. "As the water temperature changes, you go from trout, the rare Gila trout, browns and rainbows, to mountain bass, and then to channel and flathead catfish."

Salmon is current chairman of the New Mexico Wilderness Study Committee, a citizens' advisory group working with the Bureau of Land Management and members of Congress on wilderness designation.

"So much has been destroyed by dams, floods and channelization," he says. "Of the few riparian areas left in the Southwest, the best are found along the Gila and San Francisco rivers." Both run through the Gila Wilderness.

Walking along this high prairie in the sombre sunset with a howling wind tossing the old cedars along the rim, and a soaring raven croaking over the abyss below, was a solemn and impressive experience. Jumped three white-tails right out on the prairie but it was too late to see horns. They were very pretty bounding over the sea of yellow grama grass with the wind blowing them along like thistledown.
—Aldo Leopold, trip to the Gila backcountry, 1927,
Aldo Leopold: His Life and Work, Curt Meine

When Aldo Leopold arrived in New Mexico in 1909, fresh out of the Yale School of Forestry, the Gila was one of only six roadless areas left in the Southwest. "By the mid-1920s, the Gila was the only one left," says Leopold's biographer, Curt Meine.

Leopold was a naturalist and a hunter who became a forester. In the years he spent in the Southwest working for the U.S. Forest Service, he founded the profession of game management and later helped create the science of ecology. He would go on to help found The Wilderness Society and write the lyrical and descriptive book, *A Sand County Almanac*. An independent and visionary thinker, Leopold also had the ability to communicate and build relationships with local hunters and ranchers alike. He spent years forging a game protection league out of Albuquerque sportsmen, an association which helped to reform the New Mexico Game and Fish Department.

Land, then, is not merely soil; it is a fountain of energy flowing through a circuit of soils, plants and animals. Food chains are the living channels which conduct energy upward; death and decay return it to the soil. The circuit is not closed; some energy is dissipated in decay, some is added by absorption from the air, some is stored in soils, peats and long-lived forests; but it is a sustained circuit, like a slowly augmented revolving fund of life.

—Leopold, *A Sand County Almanac*

Leopold came to the Southwest as a utilitarian forester. But his experiences in the region become a source for his developing sense of the interconnectedness of all species to the land. He would eventually conclude, and express in *A Sand County Almanac*, that wilderness, in addition to its material value, was essential for scientific, cultural, recreational and aesthetic reasons.

As assistant forester in charge of operations, a post he acquired in 1919, he studied and inventoried the Datil, Carson, Manzano, Gila, Santa Fe and Apache national forests. He was alarmed by overgrazing, soil erosion and diminishing game herds. But his primary concern was the disappearance of large roadless areas.

Leopold was not alone in his growing recognition that the nation's forests and wildlands had worth beyond their material value. The National Park Service had eagerly embarked on a "good roads" plan aimed at bringing the newly motorized nation to the scenery and recently constructed visitor centers of its national parks. The Forest Service itself was just beginning to promote scenery and recreation as forest "products." But Leopold had another kind of sport and beauty in mind.

"Mechanized recreation already has seized nine-tenths of the woods and mountains," he would later write. "A decent respect for minorities should dedicate the other tenth to wilderness."

Our ability to perceive quality in nature begins, as in art, with the pretty. It expands through successive stages of the beautiful to values as yet uncaptured by language.

—Leopold, *A Sand County Almanac*

In 1919, Leopold found a kindred spirit in Arthur Carhart, a landscape architect working for the Forest Service in Denver. The agency asked Carhart to design the placement of vacation homes around Trappers Lake in western Colorado. He had also toured the Quetico-Superior region between Minnesota and Ontario. In both cases he suggested that the areas remain undeveloped and that the Forest Service manage the land for wilderness scenery and recreation.

"The thought of preserving portions of the national forests in their wild state seems to have occurred to Leopold at least as early as 1913," writes Meine. "He did not advertise the thought. It was, quite simply, a radical notion, and it developed only slowly."

Finally, in 1921, Leopold went public with his ideas about wilderness protection. He wrote "The Wilderness and Its Place in Forest Recreation Policy," which appeared in the November issue of the *Journal of Forestry*.

In that article, Leopold wrote that the policy of "greatest good for the greatest number" in forest planning "had already done enough to raise the question of whether the policy of development…should continue to govern in absolutely every instance, or whether the principle of highest use does not itself demand that representative portions of some forests be preserved as wilderness."

Leopold did not stop with the general idea of wilderness preservation. He also proposed "setting aside the headwaters of the Gila River, high in the Mogollon Mountains of west-central New Mexico." According to Meine, Leopold's main concern in preserving the Gila as a primitive area was that it was a prime hunting ground. Its economic value was slight. "There was only a bit of logging," says Meine. "Its main value was in recreation and in preserving the watershed itself."

By "wilderness" I mean a continuous stretch of country preserved in its natural state, open to lawful hunting and fishing, big enough to absorb a two weeks' pack trip, and kept devoid of roads, artificial trails, cottages, or other works of man.

> —Leopold's initial definition of wilderness, from "The Wilderness and Its Place in Forest Recreation Policy," 1921

By today's standards the Gila is still a remote wilderness. No other wilderness receives fewer visitors. The nearest big cities, El Paso and Tucson, are both over 200 miles away, and nearby Silver City has a population of only 12,000. It is the biggest wilderness area left in the Southwest, and as Dutch Salmon puts it: "You can really get lost in there."

"The Gila was a benchmark in Leopold's thinking about wild lands," says Gulliford. It was also the platform from which he sprang into an understanding of ecology. Leopold hunted and fished in the Gila. In the early years he was concerned about the disappearance of big game herds, and that meant that he was a proponent of predator control. His thinking about predators and their role in the health of natural systems would change, but only gradually.

The disastrous occurrence of over-populated deer in the Kaibab National Forest caused Leopold to rethink some of his game management theories, especially when the same kind of range destruction and subsequent mass starvation threatened to repeat itself in the Gila and elsewhere.

We all strive for safety, prosperity, comfort, long life and dullness. The deer strives with its supple legs, the cowman with trap and poison, the statesman with pen, the most of us with machines, votes, and dollars, but it all comes to the same thing: peace in our time. A measure of success in this is all well enough...but too much safety seems to yield only danger in the long run. Perhaps this is behind Thoreau's dictum: In wildness is the salvation of the world. Perhaps this is the hidden meaning in the howl of the wolf, long known among mountains, but seldom perceived among men.

— Leopold, *A Sand County Almanac*

In 1924, when the Forest Service created the Gila Wilderness, most native predators had been exterminated. Ben Tilly, a contemporary of Leopold's, was a mountain man who killed grizzly bears and mountain lions for both the Forest Service and the U.S. Biological Survey.

Tilly tracked large predators in the Gila area from 1916 to the 1930s. "He traveled with his dogs, his frying pan, his rifle and his knife," says Gulliford. "He was an extraordinary hunter and tracker. He made his own knives, never bathed or shaved, never drank and never killed anything on Sunday. But he could tree a bear on Sunday and hold it with his dogs while he waited for Monday."

In 1931, the last grizzly bear was trapped out of the Gila. "In 1909, when I first came to the West," Leopold wrote later in *A Sand County Almanac*, "there were grizzlies in every major mountain mass, but you could travel for months without seeing a conservation officer. Today there is some kind of conservation officer 'behind every bush,' yet as wildlife bureaus grow, our most magnificent mammal retreats steadily toward the Canadian border. Of the 6,000 grizzlies officially reported as remaining in areas owned by the United States, 5,000 are in Alaska. Only five states have any at all. There seems to be a tacit assumption that if grizzlies survive in Canada and Alaska that is good enough. It is not good enough for me. The Alaskan bears are a distinct species. Relegating grizzlies to Alaska is about like relegating happiness to heaven; one may never get there."

"By officially designating the Gila a wilderness," writes biographer Meine, "Western culture had in fact taken final possession of the wilderness. It was a conquest, albeit a conquest of the gentlest kind. It conquered by recognizing that there is a point beyond which the spoils of conquest are no longer commensurate with the value of the vanquished. For all the settlers' energy and impertinence, here was a sign of cultural foresight, a willingness to let a wild place be."

Wilderness is a resource which can shrink but not grow. Invasions can be arrested or modified in a manner to keep an area usable either for recreation, science or for wildlife, but the creation of new wilderness in the full sense of the word is impossible.

It follows, then, that any wilderness program is a rearguard action, through which retreats are reduced to a minimum.

— Leopold, *A Sand County Almanac*

A "Beauty Engineer" Births the Wilderness System

BY PETER WILD

Feel pent up in a "heat-cursed" city? Do you yearn for "the music of water splashing through a rocky stream bed mingled with the chuckle of a diminutive waterfall"? You're in luck. Now, for a fee of between $10 and $25 per year, "every citizen of the country is given the opportunity to own a summer home built on forest land." Interested? Just contact your local national forest ranger, a "generally well-known and liked" fellow.

This was the unblushing come-on of a Forest Service propagandist celebrating Public Law 63-293 of 1915. Under its provisions, common folk like you and me could lease a few acres from Uncle Sam, build a vacation home and sit back to enjoy "reflected light, flashing from snow-capped peaks."

In its day, the plan seemed a grand step for democracy on the nation's forest lands, but in the 68 years since its passage, many a "generally well-known and liked" ranger has torn his hair in distraction over the biting dogs, sewage overflows, traffic jams and family shootouts he's had to contend with owing to the presence of summer homes on his district. No wonder that in recent years Forest Service officialdom has smilingly tried to nudge these formerly blessed interlopers off the public's lands and back to their "heat-cursed" cities.

Curiously enough, this plunges us immediately into a quite different but equally knotty tussle. Who was the "father" of America's wilderness system? The two seemingly opposed events—the opening of forest lands to officially encouraged squatters and the founding of our chain of wilderness preserves—are bedfellows.

"Forestry is tree farming," pontificated Gifford Pinchot, who in 1905, with bumptious help from President Theodore Roosevelt, established the U.S. Forest Service. Its job: to grow and cut trees. About as simple as that. But by World War I, and especially in the years immediately following, the rapidly industrializing society was foisting unexpected pressures on the national forests. Not least among the causes were the expanding population, growth in leisure time and Henry Ford's sputtering but threatening-to-become-ubiquitous Model T. In sum, people wanted to travel, and they now had the means to do it. The somewhat bewildered ranger stepping forth to cruise timber found them camping out in increasing numbers on his tree farm. That brought the timber-oriented agency on a collision course with recreation. "Well, what the heck," reasoned the Forest Service. "Give them a few roads and campgrounds"—and with mounting enthusiasm for the agency's new mission of public service—"why not leases for summer homes to boot?"

That decision brought a young man striding in backpack to the shores of Trappers Lake in Colorado's White River National Forest, where he rested his bones one evening in Scott Teague's ramshackle fishing camp. In 1919, armed with a degree in landscape architecture from Iowa State College at Ames, the recently discharged first lieutenant managed to talk his way into the Forest Service as its first "Recreational Engineer."

"Beauty engineer," winked the callused old hands, but he seemed harmless enough, "a good fellow," judged an in-house publication for Forest Service employees. His mission: stomp around the lake a bit, take out his pencil and map and draw in sites for a few hundred summer homes. Then, survey a road around the pristine body of water.

He was still young, only 27, feisty, and open to new ideas. One night around the campfire, two of Teague's guests, Paul J. Rainey and William McFadden, began filling his head with them. One can imagine the conversation.

Rainey and McFadden: "What do you want to hack out hundreds of cabin sites and a road for?"

Recreational Engineer: "Dunno. That's what they told me to do."

R & M: "Son, that'll bring the unwashed herd in droves. They'll ruin this isolated place with their screaming kids, marshmallow wrappers and ukulele strummin'. You want that?"

The young man leaps defiantly to his feet. "By gumbo, no!"

The young whippersnapper runs back over the Rocky Mountains to his office in Denver and draws up the plans as directed, but also inserts, entirely gratis, a strong opinion opposing "improvement" to the area.

His boss sees his reasoning about the dangers in too much of a good thing, scraps the road and starts withdrawing the permits for vacation homes. An unprecedented step in Forest Service history, this championing of beauty over use. And there we have, at Trappers Lake on the West Slope of the Colorado Rockies, the first official act of wilderness preservation.

This is heresy among some historians. We all know, or at least thought we knew, that Aldo Leopold, a forest ranger in New Mexico, was the motivating force behind setting aside the Gila, the world's first wilderness preserve, in 1924. Most of the books on conservation history cite the Gila as the beginning milepost, and many of them skim over, or fail to mention, upstart Arthur Carhart and his successful proposal for Trappers Lake. Added to that, we all recognize Leopold's lucid mind, professional generosity and activities in The Wilderness Society. The eloquence of his classic statement on land care in *A Sand County Almanac* charms us. Out of sentiment and habitual thinking, we hesitate to begrudge Aldo Leopold the honor of "father" of the wilderness system.

Human nature being what it is, we cling to the idea of "firsts." It makes us comfortable in a mutable world to have solid reference points. We're glad to declare, without much chance of being wrong, that Sir David Brewster invented the kaleidoscope in 1816. But things aren't always that simple. Did Columbus really discover America? Evanescent Vikings scouted our shores hundreds of years before him. Did Leibniz or Newton create that bane of math students, calculus? Often in this business of "firsts" we plunge into murky waters. We know, for instance, that Alfred Russell Wallace and Charles Darwin hit upon the theory of evolution about the same time. The idea was "in the air," as they say. It took someone with vision to snatch it and tie it down. So the credit goes to Wallace and Darwin, though the popular mind conveniently anchors the credit to Darwin.

A similar process was at work in the unfolding of the wilderness idea. A host of thinkers in the nineteenth century—from George Catlin and Henry David Thoreau right on down to Frederick Law Olmsted and John Muir—advocated preserving wild nature. But we're looking for something concrete, the first solid link in the chain of events that leads directly to congressional creation of the Wilderness System in 1964.

In an article appearing in *The Living Wilderness* of December, 1980, Roderick Nash staunchly defends the Gila and Aldo Leopold on this score. In contrast, Donald Baldwin's book *The Quiet Revolution,* expends 295 pages documenting his decision to lay the laurel at the feet of Trappers Lake and Arthur Carhart. Despite Nash's well-deserved reputation as an historian, Baldwin may be right.

Soon after the discussion with his Denver supervisor over the future of Trappers Lake, Carhart drew up a broad plan for the area, thus formulating in 1919, according to Baldwin, "the first written blueprint which spelled out the wilderness concept as it is understood today." Added to that, the peripatetic "beauty engineer" subsequently traveled to Minnesota. Inspired by his canoeing through the lake-and-forest country, Carhart wrote a second document recommending "immediate action toward general preservation of good timber stands" so that "aesthetic qualities shall, where of high merit, take precedence over…commercialization" on the Superior National Forest. With Carhart's continuing activities, and with support from the Izaak Walton League, Zane Grey and Herbert Hoover, the region eventually won protection as the renowned Boundary Waters Canoe Area.

Thus, acting in 1919 and again in 1922, Carhart had taken the first two steps for wilderness. Chronologically, Leopold took the third. As Baldwin puts it, the outline for Trappers Lake set the "guiding principles." Then "Carhart's plan for the Superior National Forest was approved in 1922, two years before the one proposed by Aldo Leopold for the Gila National Forest, New Mexico, which was not formally approved until June 3, 1924."

Carhart, we might note, followed up his early environmental interests by becoming an outdoor writer of note, by speaking out in the movement that culminated in passage of the Wilderness Act of 1964 and by founding the outstanding Conservation Library of the Denver Public Library.

One more nail needs to be driven in the Carhart-Leopold controversy. Back in 1919, down in New Mexico, ranger Aldo Leopold caught wind of his colleague's first radical suggestions for Trappers Lake. Carhart's preservation stance so appealed to Leopold that he traveled to Denver to see what was boiling in the beauty engineer's pot. Nash pooh-poohs the meeting: "Leopold was five years older than Carhart, was a graduate of the prestigious Yale School of Forestry and was far senior to the recreational engineer in terms of Forest Service status. He was well on his way toward a philosophy of the value of wilderness, and it is logical to presume that he impressed his younger colleague rather than vice versa."

Nash's first sentence is accurate, but his conclusion does not necessarily follow from his premise. In fact, after the Denver discussion, it was Leopold who was so intrigued by the younger man that he asked Carhart to put down his ideas for him in writing. The resulting four-page "Memorandum for Mr. Leopold, District 3" questions the proliferation of "manmade improvements" at

Trappers Lake in particular and on forest lands in general. It goes on to state prophetically: "Time will come when these scenic spots, where nature has been allowed to remain unmarred, will be some of the most highly prized scenic features of the country…" As the document unfolds, it sounds very much as if the younger Carhart were instructing Mr. Leopold, not vice versa.

In any case, the Carhart-Leopold dispute is a controversy born of historians. In their day, the two foresters did not perceive themselves as combatants for first place. In fact, the men's lives are striking in their similarities. Both were from Iowa; both shared broad wilderness concepts; both worked for the Forest Service, then quit in frustration to become writers on conservation issues. Both played significant roles in gaining, nearly twenty years ago, congressional recognition of the areas protected for decades as wilderness by the Forest Service.

And both, we might imagine, now stand in that Great Wilderness in the Sky, their arms around each other, chuckling down on the Carhart-Leopold debate.

Bob Marshall: Last of the Radical Bureaucrats

BY PETER WILD

The woodsman undressed, cranked up his record player, then leaped into bed. He lay there, listening to Schubert's "Unfinished Symphony" while watching the northern lights twitch in the Arctic night outside his cabin window. Before drifting off to sleep, the millionaire thought about his Eskimo and sourdough friends and reminded himself that he had again returned to "the happiest civilization of which I have knowledge."

Years later, hikers in the Lower 48 remembered that their famous companion preferred riding to trail heads on the running board of a car—the better to awaken his senses to the coming experiences. A romantic indeed, some might conclude—one of those exuberant and wealthy few who can afford to indulge occasional whims for rustic adventure.

On the trail, however, Robert Marshall quickly proved to be more than that. A typical day for him was 40 miles over rugged terrain with a full pack, and he was known to do 70 miles cross-country—no pace for a dilettante.

He was indeed a millionaire, a man of culture with a Ph.D. in plant physiology, who could quote as easily from the Latin poets as from Bertrand Russell and who could build a boat with an ax to cross an Arctic river. He was a best-selling writer, a radical and, for all that, one of the government's most effective bureaucrats. Historian Roderick Nash calls him "one of the most colorful figures" in conservation.

Shortly after his death, an unusual accolade to a bureaucrat appeared in the *New Republic*. "Gap in the Front Lines" testified to his abilities to move others: "He was an unwearied, unsentimental, common-sense radical who never supported any movement without participating in it wholeheartedly and responsibly. He was the one guy who could always pull you out of the squirrel-cage and make you feel again the excitement, importance and opportunity in what you were trying to do." Little wonder that Eskimos, Washington socialites and fellow bureaucrats—whether or not they agreed with his politics—enjoyed Marshall's company.

The movement that Marshall crystallized had a long but disconnected history. In 1864, Frederick Law Olmsted and other Californians persuaded the government to set aside the Yosemite Valley as a scenic preserve. Prodded thereafter by various citizen groups, Congress added units over the years, and in 1916 brought them together under the National Park Service. In the 1920s, a hesitant Forest Service began a policy of creating primitive areas when a young ranger, Aldo Leopold, convinced the agency to forbid exploitation on one-half million acres of New Mexico's Gila National Forest.

The concept of keeping part of America as wilderness was slowly taking hold, but by the 1930s, it still lacked a spokesman to consolidate the often vague notions of preservation into national policy. Aimed at moving citizens both inside and outside government, Marshall's articles in *The Nation*, *The New York Times* and *Nature Magazine* pressed that wilderness "is melting away like the last snowbank on some south-facing mountainside during a hot afternoon in June."

Uniquely talented and well-connected, Marshall became the pivot on which the country turned toward a firm wilderness commitment. The legislation implementing his ideas, however, came 25 years after his death, and since history often is slow to sort out individuals responsible for change, he has yet to receive full credit for the accomplishment.

"As a boy," reflected this founder of The Wilderness Society, "I spent many hours in the heart of New York City, dreaming of

Lewis and Clark and their glorious exploration into an unbroken wilderness which embraced three-quarters of a continent. Occasionally my reveries ended in terrible depression, and I would imagine that I had been born a century too late for genuine excitement."

Pioneers straining to hack and hoe a livelihood from the wilds rarely thought of their awesome surroundings in such wistful terms. But the city boy's dreaming, an intensified version of America's yearning for a lost past, formed the mainspring for Marshall's future activism.

The son of a Jewish immigrant, Robert Marshall's father remembered family stories of repression and hardship in European ghettos. As did other newcomers' sons, he strove to make the most of the opportunities America offered. A legal genius who completed Columbia University's two-year law course in half the usual time, Louis Marshall became a wealthy and internationally famous lawyer. But though he spoke half a dozen languages and frequently appeared before the U.S. Supreme Court, he never forgot his humble origins. To him, as to immigrant Carl Schurz, America represented a liberal dream for humanity not yet fulfilled, and he spent much of his life arguing for the civil and religious liberties still denied to many Jews, blacks, Roman Catholics and American Indians.

As part of his vision of America as a land of potential justice and plenty, he also shared George Perkins Marsh's concerns about the country's hasty dismantling of her natural heritage for the benefit of a few. Putting his legal skills and prestige to work for conservation, he supported bird-protection reforms, and during New York's constitutional convention of 1914, led the fight against lumbermen to retain the "forever wild" guarantee for the immense reserve of Adirondack State Park. For 20 years, he served on the board of trustees of the New York State College of Forestry. Friends summed up his career by praising his victories for civil rights and "his championship of the American forests and of all America's natural resources."

. . .

A lover of what he defended, the lawyer built a vacation home in the heart of the Adirondacks. His son grew up, then, not only among the refinements of wealth and the reformist commitments that shaped his outlook but also with opportunities to indulge his wilderness reveries. Still yearning for the days of Lewis and Clark, the boy backpacked through the mountains around the summer retreat. It came as no surprise to his family when he decided to become a forester. The choice of profession was motivated by the incipient strivings for reform reflected in lines he wrote at the age of 8 after a trip to Lake Champlain: "Where once the Indians used to dwell, From the steamboat comes a smoky smell."

Robert Marshall's professional life can be capsulized in one paragraph. After receiving a Bachelor of Science degree in 1924 from the College of Forestry at Syracuse, N.Y., he went on for advanced degrees from Harvard and Johns Hopkins University. With the exception of four years as director of forestry in the Office of Indian Affairs, he spent his entire career with the U.S. Forest Service. Various positions involving field work, laboratory research and administration took him to the state of Washington and to the Northern Rocky Mountain Experiment Station in Missoula, Mont. In 1937, the head of the Forest Service, Ferdinand Silcox, appointed him chief of the Division of Recreation and Lands, a post created especially for Marshall.

Such an outline might summarize the careers of many bureaucrats who leave behind little more than undistinguished legacies of dutifully performed functions. It gives little idea of Marshall's influence both inside and outside government, of the hard-working yet essentially artistic personality responsible for major shifts in public policy.

As a millionaire, Robert Marshall didn't have to work at all. But having made a commitment that involved his entire outlook, he threw himself into work with a drive, daring and creativity that most men with families to support and bills to pay would not have risked. His exploits as a hiker, his father's reputation as one of the nation's foremost constitutional lawyers, and his credentials as a researcher and a best-selling author allowed him to move somewhat with the aura of a wunderkind among hidebound government bureaucrats.

But many bureaucrats weren't as hidebound as might be supposed. The Depression was on, with millions of people out of work and listless in the world's richest country. Obviously, some traditional ways of doing things had gone wrong, and the New Deal administration of President Roosevelt made Marshall's socialist approach to resources seem far less radical than it would have appeared in more prosperous times.

Though the profit-hungry timber industry continued to wreak havoc on privately owned forests, it hadn't as yet begun to eye the public domain. With notable exceptions, the Forest Service, responsible for most federally administered timberlands, protected them with much of the progressive zeal inspired by Gifford Pinchot when he founded the agency in 1905.

Added to that, the traditional rivalry between the preservation-oriented Department of Interior and the use-oriented Department of Agriculture flared again under Interior Secretary Harold Ickes. It played directly into the hands of a small but earnest and politically sophisticated band of wilderness advocates led by Marshall. Temperamental Ickes pointed to abuses on Agriculture's domain and demanded that the national forests be transferred to his own department, brought "home" under the protective wing of Interior. His repeated campaigns, launched with nearly the fervor and acerbity of a religious fanatic battling the heretics, were unsuccessful, but they jolted Secretary of Agriculture Henry A. Wallace into action.

Publicly railed at by Ickes from without and gently prodded by liberals Silcox and Marshall from within, Wallace strained to make his Forest Service seem the model of conservation. Among other changes, he consented to wilderness expansion in order to placate both factions.

As for Marshall's techniques, friends recalled his diplomatically tempered chutzpah at work in an atmosphere ready for change: "Bob had the nerve to get all kinds of people together—congressmen, prima donna braintrusters, professional civil servants, promoters of this or that—hand them a dubious drink, and then insist that they debate the public ownership of resources."

He backed up his lobbying efforts with an array of alarming statistics, all pointing to one central fact: 20 percent of the nation's forests enjoyed conscientious stewardship from the U.S. Forest Service, but the other 80 percent remained in careless, private hands. Driven by the necessities of the capitalistic system, the timber companies were competing to see who could cut the fastest on the major portion of the country's forest resource—with profits, rather than the future, in mind. As George Perkins Marsh had predicted, the results of the profligacy were beginning to show: timber shortages, floods, erosion—the loss of America's once scenic and bountiful woodlands.

In short, despite their efforts since the latter years of the 19th century, conservationists had failed. "The proof," warned Marshall, "is the condition of our forests: unbelievably worse than before the conservation movement started." Supporting his judgments were the writings of such professional foresters as Gifford Pinchot and George P. Ahern. In 1929 Ahern had published a documented account of abuses, bleakly entitled *Deforested America.*

Basically, Marshall offered a twofold solution. Since private enterprise was not working for the nation's good, he wrote in *The People's Forests* (1933), timberlands should be nationalized, placed under control of the federal government to ensure rational, long-term use. This, Marshall reassured Americans, was not a radical step: "Most of the older countries have public control of private forests, from the well-nigh complete control of Sweden, Japan and Switzerland, to the partial control of France and Germany. In most countries, public control of forests needed for protecting mountain and river systems is taken for granted."

Despite the precedents, the suggestion was branded "communistic" by many, and it failed to take hold, though it did result in some nominal changes in forest regulation.

Closest to Marshall's heart was the preservation of wild America, and in this effort he enjoyed a nearly phenomenal success. From his vantage point as a high official within the Forest Service, he prepared inventories of roadless areas. By skillfully playing on interagency rivalries, he single-handedly added the immense figure of 5,437,000 acres to the government's preserve system—all of which was to be kept as pristine as when the first white man laid eyes on it.

Still, a shadow of instability hung over the coup. The new reserves, set aside by administrative decree, could just as easily be opened again to exploitation by the pen of a future head of the Forest Service not sympathetic to wilderness. The solution lay in protecting the gains under the far more permanent sanction of Congress. To accomplish the feat—and to add further units to the wilderness system—Marshall, for all his talents, clearly needed the broad-based political backing that could come only from a national organization. Yet at the time, remembered one of his hiking cronies, "there was no strong body of wilderness sentiment in existence." Marshall, it seemed, was standing alone.

The organization came about almost by happenstance. In 1934, Marshall joined Benton MacKaye and Harvey Broome for a jaunt into Tennessee's Great Smoky Mountains. There they witnessed the negative side of the New Deal. While many of Roosevelt's public works projects served useful ends, others did irreversible damage by extending unneeded roads into the hinterlands. Partly the upshot of the hikers' grousing, The Wilderness Society was founded in 1935 to save the remaining remnants of wild America from all technological invasions.

The society began with eight dedicated and politically active members. Besides Marshall, who provided the financial backing, they included lawyer Broome; MacKaye, the planner of the Appalachian Trail; wilderness celebrant Aldo Leopold; wildlife specialist Olaus Murie; and Robert Sterling Yard, an editor with a long career of publicity work for conservation that went back to the early days of the National Park Service.

The organization, one of the most effective lobbying groups of its kind, has served its purpose well, today boasting tens of thousands of wilderness supporters. Without their combined efforts, which resulted in passage of the Wilderness Act of 1964, the nation would not have the splendid and still-expanding wilderness system envisioned by Marshall nearly 50 years ago.

Behind Marshall's successes in the political arena lay one central ability. Through his personality and his writing he was able to make people feel his deep love of wild lands. Author Paul Schaefer recalls his first chance meeting with the bureaucrat on an Adirondack peak: "As we spoke he seemed to be chafing at the bit. A strong, cool wind whipped his hair. He exuded a restless, dynamic strength of purpose—strength which had been nurtured in the remote Arctic wilderness."

Marshall's books and articles projected the same simple power. They spoke about the need of wilderness preservation, but they emphasized the author's own explorations, adventures infused with personal thrills and spiritual enrichment. "He seemed," testifies one admirer, "to personify the limitless sweep of mountains, the ancient rocks, the unbroken forests…"

In brief, Marshall reawakened people to what for many is a fundamental, if at times dormant, love of nature.

Realist that he was, Marshall didn't gloss over the complexities of preserving wilderness in a society that glorified the machine. In a time when such questionings had not yet become fashionable, he asked whether adding more technological gadgets to the gross national product each year was bringing the fulfillment to people that should be the goal of a truly humane society. In fact, while giving the scientific and economic benefits of preservation their due, he used the psychological necessity of wilderness as the pivot on which his arguments turned.

Echoing psychoanalyst Sigmund Freud, he pointed to the

"horrible banality" of an over-civilized society that repressed rather than encouraged diversity and creativity. In contrast, he suggested that wilderness not only made badly needed physical demands on a sedentary society, but also provided a retreat to the freedom of the primitive. "It is," he said, "the last stand for that glorious adventure into the physically unknown that was commonplace in the lives of our ancestors and has always constituted a major factor in the happiness of many exploratory souls. It is also the perfect aesthetic experience because it appeals to all of the senses."

Thus Marshall combined conservation with social theory, for in his mind untrammeled nature served the public good. He advocated not only great swaths of wildness preserved for the exhilaration of the backpacker but summer camps for ghetto children and rustic facilities for the less hardy among the general public. The stance placed him in line with America's pastoral counter-vision espoused by such diverse thinkers as Thomas Jefferson, Henry David Thoreau and John Muir—and continued today by such environmental leaders as David Brower and Edward Abbey.

For all that, Marshall didn't lose his readers in social theory. Instead, he enlivened his writing with anecdotes, humor and curious facts. He once made an analysis of loggers' parlance based on 10 conversations. His report informed the public, "Of this record it transpired that an average of 136 words, unmentionable at church socials, were enunciated every quarter hour by the hearty hewers of wood."

He drew on his wide-ranging knowledge to entertain and inform with such pieces as "Lucretius on Forest Fires" and "Precipitation and Presidents." The latter made a statistical and only partly tongue-in-cheek case for predicting the outcomes of presidential elections on the basis of annual rainfall.

His turns of phrase went far beyond statistics and formal argument to drive a point home. Once challenged to state the specific number of wilderness areas the country should have, he countered, "How many Brahms symphonies do we need?"

The wilderness ideal that Marshall held up—as well as his effectiveness in stating it—can best be seen in *Arctic Village* (1933). As an adult still haunted by the exploits of Lewis and Clark, he made several trips to map the unknown territory of the Koyukuk River drainage near Wiseman, Alaska, a tiny village just above the Arctic Circle. There he found a self-sustaining hunting and mining society of 77 whites, 44 Eskimos and six Indians spread over an area as large as the combined states of Massachusetts and New Jersey. His book included more than the revels of standing on peaks to survey Arctic vistas never before seen by any human.

With a thoroughness reminiscent of the classical sociological study *Middletown*, he analyzed the economic, communal and sexual activities of the hardy wilderness dwellers. Despite the demands of their harsh surroundings, they knew almost no crime, racial strife or poverty. Instead, "People in the Koyukuk realize that they are living together in an isolated world, sharing its work, its dangers, its joys, and its responsibilities. They recollect countless personal associations of the most intimate character imaginable. Such factors seem to furnish them with an urge to act decently which in most cases is sufficient to obviate any necessity for the more usual compulsions of law," he wrote.

After reading *Arctic Village*, even H.L. Mencken couldn't contain his amazement. "How peacefully they live together, how easily they escape most of the evils that go with the Outside, and how content they are to remain in their remote isolation," he marveled. Reviewers in *The New York Times*, *The Nation*, and the *Saturday Review* praised the world of *Arctic Village* with similar enthusiasm. The book quickly climbed to the best-seller list. Caught in the malaise of the Depression, the public was questioning the validity of its highly urbanized, crime-ridden and often lackluster culture. And Marshall, while not suggesting that people strike out for the Arctic wilds as a solution to their ills, had proved his point. He had shown alternatives, values that might be found and fostered through experiences in the wilderness areas he was fighting to preserve.

. . .

When Robert Marshall died in 1939 at the age of 38, friends said that his sudden heart attack resulted from his strenuous pace. In spite of the successes of his short life, it should be remembered that many people viewed him as a maverick within government, one who, as Nash says, "broke sharply with existing government policy and marked (himself) as a radical, especially among foresters." He was among the last innovative conservationists in the federal bureaucracy who had hope that the government could be flexible and idealistic enough to make changes for the public good.

Though his tactics worked in his own time, in this belief he was wrong. After World War II, the growing corporations that came to dominate America's economic system also gained decision-making powers in the federal agencies designed to regulate them. Wilderness advocate Michael Frome reflects on the present Forest Service, now dominated by the interests of the timber industry: "Innovative thinking like that of such figures as Robert Marshall is not encouraged."

Since the days of Marshall, activists such as Rachel Carson and Ralph Nader have had to take up bitter adversary positions outside government, depending on massive public outcries to move the bureaucracy toward environmental reforms.

Howard Zahniser:
The Gentle, Genial Man
behind the Wilderness Act

BY PETER WILD

Throughout the Depression, urbane conservationist Robert Marshall was selling the concept of a national wilderness system. He buttonholed Washington's elite and cajoled the Forest Service into designating lands to be set aside as inviolate.

On the verge of success in the late 1930s, Marshall rallied his followers for the final push. But World War II and Marshall's untimely death from a heart attack in 1939 postponed the victory.

Then, the year after the worldwide conflict ended, the Forest Service experienced a change of heart. Pressured by the timber lobby, it began disassembling the units of wilderness that Marshall and others had hoped would become the seedbed for a series of reserves stretching across the country.

Clearly, if America were to save even tokens of its once-pristine land, someone would have to take up Marshall's standard. And, facing the new postwar enthusiasm for economic growth, that person would have to begin well behind where optimistic predecessors had left off.

The task fell to an unlikely candidate. A former high school English teacher, Howard Zahniser had little of Marshall's chutzpah, and certainly none of his wealth. His delights centered on a private collection of nature books and on writing bits of puckish verse for the entertainment of friends. Bespectacled and heavyset, he hardly looked the part of such forerunners as John Muir and

Marshall, men who had captured the public imagination with a combination of intellectual toughness and physical exploits. Once thrust into the complex political struggles for passage of wilderness legislation, however, Zahniser soon developed his own vital, if humble, style.

His son recalls, "Even toward the end of the eight-year legislative battle to pass a wilderness bill, when success was in sight, he saw himself as a mere cog in an inexorably turning wheel. He would joke that whoever had designed the wheel—Zahniser means 'gear maker' in German—might have made a better choice of materials."

Gentle Evangelism

"Nature was his God," observed a colleague. The gentle evangelism that marked Zahniser's conservation career had roots in his upbringing. His father was a minister, his mother a minister's daughter.

The future leader of The Wilderness Society grew up in the docile beauty of Pennsylvania's Allegheny River Valley. But young Zahniser's eyes were bad, and the family had no money for optometrists. Howard saw only blurs when the teacher pointed to birds. In his teens, he finally received a pair of eyeglasses, and his reaction is telling. "Putting them on for the first time, he jumped fences and ran through fields," said his son, "marveling at how much there was to see and how distinctly beautiful it was."

At Greenville College in Illinois the minister's son reveled in literature courses—at the expense of fulfilling the standard requirements. "I crammed four years of college into five," he quipped. Despite his literary self-indulgence, Zahniser worked hard, graduated, became a reporter for the *Pittsburgh Press* and later an English teacher in Greenville's high school.

Beginning in 1930, employment with what is now the U.S. Fish and Wildlife Service provided him a satisfying niche for 15 years. In addition to his editorial and broadcasting work for the government, he had freelance projects. From 1935 to 1959, Zahniser turned out essays and a regular book-review column, "Nature in Print," for *Nature Magazine*. True to the gentle Zahniser form, he avoided the thrusting and cutting of many reviewers; instead, he emphasized new volumes that would prove useful and enjoyable for his readers.

Meanwhile, he was also cutting "his wilderness teeth," to use his son's phrase, on backpacking trips into New York's Adirondacks and Tennessee's Great Smokies. On the vacation forays, Zahniser became friends with wilderness advocates Paul Schaefer and Harvey Broome. Through them, he absorbed the ideas of Marshall and Benton MacKaye.

The death of Robert Sterling Yard in 1945 left The Wilderness Society's two major positions vacant: executive secretary and editor of the magazine *The Living Wilderness*. By then Zahniser had developed his own visceral "relationships to the primeval." Compelled by the wilderness crisis and fired by Marshall's vision, he quit government employment to become the Society's paid professional staff of one.

Windmill Tilting

In the mid-1940s, the ambitions of The Wilderness Society had the charming but fey aspects of windmill-tilting. The Society's 2,000 members stood enthusiastically behind passage of legislation ordaining a national wilderness system. To accomplish this, they would have to ride over the roadblocks thrown up by the mining and timber industries, among the country's most politically adept and financially well-heeled lobbying groups. Secondly, the band would have to rouse a nation—one traditionally careless of preservation and now drowsy with postwar prosperity—to its diminishing natural heritage.

The Society's hopeful leader, approaching middle age, had exchanged government security for a shaky financial future. His new salary was only half his modest government pay, and his wife

Alice was expecting their fourth child. Zahniser had stripped himself for battle.

A national furor concerning a park prepared Zahniser for his ultimate accomplishment. To satisfy scientists rejoicing over a treasure trove of fossil bones, in 1915 President Wilson declared 80 acres on the Colorado-Utah border a national monument. For years, it lay baking under the Western sun, rarely visited except by an occasional paleontologist. In 1938, Franklin D. Roosevelt expanded the protected area. Few entrepreneurs objected. Dinosaur National Monument's 200,000 sprawling acres consisted of jumbled, seemingly useless desert landscape. But by the late 1940s, the Bureau of Reclamation was eyeing Dinosaur's Echo Park as a dam site—as well as places in Glacier and Grand Canyon national parks.

Meanwhile, taking advantage of its new affluence and mobility, the public was driving around the country, visiting national parks in record numbers. It was taken aback by the issue of Dinosaur. Were park lands, touted as belonging to all the people, truly inviolate? Apparently not. Encouraged by conservationists, the public shook itself from years of lethargy to make Dinosaur's harsh real estate a cause célèbre for park integrity.

Quickly developing his talents through the campaign, Zahniser, along with David Brower of the Sierra Club, argued that the dam was a financial mistake and actually a water-wasting project—an ill-conceived scheme designed to benefit a privileged few, using tax dollars and ruining wild lands. On the floor of the Senate, wilderness allies Richard Neuberger and Hubert Humphrey spoke out against the vast engineering plan.

Finally, after years of interminable hearings and several failures, Congress in 1956 passed a law forbidding dams in national parks and monuments. The prolonged debate had united conservationists for the first time in years; it had shown them that Americans would rally to support wild places.

Couplets for Wilderness

Counting on the momentum, Zahniser drew up plans for a national wilderness system. Characteristically, while struggling over the wording he joked that he'd "much prefer to state all this in iambic rhyming couplets." Sen. Hubert Humphrey and Rep. John P. Saylor introduced the bill—unrhymed but in Zahniser's exemplary prose—in the 84th Congress. Its uncertain progress proved less dramatic than the sharp debate over Dinosaur, but the eight-year struggle eventually resulted in a far larger gift to the nation.

Zahniser proved just how far the talents of a seemingly ordinary man can be developed carrying out goals on a national scale. Lacking Marshall's originality, he possessed important qualities that foreshadowed a new kind of conservationist who built on the accomplishments of more dashing mentors. For one thing, he could write. When he lectured that we are projecting "into the eternity of the future some of that precious unspoiled ecological inheritance that has come to us out of the eternity of the past," Zahniser was linking citizens with a cause beyond their ordinary, mortal lives.

As to practical affairs, he handled the details of a volunteer organization entering the upheavals of phenomenal membership growth, while loosening the purse strings of wealthy supporters. The man who enjoyed nothing more than to read *The Divine Comedy* or *Walden* aloud with friends campaigned in a kindly, avuncular manner. In the face of granitic opposition, Zahniser persuaded, drawing people into the movement.

Paul Oehser, a retired official of the Smithsonian Institution, capsulizes the method: "Zahnie was famous for getting along with people. He had a way about him. Even his adversaries grew to respect and love him. He was never caustic or vindictive."

Typically, when invited to justify his wilderness views to the assembled Society of American Foresters—a group opposed to preservation—he began his speech, "I do not come here to quarrel..." After the talk, the foresters peppered their guest with questions. By the end of the session, they couldn't help but respect the gentle man who had entered enemy territory full of good will and humor.

Preaching the transcendental view that "We are a part of the wilderness of the universe," Zahniser scurried about lecturing, distributing conservation literature from large pockets sewn inside his suit coat. David Brower, now president of Friends of the Earth, remembers that for Zahniser "the hardest times were those when good friends tired because the battle was so long. Urging these friends back into action was the most anxious part of Zahniser's work."

In many ways, buoyant Zahniser was exactly the man for the job. Like Marshall before him, he drove himself until he died in the harness, still fighting for what he saw as an essential cause for the nation.

Irrational Fears

In all likelihood, anything less would not have been enough. Exploiters of natural resources reacted to the new environmental enthusiasm by launching an anti-wilderness campaign. As far as wilderness was concerned, the lands under question—much of them rocky peaks and high valleys—were not especially lucrative for mining or lumbering. Yet as with almost all the battles for preservation in America, the wilderness movement generated fears, some of them irrational. Accustomed to centuries of doing what they wanted to the land, some Americans looked upon the idea of leaving a mere 2 or 3 percent of the nation untouched as heretical.

Some Forest Service officials also felt threatened. If some of their bailiwick—even a small portion—were withdrawn from exploitation, wouldn't that mean fewer rangers on its payroll, and hence fewer secretaries, pickup trucks, hard hats, paper clips and forms in sextuplet—in short, a smaller bureaucracy? Even the traditional land-preserving agency, the National Park Service, suffered from the trepidation, worried that curbs on future access roads, scenic drives and tramways would mean a loss in bureaucratic status.

In response to these objections, Zahniser emphasized the basic issue—the preservation of "our oldest resource," as he called it. Alerted to the urgency of the problem, the public generated thousands of pages of hearing testimony and tens of thousands of letters to its representatives in Washington.

Yet for eight years, Congress vacillated, tugged by exploiters on the one hand and the clamors of their more ordinary constituents on the other. Sixty-six different times the wilderness bill was rewritten and resubmitted into the legislative mill.

Meanwhile, weary Zahniser was crisscrossing the country, attending each federal hearing on the issue, repeating the words that for all their repetition represented a fresh vision: a national program establishing wilderness for "the first time in the history of the earth." It was a step that no civilization had taken before, a test, as he saw it, of our cultural development. Zahniser answered critics from the timber industry: "We are not fighting progress. We are making it."

In the spring of 1964, Zahniser sensed victory, but he would not taste it. He died of a heart attack at the age of 58, only a few weeks before Congress passed the Wilderness Act.

Granted the help of others, the Wilderness Act of 1964 remains Howard Zahniser's monument. As might be expected from such a prolonged legislative storm, the bill emerged with flaws of compromise. The act allowed mineral exploration on wilderness lands until 1984, and it did not entirely eliminate the motorboats and aircraft that hikers come to wilderness to escape. But in one sweep it did establish 9 million acres of untrammeled land, while creating a review process for possible inclusion of other areas. As the provisions of the act are implemented, Zahniser's legacy to the nation grows.

"The Poor Man's Wilderness": How the Wilderness Movement Got its Start

BY TOM PRICE

For all its current political influence and professional staff, today's wilderness movement owes much of its start to a hardware store-owner from western Montana. His name is Cecil Garland.

It happened this way. In the days leading up to the passage of the 1964 Wilderness Act, a final compromise forced its backers to agree that all future designations of wilderness areas would be made through additional acts of Congress.

But in practical terms, nomination of new areas was still up to the Forest Service, an agency in no hurry to set aside new areas.

Staffers planned to manage wild lands as they saw fit, leaving some alone and developing others. One such place on the latter list was what the agency called the Scapegoat Backcountry, outside Lincoln, Mont.

Called the "poor man's wilderness" because anyone with strong legs could experience it, the 240,000-acre Lincoln Scapegoat sat hard against the massive Bob Marshall Wilderness, one of the trophy areas designated when the Wilderness Act passed.

High-winding mountain slopes fed crooked trout streams, their waters the setting for Norman Maclean's *A River Runs Through It*. At the Lincoln-Scapegoat's entrance, a sign prohibited motorized vehicles, and Cecil Garland was among those who believed that the area had official protection as wilderness.

When, in 1960, he learned otherwise, Garland decided to do something about it. Although most of the key players are older now, with fading memories, Dennis Roth captured much of the action in a little-read 1995 book, *The Wilderness Movement and the National Forests*. By the time Garland was finished with his 12-year crusade, Roth recounts, this small-town fight had forever changed the protection of public lands.

Garland was no professional environmentalist; he was a hunter, a fisherman, and a rancher who owned a hardware and sporting-goods store in Lincoln. He also had a remarkable memory and a gift for understanding complicated planning documents. He used these talents to rally opposition to the agency's planned roads for logging and campgrounds in the Lincoln Scapegoat.

"He may have been uneducated, but he was no fool," recalls Doris Milner, a key volunteer with the Montana Wilderness Association. "He had vision and knew how to get people to act."

Along with new allies such as the Montana Wilderness Association and The Wilderness Society, Garland picked apart the Forest Service's carefully constructed plans. He rallied development opponents, who packed Forest Service hearings and traveled to Washington to plead the case for wilderness protection.

One story told by Roth illustrates Garland's persuasiveness. The Forest Service, although concerned about the opposition, announced in March 1963 that its plans for road-building in the Lincoln Scapegoat would go forward. An alarmed young Forest Service engineer slipped quietly into Garland's store, telling him that the roadbed had already been flagged, and bulldozers were parked at the end.

Frantically, Garland called Montana Rep. Jim Battin, R. "I began to pour my heart out to him in a most pleading and earnest manner," recalls Garland. Battin was so moved by Garland's passion that he dialed up the regional forester, asking for a 10-day delay to study the issue. The forester replied he didn't have 10 days, saying the bulldozer was ready to go.

Battin bristled and replied, "By God, we'd better have 10 days." They got the delay, and Garland used the time to organize local opposition. A Forest Service hearing a month later drew 300 near-riotous citizens.

The agency, to its dismay, was losing its grip.

The Grassroots Gains Clout

As Garland's cause gained more grassroots support, new Helena Forest Supervisor Robert Morgan decided in late 1963 to put development plans on hold. The following year, he told higher-ups that "we will get no support from the man on the street" if the agency proceeded with its plans for the Lincoln Scapegoat.

In April 1965, the stakes were raised when the Montana delegation introduced a bill designating the 240,000-acre Lincoln Scapegoat Wilderness Area.

"It set a precedent," recalls Clif Merritt, a former organizer with The Wilderness Society, as the first-ever citizen-drafted wilderness bill. Field hearings in 1968 showed the entire Montana congressional delegation and most of the citizens in favor of the bill, with the increasingly out-of-touch Forest Service among the only opponents.

Regional Forester Neal Rahm vented his frustration over the agency's changing fortunes at a meeting of agency leaders in the spring of 1969: "We have lost control and leadership in the sphere of wilderness philosophy," said Rahm. "The Forest Service originated the concept in 1920 and, practically, has been standing still since 1937. Why should a sporting goods and hardware dealer in Lincoln, Mont., designate the boundaries for the 240,000-acre Lincoln Backcountry addition to the Bob Marshall?"

One month later, in an effort to forestall congressional action, Forest Service Chief Ed Cliff told a Senate Interior Committee that the agency would "take another look" at the Lincoln Scapegoat. It was too late. The Forest Service was no longer the sole decision-maker.

Later that year, the Senate passed the Lincoln Scapegoat bill. After a few more years of struggle, the Scapegoat Wilderness was signed into law in 1972, becoming the first national forest wilderness area designated at the initiative of anyone other than the Forest Service.

In demonstrating what Stewart Brandborg of the Wilderness Society calls "the strength of determined citizen leaders who have realized their own power," Garland had rewritten the rulebook for protecting public land, and had created a model for activists throughout the country to follow.

Back to the Future

Fast-forward some 25 years, and the change is remarkable.

The growth in the West is nothing less than explosive, and partly in response, the last two years have seen a dramatic increase of interest in wilderness designation. Yet many young activists have never heard of the Lincoln Scapegoat or the man named Cecil Garland.

This story would have a tidy ending if it came here, but it doesn't.

Following the passage of the Scapegoat bill, Garland and his wife decided they had had enough of the fighting and turned the store over to his daughters. Then the couple divorced, and he drifted south and west, to Utah.

Now remarried and living in the desert, Garland occasionally rails against a vast media conspiracy. Visitors to his dusty ranch are also likely to hear a perspective on the world's problems that is, to put it politely, somewhere to the right of the late Ed Abbey's anti-immigrant views.

Still, Garland's legacy is clear. Doug Scott, policy director for the Pew Wilderness Center, credits Garland for helping show the way to citizen action. "Folks reacted to threats to roadless areas by going directly to their congressional delegations for help," he says. "The new path they followed was marked for them by the fresh blazes and cairns set out by Cecil Garland."

JANUARY 27, 1978

The West Loses Lee Metcalf's Environmental Voice

BY ROBIN TAWNEY

With the unexpected death of Sen. Lee Metcalf, D-Mont., on Jan. 12, 1978, conservationists lost one of their dearest friends in the U.S. Senate.

Metcalf was a "bear of a man," fiercely private and independent, yet one who could usually be counted on to advocate for wilderness issues and to support other environmental legislation. But, as the senator said shortly before his death, "I don't jump every time (environmentalists) holler 'frog.'"

Metcalf made the wise use of natural resources one of his prime concerns during his 26 years in Congress. He was first elected to the House in 1952, and then joined former Majority Leader Mike Mansfield, D-Mont., in the Senate in 1960. Metcalf was finishing his third term there when he died of a heart attack at his home in Helena.

He had announced his intention not to seek re-election to the Senate seat, but Metcalf was determined not to let that decision make him a "lame duck" in his legislative work. When Congress resumed its chores on Jan. 19, Metcalf had planned to be there pushing for what he said were his last "objectives for wilderness in Montana." He was planning to introduce legislation for a Great Bear Wilderness, linking Glacier National Park with the Bob Marshall-Scapegoat wilderness areas and providing his favorite wild animal, the grizzly bear, with vital habitat.

This session, Metcalf also hoped to see Congress pass his bill calling for the creation of a unified Absaroka-Beartooth Wilderness in south central Montana, more than 900,000 acres in size. This and other bills Metcalf had introduced are very much alive, but they will require strong support from other senators—and from Metcalf's replacement, Paul Hatfield, D, a former chief justice of the Montana Supreme Court.

Metcalf also planned to hold hearings this month on one of the most important environmental questions facing Congress—his bill to set aside 120 million acres of Alaska for national parks, wilderness areas and wildlife refuges.

Why did a senator from Montana introduce the Alaska National Interest Lands Conservation Act? Because the "senators from Alaska are of the Melcher (Sen. John Melcher, D-Mont.) philosophy," he said recently. That is, he explained, they don't believe in setting aside land for wilderness. And, the bill had to be introduced by someone on the Senate Natural Resource and Energy Committee.

Metcalf also initiated the Montana Wilderness Study Bill and wilderness legislation for Montana's Elkhorns and Spanish Peaks, although he hadn't expected them to be passed before he retired.

Metcalf left a legacy of important wilderness legislation. Among his accomplishments is the inclusion of more than 150 miles of the Missouri River in the National Wild and Scenic Rivers System (which was established by the Wild and Scenic Rivers Act of 1968). After Metcalf struggled for wild river status in three sessions of Congress, the river was finally added in 1976. He also worked for passage of the Wilderness Act, which he co-sponsored in 1964, and on efforts to reform management practices on the national forests.

For these and other efforts, Metcalf received dozens of conservation awards.

His interest in wilderness began in the Bitterroot Valley of western Montana, where he was born on Jan. 28, 1911. Although in later years, heart trouble and a crippling knee injury prohibited Metcalf from traveling farther than a quarter-mile from any road, he remained a staunch supporter of wilderness.

Quarrelling with those who say wilderness designation unfairly excludes the elderly and the handicapped, he said recently, "The way to deny (wilderness) to everybody is to cut all the trees down and to not have a wilderness. People who are physically disabled are always going to be disadvantaged whether there's wilderness or national forest. The worst disadvantage is not to have any wilderness at all."

Reminiscing about his wilderness battles over the last two decades, Metcalf said, "It will be a long time before there is another senator from Montana who has the special interest in wilderness that I have had."

Indeed, it probably will be.

Congress passed the bill to create the Absaroka-Beartooth Wilderness in March 1978, and formally designated the Great Bear Wilderness that October. Two years later, Congress passed the massive Alaska National Interest Lands Conservation Act, which designated more than 56 million acres of wilderness in Alaska. President Jimmy Carter signed the act into law on Dec. 2, 1980.

Construction Workers for Wilderness? You Bet!

BY JILL BAMBURG

There's a new voice for wilderness in northwestern Wyoming, a voice that could carry all the way to Washington, D.C.

It's the voice of the blue-collar worker, organized last summer into Construction Workers for Wilderness (CWW).

The organization is the brainchild of Howie Wolke, Wyoming representative of Friends of the Earth and a man who's subsidized his work in the environmental movement by working construction four to five months a year.

Wolke got the idea last spring when he began collecting his co-workers' signatures on a petition supporting wilderness designation for the DuNoir area near Dubois, Wyo. He found considerable support for the DuNoir proposal and for wilderness in general, but what got him going was the crowd's reaction at the hearing to the petition signed "Jackson Construction Workers for Wilderness."

"They loved it," he says.

There was something powerful in the incongruity of rank-and-file members of a timber-dependent industry coming out in support of a policy that industry spokesmen claimed would put them out of work.

The political significance of the event was not wasted on Wolke, a down-to-earth environmentalist who's long been distressed by the elitist image he feels has been foisted on the environmental movement.

"The charge that environmentalists are a bunch of rich,

leisure-class-type elitists has been with us for a lot of years," Wolke says, "and I think it's invalid."

Construction Workers for Wilderness is, in part, intended to counter that image.

"If for no other reason, it's important politically," Wolke says. "Let's face it: For protecting wilderness, we're dependent upon the political process. A bill has to be introduced into Congress and it's got to be passed."

"If at a wilderness hearing the only people who get up and testify are a few well-known environmental crazies and a couple of university professors or whatever, a politician who may be sitting on the fence at the time is going to look at that and is going to say, 'Well, there doesn't appear to be broad support. I'm not going to introduce a bill on this.'"

"But if he can look and see that there really is broad support, politically, it makes an awful lot of sense."

Wolke served as a consultant when the new group was chartered July 1. Under the leadership of journeyman ironworker Bill Gill and carpenter Obed Martinez, the group has grown to 65 or 70 members in a matter of months. Members are mostly construction workers based in Jackson, Wyo., but the list includes at least one oil-rig worker, logger and mill worker and a handful of members from Kemmerer and Rock Springs, Wyo., and Driggs, Idaho.

Recruitment is easy, according to Gill and Martinez, and the demands upon members' time and pocketbooks are minimal. Members allow their names to be used in pro-wilderness testimony submitted by the organization, receive occasional mailings on wilderness issues and are encouraged to submit individual statements when opportunities such as the Forest Service's Roadless Area Review and Evaluation, an inventory of potential wilderness areas, present themselves.

Unlike many other environmental organizations, Construction Workers for Wilderness is a one-issue outfit, and it appears likely to remain so.

"Wilderness is something that an awful lot of people with diverse interests can often times come together and agree on," Wolke says. "A lot of working people who really don't have much spare time but who like to go out and hunt and fish when they do have time can really see the need to protect wilderness.

"If, on the other hand, we were to have the organization become involved in things like air and water pollution and strip mining and nuclear power and other issues like that, it would be an administrative nightmare to try and reach consensus among people with such diverse backgrounds and interests."

At some point, worries about jobs might begin to enter the picture. On the wilderness issue, however, the apparent contradiction between preservation and the pocketbook has not been a problem.

Wolke says, "The Rocky Mountain region contributes very little to the national timber supply. When you couple that with the fact that even in the Rocky Mountain region, the most productive sites are not being considered for wilderness, I think people really start to see that there's no basic incompatibility between construction workers and wilderness.

"I think a lot of these guys are starting to realize that and they're not buying the old industry arguments that conservationists are going to put people out of jobs."

Gill arrives at the same conclusion from a slightly different tack, pointing out a connection between wilderness and construction that hinges on tourism.

"Our economy here (in Jackson) is definitely tourism," he says, "and most of the people who live here work construction. As long as tourism is up, construction is up.

"Jackson Hole is considered more or less a wilderness-type setting. The fact that there's the beautiful Tetons, two national parks and a great amount of wilderness and potential wilderness draws people to this area. That is actually the future of the economy of this area, as opposed to mining, oil or logging."

For Martinez, the motivation is different still. He grew up an avid outdoorsman in Colorado, and moved to Wyoming to be closer to the wilderness values that he'd seen destroyed in his native state. To him, it's a fight that has little to do with economics.

"We want to show the people in Washington that it's ours, too, the working class; it's everybody's land. We want to draw a bottom line. You can't make wilderness. You have just as much as you have to work with and that's all.

"Sure, we want to see wilderness areas stay wilderness. We don't want to see it depleted and to hear, 'You can't go hunting any more, boys, 'cause there's an oil well up there, and the game's all gone. And there's no more elk 'cause all the calving areas are destroyed; no more fishing 'cause there's pollution.'

"You just start from there. If you're not going to designate a wilderness area, then pretty soon you're going to have tract houses there, maybe. I'm a construction worker—so what? I don't want to see those houses in there."

Construction workers aren't "the dumb, cinder-block-toting gorillas you might think," says Gill.

Howie Wolke went on to co-found Earth First! in 1980, and now runs Big Wild Adventures in Emigrant, Mont.

The Wilderness Society's Outstanding Alumni

BY ED MARSTON

In 1979, William Turnage, who had just become The Wilderness Society's president, fired the group's entire field staff. Members of the diaspora went on to become some of the most influential figures in the wilderness world, but the shakeup also highlighted some of the fundamental disagreements about tactics that continue to this day.

The good old days of America's wilderness movement, says Jerry Mallett, were the 1970s: "We could send five to six guys into a state and just wreck it with phone calls, coalitions with sportsmen, the whole thing." Mallett says it was a time of skilled grassroots organizing by good-old-boy environmentalists who happened to have degrees in natural resource management.

"I remember on the Flat Tops (then a wilderness candidate in Colorado), we had a problem with (Colorado Sen. Gordon) Allott. So we cranked up several hundred letters to him from his voters. Then, after a couple of weeks, we went to see him. He told us: 'Boys, I'm glad you're here. I have a real problem back home. What can I do about the Flat Tops?' He'd gotten letters from sportsmen, county commissioners, people like that."

The good-old-boy environmentalists worked for The Wilderness Society. Clif Merritt, who put the 19-person field staff together, says he looked for knowledge of resources, ability to talk to all sorts of people, and dedication. Mallett recalls how that worked in practice:

"Bart Koehler would spend all night driving to a hearing to

save on a motel. Dave Foreman once sold his mule so he could do a mailing." Mallett suggests that the grassroots work done in the 1970s helped lead to 1984, when Congress created 8.6 million acres of wilderness, most of it in the West.

Ten years later, that staff is in large part still doing grassroots wilderness work in the West—but not for The Wilderness Society.

Best known of the alumni is Foreman, a founder of Earth First! and its current head. Another founder, Bart Koehler, is with the Southeast Alaska Conservation Council in Juneau. Sally Ranney founded and is president of the American Wilderness Alliance. Merritt is the Alliance's executive director. Jerry Mallett is head of the Western River Guides Association. Jim Eaton heads up the California Wilderness Coalition. Dick Carter founded and leads the Utah Wilderness Association. Bill Cunningham directed until recently the Montana Wilderness Association. Roger Scholl works with the Nevada Wilderness Association.

Jim Eaton, speaking from California, says Earth First! "came out of The Wilderness Society staff sitting around the campfire talking about being reasonable and losing wilderness. We talked about what we really wanted to do."

William Turnage, who came in as president of the Society in 1978, gave them the unhappy opportunity to do just that. According to Eaton, "Turnage was the first of the conservation leaders to not come from conservation ranks—he came from business."

Mallett adds, "Turnage didn't feel comfortable with the field reps. They were all personable and down-home, sleeping on people's floors while travelling, grateful for a meal, and working 60 hours a week for $400 a month."

Within 18 months of Turnage's arrival at The Wilderness Society, the 19-person field staff was essentially gone. Merritt, who had put the 19 together, says today: "Bill Turnage decided to scuttle the strongest field force for wilderness" this country ever had.

Earth First!'s Dave Foreman, famous for his lambasting of three-button-suited professional environmentalists, sees a silver lining in Turnage's action. "I think it was a good thing, the way we spread out and did things."

The firings and resignations had meaning apart from the creation of the Utah Wilderness Association and Earth First! and the strengthening of existing groups such as the Montana Wilderness Association and the Oregon Natural Resource Council. Foreman says there was a certain internal logic to the transformation of The Wilderness Society from a grassroots group based on a national membership to a centralized group lobbying in D.C. and raising money from a big-city constituency.

"After RARE II (the Forest Service's 1970s wilderness planning effort), everyone was burned out. So we let the pros take over." The change may also have been related to the size of the Society. Mallett says, "It's inevitable that a group, at a certain size, will abandon the grassroots—look at the National Wildlife Federation or Audubon."

Plus, the alumni agree, a presence in Washington, D.C., is necessary to the wilderness movement. And under Turnage, The Wilderness Society has gone from about 40,000 members to some 140,000 today. Its budget is $6 million and its staff numbers 85, including six regional representatives in the West.

That kind of a rich, large, centralized operation lends itself to Turnage's approach to conservation. In the summer 1985 issue of *Wilderness,* in a lavishly illustrated article typical of those about chief executive officers of large operations, Turnage said:

"A vital part of the job is a willingness to aggressively sell, to sell ideas, to sell the organization, and that relates to everything. It relates to persuading a donor to support the organization, persuading a reporter to do a story about an issue about which the public should learn.

"It involves a willingness to go out and vigorously advocate and sell our point of view to corporate leaders and opinion-makers, a willingness to sell ideas and ask for help from members of Congress and other government leaders important in the decision-making process."

It's an approach that requires well-paid expertise, a lifestyle that at least approximates that of congressmen and corporate heads and presence in the power centers. But while the Society's alumni agree that Washington is necessary, they believe that the real action is in the field.

Mallett recalls, "Clif and I just laughed when we realized Turnage was going to center things in Washington. We knew he couldn't touch (Nevada U.S. Sen. Paul) Laxalt from there."

The alumni praise some of The Wilderness Society's field reps, but they say that a centralized, top-down style dominates other of the Society's regional offices. Eaton, the head of the California Wilderness Coalition, says: "The California regional rep hasn't worked with the grassroots. She talks to legislators, she gets editorials in the paper, but she doesn't use her membership at all. Their style is to meet directly with decision-makers. Our style has been to have (local members) meet with decision-makers. That's especially important here in California—one person can't know 43 congressmen."

What's wrong with working the media and Congress? "The media is fine, but you have to have folks out there working on the issues. Even in California, most potential wilderness is in rural, conservative areas. You have to get those congressmen. And you can't do it from San Francisco or Los Angeles. You need to have local people."

Another product of centralization is a staff of lawyers. But Eaton says court victories are also of limited use: "They stopped the Trans-Alaska Pipeline and clear-cutting with lawsuits, and only gained a year or two. It's not a solution if you win without popular support."

How does one use the grassroots? The alumni have different approaches. Mallett's is political. He recalls coming to Washington, D.C., a few years ago with a group of guides and outfitters—men of no particular polish or apparent connections with the power centers. "Within a half hour we had an appointment with George Bush. And before we left, we had what we wanted out of the Forest Service." The guides and outfitters, he says, are incredibly well-connected because their work brings them into intimate contact with the wealthy and powerful.

How did he work in the 1970s as a Society rep? "I would go into a town with a list of members. If it was Escalante, Utah, and there were no members, I'd go to the local newspaper and ask who's interested in resource issues. From there I'd go to the local doctors and lawyers—they were usually prominent people involved in civic and resource issues. I was after somebody we could talk to. My job was to build coalitions. But I was an outsider. I couldn't go to a congressman."

Dick Carter of the Utah Wilderness Association had a different approach. "I'm still of the school—I can't be convinced otherwise—that the way you do it is to get people emotionally involved in their on-the-ground concerns. Get people who have an attachment to a free-flowing river, or an elk band, or a stand of trees."

That concern, in Carter's view, should not lead only to pressure on Congress. He prefers to work with the land managers. "Sit down with the Forest Service and see if the conflict can be resolved. We have to go back a few steps—we have to get back to Leopold's land ethic—what the land tells you you can do with it. Then you meet on this common ground with the Forest Service—the common ground of what the land can do."

Carter thinks those who try to match wits with the Forest Service's computer jocks and economic analysts are heading in the wrong direction. "You can't put a piece of land into FOR-PLAN (the agency's land-planning computer program) and have it mean anything. It takes the public out of the planning process."

The recent involvement of The Wilderness Society in 16 forest plans has been seen as a possible return by the Society to the grassroots. But Carter, who is negative on the analytic approach the Forest Service is taking toward planning, doesn't see much point in the Society's meeting them on their own turf:

"What I see is a very centralized Washington, D.C., effort—the Society is going to out-plan, out-computer, out-spend the Forest Service. They'll provide a bit of information to the grassroots. But it won't even approach what the Utah Wilderness Association provides to local people" at a fraction of the cost.

Earth First! head Foreman is more positive. "I'm encouraged by their forest-planning effort. It is something of a return to the grassroots. And I've been quite surprised that Turnage has been able to hire good people. But there's still a tendency to think the real action is in Washington, D.C."

Foreman, who traces his organization's roots back to the Luddite machine-smashing movement in England, thinks in historic terms. The Wilderness Society, he says, is responding to a shift in the forces that in the late 1970s pushed it toward a centralized existence in the urban centers. In his view, the grassroots activists were burned out and discouraged in the aftermath of RARE II. They needed time to catch their breath and recruit new people.

"Now the committed people are recharged. The Wilderness Society was sort of forced into making forest planning more grassroots because the grassroots were taking over. There have been little Sagebrush Rebellions within the national environmental groups—it's caused lots of state and local groups to form and to take action. The Wilderness Society may be hustling to get in front of the parade.

"But it may be a good thing, more of a relation between equals—because the Society needs the local people. They're the ones that know the forests."

Eaton, however, wonders how much attention the Society will pay to the grassroots, even on forest planning. "I suspect they'll work directly with the Forest Service."

Eaton says it is not only The Wilderness Society which is neglecting the ground. "There is less and less grassroots organizing going on. Only a few groups are working in the old style." He thinks environmental causes may still be getting a free ride on past efforts. "I'm afraid people may perceive we're stronger than we are. Media coverage is fine. But there have to be folks out there working on the issues."

Do the alumni ever question their approach to the issues? Only Eaton admitted to a bit of doubt. "I have very fond memories of working for The Wilderness Society in those days. But it was a shock to be fired while earning $12,000 a year and have your replacement earn $43,000. It made me wonder what I'd been doing all those years."

Eaton's wondering apparently didn't last long. Today, he says, he earns even less as head of the California Wilderness Coalition than he did in his Wilderness Society days.

To Save a Utah Canyon, a BLM Ranger Quits and Turns Activist

BY ELIZABETH MANNING

Floating past cottonwood trees and tamarisk just before dusk, Skip Edwards deftly keeps his raft within earshot of ours so he can pummel us with facts about the Wilderness Act. But around the next bend, the former Bureau of Land Management river ranger falls silent and points to a massive red and orange sandstone wall marking the entrance to Utah's Westwater Canyon. Though he's logged more than 200 trips down this section of the Colorado River, he is still awed. He shakes his head in total disbelief. "This is not worthy?"

Worthy of wilderness, he means.

For 15 years, Utahns have fought bitterly over which BLM lands in their state should be designated wilderness. A stew of wildly differing proposals reflects just how much the issue has fractured the state.

But in one rare fit of consensus, all parties agreed that Westwater Canyon in Grand County should be wilderness, even nodding to roughly the same boundaries.

"They all pointed to Westwater and said, 'This is what we mean by wilderness,'" says Bill Hedden, Grand County Council member.

Then, suddenly, in the last step of the process, the first mile and a half of the canyon, just over the Utah-Colorado border, slipped through a crack.

It was a crack created by Ron Pene last March in Moab. Pene, twin brother of Grand County council member Ray Pene, presented a report to the council on his family's mining claims within BLM's 31,000-acre Westwater Wilderness Study Area. He argued that because of the claims, old mining scars, historical mining shacks, an agency fence and "three and a half miles of county roads," the area was "trammeled"—too trammeled to be called wilderness.

Based on Ron Pene's testimony, council members—including his brother—voted 4–3 to delete 1,800 acres in Westwater from H.R. 1745, a 1.8 million-acre statewide wilderness bill. The Utah Republicans in Congress acceded to the county's wishes.

No Need for Wilderness

What nobody realized then, says Hedden, was that Ron Pene, 49, had illegally driven a bulldozer into his family's claims at Westwater. While Pene admits to bulldozing the road, he insists he didn't break the law.

A lot of people in southern Utah sympathize with Pene, who has worked as a miner, a heavy-equipment operator and a chemist for a mining company. Mining is what his family has done for three generations and mining is what he still plans to do. The fact that he has valid claims inside a wilderness study area is the BLM's problem, not his, says Pene.

Ray Pene isn't a fan of wilderness legislation.

"I am completely opposed to the taking of lands from multiple use," wrote Councilman Pene in a letter last spring to the delegation. "I have heard the argument that if we don't designate the lands wilderness, we will lose them forever. I say if we do designate the lands as wilderness, we do lose them forever."

Environmentalists say Pene is exactly the kind of council member Utah's congressional delegation hoped they would find when they asked leaders in rural counties to recommend wilderness. The delegation says they wanted approval from those who would be most affected.

Environmentalists charge that the consultation with rural counties was a ploy to make the 1.8 million-acre bill look generous, knowing that most rural counties would recommend little to no wilderness.

That happened in most of rural Utah. But in Grand County, even though at least three council members are anti-wilderness, as a group they called for more wilderness than the delegation. Hedden says the Pene claims in Westwater were deleted as part of the give-and-take needed to keep Grand County's proposal intact. This was one of the dumber things the council did, Hedden says now.

"It's not a gigantic piece of wilderness, but it makes you sick to see the most blatant conflict of interest blessed and rewarded. It's in the delegation's bill," he says. "It changes national law in Pene's individual favor."

Activist Turns Detective

The Westwater deletion seems like the kind of thing that should have galvanized environmentalists and the 20,000 boaters that paddle through Westwater each year. The canyon is home to native endangered fish, bald eagles, golden eagles, blue herons, peregrine falcons, a rare species of butterfly and scores of archaeological sites. It is also a whitewater run of near-cult status.

But while environmentalists say the Pene deletion is a terrible mistake, they have bigger battles—whole chunks left off the bill, "hard-release" language that would prohibit future wilderness designations in Utah, and disclaimers that allow dams, motorized vehicles, overflights and pipelines inside wilderness areas.

That's where Skip Edwards, our guide through the canyon, steps in. Westwater is one of his favorite wild places, and he's not about to see even a piece of the canyon let go.

He and his partner, Doreen Dethmers, worked for the BLM and lived at the ranger station, a mile or so upstream from the canyon's entrance, from 1988 to 1993. They know every side canyon, every submerged feature of the river bottom, every eddy. Though they could rarely find time away from the boaters to have a quiet evening alone, Edwards says one of the joys of working at Westwater was watching people fall in love with the canyon.

He resigned from the BLM a few months ago in disgust, in part because of the BLM's refusal to protect Westwater from Pene.

"(Edwards has) given up everything to work on this, which is amazing to me," says Hedden.

Edwards, 50, has turned detective as well as activist, obsessed with every detail of the Penes' mining claim. What he found was that the conflict was partly the BLM's fault. In 1975, an amendment to the Wild and Scenic Rivers Act protected a quarter-mile on each side of the canyon from new mining claims.

Unfortunately, the agency forgot to file for an extension in 1982, creating a three-year loophole through which Pene drove his first six claims. Pene's other claims were filed in 1991, after protection had been reinstated. BLM geologist Sal Venticinque thinks the agency could kill at least some of the claims simply because of their filing date.

The agency could also get rid of the rest of the Pene claims if it can prove mining can't make a reasonable profit, says Kate Kitchell, the BLM's Moab district manager. So far, the agency hasn't tried. Although a 1989 study by the Bureau of Mines estimated the claims wouldn't produce much gold, Pene believes he may have found the mother lode.

But Edwards and Hedden wonder if Ron Pene is working the claims mainly to gain ownership of the land through the 1872 Mining Law. His claims are at the edge of a spectacular canyon slated for wilderness.

Pene says if he had the money, he would patent the claims— but only to protect his mining rights. "I don't want to build a resort," he says. "This is strictly for mining, and that's the way it is."

Though the BLM is now trying to actively manage Pene's claims, its attempts to enforce the law have been ignored. Alex VanHemert, a recreation planner for the BLM, says Pene continues to work his claims without BLM permission. He no longer uses the bulldozer, but he still maintains the road with a metal drag that he attaches to his truck.

Pene says the BLM is harassing him and that it has changed the rules. "The bottom line is, I'm not getting a fair shake."

But Edwards says agency officials haven't been aggressive enough. He thinks they're scared Pene might do serious damage to the land. Given agency inconsistencies and lax enforcement, Edwards also raises the question of collusion with former BLM staff. "It's too hard to trace," says Hedden. "But it wouldn't take your breath away."

Taking it to D.C.

"Mining is what put Moab on the map, and everyone hoped mining would pull the county of its slump in the 1980s," explains BLM geologist Terry McParland. "Instead, recreation turned out to be the answer. That's been both good and bad. It's hard to convince locals they have to change their ways."

She says old-time county residents and recreationists are still learning how to respect each other. "For some people," she adds, "that learning curve may not be very fast."

Despite the canyon of disagreement between them, Skip Edwards and the Pene brothers have more in common than they might think: The three are intimate with and passionate about the land in a way that those making the decisions in Washington, D.C., are not. They just see it differently.

When Edwards talks about Westwater, his reference points are nesting grounds, rapids, a certain arch, a beach swallowed by high water. When council member Ray Pene talks about his native Utah, his landmarks are those created by extraction and industry: mines, diverted rivers, power plants, the new Micron computer chip manufacturing factory near Lehi.

A decision on the Utah delegation's bill, H.R. 1745, is imminent, says Ken Rait of the Southern Utah Wilderness Alliance. He says it will probably pass the House easily, but may be defeated by the Senate, or possibly vetoed by President Clinton.

Edwards is optimistic, but he hasn't stopped fighting for the canyon. He recently bought a secondhand suit at a thrift store and traveled to Washington, D.C., to lobby Utah lawmakers. He wore dress shoes, not river sandals, and grew big blisters on his ankles. He told lawmakers they must put the Pene deletion back into H.R. 1745.

"I want to believe some people heard what I was saying," reports Edwards.

Aaron Edens, aide to Rep. Enid Waldholtz, R-Utah, says the congresswoman is looking into the possibility of adding the deleted portion of Westwater to the 300,000-acre amendment she plans to introduce when the bill hits the House floor.

Meanwhile, Pene vows to hold onto the claims he considers his: "Am I going to let the property go? No!"

The controversy over BLM wilderness in Utah is described in more detail in Section 4.

DECEMBER 25, 1995

How to Influence Congress on Just Dollars a Day

BY RAY RING

Ray Wheeler, who has a history of determination that includes hiking nearly all the way across Utah, climbed on a jet in Salt Lake City last July 12, bound for the nation's halls of power.

The occasion was an emergency, he felt: Congress seemed about to ram through a bill that would open much of Utah's wilderness to development.

Wheeler had snatched four hours' sleep during the previous two days; he'd been scrambling to gather materials, writing and rewriting a statement that he was going to read to senators in a hearing he saw as crucial. In Washington, D.C., he was in motion again, assembling a packet that included news reports and first-hand observation from his many hikes, a dozen large color photos and a 12-square-foot poster, all portraying the Utah wilderness that he knew so well—the canyon of the Dirty Devil River, for example, Labyrinth Canyon, Happy Canyon, the San Rafael Swell around Muddy Creek.

Only by working through his third all-nighter was he ready to walk into the hearing room the next day when his name was called, and sit at the witness table. There, he was stunned. Only a half-dozen or so of the subcommittee members had bothered to attend the hearing, and by the time Wheeler got his chance, only one senator, Mark Hatfield of Oregon, remained on the dais. Nudging another Utah activist to hold up his photos at the proper time, Wheeler read his statement in the direction of the mostly empty senators' chairs.

The Oregon senator, in animated conversation with an aide, paid little attention, until it was time for him to bring down the gavel on Wheeler's seven allotted minutes.

Wheeler had picked the redrock country as his home more than 20 years ago, after scouting much of the West as a river guide and backcountry lodge worker. With a degree in English Lit as a springboard, he'd arranged a life around chronicling Utah's wilderness. He had a day job at the University of Utah with one-quarter time off, so he could go on expeditions, and a wife, Amy O'Connor, who shared his politics and his love for the outdoors.

Over the years, Wheeler had mapped a route and come within 15 miles of hiking mostly contiguous wilderness from Colorado to Nevada; he'd inventoried wilderness all over Utah, acre by acre, helping to spur protection of some U.S. Forest Service areas; he'd helped put together a coffee-table book, called *Wilderness at the Edge*, detailing the wonders of areas that the Bureau of Land Management was temporarily protecting and evaluating.

He'd come to understand how special Utah's wilderness is— hunks as large as 1 million acres almost blending together without interruption from people. He believed that the decision on wilderness managed by the BLM—Utah's biggest landlord, managing 44 percent of the state's area—would leave a permanent imprint. The BLM process of studies, comment periods and recommendations had dragged on all the years he had been in Utah, and he'd gotten cynical about the lack of victory. Then most of Utah's congressional delegation had united behind what seemed like the ultimate disastrous bill.

Wheeler, 43, felt he couldn't live with himself if he didn't go down fighting.

He had planned his D.C. trip to last only a few days, but after the hearing went so badly, he extended his stay. He'd been associated with groups such as the Southern Utah Wilderness Alliance (SUWA) and the Utah Wilderness Coalition, but at this point he was freelancing in a niche he'd discovered: The groups had concentrated on lobbying the House of Representatives, so he'd conduct a personal campaign targeting senators.

His first problem was to persuade busy political people from New York and California and other urban power bases that a bunch of rock and sand in Utah mattered.

By trial and error, he perfected his method: call the senator's office and get the name of the staffer who would handle such approaches. Above all, don't leave a message saying that some unknown, waffle-stomping maverick named Ray Wheeler was calling blind about Utah wilderness. Instead, leave no message, but call back later acting like Ray Wheeler the insider, who of course expected his call to be put through. Wheeler would keep pressing until the staffer agreed to a meeting, where he could make eye contact and present his photos and poster.

Wheeler operated out of SUWA's national office, which sits over a Chinese restaurant a few blocks from the Capitol, and out of the Sierra Club office, which is closer to the Senate side. Other than the plane ticket and two nights at a cheap bed and breakfast, which SUWA funded, Wheeler was paying his expenses. He was on foot pretty much everywhere he went, in a city that was sweltering in a record heat wave.

Some nights he slept on the carpet of SUWA's office. One night he slept on a sheet of cardboard on the fire escape outside the office, feeling not too different from the homeless people who scrounged on the streets below.

Always on deadline or running late, Wheeler would show up for his meetings with the key staffers carrying all his props, sweaty and out of breath; he'd try to persuade the stranger from another culture to imagine what his material and photos represented. He'd pull out one photo and say, "I've stood right on that spot— pretty awesome, isn't it? That's where the tar sands development would go."

One meeting, with Martin McBroom, a staffer for heavyweight Sen. Robert Byrd of West Virginia, looked to be especially difficult. McBroom interrupted Wheeler's spiel, taking charge, firing skeptical questions and pawing through the supporting evidence. "Aren't you really overstating your case?" McBroom wanted to know. Then he noticed the portfolio, and took possession of it, much as he had taken possession of the meeting. As McBroom looked through the photos, he warmed. It turned out that McBroom was also a photographer who had tried to capture landscapes; he began to admit some enthusiasm for Utah's sand and rock. He also offered advice.

"Senate staffers are snobs. You look sloppy. We don't appreciate that," McBroom said. He reached out and straightened Wheeler's tie.

In two intense weeks, Wheeler managed to meet with staffers for 34 senators. Then he dragged himself onto a jet and flew home.

MANAGING THE WILD
Too Many People

The following stories, as well as others located in later "Managing the Wild" subsections, delve into the galaxy of management issues that arise when wilderness is formally protected.

Once wilderness areas began to be designated, it didn't take long for some of them to start suffering from their own popularity. The impacts that an increasing number of visitors have had on wilderness—and some possible solutions—are explored in more detail here.

Wilderness Exists in Name Only

BY PHILIP FRADKIN

The best way to read an account of John Muir's ascent of Mount Ritter 100 years ago is to dine on ox-tail soup, beef stroganoff, chocolate pudding, cookies and a shot of brandy. Then curl up with a cigar in a warm sleeping bag snuggled between two rocks at the west end of Thousand Island Lake. At the 9,800-foot level of the lake, the glow of the setting sun lingers on the crenellated peak, thought to be inaccessible until Muir made his solitary climb.

Wrote Muir: "After gaining a point about halfway to the top, I was brought to a dead stop, with arms outspread, clinging close to the face of the rock, unable to move hand or foot either up or down. My doom appeared fixed. I must fall."

After mastering this temporary stroke of fear, Muir scrambled to the top and then discovered that the sun was setting. With only a crust of bread to eat all day, he had many miles of hiking in the night to return to his camp in a pine thicket, where he slept without blankets in "the biting cold."

These instructions are now given to hikers along the Muir Trail in Sequoia and Kings Canyon National Parks. They state in capital letters:

"RECOMMEND THAT ALL DRINKING WATER BE TREATED WITH PURIFICATION TABLETS OR BE BOILED BEFORE USE. (BOIL 10 MINUTES)"

Park Superintendent John S. McLaughlin says that tests of

backcountry lakes and streams had shown that the bacteria count from human wastes exceeded U.S. Public Health Service standards.

In the Inyo National Forest, where the John Muir and Minarets Wilderness areas are located, the Forest Service has hired a hydrologist for the first time to test High Sierra water this summer for pollution.

In Yosemite National Park, the Park Service has hired a hydrologist for the first time to test water there.

In Yosemite National Park, the Park Service is so leery of the drinking water in the Merced River below the heavily used Little Yosemite area that it has closed its drinking facilities at the top of Nevada Falls.

Says Superintendent Cone: "Because of the human wastes emptying in from the back country, we don't feel confident of the water source. The only way we could feel confident is to chlorinate the water."

Overcrowding has contributed to water pollution, according to the experts, in the following manner:

—Because there is very little or no topsoil in the High Sierra and because warm temperatures exist for only about 1½ to 2 months, human and animal feces have little chance of decomposing.

—More likely, waste is liable to be washed undiluted into lakes which at the height of the hiking season have little or no outflow.

Water pollution is not the only evidence of overuse of certain wilderness areas. A Forest Service report on the John Muir Wilderness Area west of Bishop states:

"This intensive use is causing site deterioration—as is evidenced by vegetation being damaged or destroyed, increasing areas of bare ground and by the invasion of sub-climax species near trails, lakes and streams.

"In many heavily used areas, most or all the dead wood has been burned for firewood. Live trees are often cut and attempts made to burn the green wood...The opportunities for camping solitude are diminishing and in many areas no longer exist during the peak-use periods...

"During the summer, human habitation seems almost permanent because as soon as a camp is vacated by one party, it is often occupied by another. This level of occupancy is in conflict with the quality levels that offer the opportunities for solitude..."

When issuing the wilderness permit needed to enter the Desolation Wilderness area, the receptionist at the South Lake Tahoe Ranger Station cautioned: "You better hold onto your backpack. We just had a guy come in here and report that his was stolen while he was asleep by Eagle Lake."

At Yosemite, a park official said: "If you put a $60 Kelty pack or a $150 sleeping bag down you just might lose them. It is sad but true."

Wayne Merry, who runs the climbing school in Yosemite, is making an attempt to educate users of the backcountry. He is conducting six-day "minimum impact trips" into the wilderness this summer. Says Merry: "It gets so bad that if you turn over a rock to hide the garbage, you find another camper has been there." So, on Merry's trips, all garbage will be hauled out, there will be no campfires and cross-country travel will cut down on trail use.

All of this would come as a shock to John Muir, should he now retrace his steps along crest of the Sierra Nevada. He would be told by a friendly wilderness ranger:

"Bullfrog and Timberline Lakes are closed to all camping and grazing, in the Evolution Basin and at Kearsarge Lakes wood fires are prohibited, and I am sorry to tell you, sir, but you can only stay one night at Paradise Valley, Woods Creek, Rae Lakes, Kearsarge Lakes, Charlotte Lakes, Sixty Lake Basin, Junction Meadow and Bubbs Creek.

"Oh, and at these last named areas you have to camp 100 feet from the lakes and streams. Thank you, and have a good trip in the wilderness."

It's Us—Not Them—
Guilty This Time: Wilderness
Endangered by Overuse

BY MARJANE AMBLER

Don't look now, but we're losing our wilderness. No, it's not an overzealous capitalistic plot designed to get the coal or the timber out when no one's looking. It's you and I who are responsible.

"It's time to blow the whistle. Unless we start managing wilderness use, we're losing wilderness just as surely as if we'd turn the bulldozers loose on it," declares Floyd Wilson, a former summer ranger in the Rawah Wilderness in Colorado.

The Rawah is, perhaps, an extreme example, but the use and abuse of the wilderness resource is proceeding much more quickly than efforts to determine any management policies. Although we like to think it has reached crisis proportions only in California, near population concentrations, the use of wilderness and primitive areas in the Rocky Mountain region increased by 100 percent in just a seven-year period, from 1967 to 1974. Use in the Rawah also increased by 100 percent, the Maroon Bells-Snowmass Wilderness in Colorado by more than 200 percent, the Glacier Primitive Area in Wyoming by more than 300 percent. And there's no end in sight.

So what's the answer? Creating more wilderness? Presently there are about 12 million acres in the wilderness system. Another 12 million acres are being studied by the National Forest Service, and 26 million more are in administration proposals now before Congress. That means that if all of these acres were designated as wilderness, the acres would increase the present wilderness system by 300 percent. But adding acreage is only a short-term solution, at best, especially in light of the fact that the additional acres are already being used.

No, the answer is tougher than that: management—even though the concept of managing wilderness seems to be a contradiction of the principles behind its establishment. Most people believe it was meant to be left alone. Probably that belief is the seed of the present problems. We've looked the other direction as our wilderness disintegrates, not wanting to interfere with the "natural process."

For many of us, it takes a traumatic experience to recognize there is a problem, such as finding a favorite remote campsite stripped of its wood supply and covered with litter, the nearby field of columbines gone.

Still, we're tempted to choose an easy solution: "If we only keep THEM out..." Wilson says he hears this often at Forest Service workshops where citizens are discussing management. "Them" might refer to horseback riders, outfitters, or large groups from schools or organizations.

However, Wilson says that much of the damage he sees is the result of small groups of backpackers. It's us—even those of us who consider ourselves experienced, but who have not adjusted our camping techniques to keep up with the growing numbers of users. We continue to pull dead limbs off trees to feed our fires, to camp in alpine meadows and to take our dogs with us on the trail.

Wince at any of those? Or wonder that they could really do any harm? There was a time when a camper with a certain amount of care and common sense could treat a campsite in a way so that it would recover quickly (meaning only a few days). But times are changing in many of our wildernesses, and it is very possible there won't be a few days leeway before the next campers come and compound our impact.

Encouragingly, 92 percent of the wilderness users would not harm anything if they knew what to do, according to Wilson, although when he started work as a summer ranger he was convinced that most people were out to deliberately destroy the wilderness. District Ranger H.B. "Doc" Smith of the Lander, Wyo., District, Shoshone National Forest, agrees that with the exception of a few "old-timers" (not necessarily old in years, but experienced) who are set in their ways, most people want to do what is right for the wilderness. "They're most receptive to information about proper use—they're hungry for it," he says.

In fact, when the users of the Mount Zirkel Wilderness of Colorado were informed in 1970 that it was suffering from overuse, they came up with recommendations for restrictions that were more stringent than the Forest Service's.

Getting the Word Out

The problem of getting the information to the users has been overwhelming for Floyd Wilson and his wife, Irene. The Wilsons have formed the Wilderness Education Foundation and given slide and movie shows to over 3,000 schools as well as universities, churches, and other groups. Whenever they testify at a wilderness hearing, they call for management of the wilderness. They took former Rep. Donald Brotzmah, R-Colo., into the Rawah Wilderness to show him the conditions and spoke before Congress in September of 1974. "(The congressmen) were not aware of the problem," Wilson says. Brotzman told the Wilsons that they were the only ones to ever write to him about the need for wilderness management.

Wilson is bitterly critical of conservation groups for what he perceives as their lack of concern. "To advocate, lobby and pressure for more and more areas to be put under the Wilderness System while ignoring and excusing the destruction of those already in the system is a form of hypocrisy that is…repugnant to us," he says.

He puts more blame on the Forest Service, which he says is ignoring the problem and is putting out printed material that does more to promote use than to control it.

Wilson is accused of being so evangelistic and egotistical in his crusade that he turns off potential disciples. Wilson admits that he and his wife are, to some extent, bitter. But he insists that we cannot wait until all wilderness areas have been designated until we start worrying about managing them, as some conservationists insist. He says the damage that is being done is long-term—that already some areas, such as the Rawahs, Maroon Bells-Snowmass and Eagles Cap are lost and cannot be saved.

The Wilsons also put some of the blame on mountain-equipment stores and on outdoor schools that make billions of dollars encouraging use of wilderness. Irene points out that most of the equipment catalogs show tents pitched in the tundra, a practice that the Wilsons deplore because of the fragility of that ecosystem. Instead, they would like to see the mountain equipment stores participate in the education of users by, for example, putting a copy of an approved code of conduct in each pair of boots they sell.

One Ranger's Use Study

Ranger Doc Smith says the Forest Service is addressing the problem of management, although he admits that the agency's efforts are not keeping pace with the growing use. There has been no attempt to standardize management of wilderness across the country, and Smith doesn't think it's necessary. Now, each district ranger assumes the responsibility and approaches management in his own way.

When Smith attends wilderness meetings with other rangers, he finds, however, that many end up turning to the same solutions. This is because many of the problems are the same: sanitation, horses, use concentration along trails, water quality, campfires that get out of control, litter.

In his own district in the Wind River Mountains, Smith used volunteers from the National Outdoor Leadership School (NOLS) as part of his study on use of the Popo Agie Primitive Area to try to measure the carrying capacity of the area.

The volunteers spent two 10-day sessions in the area the summer of 1974, and then prepared a 26-page report that included recommendations on carrying capacity and ways to reduce the abuse of the area. Smith emphasizes that the study was only one of many recommendations he is taking into consideration in making management decisions.

The study utilized one innovative measure that might be useful for future studies by others: Volunteers assessed the experience level of the campers they encountered, as well as their numbers. They concluded that the carrying capacity of the area for experienced visitors is twice what it is for in inexperienced visitors.

Smith explains with an analogy: If you had eight slobs in your living room who didn't use ashtrays, who spilt drinks on the carpet and who were loud and obnoxious, the use of the living room would have passed its carrying capacity. However, 16 or 20 courteous visitors would have far less impact. Still, he says, there would obviously be a limit to the number of courteous users since you're dealing with a finite resource.

The Popo Agie study indicated that as many as 75 percent of the users were inexperienced. Smith admits that the figure is a very subjective analysis and could be affected by the volunteers judging the visitors by their deviations from NOLS practices rather than deviation from more broadly accepted standards.

However, he says, the figure still indicates the size of the problem and the need for education. The volume also recommended several solutions for educating visitors, including some that others have recommended, such as certification and the use of Forest Service printed material and seminars.

Smith says he is very interested in one of their suggestions— development of a slide show and script dealing with proper backcountry conservation techniques, which would be required for groups applying for permits.

This summer, more NOLS volunteers are working in the Popo Agie Primitive Area as backcountry teachers. One of their duties will be taking pictures that could be used in slide presentations.

But principally, they will be offering their services as teachers to campers at their campsites. Smith says he doesn't know how receptive the campers will be to the intruders and their information. He says he realizes it will be a delicate situation, and the four teachers were chosen partially on the basis of their diplomacy.

Dollars Dictate

However, Smith says this program, like all other management suggestions, requires more money and more administration than the Forest Service now has available.

The Lander District now requires permits for groups using the Popo Agie Primitive Area and recently began requiring them for horse users. Even that minor change required signs, bookkeeping, and the time of a wilderness ranger who could keep track of grass conditions and notify the district office, which determines where horses will be allowed.

Volunteers are a big help, Smith says, but if more volunteers would come to him now, he would have to refuse their services because of the lack of administrative manpower. For the NOLS volunteers, NOLS provides the food and equipment, and the Forest Service provides administration, and transportation and lodging when they're in town.

"I don't think there's a wilderness area in the country that's funded anywhere near adequately," Smith says.

The Wilderness Act of 1964 offers no help in this regard. It states: "No appropriation shall be available for the payment of expenses or salaries for the administration of the National Wilderness Preservation System as a separate unit nor shall any appropriations be available for additional personnel stated as being required solely for the purpose of managing or administering areas solely because they are included within the National Wilderness Preservation System."

This section perhaps reflects the thinking at the time the act was written: that wilderness areas could be set aside and left alone to assure their protection. However, Floyd Wilson says that the condition of the wildernesses today was not what he nor any of the others who pushed for the act had in mind at that time.

When Wilson testified before Congress last year about the need for management, he said there was no need to change the act nor to make a specific enactment for wilderness funds.

Smith agrees, and says the best tactic would be to increase Forest Service funding for all recreation; the money would be distributed from that for wilderness management.

"Look at the figures on use. It's so obvious that recreation needs more money than it's getting—more than timbering... The conservation groups could help by encouraging management and limited use. If they can take the Forest Service to court over timbering, then they could also do it over management," Wilson says.

"If we're going to have wilderness, we've got to pay the price," Wilson says, which includes both federal dollars and personal sacrifices when the use of the wilderness is limited as it must be.

"If we can't do this, then let's just do away with wilderness and get away from being hypocrites."

Budding Bureaucracy Copes with Crowds, Confusion and Conflicts

BY LOUISA WILLCOX

Originally, the word "wilderness" connoted mystery, danger, the presence of wild beasts and the absence of human control. However, one finds in today's wilderness a plethora of signs, trails, campsites and people. Many feel that the kind of wilderness experienced by Lewis and Clark and John Wesley Powell is rapidly becoming a thing of the past, preserved only in books and the memories of old-timers.

Schemes for rationing the number of visitors have been implemented in 27 designated and proposed wilderness areas, which make up 8 percent of the U.S. Forest Service wilderness and 42 percent of the National Park Service wilderness.

At the same time, resentment has been brewing against such heavy-handed methods of control. A recently filed lawsuit and numerous threats of legal action against the agencies that manage wilderness indicate the heat of public concern. Managing agencies, particularly the Forest Service, are beginning to explore other techniques, such as education and wilderness zoning, which in some cases could reduce the need for rationing.

At the root of the problem is a steadily growing group of wilderness-hungry recreationists. Despite the increased cost of gas, use continues to rise at an average rate of 8 percent to 10 percent a year, so that now, more than ever, backpackers are threatening to "love wilderness to death." At the same time, the number of new areas suitable for inclusion in the 19 million-acre National Wilderness Preservation System is dropping every year. And increasing pressure from timber and mining interests could make large increases in the system politically impossible in years to come.

A New Profession

Keeping some wildness in wilderness has become the goal of a new profession: wilderness management. In recent years, even wilderness, a symbol of freedom from the constraints of government institutions, has become host to a bureaucracy.

Due to the newness of the profession, many of its practitioners are old-school foresters, trained in the biological sciences and timber cruising, not social engineering. Others in the National Park Service are steeped in the "parks for the people" philosophy, accustomed to designing campsites and trails and posting signs.

When the Wilderness Act was passed in 1964, anyone who suggested that wilderness needed managing would have been laughed at. All you had to do was draw a line around it and leave it alone. But as use has escalated, so have problems of trail erosion, water pollution, tree stripping and wildlife disturbances.

Faced with signs of degradation of the resources and conflicts among users, managers are increasingly compelled to act. Many managers in this situation have decided to make recreationists bite the bullet by limiting their numbers. Other options include educating campers to leave fewer traces, and engineering projects — such as huts, privies and improved tent sites—that increase the amount of use a wilderness can sustain.

The administrators of all wilderness areas are currently developing wilderness management plans. The National Park Service's in-house handbook "Management Policies" directs the planning process with some general rules of thumb, such as flexibility, fairness, respect for visitor freedom and the application of the "minimum tools necessary for management purposes."

The Forest Service is subject to a more detailed set of require-ments, some established by the National Forest Management Act of 1976. These include public participation in the planning process, as well as setting wilderness capacity limits.

Philosophical Disagreements

Despite statutory planning requirements, however, the direction of wilderness management is bogged down in fundamental dis-agreements over philosophy.

One side in the argument favors human "use and enjoyment," in the words of the Wilderness Act, as the highest goal of wilder-ness use. For them, engineering and education are generally appropriate solutions to overuse problems. On the other side are wilderness purists, who lean toward preserving natural processes and an aura of solitude in an area, even if it means less conven-ience for people. This group tends to support strict control of visitors through rationing in crowded areas.

Congress, anticipating that commodity interests, not recre-ationists, would represent the major threats to wilderness preser-vation, has provided little guidance for developing a wilderness management philosophy.

A survey of wilderness managers conducted last year by the Northeastern Forest Experiment Station in Durham, N.H., found that most of the administrators who responded are confused about the basic meaning of wilderness. One manager wrote, "Public administrators, experts and professionals do not agree about what wilderness is or how it should be operated—if we could decide what wilderness is, then we might be able to elimi-nate non-wilderness happenings in it."

Although study techniques have increased in sophistication, with computers that simulate hiking patterns and calculate the number of encounters on the trail, the question of where to set capacity limits remains largely speculative. Many researchers have concluded that the idea of a cut-off point for ecological or social wilderness quality may, in fact, not exist. Ecologist William Moen says, "The complexity of the dynamic relationship between an animal and its environment is so great that the human mind cannot fully comprehend it. Carrying capacity is not a straightforward, definable biological relationship."

Currently, proponents of the wilderness "use and enjoyment" philosophy are using studies that debunk the carrying capacity theory to support their preference for engineering solutions and visitor education over rationing. In the hands of a bureaucracy, rationing has enormous potential for abuse, some say. Others, including the managers of a number of Eastern wildernesses, feel that rationing is unfair and impractical in areas that traditionally host many visitors.

Defending Rationing

On the other hand, members of the wilderness purist school, such as George Stankey and Robert Lucas, researchers at the Rocky Mountain Forest and Range Experiment Station in Missoula, Mont., are using their calculations of carrying capacity to defend rationing systems. These include rationing by reservation, first come-first served, lottery, fees and outdoor proficiency certification. Among the suggested methods, the last two have not yet been tried. However, momentum is building to experiment with certification. Under such a system, admission to wilderness would depend on proving skills and knowledge that protect the user and the wilderness.

While certification would be an expensive rationing technique for both visitors and the managing agencies, so are the reservation and first-come, first-served methods used today. According to recent calculations of permit costs conducted outside the agency, wilderness managers (and in turn U.S. taxpayers) spend $5 to $20 to issue one "free" user permit.

Responses to a recent survey of the 27 managers who currently ration use indicate that many user limitations are being set "arbitrarily" and "without previous study." "It was a seat-of-the-pants guess," says one manager. "We might as well have flipped a coin," says another. Many blamed insufficient funds and staff to measure use and study impacts.

Some researchers and agency critics feel that the decision-making process would not greatly improve even if the money were available. John Stanley, co-author of the Sierra Club's 1979 Wilderness Impact Study, says: "Both the Sierra Club and wilderness managers end up reacting to peer pressure from other wilderness users when making policy decisions regarding the kinds and amounts of wilderness use."

Some users, frustrated with permits and seemingly capricious limits, are threatening legal action in Washington's Mount Rainier National Park Wilderness, in New Hampshire's Great Gulf Wilderness and in Great Smokies National Park Wilderness in Tennessee.

Rationing systems in the nation's popular whitewater rivers, such as Idaho's Middle Fork of the Salmon and the Grand Canyon in Arizona, have also been subject to similar threats by river runners—and in the case of the Grand Canyon, to a legal suit. Among charges against the National Park Service, which recently instituted a phase-out of motorized boat travel through the canyon, the plaintiffs, a group of commercial boatmen, accuse the agency of adopting an elitist rationing policy. By increasing the time, money and stamina required to run the river, the boatmen charge that the Park Service is discriminating against the old, the weak, and those with tight schedules.

Different Approaches

Some administrators, mostly from the Forest Service, are experimenting with ways of doing things differently.

Managers of the Selway-Bitterroot's Moose Creek District in Idaho are finding that teaching minimum-impact camping techniques in the area's public schools is reducing some types of impacts along several drainages. While the Forest Service used to take out several pack trains of trash a season in these areas, the district ranger says that since the education program began, the amount of garbage has dwindled—to less than one backpack-full last year. For this area, at least, education has so far eliminated the need to ration. The program—cheaper, easier to administrate and less controversial than rationing—has spread quietly to several other Forest Service wilderness areas.

In the White River National Forest in Colorado, administrators of the Maroon Bells-Snowmass Wilderness are developing a plan that aims to avoid a blanket approach to user restrictions, by tailoring management practices in different areas to the interests of various groups of users.

Instead of assigning one overall carrying capacity for the wilderness, the plan would establish several. This approach sets up different zones of experience within the wilderness. These zones include an outer "transitional" corridor, which would bear higher concentrations of use, and a series of more natural areas as one penetrates into the inner core of the wilderness. The pristine inner sanctum would have no trails or signs.

The plan, due to be published in several weeks, seeks to provide opportunities for four distinct categories of users that have been found to frequent that wilderness area: the elbow-rubbers, the hard-core hikers, those who try to avoid risky situations and a group that possesses several of these attributes.

If the public is satisfied with the way the plan works, it will be incorporated in the forestwide plan for White River National Forest, slated for completion in 1985. Managers currently involved with the wilderness planning process nationwide look upon the Maroon Bells-Snowmass plan as a potential prototype for their own plans.

While the plan does not solve the rationing issue, it avoids it by giving purists and non-purists separate niches.

Ultimately, Congress or the courts may be forced to give wilderness management a clearer direction. In the meantime, experiments such as those in the Selway-Bitterroot and Maroon Bells-Snowmass may keep complaints from various factions down to low decibel levels.

Agency Hopes Fees Will Protect a Crowded Wilderness

BY JERRY THULL

Desolation Wilderness in eastern California is one of those places that don't come close to living up to their names. Its beauty, some say, is only matched by its crowds.

Thanks to its accessibility from San Francisco (three-and-a-half hours away), Sacramento (two hours away), and Lake Tahoe (just a few minutes away), the wilderness is booming.

Last Memorial Day, for instance, 700 visitors flocked to its Eagle Falls Trailhead near Lake Tahoe. Last year, a total of 67,000 day users visited Desolation Wilderness, while 18,000 people camped overnight. Of the 380 wilderness areas in the country, Desolation had the fifth-highest use according to 1993 figures— and was the most visited for its 63,600-acre size.

That could change, thanks to the area's participation in a pilot project that allows the Forest Service to set fees for uses that have formerly been free. Congress approved the experiment for some public lands last year, and under the law, wilderness managers get to keep 80 percent of any fees collected instead of sending the money off to Washington. How much to charge is the question.

When the El Dorado National Forest first proposed fees for both day and overnight use, many hikers, campers and anglers complained that they'd be paying a disproportionate amount of money. In late February, the agency announced it would drop any fees for day use, though other fees were still in the works. Forest official Frank Mosbacher says a day-use fee would be difficult to collect "without an army of cops" since wilderness boundaries are both rugged and not clearly marked.

Mosbacher also says an overnight camping fee makes sense, since quotas and reservations are already in place. He says the agency is now proposing an overnight camping fee of $5 a night, with two or more nights for $10, and a total of up to 14 days of camping permitted.

Some members of the High Sierra Hikers Association called the new fees discriminatory because they aren't applied to all users of public land, such as ranchers, miners and outfitters. While some critics feared the fees would be prohibitive for groups such as Tahoe Turning Point, an outdoor education program for troubled teens, Mosbacher says a maximum fee of $100 per permit for 15 people should resolve that objection.

No one disputes the wilderness is heavily used and bears the scars of too many people. Mosbacher ticks off the damage: not enough bathrooms at popular trailheads, compacted soils and damaged vegetation around lakes, not enough money to clear trails in time to head off hikers who make new trails, and not enough money to work up and present materials educating visitors about wilderness ethics.

Mosbacher, who hopes Desolation Wilderness can begin its experiment with fees by Memorial Day, projects they can raise $180,000 a year. Since the Forest Service budget for maintenance has declined by 50 percent over the past three years, he says, "we can use the money." He also hopes a "stakeholder process" that includes an annual meeting and more consultation with users will improve the way the wilderness is both managed and treated.

DECEMBER 17, 2001

A Crowded Washington Wilderness Gets Ugly

BY JAMES MORTON TURNER

In northern Washington state, the Pasayten Wilderness stands out. Its 530,031 acres of wild land buttress the Canadian border. It offers the promise of grizzly bear, lynx and wolf in the Pacific Northwest, and it has a unique geological history that left the area dotted with rare boreal hummocks. Even so, when Congress established the remote area as wilderness in 1968, it received little attention. George Wooten of the Kettle Range Conservation Group remembers the Pasayten "as our own secret wilderness— the last wilderness." Now, he says, "you can drop that. The Pasayten has been discovered."

The Pasayten, like so many Western forests, has been discovered by recreationists. Its promise as an important low-elevation biological reserve has been discovered, too. And that has placed the Forest Service, which administers the Pasayten, in the middle of a sharp controversy over how to manage this tract of the Okanogan National Forest. The problem stems from a paradox rooted in the Wilderness Act: how to manage the National Wilderness Preservation System both for recreational use and as an ecological reserve.

In the Pasayten, some say the Forest Service's bias has been made abundantly clear. For the past three summers, Martha Hall, a former schoolteacher from Anacortes, Wash., has painstakingly documented the threat that poorly managed recreation poses to the Pasayten's wilderness habitat. Hall is entranced with the Pasayten because she believes it "is one of the most valuable wilderness areas we have" for its biological diversity. But her field notes reveal a wilderness laced with eroding trails, pockmarked by overused campsites and sullied by trampled wetlands.

With her evidence in hand, Hall has raised the alarm over backcountry conditions in the Pasayten. Hall's criticism, however, has not been limited to the Forest Service. She has taken on a well-entrenched tradition on the Pasayten: its community of commercial outfitters.

"She Was Hunting Us"

The five outfitters on the Pasayten, with special permits from the Forest Service, advertise a cowboys' wilderness replete with rustic camps, roaring campfires and good hunting. While initial Forest Service research reports corroborate much of the overuse Hall has reported, all told the trampled trails, campsites and wetlands add up to only a fraction of this large wilderness. To the horse-packers, those worn areas are like small stains on an old, familiar shirt. Claude Miller and Aaron Lee Burkhart, who each earn upwards of $3,000 in revenue every week that they pack customers into the backcountry, believe conditions on the Pasayten have improved recently.

Until last year, sheep and cattle had grazed the Pasayten for decades, and the outfitters argue that much of the damage Hall has focused on is actually the legacy of that grazing. Miller is quick to criticize Hall's work on the Pasayten. Not only is she relatively new to the wilderness, he said, "she was hunting us: coming into our camps, and chewing out me and my guests."

In July 2000, the Pasayten no longer seemed large enough to comfortably accommodate the different views of wilderness held by Hall and the packers. Hall ran afoul of one local horsepacker when she and her sister were spotted taking photographs in the backcountry. Hall says that the outfitter lost his temper, pushed her sister, and "kicked her backpack around like it was a football." The outfitter denies the allegations and counters that Hall and her sister had been impersonating Forest Service personnel. In turn, the five outfitters sued Hall for harassment, leading to a settlement and a restraining order requiring Hall to keep away from the packers' backcountry camps.

In the middle of the controversy is the Forest Service, which is trying to balance recreation and ecology, says Jim Archambeault, a recreation planner for the Okanogan National Forest.

Last summer, the Forest Service deployed botanists, range specialists and recreation specialists into the Pasayten to assess the wilderness area's condition. In the next few years, the agency must renew the packers' special-use permits and prepare a new management plan. Already, the Forest Service has begun to coordinate outfitters' backcountry itineraries and enforce limits on oversized parties. The agency has reintroduced wilderness permits and considered closing some campsites.

"The (Forest Service) is pulling the present knowledge together, saying, 'We've got some problems on the Pasayten, and we are going to work on them,'" says Archambeault.

The Root of Conflict

Hall and regional conservationists say they are relieved to hear that the agency is trying to make some changes, but they worry that just changing the management of the Pasayten won't get to the root of the problem: an agency policy that, historically, has ignored ecology.

At the Forest Service, wilderness management falls under the Division of Recreation at both the national and regional level. "There is very little in existing Forest Service management that seeks to promote the ecological values of wilderness," says Andy Stahl, executive director of the Forest Service Employees for Environmental Ethics.

Since the passage of the Wilderness Act, environmental groups have expended most of their energy lobbying for the designation of new wilderness lands. Now that the National Wilderness

Preservation System includes over 105 million acres, some groups say the environmental movement should start to focus on resource management.

"Grazing, timbering and mining are on the way out," says George Nickas of Wilderness Watch. "But recreation demand is going to grow and grow and grow." In the long term, he says, "that poses a much greater risk to changing the character of our public lands than did all of those extractive industries of the past."

Finding the Wild

The Frank Church-River of No Return Wilderness in Idaho.

—PHOTO BY LELAND HOWARD

The Wilderness Act immediately designated 9.1 million acres of wilderness. It also initiated a series of inventories in which the U.S. Forest Service, National Park Service and U.S. Fish and Wildlife Service sent staffers into national parks, national wildlife refuges, and the Forest Service's "primitive areas" to identify lands eligible for wilderness protection and, ultimately, recommend them to the president and Congress for formal designation.

Much of the early drama played out in the national forests. While the Wilderness Act required the Forest Service to evaluate its primitive areas, it said nothing about the agency's much larger holdings of roadless lands. But starting in 1965 with the citizen-initiated Lincoln-Scapegoat wilderness proposal, ordinary citizens began forcing the agency's hand by developing their own proposals to designate roadless land as wilderness. Recognizing that it was only a matter of time before citizens' groups would do the same elsewhere, the Forest Service took the initiative to inventory its roadless areas and determine which lands might qualify as wilderness—and which could be kept open for logging.

In 1971, the Forest Service began the Roadless Area Review and Evaluation (RARE) process to evaluate some 56 million acres of roadless national forest lands. The process slogged along, dogged by serious questions about the adequacy of the Forest Service's findings, and by a Sierra Club lawsuit, which alleged that the Forest Service was using rigorous "purity standards" to disqualify large amounts of land from consideration as wilderness. In 1977, the original RARE inventory was reincarnated as a more comprehensive program called RARE II, which ultimately identified approximately 62 million acres of roadless land.

In the meantime, Congress refined the concept of wilderness. The 1978 Endangered American Wilderness Act, for example, jettisoned "purist" requirements and allowed land with some marks of previous human activity—such as limited logging, or roads that had fallen into disuse—to be considered for wilderness protection.

Then, RARE II was itself killed by another lawsuit, this time from the state of California. For a time, it looked as if the Forest Service might be forced to do yet *another* assessment. But Congress began moving to break the impasse—and to avoid the possibility of a court injunction on development on roadless lands until the wilderness inventory issue was resolved. In 1980, Congress designated more than 56 million acres of wilderness in Alaska, along with more than 4.4 million acres of wilderness in Idaho, New Mexico and Colorado. Then, in 1984, it passed wilderness bills for Oregon, Washington, Arizona and Utah, as well as Vermont, New Hampshire, North Carolina and Wisconsin, designating more than 8 million acres of wilderness in the Lower 48.

Idaho's Chamberlain Basin: "Either We Share It or We Lose It"

BY CARL BROWN

This story about the Idaho and Salmon River Breaks Primitive Areas gives a glimpse of the kinds of issues that arose once the Forest Service began evaluating its primitive areas for formal wilderness designation. Many similar issues arose with the much bigger group of roadless lands that the agency would consider for wilderness designation under its Roadless Area Review and Evaluation process, described in subsequent stories.

How do you keep 1.5 million acres of prime wilderness a secret from the nation for over 40 years? Somehow, they have done that in Idaho, watching quietly while the crowds flowed into the Sawtooths and the Selway-Bitterroot. Now those who know Idaho best are letting out the word. Why? A tobacco-chewing local explained, "It looks like we have our backs to the wall. Either we share it or we lose it."

The Idaho Primitive Area and its neighbor, the Salmon River Breaks Primitive Area, are the largest single block of wild land in the Lower 48 states. Ironically, the threat to them is the result of an attempt to grant them permanent protection in the National Wilderness Preservation System. If admitted, the two areas will be combined and renamed as the River of No Return Wilderness.

The difference between a primitive area and a wilderness is, essentially, a matter of bookkeeping. Primitive areas are managed under wilderness criteria, but without the legality and permanence of wilderness classification. The Wilderness Act of 1964 required that all Forest Service Primitive Areas be reviewed by 1975 and be recommended for either wilderness classification or declassified and opened to multiple-use management.

Most wilderness advocates felt that reclassification of the two primitive areas would be a mere formality. After all, they are remote and of unquestionable wilderness quality.

Nonetheless, advocates enthusiastically joined in the ritual of public hearings, turning out en masse for workshops and sending reams of letters to forest supervisors. All the other special interest groups showed up according to script. Livestock associations gave testimony to the salvation of government subsidized grazing. Prospectors left over from the 1860s warned of the Communistic takeover. Straight-faced corporate foresters suggested we acknowledge the right of all citizens to visit the area by crisscrossing it with roads which would intersect at dead center. Burned-out freaks pilfered the words and garbled the messages of John Muir and Ed Abbey. It was fine entertainment.

Council on the Offense

The real battle was not to save the primitive areas, but to enlarge them and give protection to the pristine headwaters of the Salmon River. Ernie Day, Ted Trueblood and several other veterans of wilderness wars joined ranks to create The River of No Return Wilderness Council. They argued that the area should be enlarged to 2.3 million acres, an almost ludicrous size to desk-bound bureaucrats, but essential to old-timers intent on preserving one integrated river system for the nation.

The proposal of the wilderness council was strengthened by similar proposals from other, more conservative groups. Idaho Gov. Cecil Andrus aggressively led a broad-based coalition advocating an expansion to 1.8 million acres, billing it as a compromise between the ideal of the wilderness council and the opposition of industry.

Surprisingly, the Idaho Department of Commerce and Development released a statement declaring, "It is very true that the exploitation of the primitive areas would play a part in improving the economy...but it would be *a short-run improvement*...Any short-term impact from development would be overshadowed by the perpetual loss of the character of Idaho's heartland" (emphasis is theirs).

Even many of those who officially endorsed 1.8 million acres were hoping for more. Martel Morache, Education Officer for Idaho Fish and Game, summed the undercurrent when he said, "We are sympathetic to the idea of a 2.3 million-acre proposal, but in light of opposition, realize that we must compromise. We will fight for 1.8 because it is the absolute minimum that will ensure our wildlife and fisheries resources."

Textbook Democracy

The machinery of reclassification takes a bit of time, but an understanding of its basics is essential to fully savor the tragicomedy which resulted. First, the regional supervisor of the U.S. Forest Service in Ogden, Utah, had to review public input before making his recommendation to the secretary of Agriculture. In turn, the secretary's recommendation was rubber-stamped by the president of the United States to become the official recommendation of the administration. Finally, the administration's recommendation became part of a bill to be voted upon by Congress. On the surface, it was a textbook example of democracy in action.

In December 1975, shortly after elections were wrapped up, the administration released its recommendation. To a person reading a newspaper in New York or Los Angeles, it looked like a great environmental victory had been won. Thirty-seven primitive areas across the country had been recommended for inclusion into the Wilderness System. Over 9 million acres were to be added. It was a day of celebration.

But supporters of the River of No Return Wilderness were shell-shocked. Ernie Day of the wilderness council said simply, "This has been the worst day of my entire life."

Andrus said, "I didn't think they had the audacity to try to cut the heartlands out of the state."

What had happened? Quite simply, the administration had mutilated the River of No Return Wilderness with a double-edged sword. Secretary of Agriculture Earl Butz had pared it to a mere 1.1 million acres. But more important was *what* he had cut out. To Idaho conservationists, it was like cutting the geysers out of Yellowstone or stopping Grand Canyon National Park at the rim. The administration had amputated Chamberlain Basin.

To even partially appreciate the loss, one must realize that Chamberlain Basin has been the secret of secrets, the one jewel that locals had hoped to keep to themselves.

Chamberlain Basin is the geographical heart of the River of No Return Wilderness. If it were an entity unto itself, it would rank 10th in size among the 126 units of the wilderness system. Anthony Park, attorney general of Idaho, described its value when he said, "It represents the best of what we in Idaho want to preserve for our children and our children's children."

The wildlife resources of Chamberlain are legendary. It is best known for its elk herd—at more than 2,000 head, the largest in the United States south of the Salmon River. The Basin is graced with 30 named and countless smaller unnamed meadows which serve as calving grounds and summer range. During winter the herd simply moves a few miles to the grassy slopes where Chamberlain breaks off and tumbles into the Salmon River, second deepest canyon on the continent.

Chamberlain is more than elk. It is a refuge for 190 species of wildlife. Martel Morache of Idaho Fish and Game says, "These remarkable lands support one of the most significant wildlife communities found anywhere in the continental United States."

A classic study of mountain lion behavior was done at the University of Idaho's research station in the basin. The largest concentration of bighorn sheep in the state, one of the largest in the nation, browses the nearby crags.

The mountain goat, mule deer, whitetail deer, fisher, marten, northern flying squirrel, great grey owl, pileated woodpecker, bald eagle, peregrine falcon, lynx, wolverine and timber wolf are also said to inhabit the basin.

Morache insists that the survival of significant populations of many of Chamberlain's species hinges upon wilderness classification. He says, "This could be the most far-reaching land management decision to ever affect wildlife in Idaho."

The fisheries resources of the area are also incomparable. According to the U.S. Fish and Wildlife Service, "The Salmon River and its tributaries provide approximately 80 percent of the chinook salmon and 30 percent of the steelhead trout in the entire Snake River System."

The quality of the fisheries is directly correlated with the quality of the watershed. Those who have battled all their lives to preserve it simply will not compromise on this issue. The granite soil of the Idaho Batholith is notoriously unstable. In the mid-1960s, a "model" logging operation promised to safeguard such soils. Nevertheless, spring rains pulled a mountain into the South Fork of the Salmon River, smothering the gravel spawning beds and destroying the anadromous fisheries of that tributary.

Nearly one-half of the watershed of the Middle Fork of Salmon River is outside the existing primitive area boundary. Although it is currently de facto wilderness, it is ripe for commercial exploitation. The contiguous areas proposed for addition by both the governor and the River of No Return Wilderness Council are intended to preserve the integrity of the Middle Fork.

Gouged by Butz, Not USFS

Why, then, was Chamberlain Basin gouged from the River of No Return Wilderness? Advocates believe that Secretary of Agriculture Butz was wooed and won by representatives of the mining and logging industries. Gov. Andrus immediately sued the federal government, forcing Butz to make public the recommendation of his regional forester.

The report showed that the U.S. Forest Service had recommended a 1.5 million-acre wilderness that included Chamberlain Basin. Andrus says this is absolute proof that an arbitrary political decision was made in Washington, a decision that ignored overwhelming public opinion and made a mockery of the entire review process.

The nitty-gritty for the administration's action seems to be to placate industry's demand for timber. Logging sales and logging roads are creeping closer to Chamberlain. In a region that is clear-cutting in between its clear-cuts in order to meet its lumber quota, 400,000 acres of virgin timber has a certain amount of attraction.

At the center of the Chamberlain timbering controversy are 300-year-old statuesque yellow pines which dot the grassy river breaks. Wilderness advocates are adamantly opposed to harvesting these giants. They fear that reforestation of the area would fail just as it has in similar areas outside the primitive area. At best, it takes 120 years for a tree to reach economic maturity in Chamberlain Basin. Also, the tragedy of the logging that wiped out the anadromous fisheries in another area is still a vivid memory.

A major concern of Idaho Fish and Game is that logging of the area would increase public access to Chamberlain, which would, in turn, erode the quality of the entire wilderness. They are vehemently opposed to trading one of the last quality elk herds in the nation, one which must be hunted with pack animals, for a quantity herd which can be hunted with a pickup truck.

Wilderness Council President Ted Trueblood dares to ask the

basic question, "Do we even need the timber in there?" He points out that even the estimates of the timber industry give a "no" answer. The sustained allowable cut from Chamberlain would be equal to one week's export of logs to Japan. Andrus says, "The quality of life in Idaho is not advanced by cutting trees in Chamberlain any more than by trying to establish an elk herd in downtown Boise."

Classic Wilderness War

It is obvious that the battle over Chamberlain is going to be a classic, a battle to be studied by generals of future wilderness wars. Where does it go from here?

According to Wilderness Society representative Dan Lechefsky, the real donnybrook will be in Washington, D.C., when the issue comes before Congress. Both the administration's 1.1 million-acre proposal and the citizens' 2.3 million-acre proposal have been introduced in House bills. Each is part of an omnibus bill including proposals for many other wilderness areas. In other words, there is an administration omnibus bill and a citizen omnibus bill.

Because it is so controversial, Idaho Sens. Frank Church and James McClure have requested separate hearings for the River of No Return Wilderness. They intend to pull the area out of both omnibus bills and have it debated on its own merits. Church's office indicates that hearings will not likely be held before early 1977.

While time erodes most conservation momentum, the River of No Return Wilderness Council is using time to refine its tactics. The group has established permanent headquarters in an office shared with The Wilderness Society and the Idaho Conservation League. They are actively recruiting members and expertise and soliciting donations to fund the showdown in 1977.

The council is also broadening its base of support, establishing a national coalition. It urges individuals to help by contacting their local representatives.

Everyone concerned about Chamberlain goes into battle realizing that the issue is probably a booby trap. They suspect that the logging industry is holding Chamberlain ransom, hoping to goad wilderness advocates into a victory-at-all costs fervor, planning to calmly sit back and use Chamberlain as a 400,000-acre bargaining chip for lands they want elsewhere.

Those lands are likely to be the timber-rich but soil-poor contiguous areas which the wilderness council and the governor have proposed for addition to the River of No Return Wilderness; lands essential to preserve the fragile headwaters of the Salmon River, lands needed to protect the integrity of the rest of the River of No Return Wilderness.

Last of the Old-Timers

Perhaps the most frustrated individuals in the fracas are local employees of the U.S. Forest Service. They know the area best. Many of them grew up there and have rambled the length and breadth of the area. They are the last of the old-timers who hired on with the Forest Service so they could be in their beloved outdoors. More than a few of them have sacrificed career advancement by refusing absolutely to accept promotions which would take them elsewhere.

These men fought hard for the establishment of the River of No Return Wilderness. But now the old-timers are between the rock and the hard spot. Their agency recommended a halfway reasonable wilderness of 1.5 million acres. Then their parent agency, the Department of Agriculture, totally ignored their recommendation.

A ranger who has spent most of his life managing a portion of the Idaho Primitive Area was asked his position on the controversy. He replied, saying, "Hell, I can't even comment on it. They went so far as to send me an official memo telling me what I can and cannot say. I better just keep my mouth shut."

Considering the circumstances, the Forest Service could be

paralyzed. Instead, it is drawing up an interim management plan for the Idaho Primitive Area, the first in the 45-year history of the area. The scope of the task can best be appreciated by realizing that it is a cooperative effort among four national forests and that it is being done under fire from special-interest groups to relax management of the area. After all, the groups reason, most of the area is going to be declassified anyway.

The rangers have responded by drafting a plan which will manage the area under the strictest possible wilderness criteria. The plan will be ready for public comment by summer 1976.

Although it is theoretically an interim plan, those in the field are prepared to use it indefinitely. One ranger said, "We have to manage the area until everyone else gets tired of political games." He recalls that the fate of the High Uintas Wilderness in Utah has been in limbo for approximately 10 years.

"Clear as Gin"

So the "biggest and best" wilderness in the Lower 48 is up for grabs. Wilderness advocates are preparing for battle, taking special precautions to guard their flanks. In a recent letter, Trueblood explained in a nutshell why he knows they will come out on top. He said:

"I recently flew home from Chamberlain after two days of steady rain which, added to heavy snow runoff, had Chamberlain Creek out of its banks. Yet its water was clear as gin!

"It was the only clear water I saw that day. Every other stream we flew over on the way to Boise was muddy, some of them almost chocolate-colored. Chamberlain Creek has no roads or logging on its watershed; all the others do. The effect of this 'multiple use' was so obvious that it doubled my determination to help preserve the River of No Return Wilderness—no matter how long the struggle may last."

When Congress finally designated the 2.3 million-acre River of No Return Wilderness in 1980, it included Chamberlain Basin. In 1984, the wilderness was renamed the Frank Church-River of No Return in honor of the senator's long-running commitment to wilderness. It is the largest Forest Service wilderness in the Lower 48 states.

Roadless Review Enters Second, Most Critical Stage

BY MARJANE AMBLER

The Forest Service abandoned its original Roadless Area Review and Evaluation (which would subsequently become known as RARE I) in 1973 after a Sierra Club lawsuit challenged the adequacy of its findings. In 1977, the Forest Service launched RARE II.

In the midst of the hottest wilderness debate since the Wilderness Act was passed in 1964, the Forest Service has released its revised figures on roadless acreage. Nationwide, 62 million acres of roadless, potentially wilderness-quality lands were found, more than two-thirds of them in the West (without counting Alaska).

The inclusion of 11 areas in the Little Missouri National Grassland of North Dakota on the list was the biggest surprise, since the regional Forest Service office did not recommend any areas in the grassland. Nine other areas in the West were added to the regional inventory by the Forest Service in Washington, D.C. Any development activities will be delayed in all the areas listed until their wilderness attributes have been considered. The Forest Service hopes many will be decided within the next year.

Conservationists say the inventory is generally good, but point out that the process has just begun. Although the inventory stage of the Resource Roadless Area Review and Evaluation (RARE II) was controversial, the debate is expected to get even hotter in the second stage, from now until next fall, when individual areas are being evaluated for their wilderness potential.

Because the first stage of RARE II was designed to list roadless areas across the nation, but not to evaluate them, the Forest Service staffs in many areas were at first surprised when the public hearings became the sites of dramatic demonstrations against wilderness. At Bonners Ferry, Idaho, logging trucks were driven to a demonstration outside a RARE meeting and a logging company helicopter buzzed the meeting when it was moved to a high school football stand, according to *Wilderness Report*, a Wilderness Society magazine. Timber industry officials in some locations wrote letters to employees asking if they wanted to lose their jobs because of wilderness.

As conceived by the Forest Service, RARE II calls for the inventory, then for an evaluation in the roadless acres found during the inventory, and finally, recommendations about which lands should be allocated for wilderness, which for other uses, and which studied further.

While the areas are being studied, the Forest Service is restricting activities that would leave a permanent mark. This means some restrictions on mining and exploration, but the timber industry is the only one that has protested the RARE II process loudly to Congress.

The timber industry sees the process as an attempt to grab thousands of acres for wilderness and to block timbering while the areas are being studied.

Anti-Wilderness

Those who opposed RARE II took their protest to Congress. Sen Malcolm Wallop, R-Wyo., told the Senate that while he generally recognized the value of wilderness, he thought the RARE II has "cemented in my state, and I suspect in a number of other Western states, an anti-wilderness sentiment the likes of which I have not seen…"

Newspapers across the region indicate Wallop's assessment may be true, although it is hard to find an adequate explanation of how RARE II inspired this.

One Forest Service official said he believed some of the negative reaction is the result of misinformation about RARE II—many people think the millions of roadless acres inventoried are all being proposed for wilderness.

Rep. Morris Udall, D-Ariz., says some people look at the number of acres that actually are being designated by Congress as wilderness each year and lose track of the overall context. "I understand the timber industry uproar," he says. "We put in a big slug of wilderness last year, we are putting in a big slug this year, and we will next year. They wonder when this will end. They have to understand we are in the closing years of a long process that started in 1964 with the Wilderness Act. It is going to take another six or seven years to complete...But when we are all through, we will have a good wilderness system on 4 to 5 percent of forest land and on 1 percent of all American lands."

M. Rupert Cutler, assistant secretary of the U.S. Department of Agriculture, told the Society of American Foresters that RARE II is actually designed to expedite allocation of forest lands to either wilderness or other uses.

Looking at the impetus for RARE II, he explained that the unit planning process used by the Forest Service tends to allow local evaluation of small areas but doesn't provide for national evaluation of a national resource nor for broader planning. Consequently, there were many appeals and court challenges, which delayed timbering and other resource development.

However, most timber representatives are not convinced and have tried to get RARE II stopped. Cutler admits that there is the potential for 307 million board-feet less timber on the market for fiscal year 1978. (The total 1977 sales were 7.8 billion board-feet.) However, he says the Forest Service could reduce this figure by finding alternative sale areas or by other means.

Whether or not the timber industry's fears are warranted will be largely determined by the next stage of RARE II. This will tell how many acres will end up in the wilderness classification and will also determine how many acres will be "tied up" by lengthy study.

Social and economic impacts of wilderness or non-wilderness uses will be evaluated during this next stage. In addition, each area will be studied to see what it would add to the quality of the wilderness system in the country. The criteria to determine this will include whether or not they represent various ecosystems and landforms, are accessible to population centers and are distributed throughout the country.

After all the inventoried areas are evaluated, it will be decided which should be proposed to Congress for wilderness designation and which should be "released" for other uses. This stage will run through the spring, leading up to the preparation of a draft RARE II environmental impact statement. More public hearings will be held during the summer, prior to preparation of a final environmental statement.

Cutler says the success of the RARE II process will be measured after the next stage. "We are not so naive as to believe that during such a short time frame, each and every roadless area can be successfully dropped into one or the other of these neat categories. Some areas will have to be remanded to the more traditional, but more time-consuming, planning and study processes. The measure of success, however, must be judged by how small we can keep the unresolved group of areas."

EDITORIAL
RARE II

BY *HIGH COUNTRY NEWS* EDITORS

RARE II—the Forest Service's second Roadless Area Review and Evaluation—is something of an obsession around here. It makes us nervous to think that the future of that much land may be largely in the hands of the side that has the most powerful and most numerous lobbyists in Washington. We're continually checking to see if the Forest Service, which we believe began the process in good faith, still has its feet on the ground. Since the publication of the draft environmental statement that we wrote about in our last issue, we're not sure.

Last summer, Forest Service officials asked conservationists and commodity interests to work together on RARE II and try to find areas of agreement. Now the agency is asking conservationists to "bite the bullet."

It seems that somehow during the innocuous-sounding inventory stage of RARE II, conservationists have been changed from consultants to casualties. Once asked for help, they are now being asked to endure the torture of losing—and to do it in a dignified manner.

In the draft environmental statement released June 15, the Forest Service claims it "mechanically" came up with 10 alternatives for the public's consideration. However, along the way someone made a very human judgement—not to consider more than the top 50 percent of potential roadless areas in any alternative. In no option does the Forest Service look at all potential wilderness and try to disturb a minimum to provide for the country's economic needs. That looks like anti-wilderness bias to us, not pure mechanics.

The "wilderness attribute ratings" are another place where politics pushed aside facts. [Wilderness attribute ratings are used to quantify an area's wilderness potential, and include factors such as "natural integrity," "apparent naturalness," "outstanding opportunity for solitude" and "primitive recreation opportunities."] The ratings reflect local Forest Service officials' feelings about the areas as well as hard data. Where wilderness ratings are low, they sometimes show more about the wilderness manager's bias than about the quality of the areas.

It is understandable that the draft was skewed in favor of commodity interests. A shrewd, year-long demonstration of anti-wilderness feeling by commodity interests forced the statement in that direction. And while wilderness foes were causing a commotion that couldn't be ignored, conservationists were quietly gathering data—just as the Forest Service had requested.

We resent the Forest Service's claims that it has been in no way swayed by the anti-wilderness demonstration of the past year. But we are not sure that an unfair draft environmental statement will harm the cause of wilderness preservation. Conservationists are angry about the draft. They are coming up with their own alternatives.

We hope that anger will give them the adrenaline they need to win during the next stage of RARE II—the stage when the Forest Service has said public opinion is supposed to be weighed. Considering the stakes—the last remnants of wild forest land—we certainly hope so.

The Forest Service's final RARE II recommendation, released in 1979, called for about 15 million acres—approximately 24.3 percent—of roadless areas to be designated as wilderness. Another 10.8 million acres were re-categorized as "further planning areas" for continued evaluation of their wilderness potential, during which time logging was prohibited, but oil and gas exploration and leasing could continue, with certain restrictions. The 36.2 million acres that the Forest Service recommended for non-wilderness—including many areas that had proven, or high potential for, oil and gas reserves and mineral deposits—were to be released for development. The Forest Service's decision was met with dismay by the wilderness community. But, as the following story shows, a challenge to the agency's final results helped put into motion a congressional effort to finally get more wilderness designated.

DECEMBER 12, 1983

1984 May Be a Wilderness Year

BY ED MARSTON

In 1980, Congress designated more than 60 million acres of wilderness, making it the biggest year ever for new wilderness. The majority of that—over 56 million acres—was in Alaska, designated with the Alaska National Interest Lands Conservation Act (ANILCA).

For the Lower 48 states, the landmark year was 1984. In response to another lawsuit, challenging the adequacy of RARE II, numerous states' Congressional delegations introduced wilderness bills intended to head off a third RARE inventory. More than 8 million acres of wilderness would be designated in 1984, but the year was also significant because the battle over the seemingly arcane, yet crucial, issue of "release language"—which determined the fate of lands that Congress decided not to designate as wilderness—was finally resolved.

Ronald Reagan could become known as the Wilderness President. He could easily end up signing more wilderness legislation into law than any other chief executive. He would set this record for historic reasons, because 1984 is ripe for a flood of state wilderness bills to pass the Congress, regardless of who is president.

States as geographically distant as New Hampshire and California, as ideologically different as Wisconsin and Utah, as climatically different as Arizona and North Carolina—could all have wilderness legislation before 1984 is over.

This ripeness for action was created mainly by an irritated reaction to repeated looks at roadless, potential wild lands, first in

RARE I, then in RARE II, and most recently in 50-year plans for 154 national forests. Elected officials especially would like to clear away the issue. Wyoming's conservative Republican congressman, Richard Cheney, said recently: "My main desire in life is to get one (a Wyoming wilderness bill) done."

Generic impatience with the slow wilderness pace was reinforced last year by a California court ruling that the nation's second roadless area review—RARE II—was fatally flawed. The federal Circuit Court of Appeals in California decreed that the RARE II environmental impact statement gave short shrift to wilderness values. The court said the Forest Service had rejected prime wilderness candidates.

The ruling brought a quick response from John Crowell, the assistant secretary of Agriculture in charge of the Forest Service. He told the 154 national forests to stop work on their 50-year plans and begin re-examining all roadless areas, saying that a defective RARE II naturally required RARE III.

RARE III is a horrifying specter to all sides of the wilderness question. It would cost the Forest Service millions, and cause industry, citizen groups and local and state government to attend yet more rounds of public hearings and prepare yet more reams of testimony and maps.

That has made wilderness bills for individual states very popular in some circles, because such a bill represents a vaccination against RARE III. A part of each state wilderness bill is a statement saying that RARE II was legal and sufficient for that state. The states of Colorado, New Mexico, Missouri and Alaska— which have state wilderness bills—will not be subjected to RARE III. Nor will states that pass wilderness bills in the next session of Congress.

Crowell says his RARE III order was simply a way to obey the court decision. Environmental opponents of the former lumber company executive view his decision more darkly. Some say he wants to reopen the roadless area question so the Forest Service can lower Carter-era recommendations. Others speculate that he hoped the imminence of a RARE III would push Congress into passing a national wilderness bill the administration liked.

Whatever Crowell's motives, it is clear there will be no national wilderness bill, and no congressional overriding of the California decision with a blanket "sufficiency" law saying the RARE II environmental impact statement was valid.

Instead, the congressional delegations are behaving as separate kingdoms: Each state is seeking its own wilderness bill. But passage of individual state wilderness bills is tempered by national interests. This is clearest in the case of Wyoming, where Ohio Democrat and House subcommittee chairman John Seiberling refuses to let the Wyoming bill passed by the Senate and unanimously supported by the Wyoming delegation go through the House. Seiberling says the Wyoming wilderness decision is not only Wyoming's business.

"They are certainly equal partners in this. But after all, this land belongs to all the people in the United States. This is national forest."

Seiberling is proposing 400,000 more acres than the Wyoming delegation. And he is opposing the "hard release" language of the Senate version of the bill. "Hard release" would forbid the Forest Service from considering protection for any land rejected for wilderness until early in the 21st century. Seiberling wants "soft release"—language that would let rejected roadless land be considered for wilderness again in this century.

For those who wish to see wilderness bills passed, it is hopeful that Congressman Seiberling and Wyoming Congressman Cheney are negotiating. If they can find a compromise, then a flood of wilderness legislation may be passed for Wyoming, Utah, Nevada, Arizona, California, Washington, Oregon, Idaho and Montana. If it is not resolved, it is possible that the Western states will have little wilderness legislation this year.

Journalistically, this is a very neat picture: a key Western wilderness bill, blocked on a central, easily understood issue, with the question dramatized by the conservative Wyoming congressional delegation struggling with Eastern liberals such as Seiberling.

There also seems to be a certain symmetry. Seiberling is clearly blocking the Wyoming bill, while conservative Western senators such as Energy Committee chairman James McClure, R-Idaho, are said to be blocking wilderness bills containing "soft release" language.

But Tony Bevinetto, a staffer on Senator McClure's Energy Committee, says from Washington that the situation is not quite so neat. He says McClure and Wyoming wilderness bill sponsor Senator Malcolm Wallop, R-Wyo., will not retaliate against "soft release" bills.

Bevinetto continues, "It probably grates on the Wyoming delegation when someone arbitrarily says your bill is no good even though the entire delegation has signed off on it." But, he said, the committee is not holding other bills hostage.

"I don't think the bills are stalled behind Wyoming. In the Senate, if a delegation is behind a bill, we can move it." He says bills such as Oregon's and Washington's, with united delegations, are moving. "We did Montana and passed out more wilderness in Missouri than that delegation wanted."

It is difficult to know if bills are or are not being held hostage to achieve passage of related bills. But it is clear that both Seiberling and the Wyoming delegation want to pass wilderness legislation, even though they differ on the details.

But the Reagan administration, despite its identification with conservative Western senators, appears to be in a different situation. Andy Wiessner, an attorney for Seiberling's Public Lands Subcommittee, says that assistant secretary John Crowell "has been telling timber interests, 'Don't push for wilderness bills. Wait until RARE III is done and we'll cut down on the amount of recommended wilderness.'" (*High Country News* was unable to check this assertion with the National Forest Products Association spokesman in Washington.)

Wiessner says that given the fact that neither RARE I nor

RARE II could pass muster in the courts, "There are considerable reasons to doubt" that Crowell can deliver a RARE III that would reduce wilderness recommendations and be legal. "But Crowell sincerely believes that he can do a good job."

Although RARE III is certainly a threat, there are other reasons given for the sudden burst of wilderness bills. Senate aide Bevinetto cautions against putting it all down to impatience with the process. He suggests that over the past several years valuable work was done and constituent opinion gathered. "People feel it's a good time to be making this decision."

Rob Smith, a Sierra Club staffer in Salt Lake City, suggests that some of the push may come from those who oppose wilderness. "The political climate will never be more favorable to anti-wilderness," with Senator McClure in a commanding position in the Senate and the Reagan administration in the White House.

He also says that the federal court decision in California may be moving bills out of more than a distaste for going through a third roadless area review. "There could be a fear that all these roadless lands could end up in some sort of limbo."

They could, but they're not likely to be pushed into that limbo by legal action from mainstream environmental groups. The California decision throwing out the RARE II recommendations in California didn't come as a result of an environmental group's lawsuit. It was brought by the state of California, under former Governor Jerry Brown.

Susan Alexander of The Wilderness Society in Washington, D.C., says the national environmental groups knew RARE II was legally vulnerable. But they feared that a national suit throwing out RARE II, and locking up all roadless lands against timbering, drilling and road building, would cause a sharp congressional reaction—perhaps a law declaring that RARE II was sufficient and adopting a small amount of wilderness acreage.

The environmental groups could probably go to court today and get a judgment blocking all further development on roadless lands. Instead, she says, the groups are being surgical in approach.

They are using the California lawsuit to block particular development projects, but not to shut down all roadless areas.

The main thrust is directed at Congress. The Sierra Club's Rob Smith says, "When Crowell came up with RARE III, it raised the specter of a nationwide lockup." But it didn't stampede Congress, he says, because there was a compromise available.

"By passing a state wilderness bill, a state could avoid RARE III." As a tactic, "It was sort of like surfing on a tidal wave."

Although risky, Smith continues, the danger was lessened by the precedent set in 1980 by Colorado and New Mexico for a state-by-state approach to wilderness rather than a sweeping national bill.

That's the big picture within which Congress will act on state wilderness bills starting Jan. 23, 1984. But each state is quirky, and anything could happen, as the following state-by-state rundown shows.

Utah

Utah, as always, is one of the most interesting of the Western states, since the battle there is a throwback to the early wilderness days. Rob Smith of the Sierra Club says, "There is an immense philosophical barrier to overcome with our delegation. It is difficult for them to acknowledge there is a wilderness constituency at all. So in Utah, it represents a truly major step to even come up with a wilderness bill that doesn't have a lot of funny items in it."

During the summer, the Utah delegation was proposing a bill which Smith says was worse than no bill at all. But since then, Utah's delegation has gone from a non-wilderness stance to introducing a bill that provides a basis for discussion.

The summer-to-winter change came about because of strong middle-of-the-road support for wilderness shown in Utah in public hearings the delegation conducted. That public support was backed by strong pro-wilderness editorials in the state's major newspapers.

Gary MacFarlane of the Utah Wilderness Association says, "(The Utah delegation) held four meetings around the state. They were told their bill wasn't big enough, that the language was poor, and that there were too many exceptions for the wilderness areas it created."

MacFarlane says the delegation, led by Republican Sens. Jake Garn and Orrin Hatch, had gone "hard release" one better, "building in what we in Utah call 'time-and-eternity-release.'" It says that land not put into wilderness by this Congress could never be considered again.

"They also said there could be road building in wilderness for control of noxious weeds. It allowed more grazing than you could have in non-wilderness areas. And it allowed for handicapped access—motorized access for the handicapped, aged and infirm."

MacFarlane says that under those conditions, even the 615,000 acres the delegation proposed at the summer hearings for wilderness wouldn't be true wilderness.

The bill the delegation submitted to the Congress this November was very different. It contains the conventional hard release language in the Wyoming bill, eliminated the road building and motorized access exceptions and upped the acreage to 707,000 acres in eleven areas around the state.

That acreage is small compared with other Western states. But it would be an incredible jump for Utah, which now has just one wilderness area—the 30,000-acre Lone Peak just outside Salt Lake City near the ski areas of Alta and Snow Bird.

MacFarlane says: "It's a positive first step. A good-faith effort." But he also says it ignores some worthy areas and doesn't provide enough wilderness in Utah's key roadless area: the High Uintas in northeastern Utah.

Arizona

The key figure here is Arizona Democrat and Interior Committee chairman Mo Udall—a congressman who has incredible clout due to his strong reputation as both an environmentalist and as the man who is moving the Central Arizona water project that every developer in the state wants. He is also taunted by Alaska Congressman Don Young, R, as the person who has locked up Alaska while keeping Arizona free for development.

Udall is said to see an Arizona wilderness bill as a major unsettled piece of business for him, with 1984 likely to be the year such a bill passes. He has said that there will be "soft release" in the bill and that he doesn't even want to be bothered with an argument about that issue.

According to Rob Smith of the Sierra Club, just as important as Udall's determination may be the astoundingly successful negotiations between industry and environmentalists over the Arizona Strip—the chunk of isolated Arizona land north of the Grand Canyon and spilling into southern Utah.

The land is empty of people, but is rich in both wilderness values and in uranium. The Arizona Strip, which is controlled by the BLM, contains 750,000 acres in wilderness study areas—wilderness-quality land given interim protection until Congress makes a decision about whether to formally designate it as wilderness. Out of that, the BLM recommended just 30,000 acres for formal wilderness designation. According to Smith, that low recommendation so inflamed the environmental community that it brought Energy Fuels Nuclear into the picture.

The uranium mining and mill company, founded by the late Bob Adams of Steamboat Springs, Colorado, had always been something of a maverick in the industry. The company, Smith says, was interested in rich uranium ore deposits in the area. But it was also interested in certainty. It didn't want to see the area tied up in litigation, and it was willing to cut a deal to gain that certainty.

The result was negotiations with The Wilderness Society, the Sierra Club and the National Parks and Conservation Association. Smith says, "It took 7 to 8 months to hammer out. There were extensive field trips." But in the end, it was decided that 380,000 acres out of the 750,000 acres will go to wilderness. The conservation groups got what they wanted, and Energy Fuels kept out of wilderness its prime uranium prospects.

The bill sealing this agreement into law was introduced unanimously by the Arizona and Utah delegations and is expected to be passed easily in the 1984 session of Congress.

Just as important, says Smith, is the tone the compromise set. "Now, suddenly in Arizona all the different interests see that a compromise can pay large dividends." It may pave the way for a fairly easy Arizona state wilderness bill on Forest Service lands.

Montana

Montana already has 3.4 million acres of wilderness, but it has never had a state wilderness bill. Its wilderness was all created piecemeal, rather than by a comprehensive act which took care of such things as release language, the sufficiency of RARE II and the like.

Bill Cunningham of the Montana Wilderness Association in Helena says his group expects to see a state wilderness bill introduced in the 1984 session. "We're pushing for 2.2 million acres more, with no compromise." If achieved, it would give Montana more wilderness than any other state in the nation. It is now second to Idaho.

Cunningham says the acreage would go into 22 new wilderness areas and eight existing areas, including the famous Bob Marshall Wilderness. Unlike Wyoming, Utah and Idaho, Montana's Sens. John Melcher and Max Baucus are Democrats and not philosophically opposed to wilderness.

Idaho

Idaho Republican Senator James McClure, as chairman of the all-important Energy and Natural Resources subcommittee, is playing a key role in the struggle over release language and the Wyoming bill. But he has yet to introduce a wilderness bill for his own state.

Idaho currently has more wilderness than any other state in the Lower 48—3.8 million acres, most of it in the River of No Return Wilderness. But it also has the largest potential for more wilderness—8 million acres of National Forest land are still roadless and technically eligible for wilderness.

Of that 8 million acres, Idaho governor John Evans, a Democrat, is proposing that one million be made wilderness. The timber industry weighs in with a 590,000-acre recommendation. At the other end of the scale, a conservation coalition is asking for an additional 2.9 million acres in 31 separate areas, with the molybdenum-rich, and controversial, 450,000-acre Boulder-White Clouds mountains area one of several to be put into protected further study status.

Colorado

Colorado is the grand old man of wilderness states. It and New Mexico were the first to have state wilderness bills in 1980. The Colorado bill set aside 1.4 million acres in 20 areas for wilderness. That gave the state 2.6 million acres of wilderness out of 14 million acres of Forest Service land.

The bill also took care of general problems. It declared that the 1979 RARE II environmental impact statement was adequate for Colorado and "shall not be subject to judicial review." It also had soft release language, saying that the wilderness characteristics of the land could be reviewed the next time the Forest Service redid its plans. Most of the roadless land freed, however, did not need to be managed to preserve wilderness characteristics.

Finally, the bill set aside 18 areas for further study, including the controversial Oh-Be-Joyful area near Crested Butte, which the AMAX mining company is interested in for its mineral content. In a bill introduced in November, Sen. Gary Hart, D-Colo., has proposed creating 10 new wilderness areas in Colorado and expanding seven existing areas. It would add 733,000 acres to Colorado's system. Included in the additions are the 5,500-acre

Oh-Be-Joyful, which would be added to the Raggeds Wilderness; the 250,000-acre Sangre de Cristo in southern Colorado near Salida and Alamosa; and the 55,000-acre Fossil Ridge near Gunnison.

The fate of Hart's bill now rests with Colorado Republican Sen. William Armstrong and Democratic Congressman Ray Kogovsek, whose western Colorado district covers most of the proposed areas. Neither man has indicated which way he will jump.

Hart aide Donald MacDonald says that Hart's bill leaves out only one of the 18 areas Congress set aside in 1980. That one is Williams Fork, "left out because of Denver's water rights in the area." Colorado's wilderness areas have been battlegrounds over urban water development, with Western Colorado interests fighting to put proposed water projects into wilderness so that Denver and other Front Range cities could not develop them.

APRIL 16, 1984

Wilderness Bills are Flooding Congress

BY PAUL LARMER

After a three-year wilderness drought under the Reagan administration in which only 340,000 acres of wilderness were added to the wilderness preservation system, more than two dozen bills covering some 10 million acres in 19 states are ready for Congress.

A number of factors are responsible for the current glut in wilderness legislation:

If states can pass wilderness legislation, an expensive and time-consuming RARE III (Roadless Area Review and Evaluation) study which national forests are beginning won't have to be performed. RARE II would be considered sufficient despite a 1983 federal Circuit Court of Appeals decision to the contrary.

The timber and mining industries which use the national forests don't want to wait for the completion of a RARE III study. They want the wilderness issue resolved once and for all, and claim that only with the knowledge of which lands will be off-limits to development can they plan for the future with accuracy.

Many of the current wilderness bills have been in the making for years. After a slew of hearings and debate, there is a feeling among all parties that now is the time to designate wilderness based upon the 1979 RARE II study. Also, some members of Congress up for re-election would like to have a wilderness bill under their belts going into the fall.

Although the time may be ripe for wilderness designation, there remains one large obstacle—release language. The two

123

central characters in the controversy are Sen. James McClure, R-Idaho, who chairs the Energy and Natural Resources Committee, and Rep. John Seiberling, D-Ohio, who sits on the throne of the Interior Subcommittee on Public Lands and National Parks.

McClure favors "hard release" language in wilderness bills, which would release non-wilderness Forest Service lands from wilderness consideration for at least several decades. Mining and timber companies dependent upon public lands agree, saying they are tired of potential wilderness areas being managed as "de facto" wilderness.

Seiberling and conservationists believe that standard or "soft release" language, which would allow non-wilderness lands to be reconsidered for wilderness designation after one Forest Service planning cycle (10–15 years), is a sufficient compromise to the resource industries. When asked if Seiberling would bend to break the release language impasse with Dick Cheney, R-Wyo., over the Wyoming bill, Andy Wiessner, an attorney to Seiberling's Public Land Subcommittee says, "We don't feel anything needs to be broken.

"We like the standard release language that was in the 1980 Colorado bill," he says, referring to one of the first RARE II bills to be passed into law.

Michael Scott, Denver-based representative for The Wilderness Society, says that the standard release language is the result of a compromise. "You have to realize that conservationists don't want any release." He adds that standard release foregoes wilderness as an option for 10–15 years, while hard release is "the process of permanently removing one of the multiple-use options for Forest Service lands."

Gene Bergoffen, resource programs vice president for the National Forests Products Association, doesn't see the release issue in the same light. "The environmentalists are not willing to draw a line and stick to it." When the land base is "subjected to consistent upheaval every five or 10 years" with new wilderness studies, there is no way that forest managers can properly determine timbering levels, he adds.

Although no one is overly optimistic, a dialogue has been going on between Seiberling and McClure over a possible resolution of the language logjam. Conservationists say they see signs that McClure is standing alone on the release provision and will search for "face-saving release language" to gracefully concede on the issue.

On May 2, Sen. McClure allowed wilderness bills for Washington, Oregon, Idaho, Arizona and Arkansas—all of which contained soft release language—to pass through the Energy and Natural Resources Committee. Soft release language became standard for all subsequent wilderness bills.

Wilderness Exceptions

The Wilderness Act contains a number of exceptions that allow "non-wilderness" uses to continue. It allows the use of aircraft and motorboats to continue in certain areas and under certain conditions; it allows grazing to continue; and, with presidential approval, it permits the construction of dams and power lines.

But in addition, each wilderness has its own special circumstances. Idaho's Frank Church-River of No Return Wilderness, described in the following story, is a case study of the kinds of inconsistencies and management challenges that come with— and are often explicitly written into—a wilderness designation.

Idaho's River of No Return Wilderness: Jetboats, Planes Are the Rule Here

BY MIKE MEDBERRY

Those who think wilderness areas are created, once and for all, by a majority vote of the Congress should look at the Frank Church-River of No Return Wilderness in central Idaho. The July 23, 1980, law which established this 2.3 million-acre area—the largest outside of Alaska and the largest administered by the U.S. Forest Service—was the culmination of a long effort by wilderness proponents.

But it is now clear that passage of the law was simply one step in determining the fate of this land and of the wild and scenic rivers (the Main Salmon, Middle Fork Salmon and part of the Selway) it contains.

The wilderness bill gave the land—which ranges from rolling hills along the Main Salmon River to rugged high country in the Bighorn Crags—a push in a certain direction. But it did not erase the effect on the area of its historical use.

One product of its past is a boundary which looks as if it were drawn by a mapmaker from the Jackson Pollock school of cartography: It twists inward to exclude developed or mineral-rich areas, snakes outward to take in desirable undeveloped areas and on occasion takes wild, improbable excursions.

In the northwest corner, for example, a long peninsula shoots out to grab land along the southern boundary of the Gospel Hump Wilderness. To the south, the boundary zigs inward to create within the wilderness cul-de-sacs of multiple-use land connected to the "mainland" by narrow corridors along roads or streams. In other places, narrow multiple-use corridors along streams or roads are ends unto themselves. The boundary gyrations come from compromises made to pass the 1980 legislation, and are found in many wildernesses.

But there are also surprising enclaves in the Frank Church Wilderness: 28 aircraft landing strips, as well as rivers open to jetboats. These exceptions are heavily used. The strips accommodate more than 4,400 landings each year thanks to 88 outfitters who fly in hunters, fishermen and sightseers. And rafting enthusiasts who win permits to float the Main Salmon River find themselves sharing their wilderness experience with visitors in outfitters' roaring jetboats.

There are other inconsistencies: several active gold mines; valid but still undeveloped claims to mineral deposits; a 40,000-acre "Special Mining Management Zone" with relaxed mining constraints to assure access to ore bodies rich in cobalt; 2,500 acres of private land; and many old cabins, including 37 identified as worth preserving. The rest tempt squatters and collect trash as they fall slowly into ruins.

All of this is in addition to the contradictions built into the 1964 Wilderness Act—the mining, the cattle and sheep grazing, and the irrigation which can occur on lands intended to be forever wild.

These contradictions would make the land difficult to administer in any case. But things are especially complicated because the 3,000-square-mile wilderness lies across two Forest Service regions—the Northern and the Intermountain; six national forests—the Bitterroot, Boise, Challis, Nez Perce, Payette and Salmon; and 12 ranger districts. In addition to the fragmented federal administration, the wilderness spans four counties.

Conflict plagued land and water decisions long before the area was designated wilderness five years ago, and it continues with the Forest Service's Wilderness Management Plan issued this

March. The goal of the $593,672 plan is easier to state than to accomplish: to manage the wilderness "unimpaired for future use and enjoyment as wilderness," while accommodating "non-conforming uses" as required by law.

For 26 years, Earl Dodds was Big Creek district ranger for the Forest Service. He criticizes the new management plan for not recognizing the administrative problems. "They can't even coordinate putting up signs," he says, and the six forests don't unite on firefighting, patrolling, issuing permits and collection of information from visitors. Dodds says the admission in the plan that there has been difficult coordination but not significant inconsistencies "borders on dishonesty."

Frank Elder, who headed the Forest Service team which wrote the plan, says the plan itself is the tool that will improve management. He says representatives from the six forests will hold periodic meetings so that differences in budget priorities can be worked out. Now at the regional office in Ogden, Utah, Elder will have no long-term responsibility for implementing the plan he helped create. Moreover, the committee that worked on the plan has been disbanded.

Whoever does it, implementation won't be easy. When the management plan for the Frank Church Wilderness was still in draft form, a proposal to close four landing strips met strenuous opposition from pilots. The Forest Service reconsidered and the just-released plan recommends only that use of the four strips will be "discouraged."

During hunting and rafting season, strips such as Cabin Creek, Chamberlain Basin and Indian Creek receive heavy use. At Indian Creek, for example, there may be 75 landings in a single day, with most concentrated during the morning, when flying conditions are best.

"A wilderness experience is no longer possible at places like Cabin Creek during hunting season," says Ed Krumpe, who directs the University of Idaho's Wilderness Studies Institute, a 65-acre research center on Big Creek. Krumpe criticizes the management plan for failing to address the issue of overuse of the landing strips.

The Forest Service "skirts the issue," he says. "They have directions throughout the plan to protect the wilderness resource, and yet they don't confront the problem. The law does not say that the strips will remain open and the wilderness experience will be allowed to go to hell."

Although the Forest Service assumes in its plan that the demand will continue to increase for use of the landing strips, there is no provision for any restrictions. According to the act which created the wilderness, only "extreme danger to aircraft" can close an airstrip.

Mike Dorris, a pilot for McCall Air Taxi, says airstrips are self-limiting because "hunters want to get away from crowds. They want a wilderness adventure and if it's too crowded, they'll go elsewhere." He opposed closing the four airstrips because keeping them open "takes pressure off places like Cabin Creek and spreads out use."

Dorris's father, Bill, who has been flying into the area since 1952, says Sen. Frank Church himself advocated the airstrips. He cites a letter by Church to the aeronautics director for Idaho before the wilderness was created, which reads: "The right conferred on the Forest Service to impose reasonable restrictions on existing airports does not include the right to eliminate the facilities altogether...I do not support Forest Service efforts to close existing airports within the proposed wilderness area."

Ed Krumpe says the Forest Service favors the outfitters at the expense of wildlife.

"At the Cabin Creek Meadow, so many horses and pack animals are allowed to graze that they preclude use by wildlife. Outfitter use also affects winter range and greenup in the spring," Krumpe says.

Scott Farr, an outfitter in the Cabin Creek area, calls the criticism "all wet. There's little grazing on that meadow. I fly in 25 tons of hay for my operation. What grazing there is improves the winter range by keeping down the tall grass and allowing younger, more palatable grass to come up in the spring."

But Farr agrees with Krumpe that camping at airstrips can be a problem. "Airstrips should not be a destination, but a link to the wilderness. Masses of people using strips as a destination defies the wilderness concept. I'd like to see camping near strips limited to one night."

In its plan, the Forest Service did initiate new constraints on outfitters, such as limiting their camps and phasing out permanent structures. That has riled the Outfitters and Guides Association of Idaho, which has appealed the management plan.

.Critics charge that problems such as the one involving outfitters cry out for public involvement to help reach solutions. But Dennis Baird of the Idaho Environmental Council says the public is left out of the decision-making process. Lill Erickson, member of the Idaho Conservative League, says the plan "was not a high-profile item."

On another subject, she says that the plan fails by trying to swallow too much. "Major issues were addressed which should have been dealt with in separate review processes," she says.

One major issue is a proposal in the plan to build a bridge over the Salmon River near Disappointment Creek. Former ranger Earl Dodds says building the bridge requires an environmental impact statement (EIS) because it will open up a new remote section of the wilderness.

The plan itself does not clearly make the case for the new bridge. On the one hand, it says: "The mix and arrangement of roads, airfields, trails, and waterways must be considered more than adequate." But it also says: "Wilderness users will expect bridges where access is needed..."

And in an addendum to the plan, there is this conclusion: "Concerns that we have not provided adequate opportunity for public consideration or adequately considered the social and environmental consequences of the proposal (for a bridge near Disappointment Creek) and its alternatives are mistaken."

The Forest Service's Elder says, "There is a 50-mile stretch of river without a bridge, and dead-end trails force people to swim the river. It's our policy to provide bridges where there is no safe ford." Elder also says the bridge will disperse use rather than encourage overuse. He adds that an EIS was not required on the bridge or any other decision in the plan. "We followed the process and put out a (less-detailed) EA (environmental assessment) with a finding of no significant impact on the plan."

The plan notes that two bridges over Big Creek have fallen into disrepair and that a "recent request to reconstruct these bridges for light truck passage has been approved."

In fact, both bridges have washed away. It was several years ago that an EA approved reconstruction of the bridges for operators of a nearby mine. Since the mine went bankrupt in 1984, no special-use permit was issued for rebuilding the bridges. Elder says a new EA is not required for their construction.

Jim Collord, a prospector who has been in the Big Creek area since 1929, needs both the bridges and a road spur to gain access to his Golden Bear gold claim.

"Potentially, we've got $12 million worth in the ground," he says. "I don't want to leave that money in there." So far, the Forest Service has balked at giving Collord road access to his claim, saying that a 48-inch-wide trail is enough.

Lill Erickson of the Idaho Conservation League agrees. "There is no justification for a new road," she says. "An EA or EIS has to be done. I don't think the Forest Service could justify building new bridges over Big Creek just to do assay work and transport samples from the Golden Bear."

Another controversial issue addressed in the management plan is water pollution caused by gold mines just outside the wilderness. Erickson says the plan relies on the state to enforce water-quality violations but that Idaho's process is "too slow and cumbersome." She refers to tailings spills at the Dewey Mine in 1981 and 1983 which eventually polluted the Middle Fork of the Salmon. According to Forest Service biologists, spawning habitat in Monument Creek was still significantly damaged in 1984.

"In 1983, the state was forced to settle out of court for $25,000," Erickson says, "which was not nearly enough to mitigate damage to the watershed. State laws are simply not strong enough to mitigate damage or assure compliance in the future."

The Forest Service's Elder says the plan calls for establishing baseline data for key streams. But, he adds, "The Forest Service can't manage lands outside the wilderness. We've relied on state agencies to enforce state water-quality standards." Erickson replies that the Forest Service could set its own standards for water quality, and act swiftly if the standards aren't met. "Yet, no monitoring is even outlined in the plan," she says.

It was a Forest Service employee, Clem Pope, who discovered the Dewey mine spill in 1981, and his report was instrumental in shutting down the mine temporarily. He says there is now more awareness and more oversight. "All precautions are being taken to protect the resource."

Whatever side you're on, and however the Frank Church Wilderness is approached, conflict seems inevitable. Ernie Day, who lobbied for eight years for the creation of the Frank Church Wilderness, recalls, "None of us conservationists liked aircraft or jetboats in there, but it was the price we had to pay to get a bill. The outfitters were very effective in lobbying for that bill."

Day says the compromises in the Act were "part of the package, part of the bargain, and we shouldn't abrogate it." But Day adds that there should be no increase in incompatible uses and no new operators allowed. On balance, he says, "We did damn well, and if it hadn't been for Frank Church we wouldn't have done nearly as well."

Sometimes, however, it is hard to sit beside the Cabin Creek landing strip in the fall and watch an uninterrupted stream of planes landing and taking off. Tom Robinson, regional staffer for The Wilderness Society, notes, "It makes you wonder what we've gained with wilderness designation back here."

Tapping the Wild

Drill rig in the Granite Creek roadless area near Jackson, Wyoming, in the early 1980s.

—PHOTO BY C.L. RAWLINS

The Wilderness Act contained a provision that left wilderness areas open to mining and oil and gas exploration and leasing until the stroke of midnight on Dec. 31, 1983. But it wasn't just designated wilderness that was vulnerable. Roadless land—the cloth from which wilderness is cut—was also at risk.

The 1973 OPEC oil embargo and the 1979 energy crisis spurred intense oil and gas development in the U.S. When the oil and gas industry began moving into wilderness and roadless areas along the Overthrust Belt, which runs from northeast Utah to western Montana, it provoked a passionate response. In 1980, *HCN*'s then-associate editor Joan Nice reported Cecil Garland's thoughts on a proposal to search for oil and gas in the Bob Marshall Wilderness:

If getting the oil and gas out of prime wild lands "were the last shot for man, I guess I'd let 'em do it. But will I tear up (a cluster of Montana wilderness areas called) the String of Pearls so some kids can go driving up and down State Street waving at one another? No, I won't.

"Will I tear up the String of Pearls so a family can go over to Hawaii and have leis put around their necks and sit in the sun and drink pineapple juice? No, I won't.

"Will I tear up the String of Pearls to fuel that vast war machine of the world? Not only no, but hell no!"

In 1981, the situation reached a fever pitch after President Ronald Reagan appointed James Watt as secretary of the Interior. Soon after assuming the post, Watt embarked on an aggressive program to promote oil and gas development in wilderness before the 1983 deadline. As the stories in this section show, Watt's agenda touched off a congressional battle royal that ended spectacularly when Watt was—for reasons unrelated to the wilderness battle—forced to resign.

Not all the endings were so tidy. Though mining in wilderness has not been as prominent an issue as oil and gas, one landmark case involving a proposed copper-and-silver mine in Montana's Cabinet Mountains Wilderness—also described in this section—is still unresolved, 20 years after the 1983 deadline. And, as stories in later sections show, the oil and gas conflict returned in the early 21st century, this time on lands proposed for wilderness protection by citizens' groups.

NOVEMBER 27, 1981

EDITORIAL

Congress Puts On a Bad Act with a Wilderness Backdrop

BY GEOFFREY O'GARA

This 1981 editorial by then-editor Geoffrey O'Gara lays out the Wilderness Act's inherent contradictions between land preservation and oil and gas development—and shows that some pro-oil and gas congressmen can have a surprising change of heart when development is bound for wilderness in their districts.

How our government decides whether it is right or wrong to explore for minerals and energy in America's wilderness areas is a drama that shouldn't be missed. Every junior high political science class should tackle this one; it is The System in action. Not since President Richard Nixon began impounding funds that Congress wanted spent have we seen such revealing confusion over which branch and which layer of government should take responsibility.

Should we feel comfortable knowing that Rep. Samuel Gejdenson, a freshman congressman from Bozrah, Conn., is one of 22 representatives who can decide for Congress and the public lands management bureaucracy what goes on in wilderness? What does he know about wilderness?

Does it make sense that Ray Hall, the Shoshone National Forest supervisor, a career forester from Missouri, becomes the nation's most prominent interpreter of what Congress intended in the Wilderness Act of 1964, a piece of legislation rife with internal contradictions?

In the environmental impact statement issued as the first step toward leasing as much as 13 percent of the Washakie Wilderness for oil and gas development and opening 88 percent of it to exploration, these contradictions are presented in adjoining paragraphs. If the Forest Service dared have a sense of humor, the provisions would have been labeled Mutt and Jeff. Instead, they are presented solemnly, straight-faced, daring the reader to laugh at the absurd.

First, there is section 2(a) of the Wilderness Act, which states that wilderness areas shall be administered "for the use and enjoyment of the American people in such manner as will leave them unimpaired for future use and enjoyment as wilderness..."

Then, there is section 4(d)(3), which allows mineral exploration and leasing in wilderness areas until 1984, "transmission lines, water lines, telephone lines," and anything else necessary to prospect and produce; it requires only "restoration as near as practical" of disturbed wilderness.

They've lived for years in the same house, but like an estranged couple, these two provisions have done their best to avoid contact. Still, there are those obligatory public appearances in any marriage, and here they are together in the Washakie environmental impact statement, making everyone else feel uncomfortable.

Students who want to understand our government of checks and balances should take note for two reasons: First, it is important to discover the sort of loony and contradictory compromises our Congress often makes when opposing lobbyists are threatening to break both arms. Second, watching our branches of government toss this hot potato back and forth provides a textbook on our way of governing: Congress dumps it on the plate of the executive branch bureaucrats; the bureaucrats interpret the uninterpretable and wait passively for the courts to write their own law; and then Congress will assuredly howl that the courts are trying to legislate.

Immediately before us are two cases of leasing or proposed leasing of wilderness—in the Capitan Wilderness in New Mexico and the Washakie Wilderness in Wyoming. Last week, moves were made to exercise an obscure provision of the 1976 Federal Land Policy and Management Act which allows either the House Interior and Insular Affairs or Senate Energy and Natural Resources committees to withdraw public lands from energy development in an "emergency." Three Montana wilderness areas have already been withdrawn under this provision.

Whether such committee-wrought withdrawals are made on a case-by-case basis, or for the entire wilderness system, there is a serious constitutional question that—here we go again—will be tested in the courts. One ought to note, at any rate, the peculiarity of a Connecticut freshman like Gejdenson on House Interior playing such a disproportionate role in the management of public lands in the West.

Rep. Manuel Luján Jr., a New Mexico Republican with no obvious "environmentalist" stigma (he voted against withdrawing the Montana wildernesses, in fact), who happens to be the top-ranked Republican on the House Interior Committee, exploded when he heard that leases had been let allowing underground slant drilling into the Capitan Wilderness in his district.

The entire Wyoming delegation—like Luján, Republican conservatives not known for tree-hugging—has objected vehemently to leasing in the Washakie.

Here we might try to construct a syllogism. Major premise: Congress must decide whether to block mineral exploration of wilderness areas, and traditionally bows to the wishes of legislators from affected states on wilderness questions. Minor premise: When leasing for oil and gas has been broached for wilderness areas, members of Congress in affected states strongly oppose it. A logical conclusion might then be: Congress should ban mineral and energy development in designated wilderness areas nationwide.

The built-in contradictions of the Wilderness Act can be tackled wilderness-by-wilderness and state-by-state; each acre can have its own piece of legislation. The contradictions can be wrestled with in forest supervisors' offices, in regional offices, in the

Interior Department in Washington, D.C., in the White House and in the congressional committees. Then they can start making appearances on court dockets around the country. Our students will see all the fine detail of the U.S. government in action, unending action, redundant action.

Hopefully, the students, after a few years of this, will ask the obvious question: Why doesn't Congress clarify its purposes in the Wilderness Act?

Ray Hall thinks it is necessary. Alice Frell, public lands specialist with the Rocky Mountain Oil and Gas Association, says Congress should do so. So does Bruce Hamilton, Northern Plains representative of the Sierra Club. Obviously, each hopes for a different kind of clarification. We happen to agree with Hamilton that the small amount of protected wilderness extant should be sacrosanct; if the future energy emergency conjured up by developers ever occurs, a simple act of Congress could change the Wilderness Act in an afternoon.

But the lesson to be learned in those political science classes should be: Track the contradictions to their source. And the trail leads back to Congress. The likes of Rep. Richard Cheney, R-Wyo., who say they want wilderness protected but fight against efforts to do it through the House Interior Committee, should be responsible for leading the fight to amend the Wilderness Act. Let us see some corrective legislation, and let us see how the big talkers vote.

It is time to clean up our wilderness act.

Oil Development Threatens Forests

BY DAN WHIPPLE

The discovery of a potential major oil and gas deposit in the heart of the Bridger-Teton National Forest in western Wyoming is creating a conflict between two of America's highly valued resources—oil and wilderness. The result is a tug-of-war among the oil industry, environmentalists and the federal government to determine the direction that the forest's future will take.

The oil discovery is the Overthrust Belt, which extends in a half-moon shape from northeastern Utah through western Montana. It was formed by a movement of the earth's crust that formed pockets, trapping organic material that eventually formed petroleum.

Major strikes were made in early 1976 along the southern leg of the Overthrust Belt. Petroleum potential from throughout the belt is enormous, according to industry estimates. It has been called "another Prudhoe Bay." The *Oil and Gas Journal*, an industry publication, calls it "the hottest new area for drilling in the U.S., offshore or on."

Part of this "hot new area" bisects one of the finest untrammeled portions in the U.S. outside of Alaska—the Bridger-Teton National Forest. The forest is a haven for wildlife, including elk, deer, and antelope, and contains the Gros Ventre, Salt River, Snake River, Wyoming and Hoback mountain ranges. It encompasses much of the scenic Jackson Hole country.

Though the forest itself is only a small portion of the Overthrust Belt, it may contain a large percentage of the available oil. A Forest Service official says, "We've got every major oil company sitting on our doorstep." A Wyoming Geological Association (WGA) report estimated that there may be as much as three billion barrels of oil in this area and up to 25 trillion cubic feet of natural gas.

All of this petroleum is only hypothetical at present, however. To actually be sure that it exists, exploratory drilling must take place.

While the forest may soon become known for its oil production, its current reputation lies in its vast wilderness and wildlife resources. There are two designated wildernesses in the forest, totaling nearly one million acres. There are also three areas that are being studied for possible inclusion in the national wilderness system. In addition to these areas, the second Roadless Area Review and Evaluation (RARE II) identified 1.75 million acres of roadless areas—making nearly all of the forests' 3.4 million acres "de facto" wilderness.

The conflict is developing because about 70 percent of the inventoried roadless lands (over 1.2 million acres) has already been leased for oil and gas. In most cases, the lease holders are guaranteed the right of access to the lease and the right to disturb as much surface as necessary to drill and develop those leases.

Generally, access to the leases requires the construction of roads. Though some old roads exist within the forest's "roadless" areas, these have been overgrown, according to the Forest Service, and would have to be substantially upgraded to carry on drilling operations. This upgrading, or the construction of new roads, would probably eliminate the areas from wilderness consideration.

Jim Connor, planning director of the Bridger-Teton Forest, says, "With the current energy situation, there is going to be tremendous competition for these lands." Connor says that the agency hasn't finished its assessment of the situation, however, and he downplays the potential problems. "There's not going to be as much of a conflict as the oil people and the environmentalists think. When RARE II is completed in December 1978, we'll know which areas will be developed and which will not. They have to let the planning process work."

However, both oil industry and environmentalists are less sanguine about a harmonious solution. Terry Martin of the Wyoming Petroleum Association says, "Of course we believe there's a conflict—it's a pretty obvious one. We just don't know whether the objections of those who don't want all of that land to be roadless will be listened to. If they put 1.5 million acres into wilderness, we'll have a tough time getting in there to drill."

Elmer Parsons, chief geologist for True Oil, says, "If you can't build roads, you can't evaluate leases. If you're not allowed to do that, there is a conflict."

Bart Koehler, The Wilderness Society's representative for the state of Wyoming, says, "Oil and gas operations are in serious conflict with the multiple-use concept of the national forest. They don't belong in potential wilderness lands. Oil and gas companies are using the energy crisis, which now ranks among motherhood, apple pie and the American flag, to justify their actions. Their profitable actions are said to be a public service."

It has been the policy of the Bureau of Land Management (BLM), which administers leasing of federal minerals, along with the tacit approval of the Forest Service, to keep the forests' oil and gas resources under lease virtually continuously since the early 1950s. The leasing subjugates other forest values, such as wildlife and wilderness, to oil and gas. Consequently, it won't be easy for Koehler and other preservationists to prevent the roads and the loss of wilderness character.

The BLM keeps the lands under lease to make as much land as possible available for petroleum exploration. Since previously the oil industry has not expressed much interest in the oil potential in the Bridger-Teton, Forest Service officials have been reasonably comfortable with BLM's policy. The agency has attached one or two stipulations to leases but, with two exceptions, these have not seriously inconvenienced the lessees.

The leasing is carried out through the BLM's "simultaneous

leasing system," which resembles a lottery more than anything else. Any U.S. citizen can pay a $10 filing fee, have his name placed in the lottery and if chosen, become the owner of an official U.S. oil lease—upon payment of his rental, which is one dollar per acre per year. [This system was scrapped in 1987 and replaced with a competitive bidding system.]

The BLM leases almost any property in demand. And demand for oil leases is running high, at least in Wyoming. In 1971, 185,366 individual filings were received on 3,725 parcels. This brought the government $1,853,660 in filing fees: In 1976, there were 1,390,185 filings on 2,836 leases, bringing in $13.9 million. These 1976 figures were surpassed in the first 10 months of 1977, promising a tenfold increase in leasing interest in Wyoming in less than six years.

There is no reason to believe that there is any oil and gas under these leased lands, and no requirement the parties that have leased them have to find out. The federal government is apparently the main beneficiary of the process. The BLM in Wyoming says that it turned a profit in 1976 on the sale of leases—the filing fees alone paid for Wyoming BLM's entire budget. Most of the leases, BLM officials frankly admit, are "worthless."

On leases within national forests, the Forest Service can approve or veto leases, or attach stipulations. Until 1972, restrictions were relatively lax, primarily because there was little concern that oil would ever be found. Some drilling had taken place on the forest in the early 1950s, but the companies abandoned the project after finding no oil at depths of around 7,000 feet. (The newer discoveries, in contrast, were at depths of about 15,000 feet.)

Sierra Club Lawsuit

As a result of a lawsuit brought by the Sierra Club, a "no surface occupancy" stipulation was attached to new leases in roadless areas beginning in 1972. Under this provision, "the lessee agrees not to occupy the surface of the (specified area) within the lease in a manner that will alter the wilderness character of the land, until an environmental statement is prepared and the propriety of surface occupancy is determined." All of the leases issued after 1972 have this provision. The Forest Service is currently compiling an evaluation of the leases to determine how much acreage is protected by this stipulation.

Under the stipulation, existing roads, if any, may be used, but not reconstituted or graded. No new roads may be built or any major scars left on the land. Two or three wells have been allowed on the forest on "no surface occupancy tracts" where there were existing roads.

For the most part, however, the "no surface occupancy" stipulation effectively prevents exploratory drilling in roadless lands.

The Sierra Club filed a "notice of appeal" with the Forest Service in November, charging that the agency has violated the National Environmental Policy Act (NEPA) because there has never been a programmatic environmental impact statement filed on the entire oil and gas leasing program within forests. The appeal concerns activities on 12 forests in Montana, Idaho, Wyoming and Utah.

The group says that the policies followed by the Forest Service regarding the leasing have varied widely among the forests, "resulting in random oil and gas development among forests without proper regard for environmental concerns." It is asking for a regional environmental impact statement on leasing and demanding that no further drilling or lease approvals be granted until site-specific impact statements are completed. Also, the club is asking that all leases in roadless areas issued after January 1, 1970 — the effective date of NEPA—be voided.

Sierra Club Legal Defense Fund attorney Allen Stokes says, "This is a chance for the Forest Service to get some order into this whole process. We particularly want to protect RARE II areas pending wilderness study."

The Wilderness Society is pursuing a different course to protect some of the forest lands. Bart Koehler is challenging the Jackson Hole Stipulation, which is attached to some leases on the Teton portion of the forest, near Jackson Hole.

A 1947 Interior Department memo stated that all Jackson Hole leases give the Secretary of Interior "control over the rate of prospecting and development, including, in particular, the spacing of wells and such other conditions as may be deemed necessary in any case for the protection of wildlife and scenic values within the area." The language later included in the Jackson Hole stipulation apparently doesn't give the Interior Secretary the broad powers referred to in the memo. Consequently, Koehler says, "many of the leases on the Teton forest may be invalid."

Caught by Surprise

The suddenness of the petroleum onslaught has caught the Forest Service by surprise, according to Connor. He says, "This has happened so fast that we really don't know the impact of leasing. The RARE II inventory brought the attention to this. If there were no restrictions, probably most of the roadless area would be explored. Even with the restrictions, we have no idea how much would be roaded."

The Forest Service regional office has sent a management directive to the Bridger-Teton forest supervisor, saying that any company holding a lease within a roadless area without the "no surface occupancy" stipulation should be allowed to develop the lease. The forest is currently in the process of determining how many acres that covers.

Meanwhile, the pressure mounts for massive oil development in the forest. There are currently about 30 proposals for drilling awaiting Forest Service recommendations. The agency is showing its concern by calling for public input on one of the first of these.

Once the land is leased, the Forest Service advises the U.S. Geological Survey on where the wells should be placed to best protect forest values. This advice, while not binding on USGS, is usually followed. The Forest Service cannot prevent drilling on property under lease, however.

Attention is now centered on Cache Creek, a stream near the town of Jackson and a major watershed for the town. The area is the site of a proposed National Cooperative Refinery Association drilling rig. The creek is classified as a roadless area, but it does have an old unimproved road up to it.

The Cache Creek well is causing more uproar than expected, largely because the area is considered "the Jackson Hole residents' private playground," according to Connor. Bridger-Teton Forest Supervisor Reid Jackson has called for public comment on the well, but his memorandum on the issue demonstrates how little authority the agency really has over already-leased lands. Jackson proposes four policy alternatives for Cache Creek regarding oil company access. The alternatives all concerned road routing and improvement, but none of them include a "no drilling" option.

The Cache Creek area is a winter range for large game animals, and the Wilderness Society and the Wyoming Game and Fish Department have recommended it for inclusion in the Gros Ventre Wilderness Study Area.

Rainbow Resources has already completed one well on Granite Creek in the forest, adjacent to the Gros Ventre wilderness study area. The company found a natural gas deposit there and is trying to get approval to explore a site further up the creek.

True Oil is requesting five drilling permits on the forest's roadless areas. The company holds leases issued in 1969, before the Forest Service began requiring the "no surface occupancy" stipulation. Other major firms interested in forest leases are Exxon, Atlantic Richfield, Getty, Mobil and Champlin.

While acknowledging that roads are required to adequately assess a lease's potential, True Oil geologist Parsons disagrees with the dire predictions of the environmentalists about the wholesale destruction of the wilderness character of the land. He says, "I don't see where there has to be any reason why we can't keep the environmental impact to a minimum."

Parsons says that the oil industry in Wyoming has long exhibited sound environmental practices. He says, "I live in Wyoming because I want to, I've been here half my life and expect to stay the rest of it. I like the scenery, the wildlife, the scarcity of people, and I don't want to see it torn up any more than anyone else does. Our company will do everything it can to protect those values. There is a very high awareness of corporate responsibilities."

Bart Koehler is skeptical about the industry's ability to preserve the wilderness. "How are they going to do it?" he asks, "Fly in their equipment in a helicopter? And, if they get a strike, they'll have to drill another well. They're looking for a field—it's not just one well here and one well there. If they drill and get a strike, it will be impossible to keep them out."

The Forest Service's Connor says, "Roads are the most controversial subject. I have no personal knowledge where they have been able to explore for oil and gas without putting in roads."

Connor says that the roads' most appreciable impact will be on forest use and big game. He says, "The oil and coal development around Kemmerer and Rock Springs (Wyo.) has already resulted in increased use of the forest. This new development will have an appreciable impact. The people who come to the area with this kind of development are usually outdoor types. They're hunters and four-wheel drive enthusiasts. The hunting pressure has already gotten phenomenal." New roads will increase access within the forest and encourage hunting, Connor fears.

Despite Koehler's fears about roads, he believes that the main danger to the forest comes not from looking for oil but from finding it. Production requires wells, pumps, storage facilities, pipelines, pumping stations, and increased truck traffic. It also results in population increases and encourages the now-familiar Western trademark, the boomtown. Oil impact has already brought new trailer courts to Big Piney, Marbleton and Evanston, Wyo.

The problem of managing existing leases in forests threatens to spread. *Montana Outdoors* reports that about 700,000 acres of leases are pending on the east slope of the Rockies in Montana. In a report on the potential impact of a natural gas strike in the Flathead Forest in Montana, planning forester Mark Ahner of the Flathead County Areawide Planning Organization estimates that one well per square mile would be required, each well site covering six acres. A refinery might also be required, covering 40 to 60 acres.

The refinery would need three water holding ponds, and an extensive pipeline system, roads, and power lines. All of this could result in wildlife habitat loss, destruction of vegetation and water quality problems. Impacts from oil discoveries would be similar, Ahner says, though a refinery probably would not be needed.

Trade-Offs

Besides the potential problems with oil and gas development in the Bridger-Teton, there lies a deeper issue—the trade-offs between energy and other resources. The country has substantial reserves of other fuels, but it is short on easily accessible oil and natural gas. Now with a large supply potentially available from the Overthrust Belt, the pressures will be tremendous to exploit the resource, even at the expense of wilderness and wildlife resources, Koehler and other environmentalists fear.

Koehler says, "Our overconsumptive society may well succeed in destroying this part of the world...without even knowing it."

Phil Hocker, a Jackson architect and head of the Gros Ventre Wilderness Committee, says, "The overall record of wilderness in this country is one of getting dribs and drabs of the unspoiled continent we started with. We're now looking at one of the last few wild areas in a nation that is almost completely developed. The question is: Which of these few areas will be given protection for our lifetimes and our children's?"

Oil industry spokesman Terry Martin asks essentially the same question, though he expects a different answer: "Which does the country need more? Do you need that acreage more for oil or wilderness?"

Which answer the country will give is not clear, but a Forest Service official, who asked not to be identified, says, "Unless people change their ideas about wilderness, I don't think you are going to see a lot more wilderness in the Bridger-Teton forest. The most spectacular, scenic, and critical areas have already been designated. The areas they are looking at now are really second-class."

Wilderness advocate Hocker says that this attitude is short-sighted. "From the point of view of the game population, having wilderness areas close to one another presents more opportunity for migration and for game populations to breed widely, and for local famine and drought to be balanced. The flow and ebb of nature can be balanced over a large area."

The Sierra Club's appeal and The Wilderness Society's research seem to be the only levers conservationists have to delay the development so that the wilderness potential of the lands in question can be assessed. However, because of the complexity of the issue and the power of their opponents, some of the environmentalists involved are not very optimistic about their chances.

Koehler says, "The oil and gas folks may have enough muscle to force this issue. I'm not sure that we can win this fight, but we have to make damn sure that we don't lose all of it. It would break my heart if, in 10 years, I would hear someone reflect on this forest and these mountain ranges and say, 'Remember how they used to be?'"

Hydrocarbon Hunt Leads to Wilderness

BY JOAN NICE

SALT LAKE CITY, Utah—Elizabeth Smith explores northwestern Montana's Bob Marshall Wilderness on foot and finds it "the home of Montana's soul." Charles Jonkel prizes the space it provides the grizzly bear. Consolidated Georex Geophysics (CGG) is after its hydrocarbons.

The U.S. Forest Service has received a request from CGG to detonate 5,400 dynamite charges in the million-acre Bob Marshall, as well as in the 240,000-acre Lincoln-Scapegoat Wilderness, which lies to the south, and the 286,700-acre Great Bear Wilderness to the north, bordering Glacier National Park. Spaced up to 320 feet apart along four east-west lines through the wilderness areas, the explosions will help CGG map the oil and gas potential of the area. The company will transport its crews and equipment into the wilderness by helicopter.

Forest Service officials say this is the first proposal to use explosives in a wilderness area, and Smith, a conservationist, is outraged: "Does the Forest Service have to capitulate to commodity interests with such enthusiasm?" she asks. Jonkel, a biologist in charge of the Border Grizzly Project, in Missoula, Mont., is indignant. "We presumed all along we had these secure areas behind us," he says.

Forest Service officials don't have an easy answer to the Bob Marshall dilemma. They are currently weighing statements such as Smith's and Jonkel's against intense pressures to produce fuels from public lands. The Wilderness Act is ambiguous. It leaves the question of oil and gas development in wilderness areas up to the land managing agency until 1984, when the areas will be closed to new leasing.

Unfortunately for those who want to keep the seismic crews out of wilderness, the Bob Marshall lies atop one of the U.S. oil industry's last big hopes—a 60-mile-wide swath of tortured geology extending from Canada to Mexico called the Overthrust Belt. Here, eager oil firms are trying everything from slant drilling under the town of Evanston, Wyo., to pushing for entry into Glacier National Park and Dinosaur National Monument, which would require congressional approval.

Public land managers, who control most of the land in the belt, haven't unrolled the wilderness welcome mat yet, but they are encouraging oil and gas exploration on other Overthrust Belt sites—some of them highly controversial.

For instance, two forest supervisors have recommended leasing on the rugged, roadless Palisades area southwest of Jackson Hole, Wyo. That decision, which may be modified by the regional forester, was preceded by assurances to the oil industry at a February workshop in Salt Lake City that exploration drilling would be allowed on tracts such as the Palisades. Such tracts are known as "further planning" areas, for which the agency has made no recommendation to Congress about wilderness status. The Forest Service also promised to speed up the oil and gas leasing process and to eliminate promptly a backlog of Forest Service lease applications numbering in the thousands.

Representatives of at least 15 oil firms attended the meeting, including Exxon, Union, SOHIO, Amoco, Chevron, Atlantic Richfield and Phillips. Conservationists, who were less numerous, included representatives of the Sierra Club, The Wilderness Society and the Montana Wilderness Association.

"We are very interested in encouraging exploration on these (further planning) lands," Thomas E. Schessler of the Rocky Mountain regional office of the Forest Service told the group.

Nationwide, the Forest Service has placed almost 11 million

acres of land in the further planning category. Until it gathers the resource data, the agency is required to defend the areas' wilderness qualities.

As Howard Banta, director of the minerals and geology office of the Forest Service in Washington, D.C., put it: "The issue is: How to entice industry to explore and still preserve the wilderness option."

Dazzling tales of the Overthrust Belt's potential have convinced many land managers that the oil and gas industry deserves cooperation in gaining access to public lands. Atlantic Richfield says that of the eight largest fields discovered in the United States since Alaska's Prudhoe Bay in 1968—so-called "elephant fields"—four are in the 50 miles of the Overthrust Belt that stretches from northeastern Utah to southwestern Wyoming. That section is the only part of the belt in the United States producing oil and gas so far.

Philip Anschutz, president of the Anschutz Corp., an energy firm with holdings in the Overthrust Belt, says that recent finds in the area are "one of the most significant developments affecting the oil and gas industry in several decades" and could possibly double U.S. gas reserves.

Optimists say that, while the field is now in the infant stages of development, it could yield even more oil and gas than Alaska's Prudhoe Bay: as much as 15 billion barrels of oil and 75 trillion cubic feet of natural gas, according to an information sheet circulated at the conference by the Inter-mountain Region office of the Forest Service. However, according to the U.S. Geological Survey, drilling so far has revealed proven reserves of only 0.5 billion barrels of oil and 6 trillion cubic feet of gas.

The Uncertainty

Amid what the *Billings Gazette* calls a "hot new black gold frenzy," what you don't hear much about is the uncertainty, the dry holes, the short number of days that even an elephant field can supply the nation's energy needs.

North of the big Overthrust discoveries, 112 exploratory wells have been drilled on the Bridger-Teton National Forest since 1926. Only two have been judged capable of production, and both of them have been capped awaiting further exploration activity. But dozens of dry holes apparently don't bother the industry or the Forest Service yet.

"Absence of evidence is not evidence of absence," the oil interests say. In the Overthrust's heavily faulted subterranean rubble, reservoirs of oil and gas are deep rather than broad, and it often takes many wells poked at various depths to hit the mark.

Old wells don't say much about today's prospects, Al Reuter, a minerals specialist on the Bridger-Teton Forest, says. In the early 1970s, the Overthrust Belt was considered only a fair-to-poor exploration risk. But seismic and drilling technology has improved dramatically over the past three or four years. What's more, prices have risen so much that many an "uneconomic" oil well may be worth revisiting. So, suddenly, the belt is the hottest prospect around.

But even if the belt fulfills its promise, it's no panacea. The energy-hungry U.S. can consume an elephant field, which is capable of producing 100 million barrels of oil or a trillion cubic feet of gas, in a matter of days. At present consumption rates, a field that big would satisfy the nation's appetite for oil for about 6½ days, and for gas for about 25 days.

Conservationists argue that sacrifices in an area such as the Bob Marshall would, at best, be made for a very temporary fuel fix. They point to energy conservation as an alternative that costs less and permanently shrinks the size of the nation's energy problem.

Few Showdowns

Except in the case of the Bob Marshall proposal, there have been few showdowns between oil interests and environmentalists so far. While there have been a few skirmishes in Utah and

Wyoming, environmental groups haven't challenged a single well in the belt's 50-mile-long productive zone.

But more conflict seems to be brewing. For one thing, environmentalists do not always agree with agencies about where wilderness potential exists along the belt. The Bureau of Land Management recently declared only one-tenth of its land in the Overthrust Belt to be worth considering for wilderness.

In a wilderness inventory completed in 1978 by the Forest Service, RARE II, The Wilderness Society charges that 95 percent of the lands considered to be high in oil and gas potential were recommended for non-wilderness status by the Forest Service, regardless of their true wilderness potential. Both decisions have been protested by environmental groups, but the figures aren't likely to change too much.

Forest Service officials say that, in most wild places, exploration shouldn't harm the environment if activities are carefully regulated. Seismic work leaves a patch of disturbed vegetation about 100 feet long and a foot-and-a-half wide that is usually easy to reclaim, says Reuter. The second step, exploratory drilling, requires a four-acre drill site and usually an access road. In gentle terrain, both of these can probably also be restored, Reuter says.

The impacts of oil and gas production, however, are a different story. Reuter explains: "You have to get power in there and a pipeline. Wells are very closely spaced."

In the case of the Bob Marshall, "It is evident that the seismic proposal is a foot in the door," says Phil Hocker, conservation chairman of the Wyoming chapter of the Sierra Club. "It's nice to think they would lose a few toes, but I'd rather not open the door in the first place."

Hocker feels differently about further planning areas. Because their status is uncertain, he is not opposed to exploration to gather information. "But it must be done in a way that doesn't completely prejudice the wilderness decision," he says.

The "further planning stipulation" that will be attached to leases in these areas apparently leaves both oil interests and environmentalists feeling insecure. The stipulation says that a decision about whether development can occur in a further planning area will be made after the lease is issued and the area's wilderness status is decided. That gives oil interests the queasy feeling that, gusher or not, they may be pouring their exploration money down a dry hole. Conversely, it gives environmentalists the impression that the Forest Service is making an unofficial commitment to development.

"Stipped" to Death

When they are handed a Forest Service lease in a further planning area, some oil developers complain that it is weighted down with so many stipulations it is essentially useless to them.

Ron McCullogh, a lands man for SOHIO based in Denver, said that he just rejected 27 leases that were offered to him on national forest lands. "They had attached stipulations an inch thick," he said. "I threw them out the window. If there's oil there, it's going to stay there."

Reuter says that with all the protective stipulations, some leases do get unwieldy. "Some industry people say we 'stip' them to death," he says. "But, on the other hand, there's a lot of super country out there."

While leasing in the Palisades seems inevitable, both sides hope that the conditions of the lease will be changed to protect their respective interests. There is intense interest because on the Palisades the pattern will be set for new leasing in further planning areas in the rest of the Intermountain region, which includes most of the agency's Overthrust Belt lands.

On the three wilderness areas in Montana, even more is at stake.

Just the mention of exploration in wilderness has changed the tone of environmentalists' arguments, which focus on mitigation measures and stipulations when less-precious categories of lands are at stake.

Says the Montana Wilderness Association's Elizabeth Smith, "To allow lines of explosions in the Bob Marshall is like slashing the face of the Mona Lisa."

Oil and Gas Hunters Locked Out of the Bob

BY STAFF

Two major skirmishes in the battle over the future of the Bob Marshall wilderness were won by conservationist forces last week, as energy exploration and development of the northern Montana preserve were blocked by Congress and the Forest Service.

Two weeks ago, the U.S. Forest Service's Northern Region Director, Charles Coston, denied an application from Denver-based Consolidated Georex Geophysics to conduct seismic testing in a search of oil and gas in the Bob Marshall, the Lincoln-Scapegoat and the Great Bear wilderness areas. Taken together, the three contiguous wilderness areas contain 1.5 million acres.

Last week, the House Interior Committee voted 23–18 to declare an "emergency situation" in the Bob Marshall area and block oil and gas leasing. The vote on the resolution, which exercised powers granted in the Federal Land Policy and Management Act (FLPMA), pitted Rep. Pat Williams, D-Mont., the author of the resolution, against Rep. Ron Marlenee, R-Mont., who opposed it. FLPMA provided that a majority vote of either the House Interior Committee or the Senate Energy and Natural Resources Committee can block action on federal lands.

The Wilderness Society's Montana representative, Bill Cunningham, said he was "absolutely overjoyed," and added, "We hadn't dared to dream of this a few months ago."

Rumors circulated in the environmental community that industry planned to appeal Coston's decision to Forest Service Chief Max Peterson and challenge the Interior Committee's resolution in court. However, Alice Frell of the Rocky Mountain Oil and Gas Association (RMOGA) said her group was still deliberating on a course of action.

Williams' resolution will block oil and gas leasing in the wilderness areas until Jan. 1, 1984—one minute after the deadline for oil and gas leasing in wilderness areas under present law. Legislation has been introduced in Congress to extend that deadline for final closure of wilderness areas; conservation groups are actively opposing any extension.

Williams told reporters that the resolution was intended as a warning to Interior Secretary James Watt, who has repeatedly stated his intention to open more public lands to development. Watt now has 90 days to tell the committee how he will implement the resolution; if he does not, the committee could take him to court.

Marlenee and Rep. Richard Cheney, R-Wyo., who voted against the resolution, claimed that allowing a congressional committee to effectively veto provisions for leasing in any federal wilderness or public lands legislation would set a dangerous precedent.

Conservationists, however, said it was unlikely that similar resolutions would be introduced to protect other wilderness areas now facing imminent processing of oil and gas lease applications. The Washakie Wilderness in Wyoming is considered likely to be the first area in which oil and gas leases are processed; it has received 72 lease applications and officials are preparing a draft environmental impact statement.

EDITORIAL

Washakie Wilds Battleground

BY GEOFFREY O'GARA

Were it not for the efforts of a few obsessive and charismatic individuals to capture the public's imagination, a great many wondrous natural areas around the country might today be filled with mine tailings or Ramada Inns. The support for preservation comes not just from those who use these areas regularly: The outpouring of sentiment for protecting the Bob Marshall Wilderness in Montana from mineral exploration earlier this year came in part from outsiders who knew the name and symbolic importance of the Bob but never set foot there.

So what happens when an equally large, equally crucial area, lacking the famous name and symbolic recognition, is similarly threatened by an invasion of seismic crews and drilling rigs? South of the Montana-Wyoming border and east of Yellowstone in the Shoshone National Forest lies the Washakie Wilderness, under siege.

That name will bring no yelp of recognition among East Coast backpackers or armchair philosophers of the wilderness movement. Yet the Washakie is about to become the first battleground of the conservation struggles of the 1980s: It will be here that resource developers and wilderness advocates go to the mat over the crucial controversy written into the 1964 Wilderness Act— the provision that allows possible development of minerals in wilderness areas before sealing them off in 1984.

Taken with the neighboring Teton and Absaroka wildernesses, various adjacent proposed wilderness and primitive areas, and the undeveloped eastern side of Yellowstone National Park, the Washakie represents a wild region equal to the Bob Marshall and its adjacent wild areas. Its beautiful lakes, mountains and wildlife are all the more crucial because they provide a natural refuge from the increasing human activity and energy development in surrounding areas.

In the case of the Bob, the developers tried to get in for symbolic reasons—there was no evidence that great oil and gas deposits were there. In the Washakie, though, the symbolism of cracking the wilderness is supplemented by a real likelihood that there is oil and gas to be found.

Public interest in the Washakie leasing plan has been low, so far. But there have been some interesting developments. Rep. Richard Cheney, R-Wyo., who opposed the House Interior Committee's withdrawal of the Bob Marshall from development, said July 9: "I do not support exploration or development of oil and gas in the Washakie Wilderness Area." And one Forest Service official said that local citizens, who adamantly opposed increasing wilderness during RARE II (Roadless Area Review and Evaluation) hearings, and many of whom work for oil companies, are equally adamant today in their desire to protect what wilderness they've got.

Public opinion matters greatly, and there hasn't been nearly enough yet. Forest Service officials will make a decision whether to approve or disapprove lease applications this fall. They must balance the volume of probable oil and gas against the public's desire for untrammeled wild areas.

We suggest that the whole nation learn the word "Washakie," and start defending it with the vehemence we showed for the Bob Marshall. What is at stake in Wyoming is reason enough; but we are, in fact, gambling with the whole wilderness system.

EDITORIAL

Oil and Gas vs. Wild Lands: Harder Choices Follow "Easy"

BY GEOFFREY O'GARA

Gov. Ted Schwinden, D, of Montana recently told the Montana Wildlife Federation that saving the Bob Marshall Wilderness from oil and gas development was "an easy one; it's a crown jewel." The public seems to be fully behind the congressional move to protect the Bob.

The same might be said of Cache Creek, site of a proposed drilling rig near Jackson, Wyo., where developers announced last week they would not erect rotary rigs. Like the Bob Marshall, Cache Creek had attracted a vocal and diverse crowd of defenders.

So much for the easy ones. Are we ready for some hard ones?

Not far from Cache Creek is Little Granite Creek. From the naked saddle where Getty Oil plans to drill, you can look across a valley to the upper end of Cache Creek, Jackson's playground. But Little Granite Creek is a little too far from the tourist mecca to upset the Chamber of Commerce; it is also within the Forest Service's proposed Gros Ventre Wilderness. Roads, the Forest Service decided in its draft environmental impact statement, will be built up the steep creek bed to the rig site.

Adjacent to Montana's "crown jewel," the Bob Marshall, is an area of public land called the Rocky Mountain Front. It provides winter range for elk, mule deer, bighorn sheep and other wildlife, and gets little public attention. It is under intense pressure from developers, and the Forest Service has leased over 350,000 acres of it for oil and gas development. The state fish and game department has been critical of road-building and other aspects of development along the Front, which it cannot control. Wildlife doesn't understand official wilderness boundaries the way the oil and gas boys do.

Then there is Wyoming's Washakie Wilderness, adjacent to another "crown jewel," Yellowstone National Park. It may be the first wilderness area in the country to have its skin punctured by oil and gas drills—but few people know about it.

All around the region, these "hard ones" are coming up. The more glamorous "easy ones" are better out of the way—Cache Creek might have raised a stink in Jackson, but Little Granite Creek matters more when it comes to habitat and wilderness preservation.

The oil and gas spear carriers get paid to fight for access to these areas. The public, on the other hand, uses its spare time to learn about the "crown jewels," but nobody is paying citizens to travel all over the Rockies learning about the values of these "hard" areas. That means the bureaucrats who make decisions on the future of these resources get more pressure from the paid industry minions. Will they correct for this imbalance?

It seems unlikely, given the current attitude at the Interior Department. It becomes, therefore, crucial that the public learn about and speak for its interests in these "hard ones." For starters, try the Washakie and the Rocky Mountain Front and Little Granite Creek. That's just the beginning.

FEBRUARY 5, 1982

EDITORIAL

Soothing Election-Year Jitters: Wilderness Closed to Drilling (for Now)

BY GEOFFREY O'GARA

The skirmishes over oil and gas in the Bob Marshall and Washakie wilderness areas were harbingers of a larger, nationwide fight.

The Wilderness Act permitted oil and gas leasing in wilderness areas until Dec. 31, 1983, but presidents and Interior secretaries had generally viewed this leasing authority as discretionary and did not issue wilderness leases.

That changed with Ronald Reagan's secretary of the Interior James Watt. Soon after his appointment in 1981, Watt circulated a memo with a list of goals for the Interior department, one of which was to "open wilderness areas" to oil and gas drilling. That October, the Interior solicitor's office issued an opinion that "...we do not believe that the secretary can decline to issue mineral leases or permits solely on the basis of a desire to protect the wilderness character of a particular area."

That decision touched off a running battle to put a moratorium on oil and gas development in all *wilderness areas until the Wilderness Act's 1983 deadline took effect.*

A Wyoming energy publication recently shared with us its wisdom that Interior Secretary James Watt would never back down—he would pursue his resource development policies with unflagging single-mindedness, and leave public relations to the politicians.

Then last week, Watt backed down—for reasons that seem, on second glance, decidedly political.

Watt has postponed decisions for leasing for oil and gas in wilderness areas until the end of the year. A sigh of relief was heard all around—politicians, oil and gas lobbyists and environmentalist lobbyists all hoisted a glass to the Interior czar.

In Wyoming, particularly, Watt has defused a ticking bomb. The first wilderness likely to test the viability of the oil and gas loophole in the Wilderness Act of 1964—the Washakie—is located in northwestern Wyoming. It was initially docketed to go on the oil and gas auction block in March, and it was creating a political furor.

After quite a bit of equivocation, the three-man Wyoming delegation to Washington, D.C., led by Rep. Richard Cheney, R, unanimously opposed oil and gas rigs in the Washakie, responding to public sentiment that, at least in comments to the U.S. Forest Service, ran over 90 percent against leasing. But none of them, and few of their colleagues in Congress, have been able to translate words into action. In fact, two of them, Cheney and Sen. Malcolm Wallop, R, have played important roles in delaying a resolution of the issue.

Cheney, working with Rep. Don Young, R-Alaska, averted a House Interior Committee resolution that would have withdrawn all the nation's wildernesses from oil and gas leasing last December. Cheney negotiated with Watt and committee chairman Morris Udall, D-Ariz., and got, in exchange for killing the resolution, a promise from Watt to delay leasing until June, and a promise of congressional hearings, to begin next month, on the wilderness issue. Cheney said he feared such a committee resolution was of questionable constitutionality.

Then Wallop and others requested a further delay of Interior action on leasing, and got it. The moratorium will run until at least December. Wallop says he did not want the wilderness issue thrown into the congressional Cuisinart with the budgetary matters Congress must give priority. But the delay could mean Judgment

Day on wilderness will not take place until after the fall elections, in which Wallop and several other key figures must face the voters.

The Wyoming delegation will introduce a state wilderness bill in the next few months—but while that may please conservationists, it will not include any provision to protect the state's wilderness from oil and gas development, for reasons of "legislative strategy," apparently.

This means it is possible that we'll arrive in November with plenty of words and no action. Wallop can say he opposes oil and gas exploration in the Washakie and all wildernesses; *and* he can say he favors a thorough inventory of resources in the wilderness system, so that we'll know what's there if we face a future emergency. The inventory might include seismic testing and more exotic forms of exploration—but that is a little unclear for the moment.

If Wallop opposes all wilderness leasing, why has he not acted? Because, he says, the chairman of the Senate Energy and Natural Resources Committee, Sen. James McClure, R-Idaho, is against such a ban. Yet Wallop chairs the key subcommittee on public lands, and he admits that if withdrawal of wilderness from oil and gas development were proposed, the Senate as a whole "would probably go along with it." For the moment, wilderness advocates look with more hope to Cheney, who is still maneuvering on the House side, and may come out with a strong pro-wilderness solution when House hearings begin next week.

There are a variety of legislative approaches that could be taken. Some brave legislator could take up the cause of changing the wilderness act to annul the unholy marriage of wilderness preservation and oil and gas development. Or, if we want to be provincial about it, a bill could be introduced to protect Wyoming wildernesses specifically from leasing. If exploration is the big hang-up, include legislation and funding for a serious inventory, not the superficial type done by the U.S. Geological Survey. Let the voters know, too, where legislators stand on the question of extending the oil and gas leasing deadline beyond

1983—an extension as dear to the hearts of the oil hunters as the elk in the Washakie are to another kind of hunter.

Combatants on all sides have welcomed a breather before the big battle, but we're sorry that Watt let everyone off the hook until after the election. Among the others from the region running for re-election this year who sit on the key committees handling the issue are Sen. John Melcher, D-Mont., and Reps. James Santini, R-Nev., Ray Kogovsek, D-Colo., and Pat Williams, D-Mont. We want to see concrete proposals from elected officials before we cast our votes.

If voters send a legislator back to Washington for another six years without knowing what he plans to do on this crucial issue, especially a congressman on a key committee, then we'll be sending a clear message that accountability is not one of the requirements for representing us in Congress.

EDITORIAL

Watt's Wilderness Proposal Sets Agenda for Energy Industry

BY GEOFFREY O'GARA

On Feb. 21, 1982, James Watt appeared on NBC-TV's Meet the Press and announced a proposal to withdraw all wilderness areas and wilderness study areas from oil and gas leasing until the year 2000. But there was some significant fine print that environmentalists missed at first: Watt did indeed propose banning oil and gas leasing until 2000—at which point he wanted all wilderness areas reopened to oil and gas development, in effect obliterating the Wilderness Act's 1983 sunset clause.

For about 24 hours, it looked as though the Reagan administration had radically turned around and favored wilderness protection. But there was a very different morning-after look. When the fine print was read, the initiative by Interior Secretary James Watt to ban oil and gas leasing from wilderness areas for the rest of the century looked more like a generous government move to do some business planning for the energy industry.

The industry has a problem. Big discoveries in the Overthrust Belt, technical innovation, and rapid expansion of public lands open to drilling have stretched drilling and exploration equipment pretty thin. Rigs are rushed to new sites as quickly as possible, but there's a chronic shortage.

The energy companies have kept their prospectors and lawyers busy as well. With the deadline for leasing in wilderness drawing near, they are trying to get their lease applications on the books in a hurry. So far, the applications blanket millions of acres in 56 designated wildernesses. Many more acres in recommended wilderness areas are also under lease application.

What in the world would the oil industry do if those wilderness areas are opened up tomorrow? Where will they get the rigs? The Wilderness Society reports that, even now, 80 percent of oil and gas leases expire without exploration. Over 118 million acres currently under lease remain untouched.

Surely the energy industry can appreciate the pragmatism of Secretary Watt's proposed closure of wilderness areas to oil and gas for 20 years. That gives them plenty of time to catch up. And during that period, if the recently introduced Wyoming and Montana wilderness bills are any indication, Congress plans to open up a lot of heretofore closed, but undesignated wilderness by simply leaving it out of state wilderness bills.

Then, in the year 2000, according to Watt's proposal, it will be back to square one—the withdrawal of wilderness from oil and gas development will just end, with no provision for further protection. The timing should be just about right—there will be some rigs available, some of the other lands will have been pumped out, and there will be more workers, too. What's more, the federal government will have been working hard to inventory minerals and energy in those wilderness areas between 1980 and 2000, so the industry will know where to lease.

Watt's move is audacious, and a little naive. He apparently is surprised that anyone is reading the fine print and criticizing his bill.

Conservationists are so busy attacking what they view as Watt's trickery that they may have failed to recognize what an opening he has given them. Watt, it appears to us, made a big mistake. While his bill may be but a thinly disguised bit of strategic planning for the energy industry, it makes an important concession by acknowledging public support for wilderness protection and the administration's willingness to accede to it at this time.

Watt has always known the value of defining the terms of the argument. By labeling his opponents extremists, he has put them on the defensive. By talking about all the acreage that is closed to multiple use, he has avoided the figures on how much more was open to mining, drilling and timbering. This time, his call for a moratorium on leasing landed him in the camp of the conservationists, even if the rest of his bill upset them. Watt's bill will not survive in its present form in a wary Congress. And the argument is no longer about whether we'll protect wilderness next year. Now we're arguing about 20 years…or longer. The terms of the argument have changed.

Watt's proposal was so outrageous that it never went anywhere. But O'Gara's speculation that it was intended to give oil and gas drillers time to regroup looked especially prescient when the industry began a second run on wilderness-quality lands—this time on citizen-proposed wilderness areas—soon after the turn of the 21st century. That story is discussed in more detail in Section 5.

No Drilling in
New Mexico's Wilderness

BY NOLAN HESTER

What began as a bizarre test of Interior Secretary James Watt's wilderness policy ended last week, with environmentalists the clear winners and a New Mexico oil firm facing a $100,000 loss.

Ruling Nov. 18 that Yates Petroleum Corporation violated federal rules, U.S. District Court judge Juan Burciaga ordered the firm to stop drilling and prepare to dismantle its natural gas rig within the Salt Creek Wilderness, part of the Bitter Lake National Wildlife Refuge.

The ruling capped three tumultuous weeks, during which the firm built a road into the wilderness, ignored U.S. Fish and Wildlife Service pleas to stop drilling and bulldozed its way through an environmentalists' blockade at the site.

The Interior Department asked Burciaga to halt the drilling nine days after it began. Environmentalists charged that the delay showed the government tacitly approved of Yates' action. The firm cut a boundary fence and moved into the wilderness near Roswell, N.M., on Nov. 1, the day its state-issued 10-year lease to subsurface minerals was set to expire. The company's earlier efforts to obtain required federal surface access permits were stymied by a temporary congressional freeze on wilderness mineral exploration.

Company spokesman Peyton Yates insisted that the state lease guaranteed its right to enter the wilderness. Consequently, the firm ignored a trespassing citation from Fish and Wildlife Service officials. The Salt Creek Wilderness was created in 1970, when the federal government bought the surface rights but left the subsurface mineral rights under state control. Though Yates was issued its 640-acre lease two years later, it made no effort to drill in the wildcat area until natural gas was found nearby three years ago.

Interior spokesman Harmon Kallman dismissed suggestions that the Interior Department supported the drilling and said its delayed response stems from the area's complex land status. Rep. John Seiberling, D-Ohio, was unconvinced, and called a special congressional hearing on the Yates case. Seiberling said he was "astounded" at the delay in seeking a simple restraining order, and called the drilling "a test of the will power of the administration to protect wilderness areas in the face of a clear violation of the law."

Prompted by the incident, a House appropriations subcommittee extended the freeze on processing any wilderness drilling permits until September 1983. In ruling against the Yates firm, Burciaga showed little sympathy for the firm's actions, calling its predicament "self-induced." Yates' attorneys said the firm would immediately file an appeal.

Under the terms of its lease, Yates will automatically lose its lease if there is no drilling for more than 20 days, according to the New Mexico State Lands Office. Acknowledging the firm's bind and the rush to appeal, company spokesman Peyton Yates said there may be no way to get around the 20-day limit to resume drilling. "Believe me, we've looked," Yates said. If the 20-day limit expires without the firm resuming drilling, Yates said the firm will have lost the approximately $100,000 it spent drilling the well.

Yates Petroleum pulled its drill rig out of the wilderness and abandoned the lease. Two decades later, the company is pressing forward with plans to drill on Otero Mesa in southern New Mexico, an area proposed for wilderness designation by the New Mexico Wilderness Alliance.

Congress Passes Leasing Ban

BY CAROL JONES

The approximately 1,000 oil and gas leasing applications in wilderness areas on file in the Interior Department will be on hold for at least a few months longer.

Early in the lame-duck session of Congress, both houses approved a ban on any oil and gas leasing in designated wilderness areas. The prohibition was attached to the appropriations bill for the Interior Department and forbids the use of any funds for the leasing process. The prohibition will run through Sept. 30, 1983.

The ban, in the view of conservationists, buys more time for stronger wilderness legislation. Although Interior Secretary James Watt has never issued a lease in a wilderness area, he has stated that the Wilderness Act of 1964 requires him to lease for oil and gas exploration.

The controversy over Watt's interpretation began last year, when a company applied to do seismic testing in Montana's Bob Marshall Wilderness Area. Watt has been stopped from approving such leases by temporary bans since that time.

In the Wilderness Act, mineral leasing is forbidden after Dec. 31, 1983. The Interior Department currently has around 1,000 leasing applications on file which involve about three million acres of wilderness.

The opposition came from Sen. James McClure, R-Idaho, who tried to add several amendments to the bill to loosen the restrictions. McClure, who chairs the Senate Energy and Natural

Resources Committee, first proposed allowing seismic testing, but that failed in committee, 13 to 11. His other attempts were defeated on voice votes.

Bill Cunningham, regional representative of The Wilderness Society, says, "The bill is a signal to the administration that they had better tread lightly on wilderness and wilderness study areas."

In 1983, Congress again attached a rider to the Interior appropriations bill, extending the temporary leasing ban all the way to the Dec. 31 deadline in the Wilderness Act itself. James Watt, who had come under increasing criticism for his ultra-conservative views, was forced to resign as Interior Secretary on Oct. 9, 1983, after describing the members of the United States Coal Commission as "a black, a woman, two Jews and a cripple."

Mining May Come to a Wilderness

BY BRUCE FARLING

Tucked away in Montana's rural northwest corner, in the Kaniksu and Kootenai national forests, are the Cabinet Mountains, a craggy range little-known outside the state. Notoriety may soon catch up with this range, because the most spectacular chunk of it is the setting for a simmering battle between powerful development interests and conservationists—a battle which could test the effectiveness of two of the nation's most powerful environmental laws.

At stake is a proposal to mine inside and next to the 93,000-acre Cabinet Mountains Wilderness, as two multinational companies plan to extract the area's rich silver and copper deposits. Taking advantage of the 1872 Mining Law and the exemption in the Wilderness Act, U.S. Borax and the American Smelting and Refining Company (Asarco) challenge conservationists who claim the development undermines both the Wilderness and the Endangered Species Acts.

That companies can mine in a congressionally protected area is grounded in legislative compromise. To appease mining interests while pushing wilderness legislation past former Colorado Congressman and House Interior Committee Chair Wayne Aspinall, conservationists accepted language in the Wilderness Act of 1964 that allows mining and oil and gas extraction in wilderness areas.

There are strings attached to the compromise: Claims and exploration had to be completed by Dec. 31, 1983, and minerals to be mined had to be discovered before the same date. Finally, mining is only allowed if it can be done profitably. So far, the companies in the Cabinets have met these conditions.

Except for a few small pick-and-shovel operations, large development interests have been rebuffed in their attempts to use the Wilderness Act's mining exemption. In 1982, pumice claims determined legal and marketable in Oregon's Three Sisters Wilderness were bought by the federal government, sparing that area a mining operation. The same year, oil and gas exploration in Montana's Bob Marshall Wilderness, encouraged by James Watt's Interior Department, was stopped by public outcry and Forest Service and congressional action.

The Cabinets issue poses a stiffer challenge. Both companies are meeting the legal requirements, and their claims are too valuable to be bought out. U.S. Borax says the Cabinet ore bodies may be worth $2 billion, with the silver deposit being the world's richest.

Unless opponents are successful in legal challenges or in marshaling widespread public support, the Cabinets may be the first designated wilderness to be commercially mined.

While containing a portion of the Revett Formation, the same layer of quartzite that has produced the nation's richest silver mines in the miles to the south, the Cabinets also harbor another kind of wealth. The area is a haven for wildlife, including elk, deer, mountain goats, bighorn sheep, Montana's highest concentration of black bears and many non-game species. Mining will affect all of these animals to some extent, but it is the area's small population of endangered grizzly bears that most concerns conservationists and biologists.

Because the grizzly is protected by the Endangered Species Act, decisions that permit mining must, by law, not further jeopardize the bears' already precarious position. Road-building, mining and logging have already hurt the grizzly in northwest Montana, and biologists now recognize the Cabinet and adjoining Yaak grizzly populations as the most threatened in the Lower 48 states.

Various estimates put the number of Cabinet grizzlies at somewhere between six and 12.

Forest Service wildlife biologist Alan Christiansen hesitates to cite a specific population figure, because so little is known about the Cabinet's grizzlies. No one can say for sure what the new mining will mean for the beleaguered bears, nor whether the animals' federally protected status is enough to halt Asarco's and Borax's plans.

It may also be difficult to turn down the companies on the grounds that wilderness values outweigh the mineral values. The Forest Service and Interior Department used this argument to halt oil and gas exploration in the Bob Marshall. But it will be harder to prove in the Cabinets.

The silver and copper claims are covered by the 1872 Mining Act, a product of an era when the government aggressively encouraged mineral development. Hard-rock miners are allowed exclusive development if their claims are proven valuable and they can meet environmental regulations. As a result, opponents must have airtight cases to stop mining—a difficult task, because both Asarco and Borax have already invested much in the venture. Allowing exploration is no longer an issue, which was the case in the Bob Marshall; now, it is a matter of whether the mines ought to be built, and if so, how it will be done.

Reflecting on the ease with which hard-rock miners can develop public lands, Karin Sheldon, an attorney for the Sierra Club Legal Defense Fund, says, "The mining law is a relic of the past. It was geared to small miners, but the giant Asarcos of the world are still using it. In the Cabinets, it might come down to: How much is a grizzly worth?"

In the early 1980s, Sheldon represented a coalition of conservationists in a lawsuit aimed at forcing Asarco and the Forest Service to prepare an environmental impact statement on the initial exploration in the Cabinets. They wanted the wilderness and grizzly questions answered before exploration was allowed, to avoid a showdown later when the decision to permit mining could be prejudiced by economics. The case was denied in federal court.

Despite the objections of conservationists, Asarco and Borax were given permission to use exploratory drill rigs inside the wilderness between 1979 and 1983. Instead of preparing an EIS, the Forest Service put stringent regulations on the drilling, in an attempt to minimize conflict with grizzlies.

Alan Christiansen says because there was little baseline information on the grizzlies to begin with, and no follow-up, it isn't known how the exploration affected the bears. The environmental analysis for the exploratory drilling also failed to investigate the impacts of full-scale mining. Until now, the Forest Service has been analyzing each step as an independent action.

The tentative operating plans submitted by the companies say there will be little physical disturbance inside the wilderness. Both companies will locate their mills just outside the wilderness boundary and use underground tunnels to reach the ore bodies inside the protected area. Claim markers and ventilation adits may be the only surface evidence of mining inside the wilderness. Slurry lines, power lines and tailings ponds will be on adjacent national forest and private land.

"The area outside the wilderness has already been roaded and logged. We won't be adding that much more disturbance," says Asarco spokesman John Balla. He also points out that the claims, named after nearby Rock Creek, are only within a six-square-mile area, in the southern portion of the wilderness. Borax's claims abut Asarco's in the same general area.

Critics say Balla's assessment is unrealistic. They argue that Asarco's mine and mill, which will employ 375 people for almost 30 years, will affect wildlife, water and recreation both outside and inside the wilderness. They say survival of grizzly bears is already threatened because of the high level of human activity in the area, and that the narrow wilderness, which is only a half-mile wide near the claims, doesn't meet the bears' needs.

Additionally, they claim blasting and other activities for building the mine and its facilities will severely affect the solitude needed by grizzlies.

Mining in the Cabinets is not a recent development. The mountains both inside and outside the wilderness are riddled with claims, and there are several defunct and active mines. Asarco is already mining in the area, at a site located six miles west of the wilderness and 15 miles south of Troy. Although the Troy Mine is the nation's most productive silver operation, its silver deposits are estimated to be only half as big as those in the Rock Creek claims.

Asarco is in the Rock Creek area because it purchased claims originally staked by a subsidiary of Kennecott Copper in the early 1960s. Since 1973, the company has been mapping, collecting samples, and then drilling from 1979 to 1983. U.S. Borax has been in the area since 1981; its drilling began in 1983.

The only study of the effects of mining in the area has been through short, individual environmental analyses for the exploratory drilling. Now that Asarco has a mine proposal on the boards, the Forest Service, with the help of the company and state of Montana, will begin preparing an environmental impact statement this year. It is expected that another environmental impact statement will be mandated when U.S. Borax firms up its proposal.

To gather baseline data for the environmental impact statements, the Forest Service is compiling an area study plan. This will project the development future for a 270-square-mile area of the Cabinets, including country both outside and inside the wilderness. The Forest Service says the study's purpose is to avoid piecemeal planning for the area's development. Jim Mershon, district ranger for the Cabinet District, says the study will look at cumulative effects on all resources from mining and other activities, such as recreation and logging. State and federal biologists will be paying close attention to the effects all development will have on the grizzly.

It appears the Forest Service is resigned to some mining in the

Rock Creek area. Mershon says, "The possibility of one mine, and possibly two, is extremely good," adding that there could be four mills and several tailings sites in the area. The agency hopes the area study plan will help identify ways to minimize the effects on recreation, water and grizzlies.

But the Sierra Club and National Wildlife Federation believe it may prove impossible to "mitigate" for mining's effects on grizzlies. Tom France of the Federation says the species is already squeezed into a tiny area: "Any more encroachment on its range may eliminate it from the Cabinets."

The Forest Service's Christiansen agrees that the bear population is in danger, but hopes that research and mitigation will provide some help. He says the most promising approach may be through trading habitat. If bears are pushed out of one area by mining, it could be made up by closing roads to recreationists or altering logging plans elsewhere. Christiansen cautions that this approach needs more research, and adds that it could cause friction with recreationists and loggers.

The mining could be an economic boon for the local counties, Sanders and Lincoln, whose unemployment rates now run around 15 percent. Asarco alone plans to employ 350 people once its mine is in full swing, and the company estimates it will have an annual payroll of $10.5 million and pay $3 million in taxes to the state.

Chambers of commerce and merchants in the towns surrounding the Cabinets, such as Thompson Falls, Noxon and Plains, have been campaigning hard for Asarco and Borax. Plains Chamber President Mary Lynn Vanderhoff says she doesn't know much about mining, but she supports the projects because of "their obvious positive impact."

Fred Roach, a Plains resident and member of a local environmental group called the Plains Clark Fork River Watchers, says he can't say for sure, but guesses local communities are "split on the mining issue," with greater support, however, for development.

While the mining companies await final approval for their plans, critics are weighing alternatives. There is a growing feeling that attempts to stop the mines could prove futile, and possibly create political backlash against the Endangered Species Act if the grizzly issue is pressed. Some local opponents say they are rethinking their position of total opposition to the projects and shifting their attention to getting the most environmentally sound mining possible.

But Tom Robinson, the Northern Rockies representative for The Wilderness Society, hasn't given up. He says the Forest Service might still reject the mining claims: "If the public knew that mining is allowed in wilderness, they would be as outraged as they were over the Bob Marshall." Robinson says it would take a large media campaign to stop the mining, but that it might work, "because the public is with us. Even in Montana."

If the mines are built, many critics question whether the companies will try to maintain environmental quality. Gene Smith, U.S. Borax's vice president for government and public affairs, says his company will consider all aspects of the environment in the mining operation. Jim Stratton, an Alaskan conservationist, says that hasn't been his experience with U.S. Borax.

Stratton, a former director of the Southeast Alaska Conservation Council, says he spent a bitter three-and-a-half years fighting U.S. Borax over its molybdenum mining proposal for Alaska's Misty Fjords National Monument. "U.S. Borax is a very powerful and well-connected company," he says. "It is a wholly owned subsidiary of Rio Tinto Zinc, a giant British conglomerate, and is responsible for all the mining compromises in the Alaska National Interest Lands Conservation Act when all the other mining companies rode happily on its coattails."

Stratton says his group was forced to go to court to get Borax to even think about protecting fisheries and wildlife in its road-building and tailings disposal. He adds: "They had no real interest in sitting down and talking to us about protecting Misty Fjords. They angered locals, conservationists and the Forest Service.

Montanans better watch out—they will build a mine as cheaply as possible." Stratton notes that U.S. Borax eventually got its way, and isn't spending the money conservationists say might have helped offset the mining impacts.

Asarco, which was largely founded by the Guggenheims in the early 1900s, and which has international connections, also has a record of stirring up opposition. Conservationists and local residents in northwest Montana have already sparred with Asarco over water quality at the company's "showcase" mine south of Troy. Asarco bills itself as "the producer of 16 percent of the free world's silver." Much of that silver comes from the Troy Mine, where mine tailings have been leaking heavy metals into Lake Creek, a pristine stream.

Asarco says the water-quality issue has been exaggerated. But local residents have appealed to the state to force the company to improve its tailings storage and water-quality monitoring. The issue is still unsettled. Some Asarco critics say that water quality may be the sleeper issue in the Rock Creek proposal. Tentatively, Asarco plans to impound its Rock Creek Mine tailings within a quarter-mile of the Clark Fork River, 25 miles upstream of Idaho's Lake Pend Oreille.

At this time, the process to get the mines started is on hold. A final decision rests with the upcoming validation of the rest of the companies' claims and environmental impact statements. Because of its legal obligations based on the 1872 Mining Law, the Forest Service may choose not to consider a no-action alternative. Rejection of the proposals rests with public opinion on wilderness and the grizzly bears' status under the Endangered Species Act.

So far, opposition has come primarily from Montanans, with the aid of several national conservation groups. Broader citizen opposition involvement may not emerge until the bulldozers are finally started up.

At that point, opponents may find that the two giant companies are not pushovers. Whatever action is eventually taken, one fact is apparent: Both companies are prepared for a fight. Though final approval for both mines may be more than two or three years away, U.S. Borax says in the cover letter for its "development concept" for the Rock Peak area: "One thing seems certain, and that is that U.S. Borax will in one way or another be in the East Fork of the Rock Creek drainage."

The conflict over mining in the Cabinet Mountains Wilderness still has not been resolved. In 1999, Sterling Mining Company bought the rights for the Rock Creek Mine and the defunct Troy Mine from Asarco. In December 2001, after completing a 2,700-page environmental impact statement, the U.S. Forest Service and Montana Department of Environmental Quality approved the mine; that decision is being challenged in court.

MANAGING THE WILD

Cows in the Wilderness

The Wilderness Act allows grazing in wilderness areas. But as the following stories show, a host of activities that have traditionally gone along with grazing—such as the use of vehicles and mechanized equipment to build and maintain water ponds and tanks for cattle, and the use of helicopters to kill sheep predators such as coyotes—have proved to be more problematic.

NOVEMBER 30, 1979

Congress, Conservationists Charge: Agency's Wilderness Grazing Policies "Too Pure"

BY MARJANE AMBLER

For 15 years, conservationists have been telling ranchers that wilderness designation would not jeopardize their grazing privileges on public lands. But when Bill Cunningham, Wilderness Society representative for Montana and North Dakota, made the statement to a group in Helena, Mont., recently, one rancher leapt to his feet and shouted, "That's a goddamned lie."

The rancher said that restrictions placed on his operation in the Absaroka-Beartooth Wilderness Area were making it impossible for him to continue raising sheep.

At the heart of the issue is a section of the Wilderness Act of 1964 that says established grazing shall continue in wilderness areas, subject to "reasonable" regulations enacted by the secretary of Agriculture, whose department includes the Forest Service.

Conservationists have publicized this section of the act, hoping it would defuse ranchers' opposition to wilderness. But such information has not stilled rancher complaints. They tell conservationists of livestock phase-outs, barbed wire and motor vehicle bans, and backpackers getting precedence over livestock and, in some cases, over resource protection in wilderness areas—all contrary to Congress' intent.

While these problems have existed on national forest grazing lands in wilderness areas since the Wilderness Act became law, they have not received much attention in the past. Most of the early wilderness areas were in high mountain country, much of it above timberline—"wilderness on the rocks," as one person put it—and grazing was only an issue on a small percentage of the areas.

Now, however, millions more acres are being considered for wilderness in the Forest Service's Roadless Area Review and Evaluation (RARE II) and the Bureau of Land Management's wilderness review. (BLM has never managed any wilderness areas before.) Many of these areas include lower-elevation lands that are now grazed.

Consequently, the question of how grazing will be managed in wilderness areas has become much more critical for both ranchers and conservationists.

Walking a Tightrope

Robert Rummell of the range management office of the Forest Service in Washington, D.C., thinks controversy is inherent in the question of wilderness grazing. "It's almost a tightrope we have to walk between production of a commodity and management for the intangibles—wilderness values," he says.

Ranchers and, ironically, many conservationists think the Forest Service has lost its balance by adopting regulations that would preserve a more pristine environment than either Congress or wilderness proponents intended.

"Any effort to manage wilderness as if it were in a straitjacket is ridiculous," says Cunningham. "I'm running out of patience with the Forest Service for its holier-than-thou attitude on grazing management, when they won't hesitate to use motorized equipment in wilderness areas for fighting fires."

Ranchers have often been surprised to find that some wilderness proponents share their concerns about the Forest Service management.

When the Absaroka-Beartooth Wilderness was proposed in Montana, rancher Teddy Thompson was one of its strongest opponents. His suspicions were confirmed when the Forest Service told him shortly after the wilderness area was designated that to prevent erosion in the wilderness, he had to delay taking his sheep to their summer pasture. Such a delay would shorten the season so much that Thompson felt it would not be worth taking his sheep into the area.

After his public confrontation with Thompson, Cunningham arranged a trip to the area with the sheep producers and subsequently wrote several letters to the Forest Service, Montana's governor and the Montana congressional delegation on Thompson's behalf. Cunningham, a professional forester by training, disagreed with the Forest Service's assessment of Thompson's grazing impact.

Cunningham emphasizes that grazing curtailments may be necessary in some cases to protect wildlife or other resources. But he feels these decisions should be made independent of whether the area is a wilderness—not because of it.

He does not think that widespread support for wilderness from agricultural groups will result from his and others' efforts on behalf of ranchers. But Cunningham does hope the agricultural community will keep an open mind and judge each proposed area on its own merits rather than absolutely being opposed to all wilderness.

He also thinks it is important to try to remove obstacles for ranchers. "Livestock production is a vital part of the Western heritage that we're fast losing. It is just as important to protect as wilderness itself," he says.

The Forest Service has not answered Cunningham's request for documentation of its decision on Thompson's allotment.

A Northern Rockies coalition called the Sheep Producer-Environmentalist Committee endorsed Cunningham's action at a recent meeting in Rock Springs, Wyo. The committee also called for an investigation of grazing policies in the Bridger Wilderness Area in Wyoming.

Disturbing Backpackers

Jim Magagna has a sheep grazing permit in the Bridger Wilderness, a backpackers' mecca with a quarter-million visitor-days each summer. His grazing permit from the Forest Service says his sheep must be herded and controlled so they won't become a nuisance to recreationists. Backpackers, on the other hand, are never told not to disturb livestock.

Magagna thinks the priority should be protection of the vegetation and the watershed—not the backpackers' esthetic experience. Instead, the Forest Service has chosen to resolve the conflict by phasing out grazing in the Bridger area by "relocation of domestic sheep from wilderness allotments to outside areas whenever it appears possible," according to a 1978 letter to district forest rangers from their supervisor. Magagna once had three sheep permits in the wilderness, and now he has one.

Mel Bacon of the Bridger-Teton National Forest office said rangers often get messages on trailhead registration forms objecting to livestock in the high country. One note at the Bridger Wilderness Area last summer said, "Hey, Forest Service, sheep shit stinks."

Recreationists say they are concerned about distractions from the natural environment and about water quality. Cattle and sheep feces can contaminate water, just as any other warm-blooded animal's feces can.

Because the Forest Service is giving backpackers priority and phasing out grazing in the Bridger Wilderness, many ranchers in the area oppose wilderness. One of those ranchers, John Barlow, whose cattle graze in several RARE II wilderness study areas in the Bridger-Teton National Forest, objects to clear-cutting and damage from four-wheel drive vehicles, which wilderness designation would prevent. He said, "I'd want my whole grazing allotment to be wilderness if I had assurance that I could continue to graze cattle in the same numbers." He thinks other ranchers in the area would also support wilderness designations if their grazing privileges were protected. "But the level of skepticism is so profound that it would take a lot of time and some very sincere effort to convince them," he said.

Congress Upset

Congress is aware that Forest Service policies are discouraging grazing in wilderness. One of the more flagrant examples the committee discovered was in North Dakota last year, where the Forest Service RARE II study report said that wilderness designations on grasslands there might result in a loss of 50 percent of the grazing potential. Then, as if to rub salt in the wound, the study said that ranchers who hold grazing permits "may be able to adjust by working part-time for the oil companies."

"These ranchers are alarmed, and I don't blame them a bit," said an aide to the House Interior Committee. "I think they've been had."

In an attempt to solve the ranchers' problems, the House Interior Committee last session sent two reports to the Agriculture Department stressing that grazing should not be curtailed. However, RARE II hearings and field inspection trips convinced the committee that Forest Service policies still do not comply with the law and are interpreted differently from forest to forest.

At one RARE II hearing, Lee Spann, a Colorado cattle rancher, told the committee he and other Colorado ranchers would like to see the law changed to protect grazing privileges, particularly to guarantee the right to use motorized vehicles under some circumstances.

Although national Forest Service regulations say motor vehicles can be used "when necessary" with permission of the regional forester, the Forest Service in Spann's region—and in most areas of the country—interprets that as almost never. Gerry Nyborg, range conservationist for the Forest Service in that area, told *HCN* that motorized vehicles can he used only when human life is in danger, such as when a helicopter is brought in to rescue a climber.

The House Subcommittee on Public Lands refused to include grazing protection in the Colorado wilderness bill, H.R. 5487. The subcommittee members think the Wilderness Act allows ample statutory flexibility, but that the Forest Service's regulations and the interpretation given to them at different levels of the agency are faulty.

Instead, the committee chose to include grazing guidelines for the Agriculture Department in a committee report. The report asks the secretary of Agriculture to review all policies, practices and regulations regarding livestock grazing in wilderness areas.

As a result of the committee's actions and boundary changes agreed upon by area ranchers and conservationists, Spann and other ranchers agreed to support the bill. Nineteen new wilderness areas totaling 1.3 million acres would be created in the state by the bill.

The guidelines suggest when motorized vehicles should be used, saying horses or other alternatives should still be used when "practical." Vehicles can be used occasionally for major fence repairs, for maintaining stock ponds and for rescuing sick animals. The guidelines also say natural materials shouldn't have to be used for repairing or replacing existing facilities if such materials would impose "unreasonable" additional costs. This means, for example, that barbed wire might be used instead of buck and pole fences.

"We haven't changed the Wilderness Act. We're just trying to get the message across to the Forest Service to be more sympathetic to the practical needs of grazing permittees," says an aide to the committee.

If the bill passes, as it is expected to, and if the Department of Agriculture abides by the committee's guidelines, which don't have the force of law, then some regulations in the Forest Service manual would have to be changed, according to Cunningham.

If changes were made, the problem of communicating Congress' intent to all levels of the Forest Service would remain. Interpretation of the current regulations vary from region to region and forest to forest. "They're scared to death that someone higher up will disagree with their interpretation, so they think, 'If I say no, I know I'm safe,'" says rancher Spann.

Conservationists charge that in some cases, Forest Service personnel use strict interpretation of the regulations as a way of deliberately arousing antagonism toward wilderness.

The Interior Committee report instructs the Department of Agriculture to distribute copies of the committee guidelines to all levels of the Forest Service and to all ranchers who have grazing permits in wilderness areas.

Still Restrictions

Bruce Hamilton, Northern Plains representative of the Sierra Club, does not think the new guidelines will eliminate the livestock industry's opposition to wilderness; their activities in wilderness areas will still be restricted. In addition, the committee's guidelines leave lots of room for interpretation. However, Hamilton thinks the guidelines are important to make the Forest Service administer the existing wilderness areas more consistently and to reassure ranchers.

Cunningham is more optimistic about the committee's action. "When the Interior Committee of the U.S. Congress lays its wishes out in that kind of detail, the Department of Agriculture has to pay attention. Especially if conservationists side with the livestock operators. Where can the department go for its constituency?"

Conservationists do not all agree on the question of wilderness grazing, however. Some have become frustrated and embittered by unsuccessful attempts to work with ranchers. Some would like to phase out all grazing on public lands.

However, Cunningham and Hamilton think there is a growing awareness of the importance of agriculture and the compatibility of grazing with wilderness. "If we continue to educate our people about grazing, and they educate their people about wilderness, we will have gone a long way toward solving our problems," Cunningham says.

The guidelines in the Committee report for H.R. 5487, which would pass as the Colorado Wilderness Act of 1980, became the standard for grazing in wilderness.

Utah's Wilderness Coyotes are Safe, for Now

BY TIM VITALE

Coyotes in Utah's Mount Naomi Wilderness may be safe from helicopter hunting this year, thanks to a joint appeal filed by the Utah chapter of the Sierra Club and the Utah Wilderness Association (UWA).

The appeal asked Forest Service Chief Max Peterson to overturn a Regional Forester ruling this February authorizing three helicopter-hunting trips to reduce the coyote population in the wilderness. Ranchers requested the aerial hunt to control what they said were significant increases in sheep kills by coyotes during the summer of 1985.

The UWA and the Sierra Club have 45 days to submit a Statement of Reasons for the appeal, and Barry Wirth, public information officer for the Wasatch-Cache National Forest, said Peterson won't rule on the case until all the information is in. Meanwhile, the hunts are on hold.

UWA coordinator Dick Carter said the appeal argues that the Forest Service is violating predator control guidelines in its own Wasatch-Cache Forest Management Plan. The guidelines say coyotes may be hunted by helicopter for up to three flights annually, but the hunters may target only coyotes that have killed sheep. According to the guidelines, the permittee must also show "special and serious losses" to domestic livestock. According to the UWA and the Sierra Club, the Forest Service is not following either guideline.

The forest plan also says that Regional Forester Stan Tixier must approve the use of helicopters. Tixier says he had reviewed the standards and guidelines in both the Utah Wilderness Act and the forest management plan before making the decision, and he felt the request was legitimate. He also says rumors were false that the Utah congressional delegation applied pressure to approve the flights. He did receive a phone call from Utah Rep. James Hansen's administrative assistant asking the status of the situation, he says, but no pressure was applied, and he never changed his decision.

Tixier says he approved hunting coyotes by helicopter because the request from the Wasatch-Cache forest supervisor included sheep-loss figures for 1985. They showed 63 sheep were killed by coyotes last year, 29 in 1984 and four in 1974.

The UWA's Carter disputes the accuracy of the sheep-loss figures: "We don't buy their figures; I don't think anyone in their agency believes them—they even put it on paper that the 1985 figure seems abnormally high." Logan District Ranger Dave Baumgartner sent the figures to the forest supervisor with a notation that he felt the 1974 and 1984 counts were accurate, but the 1985 reported losses seemed high. "The Forest Service itself has expressed skepticism on paper, and we're flatly rejecting the figure," Carter says.

"We're not opposing grazing in the wilderness," he adds. "We are saying they are violating the intent of their own guidelines. They cannot prove special and serious losses; they cannot target the offending animal, and helicopter gunning will denigrate the wilderness values in the area."

Tixier said he had no reason to doubt the validity of the reported sheep-loss figures, and he doesn't understand why the Logan District Ranger doubted them either.

Rudy Lukez, Cache Valley representative for the Sierra Club in Utah, said whatever decision the Forest Service makes will have national importance. "If it is allowed here, it could be used as a precedent in other wilderness areas in the country," he said.

Carter said the UWA contacted each of the 18 forests in the

Forest Service's Intermountain Region and asked for a summary of coyote-control efforts in the wilderness areas each managed. Carter said almost all forest managers prohibited predator control in wilderness. Not one targeted coyotes.

"But absolutely none allowed helicopter gunning in the wilderness," he said. "They seemed incredulous that I would even ask the question."

Clair Acord, executive director of the Utah Woolgrowers Association, said he was "rather bewildered" by the appeal from the conservation groups, since the groups did not oppose grazing in wilderness areas before the Utah Wilderness Act was passed in 1984. "They are turning tables on their own ideas.

"We need the predator control to run sheep," he said. "Helicopter hunting is one of the good tools we have."

That style of predator control, plus hunting from fixed-wing aircraft, has been common throughout Utah for years, he said. Helicopter hunting "is consistent with wilderness," since grazing and predator control are both allowed in wilderness.

But the Sierra Club and the UWA both said the issue is not grazing in wilderness. Jim Catlin, conservation chair for the Sierra Club, said neither group opposes grazing, and "it would be malicious for opponents to claim that. We believe, in this case, the Forest Service has made some gross assumptions in order to justify conflicting activities that could jeopardize wilderness management all across the state."

Carter said although he does not like coyote hunting in wilderness areas, "we'll turn our heads to legitimate predator control efforts."

The Forest Service recognizes the issue as a controversial one, and Tixier has directed the forest supervisor to look for acceptable alternatives aside from aerial gunning to deal with the problem of coyote predation in the future.

His authorization statement said approval was for 1986 only and could not be considered a precedent.

The Diamond Bar Saga Goes On—and On

BY TONY DAVIS

For five years, 15 livestock watering tanks planned for the Diamond Bar grazing allotment in New Mexico symbolized a fight over cows in America's oldest wilderness. Now it appears that the stock tanks may never be built.

In a precedent-setting decision in February, Forest Service Chief Jack Ward Thomas' office ruled that congressional grazing guidelines for wilderness don't allow construction of "a substantial number of new improvements" in a wilderness. This overturned a 1995 Gila National Forest decision authorizing 15 earthen impoundments for Diamond Bar rancher Kit Laney in the Gila and Aldo Leopold wilderness areas.

Although the proposed water holes were meant to move cows uphill from degraded rivers and streams on the 227-square-mile grazing allotment, environmentalists contended the tanks would degrade upland areas by causing more cattle pressure on them.

The Diamond Bar ruling clearly favored wilderness values. The chief's reviewing officer, Sterling Wilcox, said that grazing was not a "historic use" under the Wilderness Act, and grazing does not require "equal consideration" to the resource needs within a wilderness.

This makes it harder to build large watering tank developments in wilderness and easier for Forest Service officials to reduce cattle numbers when the land is in bad shape, agreed Forest Service official Dave Stewart, Arizona State University law professor Joe Feller and Bill Worf, a retired Forest Service wilderness chief who now is president of the Montana-based Wilderness Watch group.

Susan Schock, director of Gila Watch, the Silver City group that led the fight against the tanks, was pleased by the decision. "These guys in the Gila National Forest tried to convolute and manipulate the Wilderness Act. They tried to kowtow to the cattle industry," she says. "But the chief caught them and slapped them down."

Bill Myers of the National Cattlemen's Beef Association said the decision was another step toward carrying out what he called the environmentalists' agenda to get livestock off public lands.

"We're getting whipsawed," said Myers. "On the one hand, they're getting livestock out of riparian areas. On the other hand, you can't construct new watering facilities away from them. That begs the question: Where will the livestock drink?"

Gila National Forest Supervisor Abel Camarena has 180 days to rewrite his 1995 decision. Rancher Laney says Thomas' ruling, if upheld, would spell bankruptcy. He says he can't survive on 300 head.

He told the Associated Press that if forest rangers come to impound his herd, "they better bring a gun. I'm not going to go. They will plant me here." But he added, "We will do everything we possibly can to avoid that type of confrontation, because that gains nothing."

The Path into the Desert

Angel Point Trail, in southeast Utah's Dirty Devil proposed wilderness.
—PHOTO BY STEPHEN TRIMBLE

The Bureau of Land Management is responsible for 261 million acres of federal land—70 million *more* acres than the Forest Service controls—yet the agency was excluded from the original Wilderness Act. That was largely because the lands the BLM managed were essentially "leftovers"—lower-elevation public lands that didn't have the right stuff to become national forests or national parks, and that the government had, for more than a century, tried to sell off under the Homestead Act and its successors.

Then, in 1976, Congress gave the BLM a new "multiple use" mission that balanced mining, oil and gas development, grazing, recreation and wildlife conservation—and formally extended the provisions of the Wilderness Act to the agency. The Federal Land Policy and Management Act directed the BLM to begin a 15-year inventory of its lands and recommend areas suitable for formal wilderness designation to the president by 1991. The president was required to forward his recommendations to Congress by 1993.

The new law transformed the wilderness issue. It gave the BLM a mandate to assert itself as a land-protection agency, rather than as the country's largest real estate developer. And it forced the nation to reconsider its wilderness aesthetic, for now deserts and badlands and sage flats—even the fringes of the West's cities— were wilderness possibilities.

The BLM's desert low country could be as stirring as the Forest Service's traditional "rock and ice" wilderness, but it was also extremely contentious ground, where wilderness proposals frequently collided with resource-development interests and off-road vehicle use.

In large part because of those conflicts, few BLM lands have become wilderness. Although the bureau recommended 26 million acres of its land to Congress for designation, only 161 areas, totaling about 6.5 million acres, have actually been designated. In 2004, about 2.4 percent of BLM land, compared to about 17.4 percent of the national forests, is protected as wilderness. More than half of the BLM's recommendations for wilderness—some

14.4 million acres that the agency now manages as "wilderness study areas"—stalled out in Congress because they lacked the support of local congressional delegations.

Once again, citizens' groups have taken matters into their own hands. They have not only championed BLM-proposed areas, but expanded the debate to include millions of acres of eligible lands that the agency left out of its official inventories.

It has been an uphill fight, and nowhere more than in Utah. There, citizens have proposed progressively larger wilderness bills that, by the end of the 20th century, had grown to 9.1 million acres—and met increasingly stiff resistance from rural Utahns and the state's conservative congressional delegation. The effort also opened up great rifts within the wilderness community itself. Ray Wheeler's two-part series, "Last Stand for the Colorado Plateau," provides one of the best inside views of the fierce debate over whether to adopt an incremental, area-by-area approach or a statewide, all-or-nothing approach.

EDITORIAL

Scenic Beauty Contest Unfair

BY JOAN NICE

Glacier-chiseled peaks, pine trees and meadows splashed with shooting stars, primroses and pasque flowers. That's the essence of one kind of wilderness—the kind that's particularly attractive to backpackers.

But there's another kind at the base of those ethereal peaks. People who venture there shiver by night and sweat by day. The sagebrush and desolation discourage them. The expanse and lack of amenities shrink their confidence.

The United States has made some progress in protecting the home of the pine. However, most of our roadless desert lands remain exploitable, and for them, wilderness designation is discouraged with a belly laugh and a "who the hell would want to go to that godforsaken place?"

But Congress did not have a geographic beauty contest in mind when it passed the Wilderness Act in 1964. Nor did it require that the lands in the wilderness system be well-endowed playgrounds for backpackers.

It did ask that the lands be roadless and at least 5,000 acres (or a manageable unit), and that they "provide outstanding opportunities for solitude or a primitive and unconfined type of recreation." It also had in mind areas that contain "ecological, geological, or other features of scientific, educational, scenic, or historical value," according to the act.

Do the harsh, brown deserts fill the bill? If we have millions of acres of sagebrush country, how can any of it be considered outstanding?

The answer should be obvious to anyone who's ever felt a yen for the frontier. In this urbanized country, any tract of land over 5,000 acres that hasn't been penetrated by a road is remarkable. Even in the relatively undeveloped state of Wyoming, 92 percent of the Bureau of Land Management's lands were declared too civilized to be considered for wilderness status.

We have lots of pine trees in the high country as well as lots of sage down below. What makes either type of country worth saving is its occurrence in a spot that remains, as the Wilderness Act puts it, "affected primarily by the forces of nature, with the imprint of man's work substantially unnoticeable."

The pretty, wooded areas chosen by the U.S. Forest Service and the National Park Service have done more to define wilderness than Congress' own dictates. The Bureau of Land Management, now engaged in its first wilderness inventory, seems all too eager to follow the precedent of those agencies.

Certainly, not every dry tract of emptiness in the public domain should be protected. But neither should an area's commonness or lack of physical appeal to backpackers or hunters preclude it from wilderness status. The desert is all the more wild for its lack of humans. While it is not a playground, it is a haven for wildlife, for silence, for space—the last remains of the Western frontier. Such land deserves man's highest respect, and the Wilderness Act was designed to protect it.

Protect it.

ESSAY

Utah's "Heart of Darkness": Wilderness Stirs Deep Emotions

BY C.L. RAWLINS

When my grandparents were still alive and living on the farm in Lewiston, Utah, that had given them and their family sustenance since the days of the Mormon pioneers, my visits often entailed a ritual which seemed to me curious.

We would drive the roads near their place and my grandmother would point with pride to the newest houses, which in her lexicon were "lovely new homes." Many of them, built in brick in shades of uncompromising glare-white or mortgage-yellow, seemed to me hideous: overlarge and at odds with the landscape of green fields and wetland. But I realize now that they were beautiful to her in what they represented: successive triumphs for an ideal, the settling of a wilderness.

I also recall her warnings, given when I recounted solo camping trips to the mountains east of Cache Valley or talked of plans for further solitary wanderings. "Be careful," she said many times, "it's so dangerous up there."

At some point early in my personal wilderness experience, I crossed an emotional divide. The mountains, it seemed to me, were the safe place. The weather and other hazards were devoid of malice, deviousness or cunning. I was most likely to suffer from my own mistakes. By contrast, the cities and highways, with human creatures driven by ambition and greed, driving home drunk at high speeds, were truly dangerous. I could make no mistakes and still fall victim.

My grandparents were the children of a generation still struggling with what Pilgrim William Bradford called in 1620 "a hideous and desolate wilderness." Their parents and grandparents had been successively driven, with violence and death, from Indiana, Illinois and Missouri into an ill-prepared exodus across what was then called the Great American Desert.

When Brigham Young called his famous halt, they faced a large, arid valley ringed with ragged peaks and containing a dead lake, salty enough "to float an anvil, if anyone is such a damned fool as to lug one over there and heave it in."

Theirs was a sort of wilderness experience unavailable today. That the Indians they encountered seemed at home and even intimate with this wilderness was considered fit proof of their innate savagery. Unable to live in this landscape and retain their own cherished culture, the Mormon settlers struggled to transform it into a model, that of the Midwestern agricultural village, which simmered in their dispossessed hearts.

The Indians, mostly nomads living in extended-family groups and traveling to seasonal food resources, were at first little competition for the Mormons. The primary demarcation of land was between what was "ours" (cabins, fields, irrigation ditches, roads) and what was "its." The Mormons were not alone in their ideal of "reclaiming" land from desolation and wildness, as if it had somehow been civilization's property from the beginning, but they were true believers in the manifestness of that particular destiny. And they were on the cutting edge.

To them, it was a matter of immediate survival, this process of changing wilderness, land that is "its," into ditches and plowed fields and fenced pastures, into land that is "ours." The width of the streets in Salt Lake City was not, to Brigham Young, a mere engineering decision. It was a psychological necessity, an assertion of character. The streets of Salt Lake are very, very wide.

When parties of scouts and settlers fanned out from the Salt Lake Valley to define the borders of the Mormon empire, they realized the awesome breadth and beauty of "its" domain, but had eyes mostly for strictly tangible prospects. The typical written accounts of the time deal less with the majesty of the land than with its prospects for farming or grazing. The tempered tone of Major Powell is absent.

It is hard to fault a practical people for exercising their will to survive, but times have changed with the presence of people on the land. Utah's population, according to the *Statistical Abstract of the United States,* is 84.4 percent urban, even though many of those urban centers are small towns. New York state's urbanization is only slightly higher at 84.6 percent, and Pennsylvania's is 69.3 percent. Still, some vestige of the pioneer instinct, the feeling of "ours" and "its," remains alive in the state.

As wilderness in its pure form was a threat to the pioneer, wilderness in its legislated form is frightening to many of his inheritors. Ads for four-wheel-drive vehicles hit hard on the note of an illusory freedom to be gained "beyond the end of the pavement." The idea that wilderness is a quantity and quality that "man can only mar" is anathema to the urban frontiersman, dispossessed of his frontier.

Much of the opposition to wilderness designations comes from those who actually use the land in question as grazing for livestock or from those who hope to, through timber sales, mines, or oil wells. Some of the truly fierce opposition, though, comes from people who have never seen the place or even want to see it.

As Thomas Lyon, professor at Utah State University and editor of the *Journal of Western American Literature,* said in a recent speech, "Opposition seems to go far beyond what the objective circumstances require. Apparently, there is something awfully threatening about wilderness. Wilderness advocates are accused of emotionalism with a fervor that approaches frenzy."

Attendance at public hearings shows that frenzy works both ways. Anti-wilderness speakers are often shouted down or rudely interrupted by the wilderness purist. At the fringe of the issue, each side has a ferocious constituency which regards any sort of negotiation as betrayal.

It is clear that some deep level of personal and cultural identity is involved in the wilderness issue—clear especially in Utah, with its tenacious frontier-pioneer heritage.

To Professor Lyon, the dichotomy our culture imposes, in which civilization and wilderness are opposing poles, makes the issue a personal one, a matter of emotion. Too much energy is given to "human-centered arguments, rather than the facts of genetic diversity or watershed preservation."

"We tend to view these remnants as symbols and they gain the power of symbols. Wilderness as 'other' threatens merely by existing."

A recent acquaintance told me, "When I can't see lights in my rear-view mirror, I get scared." It is, just maybe, this sort of fear—of darkness, of chaos, of aloneness—which is projected into the landscape.

The Anglo-Saxon *wylder ness* means the den of a wild beast. There is, in the history of the word wilderness, a sense of lurking danger, of claws and teeth. That the Christian pilgrim to this continent chose this word above all others to denote the mountains and forests was revelatory of his fear of the vast, unknown land and his personal feeling of separation.

In his book *Common Landscape of America 1580–1845,* John R. Stilgoe sums up the importance of this encounter: "It meant confronting the fragmented former oneness of man and nature, and it meant knowing the true fragility of civilized order. *Wilderness* identified those spaces beyond human control, the spaces of bewilderment, the spaces of heathen."

In a variety of ways, this interpretation has become locked in our tradition, and Utah is a traditional state. But there is an equally strong case for finding in wilderness a source of values and a sort of shrine:

We do therefore…dedicate and solemnly devote this tree to be a Tree

*of Liberty, May all our councils and deliberations under its branches
be guided by wisdom and directed to the support and maintenance
of that liberty which our renowned forefathers sought out and found
under trees and in the wilderness.*

—From a dedication of a Tree of Liberty
Providence, Rhode Island, October, 1765

In 1797, George Washington wrote:

*We ruin the lands that are already cleared and either cut down
more wood, if we have it, or emigrate into the western country...
A half, a third, or even a fourth of what land we mangle, well-
wrought and properly dressed, would produce more than the whole
under our system of management; yet such is the force of habit that
we cannot depart from it.*

In 1976, Andrew V. Bailey, then Chief of Mining Operations for
the Department of the Interior, included the following in
a letter:

*When the Geological Survey has the lead in preparing environmen-
tal statements, inflammatory words such as disturbed, devastated,
defiled, ravaged, gouged, scarred and destroyed should not be
used. These are words used by the Sierra Club, Friends of the Earth,
environmentalists, homosexuals, ecologists and other ideological
eunuchs opposed to developing mineral resources.*

What is evident in the contrast between the last quotes is how
land-use issues, including wilderness, have become increasingly
ideological and bitterly political. Wilderness has become an
emblem, a symbol for what is loved and valued or for what is
hated and feared.

On this level, the wilderness itself—the actual land—is less
important than the struggle with personal demons. The power of
wilderness, or our image of it, in shaping the American character

is supremely evident in the ferocity with which we contest the issue. That our fears and failings as humans will so largely influence the fate of these few roadless remnants is a sad paradox.

A part of the land that has given us as a nation so much deserves to be left to itself, to its own rhythms and purposes. We may hike it, graze it, photograph it, get lost in it, fry its trout, curse its mosquitoes or ascend its peaks. What is forbidden, to use George Washington's inflammatory word, is to mangle it.

Will Mancos Mesa Make the Wilderness Grade?

BY JOAN NICE

Each year, thousands bounce over the rapids in Cataract Canyon or make a wake in Lake Powell. But few visit Mancos Mesa, only a few miles away. And why should they? It's wide-open Colorado Plateau country, where an occasional piñon pine or juniper is a relative oasis.

Nevertheless, Mancos Mesa and 174 million equally obscure acres in the West have been spotlighted for the past two years in the U.S. Bureau of Land Management's public-land wilderness inventory.

Now the inventory phase of BLM's wilderness search is ready for public scrutiny. With all but 5 million acres of land assessed, the agency has proposed that about 12 percent, or some 21 million acres—an area slightly smaller than the state of West Virginia—should be studied for possible wilderness designation.

In individual states the percentage varies, from 14 percent of BLM lands in Idaho to 3 percent in Wyoming. The BLM's recommendations in Colorado and Montana are about 10 percent.

In Utah, where some of the agency's most spectacular lands lie, 2,179,000 acres, or 10 percent, have been recommended—an area smaller than Yellowstone National Park. Here, too, the agency has met some of its most spectacular opposition.

Lonely Mancos Mesa in the southeastern part of the state didn't make it. At 51,000 acres, it is big enough—10 times bigger than the Wilderness Act requires. And it's natural enough. The imprint of man in a wilderness must be "substantially unnoticeable." Only 25 percent of Mancos Mesa would be disqualified because of drill sites and roads, the BLM says.

But Mancos Mesa and many other wild, open spaces in the West fell short on utilitarian grounds. The Bureau didn't think they measured up to the act's requirement that an area provide "outstanding opportunities" for either "solitude" or "primitive and unconfined recreation."

The mesa is clearly no traditional outdoor fun spot. It's windy, hot and—except for the occasional canyon—a plain blend of bare ground and hardy buffaloberry, Mormon tea, cliff rose and Indian rice grass. The BLM doesn't go so far as to call the terrain monotonous, but in its April 1980 Wilderness Inventory document, it does say it lacks "focal features."

In the Bureau's words: "Opportunities for primitive and unconfined recreation are considered to be less than outstanding. This is attributed to the limited natural screening and the lack of focal features that would provide an environment for either a variety of primitive recreation pursuits or an outstanding experience in any one primitive recreation pursuit...Opportunities for solitude...are less than outstanding."

That means Mancos Mesa may be big and wild, but in the Bureau's opinion it hasn't got what it legally takes to be wilderness. Apparently, if a van full of Boy Scouts arrived at the other end of the mesa, you would feel pretty silly seeking cover behind a gossamer clump of rice grass.

The San Juan County commissioners are pleased. What with Arches and Canyonlands national parks next door, they think they have enough sanctified scenery.

"We think enough land in our county already has been taken over by the federal government," said Commission Chairman E.S. Boyle. "Of course, we're opposed to wilderness proposals."

"Atrocities"

"They say you can't find solitude here," said Dick Carter of the Utah Wilderness Association. "But based on the isolation and size of the unit and the canyon systems, we say you can." Carter goes so far as to list this decision among "the great BLM atrocities" that he feels have been committed in the wilderness decisions in his state. Among the other expansive, remote areas that he said have been unfairly thrown out of the running are Wahweap on the Kaiparowits Plateau and part of Mount Ellen in the Henry Mountains. Both contain well over 100,000 acres, but the BLM rejected them on the grounds that they don't offer "outstanding" opportunities for solitude or recreation.

"Solitude is inherent in areas of this size," Carter said.

Unfair interpretations of the solitude-or-recreation requirement have resulted in homogeneity among the proposed wilderness study areas, Carter said. Lots of canyons and buttes make it, but the rolling or flat, open areas generally don't.

"A flat or rolling area in this country that has managed to stay pristine is very, very rare," said Debbie Sease, who is coordinating several pro-wilderness groups' work on the BLM inventory from Washington, D.C. "It should be a top wilderness priority."

BLM's Utah Wilderness Coordinator, Kent Biddulph, makes no apologies for the discrimination against flat areas. "Look at the criteria in the Blue Book for determining 'outstanding,'" he said.

BLM's blue-colored *Wilderness Inventory Handbook* states, "Factors or elements influencing solitude may include size, natural screening, and ability of the user to find a secluded spot...It may be difficult, for example, to avoid the sights and sounds of people in a flat open area unless it is relatively large."

Biddulph's conclusion is: "So a flat area with sparse vegetation and little topographic variation probably is not going to stay in."

However, a July 12, 1979, memo to state directors from the associate director of BLM warns against narrow interpretations: "It is erroneous to assume that simply because a unit or portion of a unit is flat and-or unvegetated, it automatically lacks an outstanding opportunity for solitude."

Carter suspects that the BLM is throwing out the big, flat areas for the wrong reasons. Kent Biddulph denies it, but Carter says that the BLM is considering Mancos Mesa's uranium potential and fears the wrath of the activist, anti-wilderness San Juan County commissioners.

The BLM is supposed to ignore resource conflicts until the next round, the "wilderness study" phase. Even if a roadless area is lined with solid gold, at this point the agency must simply concentrate on whether its wilderness characteristics meet the minimum requirements of the law.

Likewise, the BLM is supposed to turn a deaf ear to wilderness polemics from the public. This has been difficult, since nearly every segment of the public participating in the process has at times ignored BLM's orderly process. The public has frequently jumped from the inventory-phase discussion of whether an area has wilderness qualities to the question that will be asked after September: whether it should be protected as wilderness.

Commissioners want to talk about economic freedom, oil companies about energy, ranchers about bureaucracy and environmentalists about the number of people who support the concept of wilderness. At this point, according to BLM's rules, all of these topics are irrelevant.

As the inventory first began, state and local officials and commodity interests scowled while environmentalists smiled. "The fruits of our input so far have been excellent," a Sierra Club news release stated last fall.

But now, Dick Carter speaks of "atrocities" and his counterparts in other states are upset, though in most cases to a lesser degree. "Utah provides an example for every problem we have with the inventory," said Sease. BLM's pats on the back are coming from outside the conservation community.

One wilderness skeptic who is a Utah state official said: "They've done an excellent job." Commissioner Boyle has only a slightly less enthusiastic assessment: "The BLM has done a fair job of following Congress' dictates."

The BLM has reached a watershed. By September, it will have completed what most observers consider to be the easiest part of its wilderness task—deciding which lands merit consideration. Next, it will plunge into the controversial business of weighing one resource value against another. In many cases, it will have to tell Congress whether wilderness or energy development is the preferred option for a given piece of land. What's more, it must protect the study areas' wilderness values until Congress takes action. The BLM's final recommendations to the president are due by 1991.

While the furor over Mancos Mesa and other wild, open lands proposed to be dropped from the inventory will have died down by September, the BLM's work will have barely begun.

July 4th Fireworks Miss Wilderness Study Area

BY CRAIG RAYLE

The early 1980s saw the rise of the "Sagebrush Rebellion," as some ranchers and local government officials chafed under increasing federal oversight that came with the national environmental laws of the 1970s. In Moab, the movement inspired a stab at wilderness that prefigured a much larger fight over roads and wilderness in the 1990s.

MOAB, Utah—The rural West celebrates the Fourth of July in many ways. Some towns have fireworks, ice cream socials, or parades.

But this year, this town attempted a break from both tradition and the federal government when county commissioners, at the request of some town residents, drove a bulldozer into a Bureau of Land Management wilderness study area.

In their first attempt at declaring independence, county officials did not find these routes to be self-evident; they misread bureau maps, and their Fourth of July sortie fell short of its target by 1,000 yards.

On July 7, however, the bulldozer driver graded an abandoned road into the study area. At that point, the commissioners said, control of all land administered by the BLM was symbolically transferred to the county.

"It's a matter of right and wrong, freedom and liberty," said Commissioner David White. "Ecology is not part of the issue."

A Constitutional Right

The go-ahead for the action was given at an emergency meeting called by the commissioners on June 25.

Resolutions were read by the Republican and Democratic Party county representatives renouncing the federal government's right to control unappropriated federal lands in Utah, and supporting Utah State Senate Bill 5, a Sagebrush Rebellion-initiated bill passed last year that challenges the federal government's control of public lands in Utah.

"We thought July Fourth would be a good day for us to declare our independence," Marilyn Cooper, Democratic Party chairman for the county, told the commission. "We want to take county equipment and upgrade a road into a wilderness study area instead of sitting here stagnant…Let's keep the Sagebrush Rebellion alive, and every three or four months, when everybody has nothing else to do, we'll stir up something."

Wilderness supporters spoke in opposition at the meeting. Tuck Forsythe, head of the Moab Environmental Council, said he was disturbed that his taxes would help pay for the bulldozer work and then for the probable ensuing court costs.

But the motion passed, and Ron Steele, head of the Utah Sovereignty Commission, thanked the commission, saying, "We've heard what we've wanted to hear."

Steele, who has been a leader of the Sagebrush Rebellion for more than four years, bases his support of the county's action on his interpretation of the U.S. Constitution.

Nowhere in that document, said Steele, is the federal government given the right to control unappropriated lands. "When Utah entered the Union," he conceded, "the territorial government agreed that the people inhabiting this state shall forever disclaim the unappropriated lands." But, he argued, the Constitution overrides this agreement.

What to Do

Bill Binge, county attorney, was placed in the unenviable position of keeping a lid on the potentially violent situation.

Binge spent hours on the phone, trying to decide whether to bring in federal marshals and weighing other options. He advised the commissioners against the action. "But they won't listen to me," he says, "So it doesn't make much difference."

In the end, only the county sheriff and his deputies were present to maintain peace.

Gene Day, district manager for the BLM, says he is growing tired of bulldozer diplomacy. Last summer, the county commission opened another wilderness study area by building a road into Negro Bill Canyon.

Rather than press charges, the BLM offered to construct a picnicking and wading area in Negro Bill Creek if the county would maintain the quarter-mile road it built and allow a fence to be constructed to prohibit vehicle traffic past that point. The county rejected the offer last month.

The Showdown

On the morning of the Fourth, a mixed procession headed out of Moab City Park. A freshly washed late-model pickup, gun rack emptied at the request of the county commissioners, was followed by a restored Dodge full of longhaired youths.

Behind them was a mile-long procession of vehicles that wove over slickrock and massive sandstone fins eight miles from town to the waiting D-6 Caterpillar tractor. A Sagebrush Rebellion sticker was attached to the blade, speeches were made, and the crowd was asked to join in the march for freedom.

A quarter-mile up the road, Bruce Hucko, head of the Slickrock Country Council, sat on the edge of the proposed Mill Creek wilderness area, determined to make a stand. But the bulldozer never came.

A thousand yards down the trail, the bulldozer halted. "You are now standing in a wilderness study area," announced Commissioner Ray Tibbetts; congratulations were exchanged, and statements were gathered from all sides by the press.

But the commissioners were wrong. The maps had been misread. The wilderness study area was unblemished.

Correcting the Problem

Three days later, at the July 7 meeting, the county commissioners were confronted with their error by BLM officials. Tibbetts at first maintained that the county had indeed entered the area and that the BLM was lying. Then he blamed the BLM's small-scale maps for the county's inability to accurately find the boundary.

Finally, Commissioner Larry Jacobs said, "The problem is being corrected." While the commission was meeting, county employees had been ordered to secretly take equipment up to the canyon rim and blaze the remaining one-quarter mile into the wilderness study area.

"The 300 people who went up there are an extremist fringe," said Sam Taylor, editor and owner of the local newspaper. "They lowered themselves to the level of Hayduke (a character in Edward Abbey's *The Monkey Wrench Gang*).

"I'm dedicated to the Sagebrush Rebellion," he said. "But the way to change a bad law is through the courts or through legislation."

Mary Plumb, BLM public relations officer, believes the commissioners may have broken the state's own Sagebrush Rebellion law. That law holds that "any person who performs any act with respect to the use, management or disposal of the public lands must obtain written authorization from the Division of State Lands."

Apparently, no such authorization was obtained, and Gov. Scott Matheson, D, reportedly came out strongly against the Moab actions.

A Determined Dogma

Sagebrush rebel Ron Steele loves the canyon lands. "We live here by choice, because this is beautiful country and we want to live here and raise our children," he said.

But Steele also judges the value of the land by weighing its utility. "I can tear off into the Kennecott copper pits and think that's fantastic—a wondrous achievement of man," he said.

Commissioner Tibbetts also loves his home, "more than you," he told a reporter. "I've been here longer and I know it better."

OCTOBER 14, 1985

Last Stand for the Colorado Plateau, Part 1

BY RAY WHEELER

July 18, 1985

"Can we get the rest of these lights out?"

A familiar moment. People groping in a dark room. An empty slide projector banks its blazing rectangle of light off a screen in the corner of the room.

"I think you're OK there, Mo."

Where I come from, out West in Utah, the "slide show" is an old and honored tradition. I don't know anybody who doesn't own a projector, and doesn't love to show slides. It's Saturday night, and your friends come over, and you look at pictures.

Almost always, they are pictures of Utah. Pictures of the land. That last hike in Canyonlands. That Lodore Canyon river trip. That weekend in Zion National Park. There is an endless supply of such pictures, yet no one I know ever seems to tire of looking at them. How come? Because there is something out there in the dark, something out there beyond the pale of the projector beam, something so ingeniously diverse, so infallibly mysterious, so complex and intriguing that it will be impossible for any of us, in a lifetime, to see enough of it. It has many names. Canyon Country. Color Country. Hoodoo or Hondu Country. Sinbad Country. The Colorado Plateau.

Someone trips over the projector cord, and the light fails.

People are snickering—a slide-show tradition. Another pedestrian steps on the cord, and the projector coughs back to life.

As we get under way, I realize with a shock of recognition that the pictures are familiar: I've been to these places. There's Mount Ellen, a forested dome floating like a cloud over the blue and grey and gold desert badlands that surround her. The complicated redrock canyon system of Indian Creek. The cool, dark narrows of White Canyon. The perfectly formed, 500-foot-deep symmetrical hairpin meanders of Labyrinth Canyon.

The pictures are familiar, but the place and the people surrounding me are not. I'm two thousand miles from home, in a hearing room in Washington, D.C. The man showing slides is Rep. John Seiberling, D-Ohio, chairman of the House Subcommittee on Public Lands and National Parks. Sitting here with me in the dark are maybe 150 people, among them Mo Udall, D-Ariz., chairman of the House Interior Committee and Donald Hodel, secretary of the Interior.

"Slide number three," Seiberling is saying, "shows the same area, which was among the most dramatic that I recall seeing in Utah. These badlands are entirely natural, have no development, and in my opinion at least, are eminently qualified for wilderness."

This is a congressional oversight hearing. Its subject: the Bureau of Land Management's wilderness program. Such hearings, like slide shows back home in Utah, have become something of a ritual on Capitol Hill. There have been five during the past three years.

"When we first initiated these hearings in December 1982," Seiberling recalls in his opening statement, "I believe it's fair to say that the BLM program was more or less of a shambles."

At that first BLM wilderness oversight hearing, Seiberling recalls, he had shown former Interior Assistant Secretary Gary Carruthers "numerous examples of inadequate wilderness inventories...initial BLM wilderness recommendation decisions that were prompting strong public criticism, and substandard wilderness reviews." From the beginning, Seiberling says, he had tried to convince the Interior Department "that it would be better to conduct a thorough initial wilderness study than to perform a hasty, superficial one that would be fraught with endless appeals and litigation."

That advice fell on deaf ears. Within weeks, Secretary Watt had ordered the BLM to drop from its wilderness review all areas of less than 5,000 acres, and any "split estate" lands (where the subsurface mineral rights were not owned by the federal government)—1.5 million acres in all. The Sierra Club promptly filed suit.

For conservation leaders in Western states, where the BLM has identified 24 million acres of wilderness study areas, the "Watt Drops" were only the latest debacle in a BLM wilderness review repeatedly marred by controversy and scandal.

In June of 1984, Seiberling scheduled a new round of BLM wilderness oversight hearings in Congress. The results were spectacular. Rather than placating conservationists, the hearings seemed to have the opposite effect. The BLM's wilderness review was evoking protest from all over the West, and at each new round of hearings the charges became more serious, more specific and better documented.

Testimony quickly focused on two species of grievances. First, conservationists charged, the BLM wilderness inventory (the initial selection process in which wilderness "candidates" were identified) had been—at best—draconian. In some states, entire natural areas—huge chunks of pristine land—had been "arbitrarily and capriciously" dropped from the wilderness inventory. Elsewhere, the original roadless areas had been mysteriously reduced in size, giants pared down to midgets.

Second, conservationists charged, the BLM was so biased against wilderness that it had actually been allowing development inside areas that had been selected as wilderness candidates. That was a violation of the agency's legislative mandate to provide "Interim Management Protection" (IMP) to all roadless lands under study for wilderness designation.

Reports of such "IMP violations" were pouring in from all

over the West. In California, the BLM allowed a thousand dirt-bikers to race across the Soda Mountains Wilderness Study Area. In Idaho, the BLM approved the construction of a 20-mile pipeline along the boundary between two wilderness study areas so as to introduce livestock grazing on a plateau whose prime wilderness values are its virgin bunchgrass and its herd of rare California bighorn sheep. In Oregon, the BLM proposed to increase livestock grazing allotments in 12 wilderness study areas.

Even these complaints, however, paled alongside those emanating from the state of Utah. In the June 1984 hearings, two Utah conservationists presented 50 pages of detailed testimony documenting 57 interim management violations inside BLM wilderness study areas in Utah—42 exploratory oil holes and 15 seismic or mining operations, with attendant roads and surface damage—and identifying nearly 3 million acres of qualifying roadless lands that had been arbitrarily dropped from the BLM wilderness inventory in Utah.

Three million acres?

"In most of the other Western states, there were some differences of opinion," says Sierra Club Washington staffer Debbie Sease. "In Utah, the BLM wilderness inventory was shoddy."

For Jim Catlin, conservation chair for the Utah Chapter of the Sierra Club, the word "shoddy" is too polite. He prefers "massive abuse."

The "inventory" was only the first phase of the agency's two-stage wilderness review process. The purpose of the inventory was to identify all roadless units that had wilderness characteristics. Once those units had been identified, the wilderness potential of each "Wilderness Study Area" would be weighed against non-wilderness uses—such as mining—in developing the final recommendation to Congress.

According to BLM policy, simply being "roadless" and "natural" weren't good enough to qualify an area for wilderness study. In addition to meeting a minimum size requirement, all qualifying areas had to supply at least one or two "wilderness characteristics" defined in the Wilderness Act of 1964—either "outstanding opportunities for solitude," or "outstanding opportunities for primitive and unconfined recreation."

Debbie Sease toured BLM roadless areas with Utah BLM State Director Gary Wickes while the inventory was in progress, and was appalled by what she found. "We stood on the edge of—far as the eye can see—incredibly beautiful, utterly wild land. Miles and miles and miles of beautiful Utah scenery. And I would say, 'Gary, why are you eliminating this?' And he'd say, 'Because there are no outstanding opportunities for primitive recreation.' And I'd say, 'And there's no opportunities for solitude either?' And Gary would say, 'You're right. You can have solitude here, but it's not outstanding solitude.' "

Since 1980, a steady flow of politicians, bureaucrats, conservation leaders and journalists have taken the same tour. Terry Sopher, then national director for the BLM's wilderness program, says he began hearing ominous rumors about the Utah BLM wilderness inventory in 1979. In the summer of 1980, as the inventory was nearing completion, Sopher visited Utah to investigate.

A single overflight, Sopher says, was sufficient to convince him that "what the BLM was trying to do was totally absurd." Flying over Labyrinth Canyon, he recalls, "you were looking down on the ground, and one side of the river was said to have outstanding characteristics, and the other side was said not to have, and they both looked identical…Based on what we had seen, there was an egregious violation of the policies."

Sopher rushed back to BLM headquarters in Washington, D.C., to report his findings to BLM Director Frank Gregg. Sopher's recommendation: "The director should intervene and take steps to stop the current direction of the inventory, to require it to be done over." Sopher fought vigorously to block the Utah inventory, he says, but was overruled by Gregg.

"In 1980, the Sagebrush Rebellion was at the height of its popularity and public presence," Sopher explains. "If the BLM national director had stepped in before the state director had reached a final decision, it would have fit the image of Washington bureaucrats telling local professional managers what to do. So the director at the national level decided that he could not take further action until the state director issued a final decision."

But the Utah state director's final wilderness inventory decision was not published until November, 1980, simultaneous with the election of Ronald Reagan. Before anything could be done to correct the BLM inventory, Reagan took office, Watt was appointed Secretary of Interior, and Robert Burford replaced BLM Director Frank Gregg. Sopher blasted the Reagan administration in a press conference. Then he resigned in protest.

Back in Utah, the situation looked grim indeed for Utah conservationists. After four years of unsuccessful protests and appeals, they might have been expected to throw in the towel. Instead, in April of 1980, they launched an omnibus appeal with the Interior Board of Land Appeals (IBLA). Running to 1,500 pages and covering nearly a million acres on 29 separate roadless units, the appeal was the largest in the history of the IBLA.

The sheer size of the action sent a shock wave of alarm all the way to Washington, D.C. In 1982, Seiberling traveled to Utah for the well-worn tour of roadless areas cut from the inventory.

Seeing is believing.

"They've left out areas that obviously qualify for wilderness," Seiberling told *High Country News* in an interview, "and I've seen a lot of them. I mean, their position is absolutely absurd where they've said that they dropped a particular area because it didn't give opportunities for solitude."

In April of 1983, the IBLA handed down its decision on the Utah appeal: In 21 of the 29 appealed units, the BLM's inventory decisions were in error. Almost 90 percent of the appealed acreage was either remanded for reinventory by BLM—or simply reinstated outright to wilderness study status.

BLM's second inventory of appealed units took a predictable course. Just over half of the remanded acreage was reinstated, and the rest, once again, was dropped from the inventory. When the dust settled, BLM had identified about 3.2 million acres of wilderness study areas in Utah — barely half of what conservationists thought should be studied.

The slide show is over. All showed portions of roadless units that, although entirely natural, were dropped from the BLM wilderness inventory. Seiberling gets straight to the point.

"If you look at these conservationist wilderness proposals in Utah, you'll find that they're all roadless and certainly have outstanding wilderness values…The Congress is going to end up, I am sure, taking a look at these, and it certainly would be helpful if the BLM had studied them in advance and given us their evaluation. But if they don't, we'll just have to proceed eventually without BLM's knowledge."

Would Secretary Hodel be willing, Seiberling asks, to review BLM inventory problems, and to add certain areas to the wilderness inventory?

Seiberling, the romantic…

July 16, 1985

Two days earlier, I had witnessed an even more compelling display of romanticism. Pale sun, and a slight breeze, under the great old pine trees in Salt Lake City's Liberty Park. Standing at an improvised podium, Clive Kincaid is reading a quote from Edward Abbey. Two television cameras peer down at him, over the shoulders of a dozen reporters and onlookers sitting in folding metal chairs.

"There is nothing like it elsewhere in this world. There are greater mountain ranges in Asia, South America, and Africa. There are vaster deserts. There are longer and deeper and more powerful rivers. There may be, somewhere, exposed rock formations equal in color, variety of form, mass, extent, and grandeur …and there might be, though I've yet to hear of them, canyons as profound and labyrinthine as those of southern Utah and northern Arizona. But where? This much we may assert with dogmatic confidence: nowhere on planet earth can all of these features...be found within one geographic region, except in the canyon country of the American Southwest."

Kincaid, representing the Southern Utah Wilderness Alliance, is here today along with representatives of four other conservation groups to announce a *5 million-acre* BLM wilderness proposal for Utah.

Local reporters sit grim and still in their metal chairs, and one can hear them thinking: "Where do these hairball environmentalists get the gall? Do they actually believe they will ever get away with this? Don't they know that Utah's public lands belong to Utahns, and not to tree-hugging, waffle-stomping, carpet-bagging, Marxist-Leninist and possibly even New York or California-based environmentalists?"

When the speeches are over, the questions begin. The tone is incredulous: "You're asking for 141 *separate* wilderness areas in Utah, is that *right*?"

Correct. A mere 141 wilderness areas will do the job.

"Do you think Utahns want to see the San Francisco and New York conservation groups heavily involved in determining the future of Utah lands?

"I'm a Utahn," says Jim Catlin, with an edge in his voice. "And I'm a member of the Sierra Club. It's my club. It's not San Francisco's club."

One has to wonder at the temerity of these conservationists. What is it about this particular country, the high desert, the mesas and plateaus and canyons of Utah, that inspires such idealism, such passion and such faith?

"Anyone who knows southern Utah at all," says Clive Kincaid, "knows that there's something that's unique...possibly, to the world. It's vast, it's extraordinary, it's difficult for a single person to assimilate, it's so big."

When these Utah conservationists talk about wilderness, they're not talking about individual areas. They are talking about something much bigger: the "integrity" of entire regions. "I'm not so damned concerned about a 40,000-acre Little Rockies Wilderness Area or a 10,000-acre Negro Bill," says Kincaid. "I'm interested in seeing the protection of the core of the Colorado Plateau. And wilderness is only an avenue, an approach to that."

Without question, the Colorado Plateau is the most charismatic of Utah's astonishingly diverse landscapes. Roughly oval in shape, its borders sharply defined by a ring of Mesozoic lava extrusions, the Plateau covers 130,000 square miles of Colorado, New Mexico, Arizona and Utah. Like much of the Southwest, it is a world of high desert, a world where the land itself is constantly in motion, simultaneously rising with the thrust of the continent and being eaten alive by erosion. Yet while the Rockies to the east and the basin and range country to the west were being thrust, warped and splintered into being, the Colorado Plateau earned a name for itself simply by remaining structurally intact—a neat, round, little sandwich cookie of sedimentary strata afloat in a sea of orographic distress.

Half of Utah—and the vast majority of its BLM wilderness candidates—lies on the Colorado Plateau. Its scenery is unfailingly spectacular, and its topography is a window into the earth. "You can't find the kinds of canyons, the kinds of stone, the kinds of plateaus and mesas, and you can't find the piñon-juniper forests together with miles of twisting rivers, and you can't find the kinds of hanging gardens and wildlife—all with this incredible geology that's laid naked throughout the Plateau—none of that is combined together in natural form anywhere else," says Jim Catlin. "It's the wholeness of it that is its special value."

In recent years, says Catlin, development has been accelerating throughout southern Utah at an exponential rate. "New coal mines. New reservoirs. New drill pads. New roads. Off-road vehicle use increasing…Every time I visit one of these areas, I find some new development going on. The Colorado Plateau is becoming a thing of the past. If we don't act now, it won't be there."

"The majority of the Colorado Plateau is BLM lands," Catlin adds. "The wholeness of it—the integrity of it—relies upon large amounts of BLM land."

July 18, 1985

Back in Seiberling's hearing room, Interior Secretary Hodel steps to the witness stand. A former assistant to Interior Secretary James Watt, Hodel is the antipode of his blunt and controversial predecessor. He is poised, articulate, polite, conciliatory and above all, adroit.

Yes, Hodel tells Seiberling, it is true that an Interior Department investigation recently revealed there had been 281 instances of "unauthorized activity" on BLM wilderness study areas during the past five years. Not to worry, however. According to the BLM, "not one of those did they recall as having had the effect of causing the area to become unsuitable for wilderness designation."

What Hodel has neglected to mention is that, according to conservationists, there have been some 1,600 instances where BLM has authorized surface disturbances inside wilderness study areas. It is the authorized activities, say conservationists, which are the most alarming.

"They have defined 'non-impairment' in a way that the law never intended," says Terry Sopher, still angry two days after the oversight hearings. "They have defined non-impairment to mean that you can go in and destroy wilderness values, just so long as you don't destroy them in toto. And I think that's just the worst kind of hypocrisy and the worst bastardization of the law that I've ever heard."

It is Rep. Jim Weaver's turn to ask questions.

"We've got an agency out there," Weaver begins, "and people in it that don't like wilderness. They don't like the idea, they don't like the policy and they're going to do everything they can to subvert it." Wearily, Weaver recites the nationwide litany of IMP violations: "Increased grazing...illegal wood cutting...illegal road building...illegal mining...ORV (off road vehicle) races..."

Weaver represents Oregon, a state that takes environmental protection seriously. Since 1982, he has sat through five BLM oversight hearings, watched three Interior secretaries come and go, and heard the same promises. Weaver's voice is rising in pitch. He is a man who has run out of patience, and he is about to ask a question so perfect and simple and obvious that it runs down the spine like a small sliver of pain:

"Would you, in keeping with what you told this committee earlier, send a directive to the BLM to leave these wilderness study areas alone?"

"The employees have been sent directives, Mr. Weaver, which make plain that they are to manage, pursuant to the law, in a way which does not impair the suitability of the land for wilderness designation," Hodel replies.

There it is again—"non-impairment"—the magical concept. Road-building, motorcycle races, oil and gas wells, mining...is there any activity which isn't "non-impairing?"

Weaver's voice rises another notch: "Mr. Secretary, let me interrupt you. I've got to interrupt you there, because that's the problem..."

Hodel: "Mr. Chairman..."

Weaver: "Mr. Secretary, they're interpreting impairment..."

Now both voices are raised. For the briefest instant, Hodel looks flustered. Then a strange light seems to spring into his eyes, and he bears down into the microphone.

"Career employees of this department have been accused by Mr. Weaver, Mr. Chairman, of purposely and intentionally subverting the law. My experience with federal employees does not support that kind of accusation..."

It is a neat trick, effortless and smooth. Pass that generous helping of blame along to the rank and file—those loyal, dedicated, hardworking, infinitely well-meaning career employees. Then, with blinding alacrity, spring to their defense.

"We political appointees come and go, Mr. Weaver, but those that keep this system working take seriously their responsibilities." No doubt about it, Hodel is quick. On this particular occasion, however, it appears that he has been slightly too quick. Apparently, no one has informed the secretary that the most detailed and damaging indictments of the BLM wilderness program have repeatedly come from former career employees of the Bureau of Land Management.

One of those witnesses was Terry Sopher, former national director of the BLM wilderness program and an eight-year veteran with the Department of Interior. Sopher himself wrote much of the Interim Management Protection policy.

Another was Clive Kincaid. During his four years with the BLM, Kincaid rose swiftly through the professional ranks, working first as a planning coordinator, then managing an ambitious district-wide range inventory, and finally earning two outstanding achievement citations for managing one of the agency's first complete district-wide wilderness reviews.

When Kincaid left the agency in 1981, he was approached by representatives of the Sierra Club. Reports of IMP violations were flooding in from all over the West. Would Kincaid be willing to spend a couple of weeks investigating violation in the Four Corners states?

Kincaid packed up his truck and set out on a tour of BLM district offices in Arizona, New Mexico, Colorado and finally, Utah.

Crossing over into Utah, Kincaid recalls, he felt a powerful magnetism radiating from the land. "I started dropping off that plateau in Monticello, and out into this redrock dome country…and I said, 'Oh, wow, isn't this wonderful country!'"

Kincaid was not the first conservationist to examine the Moab district wilderness inventory files, but he brought something new and important to the task: the instincts and experience of a trained professional. The first thing that caught his eye was a boundary map for the Indian Creek unit, a spectacular redrock canyon system bordering Canyonlands National Park.

The eastern boundary of the unit was like no other wilderness area boundary Kincaid had ever seen. "It was absolutely squared off," he recalls. "And there would have been no policy application that could have provided for that kind of a boundary."

Intrigued, Kincaid drove out to the Indian Creek unit and spent four days wandering through its maze of canyons and side canyons. "It was some of the prettiest country I'd ever seen," he recalls, "all land just like what was in the (Canyonlands) National Park."

In the field, the unit's eastern boundary looked even stranger than it had on the map. BLM policy was clear: Wilderness study area boundaries must be drawn along the perimeter roads that define a "roadless" unit, deviating only where necessary to exclude a major human impact. Yet this boundary sliced right across the center of the original roadless unit, straight as an arrow, miles from the nearest roads or human impacts. More than two-thirds of the original unit had been dropped from the WSA.

Back in the Moab district office, Kincaid began examining other inventory maps. To his astonishment, dozens of them contained similar boundary anomalies. Something, he concluded, had indeed gone wrong with the Utah inventory.

"I knew much of the BLM wilderness study lands in Arizona, New Mexico and Colorado," says Kincaid. "And I was looking at landscape in Utah, which for no apparent justification was eliminated—and improperly so—that outweighed everything that I'd seen in the other states."

Kincaid decided to do a thorough investigation of Utah BLM wilderness inventory problems on his own. It was a huge project. There were hundreds of wilderness inventory units in southern Utah. Patiently, Kincaid began examining them one by one. He bought a complete set of topographic maps and spent thousands of dollars copying documents in the inventory files. Commuting between his home in Santa Fe, New Mexico, and BLM district offices in southern Utah, he stayed with the project for an entire year.

Perhaps Hodel is right, I muse. Perhaps these BLM professionals really do "take seriously their responsibilities." Asked why
he was willing to spend a year of his life and some $5,000 of his
own money on the project, Kincaid says he felt driven by "the
injustice of it all, as much as anything. I'd probably never felt like
I stopped working for the Bureau, actually."

What the Utah BLM had done, Kincaid came to believe, was to
manipulate wilderness inventory boundaries wherever possible
so as to exclude lands containing mineral leases, known mineral
deposits or other potential resource development conflicts. "It
wasn't accidental. It wasn't something that was happening coinci-
dentally," he says. "It was a manipulation, a well-thought-out, systematic plan."

To test his theory, Kincaid spent 10 weeks in the Utah BLM
state office mapping the exact location of every mining claim on
dozens of BLM roadless units with boundary anomalies. He came
away with a mountain of documents, a $300 copying bill—and a
conviction that he had solved the mystery.

Kincaid testified before Seiberling's committee in March, 1985,
four months prior to Hodel's appearance before the same committee. A walking arsenal of maps, photographs and documents,
Kincaid was a formidable witness. Patiently, he outlined five case
studies of BLM wilderness inventory "violations" in Utah, while
Seiberling helpfully sketched in wilderness study area boundaries
on large color photographs. In the San Rafael Swell area, said
Kincaid, the BLM had slashed 80,000 acres from the huge Muddy
Creek unit by simply adopting a county line as the boundary. In
the Henry Mountains, the BLM had dropped more than 100,000
acres of spectacular, rugged, pristine mesas and badlands.
Elsewhere in Utah, the agency had dropped entire areas, including a 37,000-acre canyon system near Natural Bridges National
Monument, and huge Mancos Mesa, variously estimated at
60,000 to 100,000 acres of critical desert bighorn sheep habitat.

These omissions, Kincaid said, were only a few examples of
what had happened throughout the inventory. He had highlighted

five case studies, but was prepared to do the same for at least 25 more.

"In my personal professional opinion," he concluded, "the entire Utah BLM wilderness review process has been so fraught with improper practices from its inception that there should be nothing less than a congressionally mandated or court-ordered review of the public lands in Utah."

Why, one must wonder, do conservationists feel so strongly about the inventory? To begin with, conservationists say, lands dropped from the inventory are far less likely to be considered by Congress for wilderness designation. What if an area has high mineral values—but even higher wilderness values? Dropped during the inventory stage, the area's wilderness values would never be reported to Congress.

But there is another, even more compelling dimension to the inventory.

A federal law passed in 1976 required the BLM to protect all of its roadless lands from development as long as they were under study for wilderness designation. While lands dropped from the inventory were immediately released from the moratorium on development, lands that survived the inventory remained "locked up" until their fate could be determined by Congress. The history of wilderness bills has been that as much or more land is "released" as is designated wilderness. If some of that land has high potential for mineral or other resource development, there is a powerful incentive for industry to cooperate in getting wilderness legislation passed.

A spectacular demonstration of the importance of that incentive came with the enactment of the Arizona Strip Wilderness Bill of 1984. The Strip is a land of volcanic mountains, enormous canyon systems, and high, forested plateaus reaching from the Utah border to the brink of the Grand Canyon.

Although BLM identified 750,000 acres of wilderness study areas on the Strip during its inventory, its final recommendation to Congress was a pathetic 30,000 acres. Yet even as Utah and

Arizona conservationists began gearing up for a long legal and administrative battle, they discovered a virtually omnipotent ally. That ally was none other than Energy Fuels Nuclear, a huge uranium exploration company with interests on the Arizona Strip.

Since many of the Strip's most promising uranium deposits were located inside BLM wilderness study areas, the company had decided to save years of delay by negotiating directly with conservationists. The result: wilderness designation for an area 10 times larger than the BLM's recommendation.

"That Strip bill was a landmark," says Clive Kincaid. "It proved that what counts is one thing only—do you have them by the balls, or don't you? Have you locked up Exxon, Gulf, Kaiser and everybody else—just like Energy Fuels was locked up on the Strip—or haven't you?"

In Utah, says Kincaid, the BLM was able to achieve precisely the opposite result by systematically removing lands with high mineral-development potential from its wilderness inventory.

And that, says Kincaid, is why the inventory is so important. "If we cannot go back and correct the inventory…if you can't build that stuff back into the wilderness review where it should legitimately have been, you're never going to get a decent and fair wilderness bill."

Given the political outlook in Utah, one has to wonder whether conservationists will ever get a "decent and fair" BLM wilderness bill under any circumstances.

Much depends upon Congress. Will deserving areas cut from the inventory ever find a constituency on Capitol Hill?

Much depends upon the American public. Does the public know what is at stake on BLM lands in Utah? Does it care?

And much depends upon Utah's beleaguered, embattled and tenacious conservationists.

Last Stand for the Colorado Plateau, Part 2

BY RAY WHEELER

Consider that rare and endangered species, the Utah Conservationist.

They have been threatened, and hanged in effigy. Their homes and cars have been vandalized. They live in a state where the word "environmentalist" is often a profanity, a state whose five ultraconservative Republican congressmen have unanimously embraced the environmental policies of Reagan and Watt and whose congressional voting on environmental questions is among the worst in the nation. They have been fighting development on the Colorado Plateau for 20 years, and in that time they have witnessed the inundation of Glen Canyon, the strip-mining of Black Mesa, the chaining and logging of hundreds of thousands of acres of forest and the systematic reticulation of the Colorado Plateau with a rapidly expanding spider web of roads.

On a bitterly cold February morning earlier this year, I observed this species in its remote and exotic habitat. Some 20 conservationists from all over the state had converged upon the old stone lodge at the Pack Creek Ranch near Moab. The setting was poignant, to say the least. Somewhere out there behind the lodge, towering over us, mantled in clouds and snow, were the La Sal Mountains. Rising to 12,000 feet, covered with forest and surrounded by exquisitely beautiful redrock canyon country for a hundred miles in every direction, the La Sals are a beacon for all of southeastern Utah.

243

For conservationists they are also a potent symbol of loss.

Since the La Sals are forested, the mountain range fell to the jurisdiction of the Forest Service, while the desert lands surrounding it fell to the Bureau of Land Management. Rejected as a wilderness candidate, the La Sals were formally "released" for non-wilderness uses by the Utah Wilderness Act of 1984. Now conservationists were meeting to determine the fate of the BLM roadless lands surrounding the range.

From the outset it was apparent that even among conservationists, the BLM lands skirting the La Sals were imperiled. The problem was not that they were lacking in wilderness characteristics. Indeed, they contain some of the most diverse and charismatic terrain in all of southeastern Utah. The problem was that they lay within the political sphere of Moab, Utah, a town with a history of virulent opposition to wilderness.

It was the residents of Moab who had celebrated the Fourth of July 1979 by slicing a new road into the heart of a nearby BLM roadless unit. Later that year, a San Juan County road crew pushed a bulldozer through a BLM barrier blocking off-road vehicles from the Negro Bill Canyon roadless unit. BLM sued, then settled out of court. The result? Both units were dropped from the wilderness inventory.

Now, conservationists had gathered to discuss a delicate question. Only two of the five BLM roadless units surrounding the La Sal Mountains had been designated wilderness study areas by the BLM—and those two only as a result of appeals. All of the units were hotly controversial. Should they be included in a conservationist BLM wilderness proposal—or were they so hot that they would only become a liability?

Most of the conservation leaders attending the meeting felt that at least four of the areas near the La Sals should be promoted for wilderness designation. But representatives of one group—the Utah Wilderness Association—disagreed.

Once again, Utah conservationists were deadlocked.

. . .

The conflicts between Utah conservation groups began to receive public exposure late in 1984, during the final negotiations on the Utah Wilderness Bill. When conservationists from neighboring states gathered in November for a two-day "Colorado Plateau Coalition" meeting, they were amazed at the level of hostility among Utahns.

"These Coalition meetings are just an excuse for Utah conservationists to kill each other off," one witness said, recalling an encounter that nearly led to blows.

The infighting among Utah conservation groups has its roots in the Utah Wilderness Act of 1984. While some view the bill as a victory, other conservationists see it as a debacle. Jim Catlin of the Sierra Club calls it the "Forest Service Development Act." Of the 3 million acres of roadless land identified by the Forest Service, only 750,000 acres were designated wilderness by the act. That was some 50,000 acres less than the agency's recommendation to Congress, and nearly 2 million acres less than the Sierra Club's wilderness proposal for the state.

"I do not believe in the short-term perspective that we've got to get it all right now," says Utah Wilderness Association coordinator Dick Carter, whose organization vigorously supported the bill. "Yes, we've gotten half of what we wanted on the Forest Service wilderness bill—and we're going to get the other half of what we want at some point in time."

One man's "half" is another man's quarter. While the Utah Wilderness Association proposed designation for 1.6 million acres, the Sierra Club's proposal was nearly twice as large. The huge difference in the size of the two proposals created tensions between the two groups from the very beginning.

If there is one thing that all Utah conservationists might agree to, it is that their state's congressional delegation is hostile to wilderness. A 1984 study by the League of Conservation Voters rated the environmental voting record of the state's three representatives as the second worst in the nation. All five are conservative Republicans, supporters of the Sagebrush Rebellion and the policies of James Watt. For a delegation hostile to wilderness, the million-acre gap between the two different proposals proved more than convenient. "The delegation had worked very effectively to exclude all other organizations and work solely with the Utah Wilderness Association," says one conservationist.

Tensions climaxed last fall in a dispute over "Box-Death Hollow," an area that all parties—including the Utah delegation—had supported from the beginning. After draft legislation including the area was introduced in both houses, a coalition of oil and gas exploration companies unveiled a plan to develop a huge carbon dioxide recovery facility in the heart of the unit.

Claiming that the CO_2 deposit was worth billions of dollars in tertiary oil recovery, the oil companies asked Congress to drop the entire area from the bill—or, failing that, to mandate development of the portion of the unit thought to contain CO_2.

The Utah delegation unanimously supported the oil company proposal. Conservationists, supported by Rep. John Seiberling, D-Ohio, fought the proposal, and threatened to withdraw their support from the bill. In the end, the unit was kept in the bill—with a specific provision that CO_2 development would be allowed to proceed within a defined area.

Although the Sierra Club and other conservation groups ultimately endorsed the compromise, some conservation leaders felt that a compromise need never have been made.

"Box-Death Hollow is perhaps one of the most extraordinary, beautiful, outrageous, scenic areas anywhere," says Clive Kincaid. Headwaters for the Escalante River, a complicated maze of narrow, winding canyons, clear streams and forested slickrock terraces, the area provides winter range for elk, deer, cougar and a small herd of pronghorn antelope. The antelope are most often seen on Antone Ridge—the area targeted for CO_2 development. If that development proceeds as planned, says Kincaid, "You're talking about nothing short of massive, full-scale industrial development of the ridge."

Like BLM lands, Forest Service lands under study for wilderness designation were largely protected from development. With the passage of the Utah Wilderness Bill, though, more than three-quarters of Utah's roadless Forest Service lands were released from that moratorium on development.

"Our goal was to have a bill within a period (of time), and then that time period came up, and we had to give up more because the time period was nearing an end—that's what happened on the Forest Service process," says Jim Catlin. "We should have said, 'No. We'll do it on our own time period. We have 4 million acres protected. Come back to us with a better bill.' And when we didn't—we rode it out—and that was a serious mistake."

Within months after the Utah Wilderness Bill was signed into law, developers were moving in on areas "released" by the bill. On Antone Ridge, Mid-Continent Oil Company—the leader in the carbon dioxide development project—cut in two miles of new road, blasted a stadium-sized clearing amid virgin ponderosa and drilled a new exploratory well. To supply electrical power for the project, developers are expected to push for new hydroelectric plants or new power line rights-of-way—or both—on adjacent roadless Forest Service lands. Across the state, on the rim of spectacular Arch Canyon, the Forest Service has proposed to chain down 1,000 acres of piñon-juniper forest in the heart of an area known for its archaeological sites.

When the BLM released its draft "wilderness suitability" recommendation for just 1.9 million acres in Utah, some conservationists recalled what for them were the bitter lessons of the Forest Service bill. Would this bill, too, mandate development for areas like Box-Death Hollow and Arch Canyon?

"The reason that the (Utah) delegation now is all of a sudden, after 20 years, hot on the idea of wilderness," says Clive Kincaid, "is that they have gained insight, through this last bill, and through what happened on Box-Death Hollow, that wilderness legislation can be the single quickest answer to what they have always wanted to do about southern Utah."

The Utah delegation sees BLM wilderness legislation as an

"industrial development bill," says Kincaid. "Every area that we have fought for for years—the Kaiparowits, the Henry Mountains, the Orange Cliffs, you name it—where there has been vital wilderness resources and an energy resources conflict, we are suddenly going to lose a large part of the potential to protect them. Because we are going to have designated wilderness in areas that have little or no conflict...a wilderness bill of 700,000 or 800,000 acres, and then what do you do to fight off tar sands, coal, uranium, oil and gas, and every other frigging thing that they can develop?"

Carter sees that as a negative approach. "The classic argument, I think, was the argument over the Box-Death Hollow area, where we couldn't get one particular region—the Antone Ridge—into the wilderness bill, and on that basis lost strong support for a wilderness bill," even though 11 other regions did get included.

Carter's view is that conservationists should focus their energies on areas of highest priority, seeking wilderness designation for as many areas as can realistically be expected to receive the support of the Utah delegation—and come back for the rest later. He points out that by introducing new wilderness areas in gradual increments, "it gets people to understand that this is not an evil thing, and you can designate wilderness and nothing happens."

Carter believes that, even after being formally "released" from interim management protection, areas not designated wilderness can be protected from development during the BLM's 10- or 15-year planning cycle, until they would again be studied for possible wilderness designation.

Jim Catlin disagrees. Once interim management protection is removed, and roadless lands are formally released, they are far more vulnerable to development, he says. "What motivated our congressmen in the first place was the ability to release a lot of lands from wilderness protection," says Catlin. "After they've released them, there's no more motivation for them to come back."

In an effort to smooth over such disagreements, and to build a united front, a dozen local and national conservation groups embarked on a series of five meetings early this year. The goal of the meetings was to draft a common BLM wilderness proposal for Utah which could be unanimously supported by all of the groups. The meetings were attended by representatives of the Sierra Club, The Wilderness Society, the National Parks and Conservation Association and 10 Utah conservation groups, including the Utah Wilderness Association, the Wasatch Mountain Club and the Southern Utah Wilderness Alliance.

At first, the process seemed likely to succeed. Conservationists from all over the state pooled their knowledge, poring over maps and sharing information. One by one, they evaluated nearly 200 roadless units, eliminating some, and carefully adjusting their boundaries for others so as to eliminate human impacts. But by the fifth meeting, it became apparent that on some areas there could never be agreement.

One of those areas was Negro Bill Canyon at the base of the La Sals. "This is an area that is one of the most outrageous examples of wilderness opposition and agency abuse," says Jim Catlin. "It's a prime candidate — riparian habitat, perennial streams, beautiful cliffs — a magnificent place."

When the BLM dropped the area from its inventory, Catlin filed an appeal with the Interior Board of Land Appeals (IBLA), charging that Moab District Wilderness Coordinator Dianna Webb had "removed field reports favorable to wilderness study for the unit, and substituted unfavorable documents which she signed." Webb had a conflict of interest, Catlin claimed, because her husband, George Schultz, was a regional representative for Cotter Corporation, which holds mining claims on numerous candidate wilderness areas.

The appeal was successful. The IBLA directed the BLM to re-examine Negro Bill Canyon, a wilderness study area. "Ms. Webb's failure to disqualify herself is highly questionable at best," the IBLA judge concluded.

A half-dozen conservation organizations, including The

Wilderness Society, the Sierra Club, the Southern Utah Wilderness Alliance and the Wasatch Mountain Club, were willing to endorse Negro Bill Canyon. The Utah Wilderness Association, however, was not.

"It's another one of those areas that we've felt all along could be protected better through another land-management tool, and take away some of the political pressure that would then be exerted against us in Grand County in southern Utah," explains Dick Carter.

At the close of the fifth and final meeting, the groups had reached agreement on all but 18 of the 172 areas they had discussed. A majority of the groups supported the 18 areas; the Utah Wilderness Association opposed them. In a final bid at consensus, the groups supporting the 18 areas agreed to drop 12 of them if the association would agree to support the other six.

The answer was no.

Five days later, the Utah Wilderness Association announced a 3.8 million-acre BLM wilderness proposal. The proposal was endorsed by the Utah Audubon Society, the Slickrock Outdoor Society and Southern Utah Residents Concerned About the Environment.

It took four months for the second shoe to drop. In July, a coalition of 18 conservation groups, including the Sierra Club, The Wilderness Society, the National Audubon Society, Friends of the Earth and four Utah conservation groups, announced a 5 million-acre proposal under the banner of the "Utah Wilderness Coalition."

Once again, conservationists would go to Capitol Hill with two vastly different wilderness proposals for Utah.

"I wish the conservation groups would have stayed together," says Dick Carter. "I am equally impressed, though, with the need for diversity."

While diversity is an asset for wilderness candidates, it may be less so for conservationist wilderness proposals. "One of the theories of any principle is divide and conquer," says Andy Wiessner, former top staff aide to Seiberling's Public Lands

Subcommittee and midwife to numerous wilderness bills. During negotiations on the Utah Wilderness bill, says Wiessner, Utah legislators "all the time trotted out the UWA proposal and said, 'the conservationists aren't even asking for this area you're asking for.'"

"The person who comes in with the smaller proposal has to be conscious of the fact that—regardless of their motivation—it will undercut the larger proposal," says the Sierra Club's Debbie Sease. Dick Carter disagrees. "What will influence the decision will be the political support for each individual area," he says. "Not the size of our proposal. So I don't think the proposal differences are even worth talking about."

Indeed, Carter suggests, a proposal that attempts to include every qualifying area, no matter how small, may present a risk. "The problem is, the large areas will end up being traded off for the small areas if we have too many small areas in our proposal."

That statement illustrates the fundamental difference of approach between the two camps.

"To make compromises prior to the political process starting is ridiculous," says Sease. "You've got to start the political process saying, 'This is what deserves wilderness, this is what we care about, this is our proposal.' And you may have to back down from that proposal. But there is, as far as I can see, absolutely no reason not to start out with what it is you want and what it is you care about."

For areas like Negro Bill Canyon, sometimes even being cared about isn't enough. While the merits of the area were being debated, word spread through the environmental community that Edward Abbey, the celebrated author of *Desert Solitaire* and *The Monkey Wrench Gang*, and a longtime member and supporter of the Utah Wilderness Association, had written Dick Carter a letter specifically requesting that the association include the area in its BLM wilderness proposal.

Abbey's *Monkey Wrench Gang*, a fantasy in which environmental commandos launch a guerrilla war against development in southern Utah, has become a symbol of solidarity and defiance for Utah's beleaguered conservationists. Surely Edward Abbey's support would win the Utah Wilderness Association's support. It didn't.

Abbey did send the letter, says Carter—and with it, a generous donation to the association. Carter filed the letter, and deposited the check.

"I respect Edward Abbey's opinion on Negro Bill Canyon," says Carter. "I just disagree with him."

Carter has strong notions about what should and should not be wilderness, and has never been timid about expressing them. During negotiations on the Utah wilderness bill, Carter argued against wilderness candidacy for Mount Timpanogos, a 12,000-foot Wasatch Front massif sculpted by glaciers and dotted with lakes.

"We were not convinced that Mount Timpanogos, at 10,750 acres, was and is a great addition to the wilderness system," Carter says. Mount Timpanogos was added to the bill, in part, as compensation for the reduction in acreage on Box-Death Hollow. It would have been better, says Carter, to add acreage on the north slope of the much larger High Uintas Wilderness.

While it may seem a incredible that conservation groups would oppose wilderness candidacy for an area, one has to remember that the political climate of Utah is as harsh as some of its deserts. Faced with a hostile delegation, limited resources and an avalanche of development threats, some conservationists seem to believe that what is necessary is a kind of triage.

If Utah had even one legislator willing to introduce a more generous BLM wilderness bill, things might be different. But since the Utah delegation is solidly Republican, and solidly in favor of developing Utah's public lands, the chances of that seem remote. "We are not going to pass wilderness legislation across the five members of the Utah delegation and the Western Republican bloc right now, unless they want it passed," says Dick Carter.

Jim Catlin seems to agree. "In order to get the right kind of wilderness in Utah," he says, "we're going to have to change the Utah delegation, and we're going to have to change the Reagan administration." In the meantime, he suggests, why not have the BLM go back and correct its inventory errors?

Dick Carter is less optimistic about the value of pursuing the inventory. "I think they have gotten it about as right as they are going to get it," says Carter. "I don't think that the inventory would be any 'righter' the next time around." The difference between the Utah Wilderness Association's approach and that of some other groups, says Carter, "is that we want to get on with the designation process to protect wilderness, and not to simply inventory and inventory and inventory."

Other conservation leaders, however, seem willing to wait for the right moment.

"If you're doing something that builds with strength and sets you in a good bargaining position, then haste is a sort of foolish thing to choose," says Debbie Sease.

"You shouldn't fall into the trap that, somehow or other, someone else is controlling the political agenda," says Clive Kincaid. "Once you do that, you sacrifice, to a certain extent, your will."

But how does one "control the political agenda" when the political agenda consists of the Utah delegation? "What we look at," says Dick Carter, "is to try and define a proposal that we feel that we can gain some degree of support for."

But Kincaid and others believe that a groundswell of public support from around the nation could force the Utah delegation to be more generous toward wilderness in Utah. "The question is whether you deal with them from a position of strength or acquiescence," says Kincaid.

"The majority of people who use public lands in Utah come from outside Utah," says Jim Catlin. "The Colorado Plateau is of national importance."

But how much does the nation know about the Colorado Plateau? And how much does it care?

After appearing on a televised talk show, says Dick Carter, he discovered that "a number of those people who called simply failed to understand what Canyonlands National Park looks like, and when they saw Canyonlands in a bus or car tour of Utah, they were not impressed. They were impressed by its aridness, by its ruggedness—not by its aesthetics. And the same holds true for a lot of the population of this country when it looks at our deserts."

To a large degree, differences of opinion between Utah conservation groups mirror the ambiguities of the concept "wilderness" in society as a whole.

For Jim Catlin, the land itself has an inherent right to exist undisturbed by man. "You should protect it because it deserves the right to live, on its own," says Catlin. Given that perspective, one can understand why some conservationists insist that every wild area in the state should receive equal consideration by conservationists. How can one area be a "better" wilderness candidate than another, if all have an "inherent right to exist?"

Dick Carter's emphasis is more pragmatic. "I don't think that man ever speaks in anything but his own self-interest," he says. "But that self-interest can be exceedingly broad." By providing a "sanctuary for non-human entities," says Carter, wilderness protection "protects the gene pool," and so benefits both humans and non-humans.

"It's obvious that we had better protect our natural gene pools, and our natural viewscape, and our natural airscapes, and our natural waterscapes, for the sake of our own survival," says Carter. "It's not just a spiritual thing."

For Carter, there are clear priorities among candidate areas, since some are better reservoirs of genetic diversity than others. "What I'm looking at," he says, "are large areas that are as close to complete ecosystems as possible." For Carter, such areas—particularly where threatened with development—should take priority over areas that are merely "aesthetic."

"The least important reason I see to designating wilderness," he says, "is because of its aesthetics."

Clive Kincaid sees wilderness as a spiritual and psychic asset for man. "That's my religion out there," he told me one cool, clear evening, pointing out the window at the jumble of slickrock and forest surrounding the town of Boulder, Utah. "Just like these people's religion in that building up the street is somewhere else."

The second reference is to the town's Mormon temple.

Yes, I'm thinking...how like the Mormons these conservationists are. Visionaries, zealots, proselytizing a new faith. Drawn to this country because only here—in this wilderness fastness—can they cultivate the values they hold most dear.

"There's a grotesque, international, worldwide change," Kincaid is saying, "that has in large measure to do with the fact that man has become over-organized."

Outside the window—beyond the sprinklers, beyond the pasture, beyond the two horses and the barbed wire fence—a hundred square miles of Navajo sandstone are sinking through a spectrum of dying colors: first yellow, then red, then orange, then pink, then violet, then blue. Soon, I will have to get in my car and return to the city, so that I can write all of this down. And what, what does it mean?

"I think there's a need to keep the 'wild' in wilderness, and to keep the 'terror' in our lives," says Kincaid. "It's the absence of that terror, it's the absence of dealing with the elements, it's the absence of worrying about whether it's going to rain this week, whether there's going to be enough snowfall...that defines humanity."

There's a painful irony somewhere in that statement, but with the whole world turning colors out there, and stars beginning to twinkle and now blaze in that India-ink sky...

"It was that receding frontier that was really significant in forming the unique sense in the American psyche, of the idea of freedom and independence. That nobody pushes you around. That's produced—for better or worse, and I'm not sure which— a unique personality on the face of the earth. And I would feel more comfortable preserving that, as a repository of something for the future...that independence..."

I'm thinking of my friends Emma and Greg in Washington, D.C. Emma is a physical therapist in a Baltimore Hospital. The hospital is in the inner city, and Emma spends much of her time treating drug addicts and mental patients. Greg, now in medical school, told me that he is certain that nuclear holocaust will come in his lifetime.

"Why bother with medical school, then?" I asked. And I was thinking: Why not come out West? Why not hike to the top of the Waterpocket Fold, or the Henry Mountains, or the La Sals. Why not sit beside the thunder of water at Lava Falls, or climb to the summit of Vulcan's Throne, or sit with your feet dangling over 3,000 feet of cool canyon air at Toroweap overlook? Why not?

There's something about this canyon country, something that makes you willing to believe in the future. Wallace Stegner called it the "geography of hope." These conservationist quarrels, I'm thinking, are a tempest in a teapot. They are also quintessentially American, full of the pain and the promise of democracy.

There's a full moon tonight. A hundred square miles of milk-white Navajo sandstone are reflecting moonlight back into the night air.

"The land," Kincaid is saying, "is our thread back from where we're at."

SEPTEMBER 23, 1991

The BLM's Proposals: Too Little, Too Late?

BY FLORENCE WILLIAMS

This fall, "BLM wilderness" will no longer be an oxymoron. After 15 years of study, the agency is ready to send a multistate wilderness package to the president, and then to Congress.

Under the 1976 Federal Land Policy Management Act, the agency was given until this year to recommend a portion of its Western lands for federal wilderness. Land in Arizona was designated last year. Now, Congress will consider Bureau of Land Management holdings in Montana, Wyoming, Idaho, New Mexico, Nevada, Colorado, Utah and Oregon.

But even after 15 years of inventories, public comments and backroom deals, the Department of Interior is still haggling over its recommendations. Final acreages in four states have not yet been settled, pending a decision by Interior Secretary Manuel Luján Jr., later this month.

The announcement will resolve a dispute that arose when the Bureau of Mines and the U.S. Geological Survey challenged the BLM's initial wilderness proposal as containing potential mineral deposits. Once land becomes a federal wilderness area, no new mining claims are allowed.

Overall, the BLM has taken a minimalist approach toward wilderness. In Montana, for example, the BLM recommended only 2 percent of its holdings. In Wyoming, the figure is even smaller: 1.4 percent. Of the land studied for protection, called wilderness study areas, only half made the final cut.

Agency officials defend the relatively small acreages, saying they had slim pickings. "The figures reflect the fact that development impacted the land to some degree," says BLM wilderness staffer Gary Pavek. "Our initial inventory found very few roadless, natural areas."

Environmentalists argue that because there are so few natural areas, all deserve protection. The BLM has consistently left out of its recommendations any land with development potential, leaving only the most remote "rocks and ice" areas as wilderness.

BLM wilderness chief Keith Corrigal sums up the agency's approach: "We thought values were higher for minerals than for wilderness."

In part, the agency's critics have themselves to blame. Most environmentalists have been asleep at the wheel during the 15-year study process. With the exception of those in Utah, most environmentalists focused on the more spectacular wilderness proposals in the national forest system.

With the BLM package slated for Congress this fall, environmentalists will have to move fast if they are to find sponsors for meatier proposals.

The two biggest winners would be Arizona, where the Arizona Desert Wilderness Act of 1990 designated 38 new BLM wilderness areas, and California, where the 1994 California Desert Protection Act designated 69 BLM wilderness areas covering more than 3.5 million acres. As the following stories show, the BLM's inventory-and-recommendation process bore far less fruit in other states.

A Wilderness War: Utah's Canyons Cut to the Bone

BY LISA JONES

ESCALANTE, Utah—Louise Liston's ranch house looks out on the Kaiparowits Plateau, a vast sandstone outcropping that stretches more than 50 miles from Lake Powell to this area of southern Utah. The remote valley where she and her husband run their cattle operation is bordered by mile after mile of red sandstone cliffs, bluffs and fins. Between these fantastic formations the creeks are running with spring melt; the cottonwoods are as green as limes. She is talking about infinity. "When I drive out to the desert with my husband day after day to check on the cows, I don't see a telephone line or a light line or anything," she says. "I see nothing but this land, and there's plenty of that out there for all of us."

Liston is an outspoken opponent of creating more federal wilderness areas in Utah. But a growing number of Utahns don't agree with her view that there's still "plenty of that out there for all of us." Much of the state's canyon country already has been paved, trampled and chipped away by decades of mining, grazing and road-building. Only a third still remains pristine enough to qualify as wilderness, environmentalists say. They want it protected.

The Bureau of Land Management administers almost all of this canyon country, and this October the agency will give Secretary of Interior Manuel Luján Jr., its wilderness recommendations for the entire West. But for Utah, the debate over how much of its canyon country will be protected as wilderness is rapidly becoming one of the state's most divisive ever.

The reason is that the wilderness issue cuts to the bone of southern Utah's attitude—and mythology—about itself and its land. The wilderness debate is forcing rural Utahns to confront their deepest hopes and fears. Should they continue to believe in the future of the traditional industries that have dominated their lives, landscape and economy for so long? Or should they embrace and protect the emerging new economy based on their region's breathtaking and nationally unique beauty?

For the first-time visitor, Utah's canyon country is a sheer, fierce surprise. Its vertical redness flips a switch in the minds of people used to country that is more or less green and horizontal. This canyon country seems to liberate people, turning them into pilgrims who become aggressively protective of its unique landscape. Visitor by visitor, hiker by awestruck hiker, southern Utah is becoming a national treasure.

An increasingly muscular pro-wilderness movement is facing off against a status quo only a couple of generations removed from the Mormon pioneers, whose distaste for federal intervention was matched only by their success in wringing a living from their parched land. Wilderness proponents maintain that more protected land could help stabilize and diversify a regional economy that has historically ridden the economic roller coaster of the mining industry. Their adversaries counter that wilderness designation will spell financial ruin for southern Utah.

A coalition of Utah environmentalists, along with Utah Democratic Rep. Wayne Owens, wants more than 5 million acres of land administered by the BLM to be designated wilderness. The BLM, which manages nearly half of the land in the state, is proposing about 2 million. Republican Rep. Jim Hansen proposes 1.4 million acres.

In Escalante, population 816 and dropping, many people consider even Hansen's proposal exorbitant. The Escalante sawmill recently laid off 30 of its 110 workers. Grazing numbers have been cut because of drought, and 21 cattle were shot last year by unknown assailants. The development of a huge coal field and power plant on the Kaiparowits Plateau—a project attacked by environmentalists—fell through when the energy market stagnated in the 1970s. Now, although another company is eager to mine the coal, parts of the plateau are being protected as wilderness study areas, and nearly the entire plateau is included in Owens' wilderness proposal. Only a handful of this year's high school seniors are expected to find jobs at home.

Here, the subject of wilderness is cloaked in emotion and fear of almost mythic proportions. "Environmental groups have sent people here *to spy*," confided one waitress. And Louise Liston, who serves on the Garfield County Commission, says: "It's a scary thing. They want all the wilderness; they want control. Control of the land. And when you have federal control of the land you take away the basis of a functional democratic society."

The BLM wilderness issue in Utah has sparked controversy from the beginning. Congress mandated the BLM to review the roadless areas under its management in 1976 to determine which had wilderness qualities and to place those tracts under interim protection as wilderness study areas. This theoretically safeguards the land until Congress passes a wilderness bill, a process that can take years. The agency was then directed to weigh the wilderness qualities of the areas against competing uses of the land and to recommend how much should be designated wilderness.

BLM's inventory process, however, generated strong criticism from environmentalists, some members of Congress and even from within the agency.

"The inventory was pretty horrible. It was tawdry. It was a damn shame," says Clive Kincaid, a former BLM district wilderness coordinator in Arizona who was urged by a friend in the Sierra Club to investigate the "outrageous" BLM performance in Utah. He took his first trip to the state in September 1981.

"I can still remember the day I drove in from New Mexico up to Monticello and Moab," he recalls. "I was blown away. We're just talking about driving down the highway. I was just utterly astonished at the grandeur of the landscape." And when he looked into the BLM's inventory process, he found "a tremendously artful and subtle attempt" to eliminate conflicts with other resources.

"It's really outrageous; the American people's posterity was thieved," he says. "It was stolen right from under them. We've lost a lot of unique and beautiful areas because of it. I mean they're actually gone. I mean places where bulldozers have scarred the hillsides, roads have been built, Anasazi ruins have been destroyed."

Subsequently, Utah's conservation groups filed a series of appeals with the Interior Board of Land Appeals, charging that the BLM didn't include about 1.4 million acres of pristine land in its wilderness study areas. It was "the cut that mattered," as Kincaid put it. Despite the board's ruling in 1983 that the BLM had erred in 90 percent of its decisions that were appealed, the BLM reinstated less than half of those lands to the inventory, putting only a total of 3.2 million acres into wilderness study areas. Oversight hearings held by then-Rep. John Sieberling, D-Ohio, and pressure from within the agency to redo the inventory were less fruitful. When the Carter administration yielded to Ronald Reagan in the White House and James Watt as Interior secretary, the upper echelons of the BLM were replaced, and all hope for reforming the inventory from within the agency died.

Utah's environmentalists then turned to the grassroots. Kincaid founded the Southern Utah Wilderness Alliance (SUWA) in 1981, basing it not in the relatively liberal, urbanized Wasatch Front, but in Cedar City, "deep in the bowels of the devil himself" in southwestern Utah. SUWA now has over 8,000 members and a staff based in Salt Lake City, Moab and Washington, D.C.

SUWA and more than 30 other state and national environmental groups have now united as the Utah Wilderness Coalition, which has developed its own proposal and a strategy to advance it. The coalition wants more than 5 million acres of wilderness, and is currently lobbing its proposal to the nation over the heads of the mostly hostile Utah congressional delegation.

In 1989 the coalition got what many environmental groups only dream about—congressional representation. Wayne Owens, a Democrat elected to the House of Representatives in 1986, adopted the group's acreage in his wilderness bill. Owens proposed 5.4 million acres of wilderness. The coalition has since increased its proposal to 5.7 million. Owens, who had served as both a Mormon Church official and an aide to Sen. Edward Kennedy, D-Mass., is an anomaly. He spent his youth on a sheep farm in Panguitch, deep in southern Utah's canyon country, but was elected by an overwhelmingly urban district, Salt Lake City.

Owens, however, must go it alone. Both of Utah's senators, Jake Garn and Orrin Hatch, as well as Rep. Hansen, are adamantly opposed to a bill of the size Owens wants. The only other Democrat in the congressional delegation, freshman Rep. Bill Orton, said through a spokesman that Owens is "asking too much." Owens admits he doesn't expect to pass a 5.4 million-acre bill. But he says he hopes to get much closer to his 5.4 than the 2 million the BLM is going to recommend.

"I think we will, but it's going to be a long process," Owens predicts. "I could get a bill through the House, but it would so embitter and divide the state it wouldn't be worth it. I couldn't get it past the Senate...You'll never get a wilderness bill past the Senate that Jake and Orrin won't buy. That's a political reality."

Hatch recently wrote: "Turning an excess of 5 million acres, which is approximately the size of the state of New Jersey, into an economic desert with no place for people would be an imprudent commitment of our resources and could well seal the fate of many rural Utah communities."

Similarly, Garn told a southern Utah high school class, "As long as I'm in the U.S. Senate with the ability to filibuster...there will never be 5 million acres of wilderness in this state. Don't you worry about that."

But Garn, whom one longtime environmental lobbyist described as "a big hitter" who will "kill it deader than hell," announced last month he won't run for office again. His term ends in 1992.

Utah's entire political structure, however, is riddled with opposition. The state Legislature passed a resolution in 1986 opposing any further designation of wilderness. It also urged Congress to exclude any state with greater than 30 percent federal ownership from the provisions of the Wilderness Act. This year, it voted 23 to 2 that no more than 1.4 million acres should be designated wilderness.

Similarly, the Utah Association of Counties believes more wilderness is unnecessary. "We're letting a handful of environmentalists try to determine what the economy is in the rural part of the state," Mark Walsh, the group's associate director, says. "I find that offensive."

And although the BLM's final wilderness recommendation is some 83,000 acres larger than its draft version, state BLM Director James Parker told the *Salt Lake Tribune* that the agency's 1.97 million-acre proposal may have been too much.

"It's not like the world is going to end if you don't designate wilderness," he says. "There are many lands out there that are almost equally protected under the planning process. It's not like they're going to be destroyed...Does it destroy a national park if you put a power line through it? Some people say yes, some people say no. I guess it depends on your definition of 'destroyed.'"

With the middle ground almost deserted, one environmental group's attempt at conciliation went nowhere. The Utah Wilderness Association—the only conservation group in the state that suggested a compromise acreage—recently abandoned its proposed 3.8 million acres in favor of Owens' proposal.

"We thought by staying where we were, we'd give a place for people to agree," explains Dick Carter, a former Wilderness Society representative for Utah who founded the Utah Wilderness Association in 1979. "It didn't work. The opponents of wilderness to this day have refused to grab hold of the peace offering on seeking compromise and consensus, and that's to their tremendous disadvantage."

The Utah Wilderness Coalition's strategy of nationalizing the issue employs a recently released book, *Wilderness at the Edge*, a document of unarguable persuasiveness. The group's other weapon is time. With 3.2 million acres already protected in wilderness study areas, environmentalists consider settling for anything less unthinkable.

"We tend to lose when we get in a hurry," says Darrell Knuffke, director of The Wilderness Society's Rocky Mountain office in Denver. Environmentalists point to the 1984 Utah Wilderness Act, which designated about 750,000 acres of Forest Service lands as wilderness. Many environmentalists consider it a tragedy because of what it left out.

"We're so much stronger now," says Scott Groene, a staff attorney for SUWA. "We don't have to take what we had to (take) in 1984. Easily two-thirds of it is long gone as far as wilderness; there's already been enough compromises made."

Where does this confidence come from, especially in a state whose environmental movement historically has had to dance to whatever tune the status quo played? Why are environmentalists so sure of success in the national arena?

Part of it has to do with Owens. Beyond that, much of the will to protect Utah's wilderness comes from the effect the landscape itself has on people. The country's love affair with Utah's backcountry was amply demonstrated when Owens' bill collected more than 100 co-sponsors in the House last year. None of them were from Utah.

The specter of wilderness designation threatens what rural Mormons revere — their ancestral past and their own continued stewardship of the land.

"They say they're going to save it. We've been here a century without ruining it; why would we ruin it now?" asks Gene Griffin, a genial rancher and hardware store owner from Escalante. Griffin made national headlines this spring when he said "We'd like to hang" Wayne Owens for his pro-wilderness stance. "My grandfather pioneered this when there were no hospitals, no roads," he says. "We should be more entitled to it (than outsiders). We pioneered it, went through thick and thin for it."

But new people are arriving all the time, and they are falling in love with what they find. They are photographing, painting, talking and writing about Utah. Edward Abbey, the Pennsylvania-born curmudgeon of the canyons, called his beloved haunt near Arches National Park the "least inhabited, least inhibited, least developed, least improved, least civilized, least governed, least priest-ridden, most arid, most hostile, most lonesome, most grim bleak barren desolate and savage quarter of the state of Utah— the best part by far. So far."

No one knows exactly what minerals lie underneath the backcountry, although estimates have been made. Russell Babcock, a board member for the Utah Geological Survey, told Owens last month that the survey "just can't see into the rocks."

Wilderness opponents say wilderness designation will lock up untold mineral wealth. Proponents counter that the pristine remnants of Utah's canyon country are still unspoiled, partly because mining has never been profitable there. But a host of unknowns throw any prediction of the economic impact of wilderness designation squarely into the realm of speculation: How much would minerals underlying wilderness areas be worth on the wildly fluctuating international market? How much can tourists be expected to spend in nearby communities? What is silence worth?

"Trying to put an exact dollar value on the costs and benefits of wilderness is a damn hard thing to do," says Brad Barber, the director of demographics and economic analysis at the Utah Office of Planning and Budget. "You're sticking your neck out there as far as you can possibly stick it."

Indeed, the only study yet completed on the economics of wilderness in Utah has sent the argument through the roof. Commissioned by the Utah Association of Counties and authored by Dr. George Learning of the Arizona-based Western

Economic Analysis Center, it concluded that more than 5 million acres of wilderness would do about $13.2 billion dollars worth of damage to the state's economy per year—a number that exceeds half of the annual personal income earned in the state. If all 3.2 million acres of wilderness study areas were designated, it would cause $9.2 billion in damage; Hansen's proposal, $1.4 billion, according to Learning.

Learning says his forecast relied heavily on estimates made in the BLM's environmental impact statement. "I tried to keep them as conservative, as cautious as possible," he said. But his findings were panned by environmentalists and economists alike.

"The claim that protecting (more than 5 million acres) of de facto wilderness will somehow cost the state the equivalent of the majority of its total annual earnings—or approximately 26 times the total earnings from all of ranching, farming, forestry, fisheries and mining for the whole state—is not only ridiculous but irresponsible," says Brigham Young University economist Arden Pope.

"This is voodoo economics at its worst," says SUWA issues coordinator Ken Rait. Barber calls the study "absolutely ridiculous."

Other studies paint a brighter picture of the economic impact of wilderness. A pair of University of Idaho geographers found that the populations of counties containing or bordering wilderness areas grew two to three times as fast as their non-wilderness counterparts from the 1970s to the mid-1980s. More than half of the newcomers credited the wilderness for their arrival.

Some 79 percent of Utah respondents to a study conducted by Pope also favored wilderness legislation.

Owens asserts that wilderness is the state's greatest economic asset. "Utah's beauty here, if we nurture it, will continue to be a magnet in bringing people into the state to live and have the economic ability to contribute," he says.

Barber calls the country's beauty "a fixed supply." "We could find more oil," he says, "but we're not going to find land with this kind of natural beauty."

. . .

By law, both grazing and mining can continue in wilderness when grazing allotments and mining claims predate the designation of the area as wilderness. New mining claims and grazing allotments, however, aren't allowed. This makes the mining industry's blood run cold, especially in an era when technology is continually opening new horizons.

Recently developed horizontal drilling techniques, for example, have opened up a potential oil boom near Moab. "Something that was worth nothing a year ago is now worth millions," says Utah state geologist Lee Allison. The area isn't protected as a wilderness study area, but part of it is in Owens' proposal.

Owens is willing to negotiate on these points. "It's not my intention to close down economic exploitation," he assured the Utah Geological Survey.

Utah's fastest-growing sector is its service industry, which now accounts for about a quarter of the state's employment. Tourism provides nearly 60,000 jobs, up by 16,000 from 1980. Meanwhile, resource development has succumbed to price decreases in uranium and oil. Also, fewer miners are needed by the new technologies of the coal-mining industry. About 8,500 Utahns mine coal today, down from 20,266 a decade ago. Mining generates 2 percent of the personal income earned in the state, while agriculture—which includes ranching—accounts for only 1.4 percent.

"There's a lot of people who would like to blame the environmental movement for the decline in the mining industry," says Barber of the Utah Office of Management and Budget. "But we know, what with international market forces, it's simply hard to lay the blame there."

Do economists expect the boom to be repeated? "No," says Barber. "Do we say it's never going to happen again? It's not very probable. But never say never."

This hope presents a psychological challenge to Utahns: "If you keep saying, 'We're a mining town and nothing else,' it becomes a self-fulfilling prophecy," says Thomas Power, a University of Montana economist and a close observer of the debate in

Utah. "There are lots of healthy economies where recreation has provided an economy without distorting life and livelihoods. The key is to think in terms of areas that are not booming but alive, rather than in terminal decline."

Moab, a former uranium boomtown on the Colorado River, is grappling with precisely this transition. It is the seat of Grand County, which was the most devastated part of the state when the bottom fell out of the uranium market. The county lost 20 percent of its population during the 1980s. But in the past few years, Moab has become a magnet for mountain bikers, rafters, hikers and jeepers who flit by the inoperative hulk of the Atlas uranium mill—which closed in 1984—on their way to the slickrock backcountry.

"This reminds me of back in '56 and '57 when uranium boomed," says Jackie Shelton, a third-generation Moab resident who works at the local information center. "It really hit, and we had people coming and pitching tents and getting rich quick," she says during a breather from her ministrations to the assembled German tourists, Canadian filmmakers and Lycra-clad Coloradans who are part of her typical daily dose of hundreds of visitors during the high season in May. "Now it's almost the same. People are trying to build a store, a cafe, anything. It's the feeling if you've got money you can make money."

But not as much money.

Shelton's husband went from making $48,000 a year in the uranium mine to $6 an hour as the caretaker of a motel after the bust hit. Shelton herself makes $4.95 an hour. And while Moab has gained enormous stature as a hub for outdoor recreation, this hasn't translated into great wealth for the community.

"People come here and ask where they can camp for free," says Shelton.

"With tourism, you have large capital expenditures while creating a lot of minimum-wage paying jobs," says Moab Mayor Tom Stocks, who started a bed-and-breakfast business last year.

"But I'm certainly grateful it came along when it did." Recreation is even gaining a tentative foothold in Escalante. This spring, a pair of former police officers from Salt Lake City opened a backcountry outfitting shop on the west side of town.

"The outdoor business is virtually untapped," says Barry Bernards, who runs the shop with his wife, Celeste. For a long time, the couple were "strangers in town," says Barry. "People just sat back and watched us for a while. But now at least half our business is local."

While the couple maintains they "are not trying to rock the boat by any means," the full coffeepot and the stools in front of the counter provide a forum for conversation between locals and visitors. No one is advocating tourism as the only economic path for southern Utah. "It's not the solution, but no solution is complete without it," says SUWA executive director Brant Calkin.

While Liston admits that tourism can be an economic help, she and others find their hopes drawn to the mineral-rich Kaiparowits Plateau. "If it helps our county for 10 years, it helps our county for 10 years," she says. "It's something we don't have now. We're at the point in Garfield County we'll get whatever we can to survive. We're going downhill fast."

To Thomas Power, this kind of thinking is not only coveting an economic base that ultimately leads to impoverishment, but is ignoring an opportunity that is staring southern Utah in the face.

"Quit the hand-wringing," he says, adding that the obvious future for the area is an amenity-driven economy that draws not only tourists but permanent residents who want to live in beautiful surroundings. "It's not crystal ball gazing," he says. "It's already happening in southwest Utah, where the focus is the national parks and other protected landscapes."

With or without wilderness designation, tourism will continue its inexorable rise in southern Utah. With or without wilderness designation, it's questionable whether the mining boom will return. While there's no question that wilderness designation will limit traditional and extractive uses of the land, there's no doubt that it also will present new possibilities and challenges. There is no other place like southern Utah in an increasingly crowded world; simple logic dictates that it will become more valuable as time goes on.

Nevada's BLM Wilderness Issue Just Simmers Along

BY JON CHRISTENSEN

The jewel in the crown of Nevada wilderness is a seemingly endless and barren alkali flat. This dry lake bed may seem an unlikely priority on a preservation agenda filled with hard-fought battles over picturesque peaks and colorful canyonlands. But for some, the immense expanse of the 30-mile-wide Black Rock Desert evokes an unparalleled wilderness experience.

"It's almost like going to another planet," says Nevada wilderness advocate Ann Kersten. "It's so unearthly."

"Nowhere else is the Great Basin Desert reduced to such simple terms," writes Stephen Trimble in *The Sagebrush Ocean: A Natural History of the Great Basin.* "Elemental time and space play round every perception of the Black Rock Desert. Some say you can feel the curvature of the earth out in the playa's center."

The Black Rock Desert—about 219,000 acres of some of the most featureless terrain on earth—is among 56 areas that have been recommended for official wilderness status by the Nevada office of the Bureau of Land Management. Totaling roughly 1.9 million acres, the wilderness areas embrace some of the most remote and least visited territory in the United States.

Utah's spectacular slickrock canyons are far better known, and the controversy over wilderness is more heated there. But the push to designate wilderness on lands managed by the BLM actually began more than 30 years ago in Nevada, the state with the largest amount of public land outside of Alaska.

In the early 1960s, wilderness apostle Charles Watson Jr., called the public domain "the lands no one knows." At the time, even the Sierra Club seemed to prefer not to let desert wastelands detract from its islands-in-the-sky approach to wilderness preservation.

Watson's missionary zeal and bulldog tenacity on behalf of unappreciated public lands got him drummed out of the local Toiyabe chapter of the Sierra Club. BLM lands were left out of the 1964 Wilderness Act; only with the passage of the Federal Land Policy and Management Act in 1976 did the untracked desert wilderness begin to gain grudging recognition.

Today, however, while Utah's redrock wonders attract national attention, Nevada's wilderness areas remain "the lands no one knows." Even among the Friends of Nevada Wilderness—a coalition that includes Watson's Nevada Outdoor Recreation Association, as well as the Sierra Club and other groups that united around the Nevada Forest Service wilderness bill in 1989—few people aside from Watson and Dave Harmon, a BLM wilderness specialist, have visited more than a couple of the 112 official wilderness study areas in Nevada.

"There is still a widespread perception that these are just alkali flats, smelly sumps and sun-baked hills," says Watson. "But we've been finding treasures out there."

Faced with the necessity of promoting these places where so few have trod, Watson long ago abandoned the notion of keeping his favorite places secret. Over the years, the photo album of Nevada wilderness areas that he faithfully lugs to environmental meetings has grown to weigh more than 125 pounds. His album is probably the best inventory of Nevada wilderness areas outside of BLM files, and the official state BLM wilderness recommendations include some of his favorites.

In the Hot Creek Range in central Nevada, a 127,588-acre wilderness peaks out above 10,000 feet where bristlecone forests overlook an ancient caldera in the sere valley below. Desert-bound waterfalls and perennial streams tumble from the mountains. Human signs are few and mostly already taken by the desert—the ruins of Shoshone wickiups, a wild horse trap, abandoned charcoal ovens.

In eastern Nevada, more than half a dozen mountains rise from a sea of valleys totaling more than 350,000 acres of wilderness. Pristine meadows and aspen forests grace otherwise rugged peaks of alpine limestone.

In southern Nevada, nearly 600,000 acres of wilderness provides additional land for the Red Rock Canyon and Lake Mead national recreation areas as well as for Death Valley National Monument. Six other mountain wilderness areas featuring remote canyons, caves and cliffs surround Las Vegas.

The state BLM's recommendations were greeted with enthusiastic support from Nevada environmentalists.

"Talk about wilderness," says Marjorie Sill, of the Sierra Club. "You can go for days and days and not see a soul in these areas."

"There will always be areas we feel have been left out," says Ann Kersten, who is coordinating the efforts of Friends of Nevada Wilderness. "But it's going very well overall."

The wilderness coalition would like to include a number of areas dropped from the BLM recommendations because of mineral potential. And Watson reels off a dozen areas not included in the recommendations because of "the Sagebrush Rebellion mentality" at the BLM district level in some parts of the state.

While Sill and Kersten say the wilderness coalition will ask for at least 3 million acres, Watson vows to fight for all of the more than 5 million acres currently in wilderness study areas, plus other areas that were not studied. But they all agree that there is no rush to win the official wilderness designations. The interim management policy for wilderness study areas protects the lands until a wilderness bill is passed by Congress.

Environmentalists confidently predict that they will help re-elect the senators who made the Nevada Forest Service wilderness bill possible—Democrats Harry Reid and Richard Bryan, who face elections in 1992 and 1994—before pushing for another wilderness bill. At 733,400 acres, the 1989 Nevada wilderness bill nearly doubled the Forest Service recommendation, but it took three sessions of Congress to pass. No one in Nevada's congressional delegation is publicly discussing a BLM wilderness bill at this time.

"We're going to face a lot of opposition," Sill acknowledges. "But we can afford to take our time."

On the other side, Grant Gerber, head of the Wilderness Impact Research Foundation in Elko and a leading opponent of wilderness designations, confidently asserts, "The longer they wait, the less they'll get."

"I don't think it's a done deal," says Gerber, who will spearhead the coalition against BLM wilderness in Nevada. "To the Forest Service wilderness debate, we succeeded in demonstrating the number of people in the opposition. They were shocked by the effectiveness of our coalition."

Gerber claims that many of the areas are not even truly roadless, a primary consideration for wilderness.

"If a rancher could haul water to sheep, there's a road," he says.

In that sense, none of these areas qualify. The questions become: Where is it worth eliminating people? It's a political decision. Who are we going to agree to hurt? Which ranchers, grazing in which areas, are expendable?

"Stories are coming out on how wilderness is affecting ranchers when they said it wouldn't," Gerber goes on. "We've got a lot of wilderness refugees coming into Nevada after being squeezed out elsewhere. They're telling stories about lockups there," he says. "There's a tension that's growing out here. Everyone is upset."

Meanwhile, as the debate over wilderness in Nevada simmers noisily on the back burner, the BLM is gearing up to be in the "show-and-tell business," says BLM spokeswoman Maxine Shane. A lot of people are interested in wilderness, she says, but few know anything about the areas.

"We'll be talking wilderness for a while," Shane sighs.

Nevada would not see a BLM wilderness bill until 2000, when Congress passed the Black Rock Desert-High Rock Canyon Emigrant Trails Act, which designated 10 new wilderness areas in northern Nevada. Two years later, Congress created 17 new wilderness areas in southern Nevada; that story is covered in more detail in Section 6.

SEPTEMBER 23, 1991

It's Colorado, but the Land Looks Very Utah

BY JOHN HORNING

The rugged mountains managed by the U.S. Forest Service, long mired in controversy over water rights, are only part of this state's wilderness story. After more than a decade of public review, the Bureau of Land Management in Colorado has started a second wilderness debate. Though overshadowed by that of the Forest Service, BLM wilderness is nonetheless a pivotal issue, one which will determine the fate of much of Colorado's arid lands.

At stake are nearly 1 million acres of pristine lands, most of which lie in the arid parts of western Colorado. The dramatic canyons of the Dolores, Yampa and Gunnison rivers are the best known, but hidden jewels abound throughout the eastern portion of the Colorado Plateau: The isolated Sewemup Mesa preserves an ungrazed desert grassland, and lands in southwestern Colorado house undisturbed remains of the ancient Anasazi.

"It's Utah-type scenery, but in Colorado," says Todd Robertson of the Colorado Environmental Coalition, a group highly critical of the BLM's wilderness proposal.

The Colorado BLM established nearly 35 different wilderness study areas totaling 783,101 acres. This October, it will submit a proposal recommending 16 new wilderness areas totaling 430,812 acres, or 5 percent of its land in the state.

"The areas being recommended are the best in terms of their wilderness values," says the state's BLM wilderness coordinator, Eric Finstick. "We were fortunate in that we had relatively few resource conflicts in our especially beautiful areas."

But one controversial location is Red Cloud Peak, a geographically atypical BLM area, located high in the San Juan Mountains of southwestern Colorado. Initially, the BLM recommended a portion of the area as wilderness, but it has recently been pressured by the Bureau of Mines and the United States Geological Survey to delete the entire area, allowing commercial deposits of alunite to be mined.

Aside from Red Cloud Peak, the traditional users of BLM lands, Colorado's miners and ranchers, seem satisfied with the wilderness recommendations. Even Colorado's oil and gas industries, which have the most at stake in this debate, came out in support.

The BLM's Finstick says pressure from oil and gas industries has not resulted in the deletion of any significant roadless areas.

"We weren't plagued with any of the problems they had over in Utah," he says, referring to that state's beleaguered inventory. "We didn't just drop areas from the inventory because of conflicts."

But Mark Pearson of the Colorado Sierra Club says that while BLM managed to identify the "crown jewels" of the more than 8 million acres they manage, numerous ecologically unique areas were omitted in the initial inventory, completed in 1980.

"Their (initial) study was skewed by the fact that they threw out nearly 300,000 acres of lands which could qualify," argues Pearson. A prime example of the conflict is South Shale Ridge, a 30,000-acre roadless area in northwestern Colorado. Despite the BLM's own recognition that the area contains unique "opportunities for solitude," it was dropped because of known gas reserves. South Shale Ridge is now slated for exploratory drilling.

Bob Moore, the head of the Colorado BLM, says these kinds of decisions are routine. "That's the kind of business we're in. If you designate wilderness, you preclude these other uses. If it were unique, then okay," Moore continues. "But to simply add another one of several (areas) when there are conflicts, then we have a problem with that."

Todd Robertson argues that this attitude results in the deletion of ecologically unique areas. "If there's a conflict between commodity and wilderness, then commodity wins out."

Many of Colorado's environmentalists point to the Piceance Basin and extreme southwestern Colorado as examples of areas that have been degraded by extractive industry.

"We're now talking about the remnants," says Robertson.

The environmental group has put forth a proposal calling for the protection of just over 1 million acres of BLM land. They hope to convince congressional delegates to include lands not recognized by the BLM's inventory.

However, all those involved in the Colorado wilderness debate recognize that the BLM wilderness issue will remain of secondary importance until the present Forest Service wilderness debate, now in Congress, is resolved.

Colorado still has not seen a statewide BLM wilderness bill pass. In 1999, Rep. Diana DeGette, D-Colo., introduced the Colorado Wilderness Act to Congress; the current version of her bill includes about 1.3 million acres of BLM wilderness.

SEPTEMBER 23, 1991

In Montana,
Not Many Cared

BY TRACY STONE-MANNING

The Bureau of Land Management holds just over 8 million acres of land in Montana; it has recommended 173,459 of them, or 2 percent, for wilderness, subject to review by the Office of Management and Budget. The BLM will release the final figure by late summer.

"Overall, the BLM has clearly set the lowest common denominator for wilderness in Montana," said John Gatchell, director of the Montana Wilderness Association, adding that they are very poor recommendations.

Despite the low acreage, no controversy rages over the BLM's recommendations. For more than a decade, Montana has been embroiled in a debate over Forest Service wilderness. Since most of BLM's wilderness study areas are small, many conservationists let BLM lands fall through the cracks during the battle for Forest Service lands.

"By and large, the environmental community did not involve themselves. The bigger prizes were with the Forest Service," said Gary Leppart, state wilderness coordinator for the BLM.

However, Leppart said, there was some controversy in 1980, when the BLM identified the 470,000 acres of wilderness study areas (WSAs) from which the BLM would draw its current recommendations.

"The ranchers got quite excited in each area," he said.

For example, the draft WSAs called for 450,000 acres along the Missouri River Breaks alone. A group calling itself the Missouri

Breaks Multiple Use Association organized to whittle that number down to 250,000 acres in the final study area draft.

"That wild country is as vital to Montana's heritage as the Bob Marshall Wilderness," said Gatchell. The BLM has completely missed the opportunity to establish wilderness in mixed or short grass prairies.

Yet Gatchell admits that his organization did not have BLM wilderness on the front burner. Neither did most conservationists.

"We won some. We lost some," said Cedron Jones, one of the conservationists who fought the draft WSAs. "The areas are smaller (than Forest Service areas), and less attractive to recreationists. They are not big peaks and alpine lakes…But now, biodiversity is starting to play a larger role."

Although a small part of the Lee Metcalf Wilderness is managed by the BLM, Montana still does not have a single stand-alone BLM wilderness area.

In Wyoming, Oil Companies Didn't Leave Much

BY MICHAEL MILSTEIN

After more than 10 years of study Bureau of Land Management officials in Wyoming have recommended 1.4 percent of its land, or 0.4 percent of the state, for wilderness protection, in what environmental groups characterize as an "anti-wilderness" proposal.

Many wilderness study areas—which were temporarily protected while under consideration—were left out of the BLM's recommendations altogether. Among these were some of the state's most spectacular areas, such as the Honeycombs, a nook-and-cranny badlands in northwest Wyoming, and the Sweetwater Rocks in central Wyoming.

Of a total of 575,000 acres considered for wilderness protection, the BLM deemed 240,364 acres suitable.

BLM officials say they used their best judgment in applying a strict set of mandated criteria to decide whether areas qualify for wilderness status. The standards required that the areas provide an opportunity for solitude and that they be essentially undisturbed by roads, structures or other development.

But environmentalists accuse the BLM of excluding areas with any potential for mining, oil and gas drilling or where ranchers might not look fondly on a restrictive wilderness designation. In one instance, Sierra Club Regional Representative Larry Mehlhaff said BLM planners dropped a study area because a dirt road ran through one edge, even though the old road is impassable and barely visible now.

Such choices left only the most commercially unproductive

and remote areas on the BLM's list, the lowland equivalent of "rocks and ice" wilderness areas in national forests. Those may be the only kind that will pass muster with Wyoming's congressional delegation, who are generally foes of wilderness, when Congress debates the designation.

"Anytime there was any possible conflict or drilling or grazing lease, even if there was no activity on the lease, they threw it out," said Wyoming Outdoor Council Director Stephanie Kessler. "They did not consider ecological concerns or try to cover legitimate examples of ecosystems—they picked those apart."

Some wilderness study areas, for instance, simply isolate certain features rather than preserve them in their ecological context, she said. It is true that BLM land in Wyoming is probably more developed than in most other states, she said, but that makes what's left even more important.

Wilderness designation only restricts mechanized activities (grazing is still permitted, for instance, and there are allowances for ranchers who need to drive to their herds), but grazing, mining and drilling groups complain that any wilderness is too much.

"Some people think it's too much, others think it's not enough," said BLM spokesman Larry Dove. "Some people think we skimped, but the complaint from the mineral and ranching industry is that we went the other way."

Several environmental groups have formed an alliance called the Wyoming Wilderness Coalition to devise an alternative proposal of 1.5 million acres, which they will present to Congress before it makes a final decision on BLM recommendations for Wyoming.

BLM officials, however, have refused requests to postpone mineral leasing of lands included in the alternative proposal. Such activity would make those lands less suitable for wilderness designation.

In 2004, Wyoming still does not have a single acre of BLM land officially designated as wilderness.

In New Mexico, the Issue is Water

BY TONY DAVIS

When southwest New Mexico writer M.H. "Dutch" Salmon visited central Arizona recently, he drove past a stretch of the Gila River that was little more than a dirt ditch. Because of irrigation, over-grazing, timber-cutting, damming and groundwater pumping, a river that 100 years ago had been a cottonwood-lined oasis has become a near-wasteland.

Salmon, who chairs the New Mexico Wilderness Coalition, doesn't want another stretch of the Gila west of Silver City to suffer the same fate. The river in New Mexico is a year-round, cottonwood-rich stream that draws river-runners, birdwatchers and fishermen. It is one reason that the debate over Bureau of Land Management wilderness in New Mexico is locked in a stalemate.

Seven years after the BLM released its first wilderness proposal for New Mexico, the state's congressional delegation has not introduced a bill. The state must rely on the BLM's proposed bill this fall, which appeals to few.

The most intractable point of controversy concerns water rights for rivers in wilderness areas. The Gila is one of only two rivers in the state that pass through BLM land. The agency has proposed preserving one section of the Gila, near the small town of Red Rock. The wilderness coalition wants to set aside another section about 25 miles west of Silver City.

New Mexico environmentalists are adamant that rivers passing through wilderness lands deserve a federally reserved water right.

A key reason is that the right of water to remain in a stream gets no legal protection from the state.

The 3,000-member New Mexico Cattle Growers Association, fearful of seeing their ability to divert water evaporate, has fiercely opposed water rights for wilderness.

Ranchers, who say their cows graze virtually every square inch of BLM land in the state, also oppose environmentalists' desire to implement Forest Service-style rules requiring advance government approval whenever they want to drive a pickup truck on the grazing land.

Republican Congressman Joe Skeen of southern New Mexico and fellow Republican Pete Domenici, the state's senior U.S. senator, say they see little reason to introduce a BLM wilderness bill while these fights continue.

Democratic Rep. Bill Richardson, who represents liberal northern New Mexico, says he'd like to get a bill introduced this year and passed in 1992.

But introducing a bill now "would be an exercise in futility," said Domenici spokesman Ari Fleischer. Environmental groups say the main obstacle to a wilderness bill is the congressional delegation's unwillingness to take a stand.

The BLM will send its proposal to the president this fall to set aside slightly less than 500,000 acres of wilderness. The wilderness coalition wants 2.3 million acres. But with the scanty BLM bill moving forward soon, pressure is on the delegation to make fast decisions.

New Mexico has not seen a new BLM wilderness area since Congress established the Cebolla and West Malpais wilderness areas in 1987.

Oregon Group Floats a Wilderness Proposal

BY TOM RIBE

In early 1990, the Oregon BLM recommended wilderness designation for 20 percent of its public land. While ranchers and miners called the proposal for 1.3 million acres of wilderness overly generous, environmental groups charged the Bureau of Land Management with an "anti-wilderness bias" for excluding millions of acres of roadless areas.

Last April, a statewide coalition of environmental groups unveiled its own wilderness proposal, called the Oregon High Desert Protection Act. The ambitious legislation would protect 5 million acres of BLM land in the state's eastern Great Basin.

In addition to creating 47 proposed wilderness areas, the environmental proposal would wrest roughly 1.35 million acres from the BLM and transfer it to the U.S. Fish and Wildlife Service or National Park Service. The lands would then become national monuments, refuges and a new national park on Steens Mountain.

Environmentalists also called for a 10-year phase-out of all livestock grazing. That provision failed to gain support from the Sierra Club and The Wilderness Society.

"We're not in any position to bust open the Wilderness Act," says Liz Frankle, a member of the Oregon Sierra Club. She and others say grazing is an ecological management question that should remain separate from the wilderness designation process.

But other groups, including the Oregon Natural Resources Council and the Oregon Wildlife Federation, say a bill is an appropriate place to deal with grazing.

"We feel it is about time someone tackled the issue of grazing in wilderness areas," says Bill Marlett of the Oregon Natural Desert Association, one of the act's chief architects. "Cows and desert wilderness are totally inconsistent."

But rancher Susie Hammond says the legislation would ruin the rural economy and social fabric of the region. "Environmentalists will only end up destroying what they are seeking to protect," she says. "What are we going to do for a living if we can't graze our cows on BLM lands? If we lose these rights, we're finished."

Oregon's congressional delegation has taken no discernible interest in the massive environmental proposal. Instead, Oregon Rep. Bob Smith and Sen. Mark Hatfield, both Republicans, have introduced the Steens Mountain National Conservation Area Act. It institutionalizes grazing, allows geothermal development and mining, and designates small wilderness areas at a higher elevation, with no water rights.

Meanwhile, the BLM wilderness proposal awaits approval by the Office of Management and Budget before it goes to Congress.

In 2000, Bill Clinton, using power granted to the president under the 1906 Antiquities Act, designated eight new national monuments in the West. In an effort to head off a similar, unilateral designation for Steens Mountain, Oregon's congressional delegation proposed protecting the area as wilderness—a move that Congress approved in October 2000.

Ranchers in the area traded grazing rights in what became wilderness for grazing rights elsewhere, and the Steens Mountain Wilderness is now the largest cow-free wilderness in the U.S., with 98,859 of its approximately 170,000 acres off-limits to grazing. It is the fourth BLM wilderness in Oregon, and the only one designated since 1984.

Utah Hearings Misfire

BY RAY WHEELER

In 1992, Wayne Owens, D-Utah, the champion of the Utah Wilderness Coalition's proposal—now called America's Redrock Wilderness Act—was defeated in his bid for re-election. New York Rep. Maurice Hinchey, D, carried the torch with a 5.7 million-acre bill. Then, in 1995, Utah's congressional delegation countered with its own wilderness bill.

From the official transcript, Salt Lake City Wilderness Hearing, April 15, 1995:

> *Unidentified speaker: What I would like to do is have a political (poll)...and just let everybody express what they can't express because of time limits; so until that red light goes off, (inaudible) make noise and...*

> *The crowd, chanting: 5.7, 5.7, 5.7, 5.7, 5.7, 5.7*

There are 400 seats in the University of Utah's Orson Spencer Hall auditorium. Every seat is filled. More than a hundred people stand or sit in the aisles; another hundred jam into the foyer, where students perch like roosting birds atop rows of cabinets. Fifty more people mill in the lobby outside the auditorium, where a harried official sits at a table surrounded by would-be speakers demanding to know why their names cannot be found on the speaker list. In all, somewhere between 700 and 1,000 Utahns will visit the auditorium during today's four-hour public hearing on BLM wilderness. One in 10 will have an opportunity to speak.

After 39 wilderness hearings held in remote corners of Utah over three months, the Utah congressional delegation's wilderness review process has arrived on the Wasatch Front, where 80 percent of Utahns live. The long wait has not made for a warm welcome. Speaker after speaker has mercilessly blasted the panel of prominent Utahns sitting before them: Utah Gov. Mike Leavitt and all five members of the state's congressional delegation.

From the beginning, the governor and the delegation made it clear that they would rely heavily on recommendations from county commissioners in crafting their wilderness bill. All but the final round of six "regional" wilderness hearings would be held at the county level and presided over by county commissioners.

Of Utah's 29 counties, only 16 were invited to hold hearings and make recommendations. The 13 mostly urban counties from which no recommendations will be accepted contain 87 percent of Utah's population. By contrast, the 16 rural counties whose recommendations will form the basis for the Utah delegation's wilderness bill contain just 13 percent of Utah's population. The 16 elect counties are in rural southern and western Utah, where the state's Bureau of Land Management wilderness study areas are concentrated.

The county-centered process is consistent with the political ideology of the governor and the delegation. But so far as Utah environmentalists are concerned, this approach puts the fox in the henhouse.

Utah's rural county commissioners have not helped matters by advertising their bias. The public notice inviting Garfield County citizens to attend the county's wilderness hearings opened as follows: "We feel very strongly that lands that do not fit the 1964 Wilderness Bill criteria should not be designated as wilderness, and we need your help in documenting proof as to why we are not including them." Garfield County wilderness hearings were chaired by commissioner Louise Liston, who has described the National Wilderness Preservation System as "a hideaway for sex and drugs."

By situating all but three of 42 wilderness hearings in cities one to four hours distant from the Wasatch Front, the Utah delegation appears to have set the stage for a hearing record heavily tilted against wilderness.

On April 1, the governor's office revealed the fruits of its wilderness review process. Utah county commissioners were recommending wilderness designation for just under 1 million acres.

The focus now turned to the final round of six "regional" wilderness hearings, where the public would be allowed to comment on the county recommendation. While the purpose of this final round of hearings was to obtain highly specific public comment on the county recommendations, no detailed maps or descriptions of those recommendations were published or made available to the public.

So today, in Salt Lake City, frustrations which have been accumulating throughout four months are being focused, like sunlight pouring through a lens, upon the Orson Spencer Hall auditorium. The air in the auditorium is hot, stale and heavy with tension.

During the past four days Utah's governor and congressional delegation have endured nearly 20 hours of hearings in five cities. Gov. Leavitt and Rep. Bill Orton still have one more hearing to go. The group looks pale, exhausted. Cindy King, chair of the Tooele Chapter of the Sierra Club in Utah, steps to the microphone. Speakers prescient enough to make telephone reservations in advance have been limited to two minutes, while those without reservations will have 60 seconds. King will have two minutes to submit detailed, area-specific comments on the 141 proposed wilderness areas in the Utah Wilderness Coalition proposal. But instead of detailed comments, she devotes her first minute to an attack on the delegation's wilderness review process, her voice shaking with anger.

She mentions "threats...to my economic livelihood from Tooele County officials." She is "appalled," she says, by "this process pitting (us) against each other," and appalled by "the greediness of the Tooele County Commissioners," whom she berates for cashiering the Stansbury mountain range "because of their vast interest in toxic pollution." (The proximity of mineral processing plants, which are among the largest point-sources of air pollution in the nation, was given by the Tooele County commissioners as a principal reason for omitting the Stansburys from their wilderness recommendation.) King derides the County's 39,000-acre wilderness recommendation, which would leave more than 80 percent of the county's roadless BLM land open to development. Her first minute is up.

"For the remainder of my allotted time," she says, "I will now stand in silence to show what this process has been trying to do to the public."

King backs away from the microphone to stand at parade rest, chin up, eyes glaring defiantly at the governor and delegation. Governor and delegation stare back, their faces hardened into statuary, their eyes glazed.

Into the void of deep silence a ground swell of applause begins to build. Hearing moderator Enid Waldholtz, a young but forceful congresswoman with an authoritative voice, has already admonished the crowd to refrain from applause. But the applause continues to build, and this time Waldholtz does nothing to stop it. It is apparent that the Will to Authority and the Voice of Prudence have been holding council in Waldholtz's mind, and that Prudence has had the final word. This auditorium is in the heart of Utah's second congressional district. The people applauding are Waldholtz's constituents.

One by one, then in groups, people rise to their feet. Soon the entire crowd is standing. People are hooting, stomping, screaming, waving raised hands and clenched fists, waving signs. The ovation lasts 38 seconds, but it seems more like 10 minutes. Finally the applause tapers off and the crowd begins to sit down.

But King's time is still not quite up.

She remains before the microphone, still trembling with anger, a lone exclamation point standing in place of a thousand unspoken sentences.

Now a second wave of applause begins to build. Hundreds of people are again clapping, stomping and chanting in unison. The rhythmic pounding is like that of a great hammer beating on the roof. The whole auditorium seems to be shaking.

The crowd: "5.7, 5.7, 5.7..."

Congress Weighs the Fate of Utah's Wild Lands

BY RAY WHEELER

When Utah's congressional delegation announced almost a year ago that it would introduce a bill designating BLM wilderness, environmentalists in the state were shocked.

They knew they faced a potentially disastrous alignment of political planets: Republican majorities in both houses of Congress, a right-wing congressional delegation determined to "solve" the wilderness "problem," and a president with a record of capitulation to the Western voting bloc.

In grim meetings last January and February, Utah Wilderness Coalition leaders made two commitments. They would urge supporters to participate in the delegation's wilderness review process. But if the delegation's wilderness bill opened far more land to development than it would protect as wilderness, they would fight to kill it.

The coalition held a meeting for supporters in Salt Lake City in mid-February, and 500 people filled the meeting hall to capacity, overflowing into a bitterly cold winter night.

The crowd was restive, vocal, eager for action. Two plastic buckets passed hand-to-hand around the room returned stuffed with over $1,000 in cash.

Encouraged, the coalition hired a full-time organizer to recruit volunteers and coordinate their work. By June, the coalition's activist database contained more than 700 names. It would grow to 1,200 by summer's end, while the number of UWC member organizations boomed from 34 to 92.

Volunteers produced and distributed 800 copies of a 40-page *Utah Wilderness Activist Handbook.* They set up an Internet web site and created an "Adopt a Wilderness" program to recruit teams of advocates for each of 13 regions in their proposal. A petition drive led by Southern Utah Wilderness Alliance (SUWA) teams contacted over 30,000 people in 10 Utah cities, securing 16,000 signatures in support of the coalition proposal.

In preparation for the final round of wilderness hearings in mid-April, volunteers staffed two phone banks which ran simultaneously on weekday evenings for over a month. Over a two-month period, the coalition sent out 10,000 pieces of direct mail and telephoned over 8,000 people to turn out supporters for county and regional wilderness hearings. It also organized car pools and chartered buses.

After wilderness opponents claimed in hearings that lands within the coalition's proposal lacked wilderness character because they contained roads, mines, cabins and other human impacts, volunteers responded within days by obtaining maps showing the alleged impacts and mobilizing photo-reconnaissance teams to investigate their existence, location and condition. With a flourish of over-the-top enthusiasm, one group of 30 volunteers, led by Salt Lake City chemist Will McCarville, surveyed every mile of alleged road within the proposed 750,000-acre San Rafael Swell wilderness and produced an 800-page report detailing its findings.

By June 1, it was apparent that the Utah congressional delegation's attempt to "balance" public comment by situating public hearings in rural Utah had not worked. Statewide, 69 percent of the written and oral public comment endorsed the coalition's 5.7 million-acre proposal; an additional 20 percent favored wilderness designation without naming a specific proposal. Only 6 percent supported the 1 million-acre proposal of the county commissioners. Even in "regional" hearings held in small-town southern Utah, 40 to 70 percent of the speakers had endorsed the coalition proposal.

Utahns now watched with interest:

After its elaborate show of soliciting public comment, the delegation found itself impaled on the horns of a nasty dilemma. Instead of creating one test of public opinion, it had created two. Instead of receiving one opinion, it had received two radically different opinions—one from wilderness supporters and one from rural county commissioners.

Now, the Utah congressional delegation had to decide on which side of the line it would stand. If the delegation's wilderness bill designated significantly more than the 1 million acres of wilderness recommended by the county commissioners, there could be hell to pay, not only with the commissioners but with ideological allies throughout the West and in the Congress. If the bill designated significantly less than the 5.7 million acres endorsed by the majority, the public would believe that the Utah delegation had forsaken the public interest on behalf of a bunch of county commissioners.

On June 6, the Utah delegation held a press conference in Washington, D.C., to unveil its wilderness bill. It was immediately clear that while the bill appeared to recommend 1.8 million acres for wilderness, in actuality the delegation had chosen to stand with the county commissioners.

The "Utah Public Lands Act of 1995" (H.R. 1745/S.884) would leave open to development nearly 4 million acres of roadless BLM land in Utah. The bill would release from "interim management protection" nearly half of the 3.2 million acres of BLM wilderness study areas where development has been forbidden until Congress enacted a wilderness bill.

The bill also contained "hard release" language prohibiting the BLM from managing any non-wilderness lands so as to preserve their potential for future wilderness designation. The BLM was also prohibiting from studying or recommending lands for wilderness designation.

The bill further stipulated that the BLM must manage all 20 million acres of non-wilderness BLM land in Utah "for the full range of nonwilderness multiple uses"—an invitation to would-be developers to argue in court that any management restriction which would have the incidental effect of preserving wilderness character was forbidden by the act.

Finally, while the bill would designate 1.8 million acres of wilderness in tracts scattered across the state, a host of special provisions would allow vehicular access, low-level military over-flights, and the construction of roads, dams, reservoirs, power-lines, pipelines and communications facilities, even within areas designated as wilderness by the act.

Reaction from Utah environmentalists was swift: They called the bill a zoning master plan for commercial and industrial devel-opment in the heart of every large BLM roadless area in the state.

"The bill mocks the concept of wilderness," said former Utah congressman Wayne Owens, now chairman of SUWA's board of directors, in a letter to the *Deseret News*.

In the blaze of publicity surrounding the Utah delegation's bill, it is easy to overlook the other wilderness bill—H.R. 1500, "America's Redrock Wilderness Act," which would protect 5.7 million acres.

Originally introduced in 1989 by Rep. Owens, H.R. 1500 had acquired over 100 co-sponsors by 1992, when Owens left Congress after losing a Senate race. No member of the Utah con-gressional delegation was willing to reintroduce the bill. Instead, SUWA lobbyist Cindy Shogan recruited New York Rep. Maurice Hinchey to reintroduce H.R. 1500 in 1993 and again in 1995. With each new Congress, coalition supporters have painstakingly rebuilt the co-sponsor base. As of this writing, the bill has 103 co-sponsors in the House.

But H.R. 1500 has never been reported out of its House sub-committee. And after nearly seven years of intense searching, environmentalists have failed to find a single senator willing to sponsor the bill: H.R. 1500 does not exist in the Senate.

A principal obstacle in the Senate is "senatorial courtesy"—the reluctance of senators to meddle with another state's issues. Press reports suggesting that Republican Sen. Orrin Hatch, chairman of the Senate Judiciary Committee, will hold hostage federal judgeship appointments have probably also helped to cool any ardor for H.R. 1500.

By comparison, H.R. 1745/S. 884 had massive backing: four of the state's five representatives and both of its senators. The delegation's bill moved ahead in the House, seemingly unaffected by all the work against it. In the House, it was shepherded by Utah's Jim Hansen, chairman of the House Subcommittee on Public Lands and National Parks.

It whipped through congressional field hearings and subcommittee markup in six weeks. On Aug. 2, it blew through the full House Energy and Resources Committee, chaired by Rep. Don Young of Alaska, on a 23–8 vote.

But then it hit the full House on Dec. 14 and suffered a startling setback, unexpected by both environmentalists and by the Utah delegation. [After a Republican leadership poll revealed that the controversial bill had little support among House members, Rep. Hansen yanked the bill.]

Hardly anyone thinks the delegation's bill is dead, but predictions that the bill would move easily through the House have been proven wrong.

The bill's progress through the Senate, shepherded by Hatch and Sen. Robert Bennett, has been slower. But at the same time, it has not suffered the kind of reverse experienced in the House. The bill has been endorsed by the Energy and Resources Committee and should go to the Senate floor in 1996.

The third player is the White House. Environmentalists hope that, if necessary, President Clinton will veto the delegation's bill. Interior officials announced that Secretary Bruce Babbitt would recommend a veto if the bill were to pass "in its present form." They stressed that hard release language was unacceptable. But in recent weeks, press reports have suggested that the Utah delegation may be willing to give up hard release language. Such a last-minute concession might grease the skids for the bill both in the Senate and in the White House.

Faced a few months ago with what seemed like a juggernaut, the Utah Wilderness Coalition, led by SUWA and the Utah Chapter of the Sierra Club, launched a nationwide campaign. Volunteers descended in waves upon Capitol Hill. Four groups of supporters from Utah and other states each spent a week on the Hill, with each group visiting over 100 congressional offices. Still more advocates have made individual visits to congressional offices throughout the year. Among the pilgrims was actor Robert Redford, a Utah resident, who reportedly met with 20 senators in a single day in mid-July.

In August and September, three national environmental groups mailed nearly 150,000 special alerts to their most active supporters in key congressional districts throughout the country, asking for letters and phone calls to congressional offices about the Utah wilderness bill.

SUWA carried the campaign to other fronts. The group drafted retiring executive director Brant Calkin to undertake the equivalent of the traditional Mormon mission, and Calkin barnstormed America in a beat-up 1977 Volkswagen van, carrying the Utah wilderness gospel to over 120 cities in 24 states. Calkin's bible was a dual-projector slide show; baptism consisted of writing letters to congressional offices, and signing up to participate in a nationwide network of grassroots "Wilderness Warriors."

While Calkin recruited grassroots supporters one handshake at a time, the public relations firm of Vanguard Communications, retained by SUWA, coordinated a nationwide media air-war. Former BLM director Jim Baca, now a SUWA board member and Wilderness Society staff member, began a national press tour in August, while Vanguard pumped out press kits and fed the Utah wilderness story to journalists.

Stories about the Utah wilderness dispute have appeared in at least a half dozen nationally distributed newspapers and magazines, including *The New York Times*, the *Washington Post*, *Newsweek*, *U.S. News and World Report*, *Country Living* and *USA Weekend*, while editorials critical of the 1.8 million-acre Utah wilderness bill have appeared in at least 30 newspapers from Maine to California.

A sampling of the editorial copy suggests that H.R. 1745/S. 884 has been taking a brutal beating:

The *Santa Fe New Mexican*: "The bill is about Utah, but if it becomes federal law, New Mexico and the rest of the West will soon hear bulldozers and blasting throughout our wildlands."

The *Kansas City Star*: "Congress needs to stop this destructive proposal dead in its tracks."

The *Cleveland Plain Dealer*: "House Republicans are about to perpetrate a massive sellout of the public interest in a spectacular corner of the West."

The *Des Moines Register*: "How ironic that the congressional delegation closest to the beauty of southern Utah should be so eager to destroy it."

The *Washington Post*: "It is a sign of the land-ravenous times, as well as the brazenness of commercial exploiters and their Utah friends Orrin G. Hatch and Robert F. Bennett in the Senate, that preserving 5.7 million acres out of 22 million is opposed."

By mid-summer, some congressional offices had begun to feel the effect of the national campaign. New Jersey Sen. Bill Bradley's press secretary, for example, estimates the senator has received 1,500 to 2,000 letters and calls, while Colorado Sen. Ben Nighthorse-Campbell has reportedly been inundated with over 3,000. Representatives in the House did not receive the same volume of mail and calls, but they too were lobbied hard, with the campaign peaking in the fall and early winter.

Now we must wait until 1996 to see the results of the Utah delegation's determination, on the one hand, to push its bill through matched against the massive media and lobbying activity expended by Utah's wilderness activists.

The stakes go beyond Utah's wildlands. If Utah environmentalists succeed in stopping the Utah delegation's wilderness bill, they will have scored a profound victory. If they fail, the Utah wilderness bill will set a devastating precedent for future wilderness bills.

In March 1996, the Utah delegation's bill, packaged in an omnibus national parks bill, made it to the Senate floor. But the fierce counter-campaign by the Utah Wilderness Coalition roused national opposition to the bill. Sen. Bradley launched a filibuster, and after Republicans mustered only 52 of the 60 votes needed to defeat it, they abandoned the bill.

On March 29 of the same year, after fundraising problems and staff departures, the Utah Wilderness Association closed its doors.

Utah Finds Three Million More Wild Acres

BY DUSTIN SOLBERG

At a congressional wilderness hearing in 1996, Rep. Jim Hansen challenged Secretary of the Interior Bruce Babbitt to find 5 million more acres of wilderness in Utah. Babbitt promptly directed the BLM to begin a second inventory of its lands eligible for wilderness designation. At the same time, the Utah Wilderness Coalition started its own reinventory.

Equipped with an old Jeep Cherokee 4x4 and a stack of large-scale topographical maps, Kevin Walker spent two years combing southern Utah. He was looking for wild, unprotected tracts of Bureau of Land Management land that might have been left out of the Utah Wilderness Coalition's wilderness proposal.

Walker helped lead the citizens' inventory, and he says his team has succeeded beyond its expectations. But Walker says he also learned that maps don't always tell the truth.

Sometimes he found jeep trails and stock tanks where the map indicated junipers and an intermittent stream. Near Glen Canyon, volunteers discovered an eight-mile road bulldozed into the desert, eliminating the area from further wilderness consideration. But mostly, when the map wasn't accurate, it was because time had obliterated or faded a two-track road.

Walker was helped by 350 volunteers from Utah and elsewhere. Some of their finds: Past inventories didn't include Utah's portion of the Great Basin, where "whole mountain ranges were left out," says Scott Groene of the Southern Utah Wilderness

Alliance, part of the 156-member wilderness coalition. In central Utah, what's known as the Price Canyon Unit was once thought to be 30,000 roadless acres. After the inventory, it grew to 100,000 acres.

Then, on July 10, in a packed auditorium at the University of Utah where a rock band played and the mood was festive, the Utah Wilderness Coalition announced the inventory results to 700 supporters—not 5.7, but 8.5 million acres was the starting point for a new wilderness bill. Rep. Merrill Cook, a Republican from Salt Lake City, showed up, too, to voice support for more wilderness. The event was in sharp contrast to nine years ago, when wilderness proponents announced their first wilderness bill to a handful of supporters and a few reporters in a quiet city park.

Not everyone trusts the results of the citizens' inventory. Last month's announcement has brought the state's contentious wilderness debate back to life.

"No one's surprised that when the wilderness advocates go out looking for wilderness they find any," says Sheldon Kinsel of Heber City, Utah, who sometimes consults for the Utah Association of Counties. "If you go out looking for wilderness and your standards are low enough, you can go out and find it everywhere but a rowcrop field."

Wilderness opponents say that a strict interpretation of an 1866 federal law known as R.S. 2477 rules out designating many of these lands as wilderness. Even if a road that appeared on a map long ago has now disappeared, the Utah Association of Counties argues that a county still has the right to bulldoze what had become a right-of-way.

"Roads can reappear and there's nothing the BLM can do about it," Kinsel says.

Environmentalists admit the law must be reckoned with. "It's a sticking point and it is a threat," says Heidi McIntosh, a Southern Utah Wilderness Alliance attorney. But it's also "a ludicrous interpretation of the law, and I don't think it will stand up."

All or Nothing

The wilderness movement in Utah has successfully challenged its opponents before. It beat back legislation supported by the Utah delegates that would have preserved only 1.8 million acres as wilderness while opening 20 million acres to development.

Until it happened, few had thought the Republican-controlled 104th Congress would quash a wilderness bill authored by one of its own, Rep. Jim Hansen.

"And they were wrong," Groene says. "It taught Utah activists that there's no end to what we can accomplish." He says a new bill, calling for the preservation of as much as 8.5 million acres, could be introduced in the next session of Congress. Once again, however, the Utah Congressional delegation is staunchly opposed to environmentalists' wilderness proposals.

"Obviously, it can be difficult to get it by Utah senators," Groene says.

But the wilderness movement in Utah has generated support elsewhere. The 5.7 million-acre wilderness bill now before Congress has 140 sponsors in the House of Representatives and 12 sponsors in the Senate. Though wilderness supporters have been quietly garnering votes for years, neither side has mustered enough votes to break the gridlock. Meanwhile, dedicated activists continue to push their strategy.

Wilderness supporters conducted their inventory without help from the BLM. They paid for full-page ads in newspapers across the nation, and a cross-country road tour to spread the word about the new inventory is in the works.

Bill Hedden of Moab, a former Grand County commissioner, says wilderness proponents have a "single-minded focus" that goes something like this: "It's the most special place you ever saw and it's going to be wrecked before you ever get out here to see it."

"And it works," he says. "They can pretty much count on support."

Signs of Support

So far, only first-term Rep. Cook has spoken out for wilderness—though not for any specific proposal—and some of his traditional Republican allies in Utah are wondering what's gotten into him. He told a Utah Wilderness Coalition gathering last month that he would not support controversial legislation authored by Rep. Chris Cannon, known as the San Rafael Swell National Heritage/Conservation Area Act.

"To be honest with you, I think he got poor advice," says Mark Walsh, associate director of the Utah Association of Counties, a group that supports the San Rafael Swell legislation.

The bill would designate 130,000 acres of wilderness while opening to development another 130,000 acres now in a wilderness study area. An additional 600,000 acres that environmentalists want preserved would also be left open to development.

Hedden says Cook's recent statement shouldn't be a surprise. "Whoever holds that (Salt Lake City) seat realizes very quickly that on the Wasatch Front, protecting a lot of wilderness is a pretty popular thing."

The Utah Wilderness Coalition uses Cook's support for wilderness protection to illustrate how Republicans in Utah are fracturing over the Utah wilderness issue, hoping it will open the door for other members of the GOP in Washington to sign on. But their critics argue that the 8.5 million-acre inventory is political: "They want to make 5.7 million acres look like a more reasonable number," Kinsel says.

The Southern Utah Wilderness Alliance insists the inventory simply tallied the roadless lands managed by the BLM. "The final number had nothing to do with political strategy," Groene says. "We've had one principle: We want to protect what's left."

Based on this reinventory, the Utah Wilderness Coalition drafted a 9.1 million-acre wilderness proposal in 1999, which was taken to Congress the same year by Rep. Maurice Hinchey, D-N.Y. Although the bill has been reintroduced in every session of Congress since then, it has not passed.

Meanwhile, the BLM's own reinventory, the results of which were released in 1999, added another 2.6 million acres of "wilderness inventory areas" to the 3.2 million acres of wilderness study areas the agency identified in the early 1980s. Under Interior Secretary Babbitt, the wilderness inventory areas received interim protection to prevent activities that would reduce their eligibility for future wilderness designation.

MANAGING THE WILD
Access Conflicts

Sometimes, simply getting to a wilderness can be tricky. The first story in this subsection focuses on an instance where access to a wilderness area on the edge of Tucson, Ariz., was cut off by surrounding development. Numerous other fights have broken out when property owners have tried to gain road access to their private "inholdings" within wilderness areas, an issue described in more detail in this subsection's second story.

Hikers Are Fenced
Out of Wilderness

BY FLORENCE WILLIAMS

TUCSON, Ariz.—Sometime between the designation of federal wilderness in the Coronado National Forest just north of town, and the construction of nearby sprawling neighborhoods, the town planners took a long nap.

To stroll through the saguaro-mesquite country just above the city, hikers must now wend through posh subdivisions, tip-toe across private land shouting with "NO TRESPASSING" signs, march through narrow, chain-linked passageways and park in the boonies.

Now, faced with a planned resort at the mouth of one of the city's most popular trails, local residents and county planners are taking steps to safeguard access to public land.

The $100 million Pima Canyon Resort, proposed by Stouffer Hotel Co., would turn a pristine, saguaro-speckled floodplain and canyon wash into an 800-car parking lot, 400-room hotel, residential neighborhood, golf course and tennis courts.

Past experience has roused Pima County residents to demand more from town planners and developers.

A mega-resort built in the mid-1980s, the posh Loews Ventana Canyon Resort, along with surrounding developments, effectively discouraged many hikers from entering Ventana Canyon. To reach the wilderness area from there, hikers must park their cars in the employee parking lot of the resort, then walk a quarter mile up an asphalt road, duck around the tennis courts of an apartment complex and finally cross the private property of the

Flying V guest ranch. The ranch demands that all hikers call ahead of time and leave their names on a recorded answering machine.

There are no signs to help would-be hikers negotiate the maze of parking lots, roads and properties.

"Ventana Canyon is a disaster," concedes Doug Koppinger, an aide to county supervisor Greg Lunn. "When the resort and apartments were built about eight years ago, there was a great deal of concern over access. But somebody dropped the ball. Now it's totally screwed up."

Tom Quinn, district ranger of the Coronado National Forest, says Ventana access is "a worst-case scenario." The forest's Pusch Ridge Wilderness, he says, lies closer to a major urban center than any other wilderness area he knows of. "Anytime you have a wilderness coming right down into neighborhoods, you're going to have conflicts," he says. "In hindsight, it would have been nice to have more of a buffer."

County planners have failed in the past to push for access to other canyon mouths as well. To reach the Campbell Cliff area, for example, climbers and hikers must walk a half-mile within a narrow corridor walled by 8-foot-high chain link fences topped by barbed wire. That is what the private surrounding landowner calls "access."

To hike up the Esperero Trail, the public must either park half a mile away and then trespass on private property, or enter a gated residential community under the pretext of visiting a property owner in order to park closer to the public trail. Even then, one must trespass several privately owned but undeveloped parcels. Although a local conservation group owns one of those parcels, it does not make that information available to the general public.

For the Agua Caliente trail as well, there exists no legal public access, says Quinn.

Aide Koppinger says the county is working with landowners to improve access, and may condemn some property or easements to secure public rights. But this is expensive, he adds, and the county should have required rights-of-way in zoning negotiations years ago.

While officials and many residents say real estate development in these foothills is inevitable, they hope to strike some compromises early in the planning stages of new projects.

"It's like a train coming down the tracks," says Nancy Kelly of the Southern Arizona Sierra Club. "But we've taken some unhappy lessons from Ventana Canyon, and hopefully we'll write stronger agreements to protect the public."

The Pima County Board of Supervisors voted 3–2 to approve Stouffer's plan in mid-October. Under the county's terms, Stouffer must build a parking lot specifically for hikers, provide easy access to the trailhead and help fund a trails access committee.

Some activists, however, remain disappointed the developer won't provide additional funding for outdoor education and interpretive programs.

"We were hoping this would be a model accomplishment for trail access, but the developers and the county weren't totally accommodating, and the hiking groups weren't unified in what they wanted," notes Jan Gingold, president of the Pima Trails Association.

"But," she adds, "I'm going to see if we can get more funding. We have to work with developers and pull together. This development could show the way for other access issues to be resolved elsewhere."

Meanwhile, some observers wonder if all the hue and cry over access is obscuring more serious concerns over increasing development in ecologically fragile areas. Much less fuss was made, for example, when the Board of Supervisors exempted Stouffer from including a riparian zone buffer.

"The Sierra Club threw a temper tantrum over not having access to hiking," notes one planner. "What happened to the idea of being good stewards? Everyone is too concerned with rights and not responsibilities."

Says forester Quinn: "It seems kind of irresponsible that the county exempted the buffer-zone requirement. It needs to enforce its ordinances." He adds, "In Pima Canyon, the access issue is going to be resolved. I would have liked more help with environmental protection."

FEBRUARY 18, 2002

Will Bulldozers Roll into Arizona's Eden?

BY TONY DAVIS

PEEPLES CANYON, Ariz.—Alaskans Erik and Tina Barnes made their fortunes working as commercial fishermen, ski instructors, veterinarians and pilots. But they'd always wanted to run a ranch. In 1990, they found their opportunity: The Santa Maria Ranch, straddling a river of the same name just outside the Arrastra Mountain Wilderness Area in central Arizona, was not only stunningly beautiful, it also had an access road, an airstrip for their Cessna 180 and proximity to shopping in Wickenburg, Ariz., about 45 miles south.

Intending to ranch part-time and continue the family fishing business, they paid $350,000 for 980 acres on the river and a 40-acre inholding along a wilderness canyon.

"It suits us better than living in a trailer park in Apache Junction or in Sun City West," says Tina Barnes.

But the Barneses' last decade on the ranch has been far from peaceful. Their plans to use heavy construction equipment to fix up old roads and livestock watering tanks in the wilderness have run up against one of the nation's top anti-grazing activists. The ensuing legal battle, which could set a precedent for how the Bureau of Land Management manages wilderness, has taken as many turns as an old river, and it is still unresolved.

"We have to remind ourselves not to stay angry," says Erik Barnes, 67. "My assumption 10 years ago was that they would take care of the inholding problem and the maintenance problems prior to declaring this wilderness. The problems are the

313

result of Joe Feller. Every time the BLM has made a decision in favor of the rancher, he's found a way to stop it. It's unfair."

Man on a Mission

Feller, of course, sees things differently. The Arizona State University law professor and activist discovered the Arrastra Wilderness a year before Congress designated it in November of 1990. Feller was looking for a riverside grazing issue to sink his teeth into, he acknowledges. After learning from a top BLM official in Kingman, Ariz., that the bureau was doing a management plan for another grazing allotment next to the Barneses' Santa Maria Ranch, Feller dove in. Drawn to steep-walled Peeples Canyon in the heart of the Arrastra Mountains, enchanted by the area's curious blend of junipers, Joshua trees and saguaros, Feller, 48, soon took the first of approximately 50 hikes in the area.

Feller wasn't alone in his attraction to Peeples Canyon. In 1990, *Arizona Highways* described it "as one of the wonders of public land in Arizona." In 1994, *Phoenix Magazine* called it "Arizona's answer to Eden." BLM reports label the canyon "a unique desert oasis" that is "among the rarest and most productive wildlife habitat."

Feller learned that the Barneses wanted to bring bulldozers and backhoes into the canyon to improve one mile of a 7.5-mile stretch of dirt road. The key stretch was 1,000 feet of a narrow, World War II-era access road that slices through hills covered with saguaro and prickly pear, and leads to the Barneses' 40-acre inholding. Erik and Tina Barnes and three other ranchers also wanted to rebuild and repair 15 abandoned and rotting livestock watering tanks. The BLM had never approved a project of this magnitude in a wilderness.

Feller discovered that the jeep road to the inholding had been closed shortly after the Arrastra became a wilderness, and that it hadn't been used since 1980. In a series of legal briefs Feller helped research for the National Wildlife Federation, the group contended that the road grading would violate a Wilderness Act ban on new roads in wilderness areas. They said the bulldozing would create long-lasting scars, and that the ensuing cattle grazing would devastate sensitive springs.

"The springs will then become livestock concentration points, and their value as oases for wildlife and recreationists will be destroyed as they are trampled, their riparian vegetation is stripped away and they are filled with cattle manure and urine," one brief argued.

The BLM's environmental assessment, completed in 1996, acknowledged that the road "would look maintained and appear to casual observers as a road receiving regular and continuous use." Increased noise could drive raptors such as peregrine falcons and zone-tailed hawks off their nests, and possibly lead them to abandon the canyon.

But the agency also said that denying the proposal might make forage in the area unavailable to livestock and force the owners to abandon their water rights to the canyon, thus reducing the value of the inholding and the ranch. Other development, such as rental cabins or other eco-tourism services, could replace ranching there, the Bureau warned.

John R. Christensen, field manager of BLM's Kingman office, says Congress gave the Bureau a "difficult set of cards to play with," with a law to manage this as wilderness while still allowing grazing: "It's hard to make those two mesh, but they wanted to allow that to happen. We're trying to have a minimum effect, yet still allow livestock grazing to continue."

The Forest Service dealt with a similar dilemma in 1996 in Catron County, N.M. There, the agency stopped a rancher from building 15 watering tanks on the Diamond Bar grazing allotment in the Gila Wilderness after five years of lobbying and litigation by local activists.

But despite the protests of Feller and environmental groups, in 1996 the BLM approved the Arrastra Wilderness projects. In November 2000, though, the outgoing Clinton administration's

Interior Department put the ruling on hold before rescinding it two months later.

Then, last fall, the Bush administration's Interior Department again authorized the road and water tank construction. But Barnes still can't start his engines. In December, with both sides pressing lawsuits, a federal judge ordered that an existing stay precluding ground disturbance would continue until the court makes a final decision.

Measures of Last Resort

Erik Barnes says that even if he gains access to his inholding, it won't make up for the lost decade. He says that he has not made a cent at the ranch, because his cattle numbers are one-fourth what they could be with road and water improvements. According to BLM's environmental assessment, though, Barnes likely would earn only $5,000 a year, even if allowed to make his improvements.

Barnes also chafes at the regulations the BLM will impose limiting motor vehicle access to the inholding to 80 to 150 days the first year and even shorter amounts of time in the future.

"The assumption that most Americans have is that if there's a road to your property, you can drive to it," he says.

Feller agrees with Barnes that the federal government has been slow to make decisions, but insists that delays don't mean environmentalists should give up their right to challenge decisions they believe are wrong. Walking down a rutted dirt road through the wilderness toward Barnes' inholding, Feller beams when he spots palo verde and mesquite trees and yellow grasses growing on the now-unused road.

"I try to imagine a bulldozer here, and that is not right," he says. "To me, this is wilderness."

But Barnes threatens to build a resort in his inholding if the case keeps dragging. The BLM offered him $200,000 for the 40 acres a few years ago. He sought $1.2 million and today contends his inholding is worth $7 million as Arrastra's "crown jewel." He envisions customers riding horseback into Peeples Canyon, just as they ride mules into the Grand Canyon:

"If we were to do that, it would be pure and simple because of the hassle Feller has caused us."

Into Thin Air

A San Juan county grader blades a road into the Harts Point proposed wilderness in Utah, 1996.

—PHOTO BY KEVIN WALKER, COURTESY SOUTHERN UTAH WILDERNESS ALLIANCE

In the 1990s, wilderness took a prominent place in the emerging discipline of conservation biology, which focuses in large part on preserving biological diversity by protecting wildlife habitat. Some citizens' wilderness groups began integrating ecology into wilderness proposals, creating large, ecoregion-based visions that strove to protect wilderness as a component of an expansive, functioning mosaic of lands whose ecological integrity remains intact.

That has led to wilderness proposals such as the Alliance for the Wild Rockies' Northern Rockies Ecosystem Protection Act, which would protect 18 million acres of wilderness in Idaho, Montana, Wyoming, Oregon and Washington. The most ambitious plan, by far, has come from a group called the Wildlands Project, which is proposing large-scale "wilderness networks" to restore habitat connectivity throughout North America.

But, as in Utah, groups that tried to sell large wilderness proposals to Congress had to rely on sponsors outside the affected states. And despite attempts to build national support, the proposals became victims of a sort of wilderness bloat when their proponents proved unable to pass such big packages.

It didn't help that the political climate in the United States underwent a major change with the 1994 elections, when the Republican party won a majority in the U.S. Senate and ended four decades of Democratic dominance in the U.S. House of Representatives.

For a time, wilderness simply went into a state of suspension. A lot of land sat in proposals, but didn't move. In Utah and Colorado, the BLM agreed to provide interim protection to citizen-proposed wilderness areas, a policy that Clinton-era Secretary of the Interior Bruce Babbitt extended nationwide in January 2001, just before he left office. At the same time, President Clinton announced the Roadless Area Conservation Rule, which placed 58.5 million acres of roadless national forest land—the shrinking remnants of the 62 million acres of roadless land identified in RARE II in 1977—off-limits to road-building, logging and oil and gas development.

Then, in 2003, the bottom fell out. On April 9, President George W. Bush's secretary of the Interior, Gale Norton, and then-Utah Gov. Mike Leavitt signed an agreement that allowed the state to claim ownership of backcountry roads across public land, along with the right to maintain them. It was a move that threatened to fragment the remaining, functionally roadless land and disqualify it from future protection as wilderness. Two days later, Norton and Leavitt reached an out-of-court settlement that scrapped the BLM's interim protection of citizens' wilderness proposals in Utah. Five and a half months after that, BLM director Kathleen Clarke extended the policy to all BLM lands in the country. Then, on July 12, 2004, the Bush administration announced what was essentially a repeal of Clinton's roadless rule.

The dream of big wilderness seemed to be in free fall.

Montana Spawns a Group that Thinks Big

BY STEVE STUEBNER

Four years ago, three Montana environmentalists worked a booth at the Montana Wilderness Association annual meeting. The trio—Mike Bader, Cass Chinske and Steve Kelly—were all wilderness advocates, but they were looking beyond the boundaries of Montana.

They pored over a map of the Northern Rockies, showing a huge expanse of unprotected, pristine forests in the Western United States and Canada. "When you look at the Northern Rockies as a whole, all of a sudden the significance of the whole region jumps out at you," says Chinske, who a few years earlier played a key role in protecting the Rattlesnake Wilderness near Missoula, Mont.

Paul Fritz, a retired National Park Service superintendent who helped protect the California redwoods, stopped by the booth and was impressed. "Geez, it's about time somebody thinks big enough," Fritz thought at the time.

Several months later, Bader, Chinske and Kelly decided to leave the Montana Wilderness Association and form the Alliance for the Wild Rockies. They asked Fritz to sit on the Alliance's six-member board of directors.

Bader, who became the Alliance's controversial and outspoken executive director, had worked for eight years in Yellowstone National Park as a law enforcement officer, firefighter and resource assistant. His duties included grizzly bear management, and he fell in love with the bears. "I spent a lot of personal time watching grizzly bears," he says.

Kelly, a Bozeman, Mont., sculptor and former tree planter, and Chinske, a former Missoula city councilman, shared Bader's view that the current state-by-state wilderness debate was too confined. "We wanted to take the ecosystem approach to wilderness," Bader says. "It seemed obvious that the statewide approach was sheer lunacy as far as trying to protect wildlife. So we had this burning desire, and we tried to work with the other groups, but we didn't think they were moving fast enough."

So in early 1989, the Alliance embarked on a mission to protect its vision of the West. Fritz, who has been pushing a Park Service study for Hells Canyon, brought in Ric Bailey, a Joseph, Ore., former logger, river guide and director of the Hells Canyon Preservation Council, as a new member of the Alliance board.

Singer-songwriter Carole King, who owns a ranch in central Idaho, helped the Alliance grab national media attention with a news conference in Washington, D.C. King promoted a 9 million-acre wilderness bill for Idaho, which fit well with the Alliance's plan to protect nearly all wildlands remaining in the state. Brian Horejsi, a noted grizzly bear biologist in Alberta, Canada, also joined the board.

Four years later, the Alliance has about 2,700 individual and over 200 business members. It is guided by a dozen-member advisory board, including respected scientists John Craighead and Charles Jonkel, as well as Buster Yellow Kidney, a Blackfeet Indian, and Steward Brandborg, a former national director of The Wilderness Society.

In October, the Alliance named a seventh member to its board of directors, Liz Sedler of Sandpoint, Idaho, who crafts string instruments and has been active in Forest Watch activities on the Kootenai National Forest.

When the Alliance first formed, a lot of people laughed at its five-state, 18 million-acre wilderness parks and wild rivers proposal, Bader said.

But today, the Alliance's plan is increasingly seen as the most visionary wilderness proposal in the West. The key question is whether shooting for the moon is the best political tactic. "I think (Pennsylvania Democrat Rep. Peter) Kostmayer described it best," Bader says. "Our proposal is a radical departure from business as usual."

Leaders of the Alliance, particularly Bader, have attracted media attention by blasting fellow environmental groups for being weak and conformist. During the debates over the Montana wilderness bill in October, Bader's barbs were quoted in *The New York Times* and *Washington Post.*

Such tactics have caused major tensions in the Western environmental community. Off the record, some activists see the Alliance as a high-and-mighty group, self-righteous and contemptuous of those who disagree.

Emily Seeger, president of the Montana Wilderness Association, said the Alliance's attacks on other environmental groups hurt the cause. "There's little, if any, disagreement in the environmental community as to what we want to accomplish," she says. "We all want to protect the remaining wildlands. It's a matter of tactics, strategy and what works best."

The Montana Wilderness Association has a policy of not attacking other environmental groups, Seeger says, and it pains her to see the Alliance personally attack veteran environmental activists. "I don't see why disagreements over tactics have to get personal, and I don't think it's effective."

Kelly says the Alliance has attacked other groups and leaders because they have compromised their goals and have not always kept their word. For instance, lobbyists tell the Alliance they will not accept release language for lands not protected as wilderness, only to suddenly support release language, he says. "If you can't trust the people you're playing with, you've got to find new allies.

"We view this as a crisis, not a career," he says. "When people get in the way, we ask them to move. And if they don't move, you've got to go around them."

Tactics, Vision Divide Montana Environmentalists

BY STEVE STUEBNER

Last month, the House of Representatives passed a 1.48 million-acre wilderness bill for Montana that brought cheers from groups such as the Montana Wilderness Association, Greater Yellowstone Coalition, Sierra Club, The Wilderness Society and National Audubon Society.

But staffers of the Alliance for the Wild Rockies, a small but influential grassroots group based in Missoula, Mont., were fuming.

Although the Montana bill would have protected new wilderness, a few national recreation areas and nearly 1 million acres of wilderness study lands, it would have released about 4 million acres of pristine mountain country for logging, mining, oil and gas drilling, grazing and off-road vehicle use.

Four million acres was too much for the Alliance to give away, says Alliance executive director Mike Bader. "A lot of people are still in shock that these groups were supportive of it. They're going to take some heat for this."

Bader applied some of the heat by sending a stinging letter to Audubon veteran Brock Evans, vice president for national issues: "Who paid you off?" he asked.

"The letter you signed to Congress (supporting) the Montana bill is the most shameful sellout ever perpetuated by you 'Beltway Bandits'...Your letter probably sealed our fate back here where the clear-cuts and the roads will actually occur."

The bill died several days later in the U.S. Senate as Congress adjourned for the fall campaign season. But the fracas over the bill still reverberates. The dispute revealed a wide gulf in the Western and national environmental community over how to protect the last remaining wildlands in the Northern Rockies, and whether an ecosystem-based, multi-state wilderness bill is politically possible.

The Alliance has its own 18 million-acre, five-state wilderness plan—the Northern Rockies Ecosystem Protection Act (NREPA). But even if that plan is the most "visionary," as Bader puts it, national and regional environmental leaders have lashed out at Bader for his outburst. They warn that unless the group changes its tactics, chances of ever winning congressional support for its plan are slim to nonexistent.

"Brutally attacking and savaging your friends is a very immature way to deal with the issue," says Evans, who claims he never bothered to read Bader's letter. "Given the way they're lobbying, it's a hopeless cause."

Adds David Alberswerth of the National Wildlife Federation, "Their attitude seems to be a bunker mentality—if you're not with us, then get the hell out of the way. To realize a vision like theirs, you have to form alliances with other groups. The course they're heading down now is doomed to failure."

Bart Koehler, a founder of Earth First! who is now with the Greater Yellowstone Coalition, called the Alliance staffers "attack-dog masters of overkill…these guys just don't know when to quit. For a group with the first name of Alliance, they've got a lot to learn."

The November election also cast a pall over the Alliance's plan. Rep. Peter Kostmayer, D-Pa., who had been the Alliance's chief sponsor and the biggest wilderness champion in Congress, lost. Two other co-sponsors of the Alliance bill lost as well.

On the flip side, incoming Vice President Al Gore is a strong supporter of wilderness, preserving ecosystems and biodiversity. Former Colorado Sen. Tim Wirth, a candidate for Interior secretary, also could help push a multistate wilderness bill.

"This is a temporary setback to lose Kostmayer," Bader says.

"We won't deny we're sad to see him go, because he's a great wilderness supporter, and he's our friend. But we're going to keep focusing on ecosystems, and we'll pick up new sponsors."

Meanwhile, the Alliance is working to broaden the grassroots support for NREPA. A four-person "canvassing" team is working the communities of the Northern Rockies, trying to increase memberships. Greenpeace volunteers are knocking on 40,000 doors a night nationwide, and an impressive group of movie and rock stars, including the Grateful Dead, Hall & Oates, Kirstie Alley, Glenn Close, Goldie Hawn and Whoopi Goldberg, among others, have backed it as well.

Singer-songwriter Carole King, an Alliance board member who owns the Robinson Bar Ranch in central Idaho, says it's important to protect wilderness for the human spirit as well as for the earth. "I definitely feel the spiritual necessity to protect wilderness as well as the physical necessity," she says. "We're also talking about protecting the health of the planet."

Adds the Dead's Bob Weir, "The timber barons and extractive industries have had their way with our national forests for long enough. Our ancient forests of the Northern Rockies don't belong to the industrialists. They belong to the children, to the future, to the earth itself."

By all accounts, the Alliance has hatched the most Utopian wilderness, parks and wild rivers plan for saving "the best of what's left" in the Northern Rockies. It's the boldest scheme to emerge in the West since Earth First! proposed turning most of the landscape west of the Mississippi River into wilderness over a decade ago.

If approved by Congress, the Alliance plan would rival the 1980 Alaska Lands Act in size and scope. The Alaska bill protected 163,000 square miles of wilderness and parks in one fell swoop.

The Alliance seeks to ban logging on nearly all the pristine national forest lands remaining in the region—some 28,125 square miles, an expanse of land larger than West Virginia. Protected lands would be scattered across five states: eastern

Washington, eastern Oregon, Idaho, Montana and northwest Wyoming.

Unlike wilderness plans limited to individual states, the Alliance focuses on an ecosystem approach that transcends state boundaries. It would add lands to improve the biological integrity of the Greater Yellowstone Ecosystem, the greater Salmon River/Selway-Bitterroot ecosystem, greater Glacier ecosystem, greater Hells Canyon/Wallowa Mountains ecosystem and greater Cabinet/Yaak/Selkirk ecosystem.

The Alliance plan calls for protecting lands that serve as wildlife travel corridors between the five ecosystems as wilderness or restricting development in them to a minimum. Other provisions would protect dozens of streams as federal wild and scenic rivers, launch studies of turning Hells Canyon into a national park and expanding Glacier National Park, and initiate a program to restore damaged forest lands.

The plan is an environmental wish list for preserving the last of the wild frontier. Instead of watching the high mountain slopes get carved into clear-cuts, open-pit gold mines or overgrazed cow pastures, the Alliance suggests the forests would best serve America as refuges for public recreation and biological diversity.

Lee Metzgar, a professor of biology at the University of Montana, argues that wilderness is the only way to protect key habitat for wildlife.

He notes that environmental groups often have to sue federal agencies to force them to make a decision on endangered species petitions. Even the scientific data for reviewing a petition can be manipulated by politics, Metzgar says.

"The system is failing, and, by default, wilderness is the only tool for saving species that we've got," he said. "NREPA is the only coherent plan out there."

Politics, it is said, is the art of the possible. Under the current political framework in Congress, passing something like the Alliance bill is considered impossible by national environmental lobbyists.

Brock Evans of Audubon notes that, for the last 15 years, wilderness legislation has been handled on a state-by-state basis. For a bill to move at all, it must be acceptable to at least one member of a state's congressional delegation. In the case of Montana and Idaho, where most—some 16 million acres—of the de facto wilderness is located, senators and representatives have never supported bills that protect even 2 million acres of new wilderness.

Nearly all the senators and representatives from the Northern Rockies are conservative Republicans who strongly favor resource development. They also receive large campaign contributions from extractive industries.

Many politicians think Montana and Idaho have too much wilderness already, and they constantly pressure the U.S. Forest Service to log roadless areas and remove restrictions to mining, livestock grazing and off-road vehicle use.

Timber industry officials say they would support a fairly large wilderness bill if environmentalists agreed to release the remaining forests for development. But since the Alliance wants it all, industry spokesman Ken Kohli says loggers have no incentive to support the plan.

"Their proposal is just too massive—it's never going to fly," Kohli says.

Given those political realities, national environmental lobbyists say a multistate bill is nearly impossible to move.

"All it takes is one senator from one state to kill a bill," Alberswerth points out. "Even if you could get even one member from the Northern Rockies interested in a multi-state bill, another member could kill it."

So unless the Alliance, Greenpeace and celebrities can rally national support for NREPA and make wilderness a national priority, lobbyists say it's futile to try to push a multistate wilderness bill over the top of the Northern Rockies senators and representatives.

Mike Bader disagrees. "The nationals have gotten so wimpy on this issue they're just willing to go along with what Congress tells them to do. No wonder we haven't broken this iron-clad grip on wilderness. We think you have to have the courage to stick by your proposal," he says.

But will the Alliance ever protect one acre of ground with that attitude? Debbie Sease, director of the Sierra Club's public-lands program, says an all-or-nothing approach could yield nothing.

"If you focus on a long-term vision, there's a big concern about what might fall through the cracks," she says. "If you go for it all, you might not get anything. But if you go for something smaller, you'll at least protect some of the critical areas, and hopefully, you'll leave a latch string so you can open the door and come in again to protect some more."

As for rolling a wilderness bill over the top of Western political leaders, Sease says it's doubtful. Even the Ancient Forests campaign, which built a strong national coalition to protect old-growth forests in western Washington and Oregon, couldn't push a proposal past House Speaker Tom Foley, D-Wash.

"There's a growing perception that our forest lands are a national legacy," Sease said. "But I just don't see a scenario where a multi-state bill could be rolled over the local delegations."

That's why the national groups supported the most recent Montana wilderness bill. It protected key areas that local grass-roots groups, such as the Montana Wilderness Association and Greater Yellowstone Coalition, have worked to protect for years, Sease says.

"Why not protect 2.2 million acres now and preserve our options in the future?" Alberswerth asks. "Let's take what we can get while we can."

During debate over the Montana bill in the House, the NREPA plan went to a vote for the first time. Kostmayer introduced a version of NREPA as a substitute to the Montana bill. National and regional groups supporting the Montana bill said that was a mistake—that the bill didn't have a chance—and they opposed it.

They were right. The Kostmayer amendment was defeated by

voice vote in the House. The version favored by the national groups passed 282–123.

"It was the best Montana wilderness bill ever passed by a house of Congress," says John Gatchell, conservation director for the Montana Wilderness Association.

But even that bill perished at the hands of Montana conservative Republicans Sen. Conrad Burns and Rep. Ron Marlenee.

So neither strategy actually protected any new wilderness in Montana. Meanwhile, the Forest Service, at the urging of Western congressmen and the timber industry, is chipping away at the final frontier—planning timber sales in roadless areas.

Region 1 Forest Service Chief Dave Jolly pledged after the Montana bill was defeated to push ahead with timber sales in roadless areas. "We did agree in our forest plans to enter some of these roadless areas," he told *The Missoulian.*

However, Jolly adds, because many people want to protect roadless lands as wilderness, he wishes Congress would resolve the issue. "It will be difficult to get the public to accept logging in roadless areas until there is a wilderness bill," he says. "As I've talked to people around the region, there is a constituency for every one of the roadless areas. When we start analyzing the effects of entering any one of them, we hear from people."

In the aftermath of the Montana bill, the Alliance, Greater Yellowstone Coalition and Montana Wilderness Association have been meeting with their members on what to do next. But Alliance backers were still so angry they refused to attend a recent wilderness strategy session with the coalition.

Mike Medberry, public-lands director for the Idaho Conservation League, says the Alliance ought to smoke the peace pipe with groups such as the Montana Wilderness Association, Yellowstone Coalition and national groups, and then work together on a multi-state bill. On the other hand, national environmental groups shouldn't settle for "political realities" as defined by Congress, he says.

But most of all, Medberry says, "We've all got to pull together, or we're never going to get anything done."

GUEST EDITORIAL

Wilderness Politics are Anything but Simple

BY LOUISE BRUCE

President, Montana Wilderness Association governing council

The case for complexity in nature grows daily The modern con-servation vocabulary swells with terms like "biodiversity," "ecosystems," "cumulative effects" and "bioregions." More people are learning that all things and processes are interconnected, and most conservationists agree that a deeper understanding of inter-connectedness will lead to better human relationships with our world.

Why, then, do some people refuse to recognize the principle of interconnectedness in politics?

The question presented itself in Stephen Stuebner's story centering on Montana wilderness legislation. The Montana wilderness bill passed by the U.S. House last fall, Stuebner writes, "brought cheers" from the Montana Wilderness Association, Greater Yellowstone Coalition, Sierra Club, The Wilderness Society and National Audubon Society.

Wrong. What brought approval from those organizations, or at least the Montana Wilderness Association, was the House's rejec-tion of a contemptible bill passed by the Senate and its amendment of that bill to include additional wilderness areas, recognition of wilderness water rights, and better release language.

We didn't "cheer" the House bill; we encouraged people in the House for making positive changes.

It's understandable why that distinction would be lost on a reporter, whose zeal to plumb the interconnectedness of things might be tempered by deadlines or bias. What's difficult to understand is why strategic subtleties are lost on the Alliance for the Wild Rockies, an organization that extols the idea of interconnectedness...except in the political realm.

As evidence that several conservation organizations sold out in the waning days of the recent congress, the Alliance points to a letter signed by groups that urged House members to support the bill from Reps. Pat Williams, D-Mont., and Bruce Vento, D-Minn., and not a measure offered by Rep. Peter Kostmayer, D-Pa., the chief sponsor of the Alliance-authored Northern Rockies Ecosystem Protection Act.

For those who admit that wilderness politics aren't always simple, two reasons for the letter stand out.

Kostmayer's Bill Was DOA

First, Kostmayer's bill was dead on arrival, having no chance to pass against the wishes of the House Interior Committee and two of the most respected environmental legislators in Congress, Reps. George Miller, D-Calif., and Vento.

Second, there was a valid fear among conservationists that Montana's Rep. Ron Marlenee, R, might succeed, if he maneuvered adroitly, in amending the Vento-Williams bill to include hard release language, the ultimate bane of any wilderness legislation. We could not allow confusion on the House floor over amendments to enhance that possibility.

Some conservationists therefore adopted a strategy that addressed perceived realities and offered the best chance for maximizing wilderness in any bill that passed the House.

Those who question—as the Alliance frequently does—the need to weigh political realities in lobbying for wilderness should examine the moves made by the Alliance's top ally in Congress at the time last fall when Montana legislation reached a climax.

Rep. Kostmayer did not share his plans with the Montana Wilderness Association and several other groups, nor did he, as it turned out, introduce the Alliance's bill on the House floor. He offered instead a substitute to the Williams-Vento bill that addressed only Montana portions of the Alliance's multi-state plan.

Even then, Kostmayer's substitute was flawed. It failed to designate as wilderness over a million acres of roadless land that Montanans have spent years trying to protect, including the Crazy Mountains, Thompson Seton, Great Burn, Trout Creek, East Pioneers and others. Oddly, the Williams-Vento bill, insufficient as it was, protected 300,000 acres that the Kostmayer substitute did not.

Quite obviously, Rep. Kostmayer was a friend of Montana wilderness. But equally as obvious, he made some decisions in the heat of legislative action that didn't toe the ideological line established by his favorite constituents. Could it be that, when crunch time arrived, even the greatest congressional ally of a multi-state wilderness bill was forced to deal with political reality, and when he did, he was bound, as all mortals are, to make some mistakes?

The All-or-Nothing Approach

None of this is to say that conservationists shouldn't support the Alliance's goal and strive to gain maximum protection for all wildlands in all states of the Northern Rockies. But the Alliance wants that protection only as it comes in one bill and at one time. Will that strategy result in maximum wilderness return?

Is it wise, for example, for Montana conservationists to immediately incorporate the roadless lands of Idaho and Wyoming into their legislative objectives? Would more of Montana's wild country be protected if its fate were heavily influenced not only by Conrad Burns and Max Baucus, but also by Alan Simpson, Malcolm Wallop, Larry Craig and Idaho's newest wilderness anachronism, Dirk Kempthorne?

Yes, of course we need to replace our local delegations. Yes, of course we need to build national constituencies for sweeping environmental legislation in the West. But how long will it take to accomplish those things, and what will we pay for the wait?

During the 1980s, over 500,000 acres of roadless land in Montana were logged, roaded or otherwise developed. More recently, areas such as the Badger-Two Medicine, Lost Silver, Mount Bushnell and Nevada Mountain have been pushed precariously close to the chopping block. The Forest Service is now jumping through the legal and administrative hoops to enter those and several other roadless areas. The idea that roadless lands in Montana (or in Idaho, where over 200 timber sales are now being planned for roadless areas) are safe until a wilderness bill passes is a costly myth.

The dilemma of timing is illustrated sharply, if unintentionally, in a letter recently sent to the Montana Wilderness Association by David Brower, celebrated conservationist and current president of the Earth Island Action Group.

In making an argument for the Montana Wilderness Association to embrace the Northern Rockies Ecosystem Protection Act, Brower refers to the Association's past leadership in gaining protection for the Scapegoat, Absaroka-Beartooth and Great Bear wilderness areas, as well as the Wild and Scenic segment of the Missouri River. By winning those past issues, Brower says, the Association has a record of uncompromising advocacy.

One Step at a Time

But look again. The Lincoln-Scapegoat backcountry wasn't entirely protected in 1972. Twenty years later, we're still trying to add 100,000 acres to the original designation of 250,000 acres.

Likewise, we didn't win everything in the Absaroka-Beartooth in 1978. We're still trying to add tens of thousands of acres—Line Creek Plateau, Republic Mountain, Burnt Mountain, Mount Rae, Tie Creek, Dexter Point, Coffee Creek and Dome Mountain—not included in the original designation.

We didn't complete the Great Bear in 1978. We're still trying to add significant roadless acreages on both the Middle and South Forks of the Flathead River.

And the Wild Missouri? We've barely begun. There are dozens of riparian BLM areas that need wilderness designation if the Missouri River ecosystem in central Montana is to remain healthy.

Brower's recommendation that conservationists settle for nothing less than immediate and complete protection of all wildlands remaining in five states contradicts the very evidence he offers to support his counsel. Would Brower—or the Alliance—argue that the Montana Wilderness Association should have opposed the legislation that established the Scapegoat, Great Bear and Absaroka-Beartooth wilderness areas because the bills didn't protect 100 percent of the areas at one time?

Victories in the conservation arena—or anywhere else—are seldom complete or static. As an undeniable element of nature, wilderness politics is defined as much by processes as by objects, and the failure to understand those processes is a failure to understand the idea of interconnectedness. The Scapegoat Wilderness victory will never be total: It will be accomplished in steps—first 250,000 acres, then 100,000 acres, then again as much acreage as necessary to sustain the area's health.

Complex as the political process sometimes is, the Montana Wilderness Association's position is straightforward: We will commit every resource we have, for as long as it takes, to protect all wild country in Montana. In the matter of wildlands legislation, we insist on optimum boundaries and maximum acreage, but our ultimate, non-negotiable interest will be statutory language that allows the American public to revisit and expand wilderness boundaries whenever it chooses to do so.

The goals of the Montana Wilderness Association and the Alliance for the Wild Rockies are similar, but our methods differ, particularly as they apply to human interconnectedness. "When people get in the way," says Steve Kelly, the president of the Alliance, "we ask them to move. When they don't move, you've got to go around them."

That's the language of exclusion and proscription, the antithesis of grassroots activism. Wilderness will endure only with popular support; people won't change their environmental attitudes simply because someone who professes to know better has told them to do so. At the Montana Wilderness Association, when people get in the way and don't move, we strive to listen, to inform and—if we're good at our work—to build new support for preservation of the wild. In a state where just six weeks ago, 47 percent of the electorate voted for Republican Ron Marlenee, that's a long-term challenge many conservation groups won't face up to.

The Alliance professes a profound belief in man's responsibility to manage ecosystems, but it practices political separatism. The Alliance wants to preserve diversity, but it condemns behavior that doesn't conform to its own.

The Montana Wilderness Association encourages the Alliance's promotion of ecosystem protection and we welcome criticism that will help the Association become a better advocate for that cause. But the Alliance's mean-spirited treatment of allies is a counterproductive waste of energy. If the Alliance really wants people to understand interconnectedness, it should lead by example.

GUEST EDITORIAL

The Only Hope for Wilderness Is to Save All the Parts

BY MIKE BADER

Executive director, Alliance for the Wild Rockies

Over four decades ago, Aldo Leopold, the father of the modern conservation movement, wrote, "The first step in intelligent tinkering is to save all the parts."

In the Lower 48 states, only the Northern Rockies support virtually all the species that roamed the area at the time of the Lewis and Clark Expedition. Free-roaming populations of grizzly bear, gray wolf, caribou, lynx, salmon, bull trout, wolverine, bison, rare plants and a host of others, both known and unknown, survive here. Most of the biological "parts" that Leopold spoke of remain—in an incredible diversity of landscapes ranging from high cactus desert to temperate rainforest. Yet today, most of the key indicators of ecosystem health and stability are on the threatened and endangered species lists, and the integrity of the Northern Rockies ecosystem is imperiled.

Politics vs. Ecosystem Integrity

Virtually everyone on the conservationist side opposes the destruction of any of our remaining roadless areas, which form the core component of our ecosystems. However, there is debate over how best to protect them. The 320 grassroots member organizations and businesses, and the supporters that make up the Alliance for the Wild Rockies, advocate a multi-state ecosystem approach based on the principles of conservation biology, economics and environmental law. This new vision is represented by the Northern Rockies Ecosystem Protection Act, whose key purpose is protection of native biodiversity. Some organizations and individuals advocate a piecemeal approach grounded in parochial politics and represented by last year's failed Montana "wilderness" bill.

In arguing for the state-by-state approach, supporters claim that wilderness advocates can return to Congress at some time in the future to seek wilderness protection for those areas released (4 million acres in the Montana bill). The Alliance for the Wild Rockies advocates that either all remaining roadless areas should be protected in a given bill, or that legal means of protecting areas not included should be maintained. Moreover, history tells us that once a statewide bill is passed, there is little or no hope of passing another before what remains is gone, or hopelessly fragmented.

Consider what happened in Oregon and Washington after they failed to protect full ranges of habitat in wilderness bills, and supported release language: The bad bills passed, the timber floodgates opened, and now an ecosystem is ravaged to the point where scientists don't even known if it can be restored. Release language is a green light for roading and clear-cutting, and eliminating citizens' rights to appeal and litigate against development decisions. People who support release language are in effect saying, "It's okay for the Forest Service to violate national environmental laws in its efforts to destroy roadless areas."

The piecemeal approach is mired in the standard political rhetoric that "passing a bill is essential to solving the wilderness question once and for all." This speaks of finality, not future protection. With the exception of Alaska, it is extremely rare for a state to add more wilderness after passing a statewide bill.

Moreover, piecemeal advocates have not articulated a strategy for how to defend the millions of acres that are released all at once. Until such a plan exists, it is clear that no bill at all is much better than a bad bill.

A Fourth of a Loaf Equals None

Some feel the ecosystem plan represents "an-all-or-nothing approach." With wildlands in the Northern Rockies now at or below the biological minimum in terms of sustaining native wildlife populations, failure to protect the remaining wild areas does mean that for certain species we end up with nothing. Grizzly bears, bull trout and other sensitive species can't survive on a fourth of a loaf. An area-by-area legislative approach can be effective—providing it doesn't give anything else away. It can work without release language or prescriptive language facilitating development actions in other wild areas. Unfortunately, the last decade has yielded no such legislation in the Northern Rockies.

Conservationists must work in the times they are in. The days of local conservation-minded legislators like Montana Sens. Lee Metcalf, D, and Mike Mansfield, D, and Idaho's Sen. Frank Church, D, who carried the great area-by-area bills of the 1970s, have passed.

Regarding the Montana bill, conservation biologist Dr. Reed Noss said in the *Amicus Journal*: "The defeatist attitude really gets me. If the compromises that a lot of the national groups seem willing to make don't maintain ecosystems and the more sensitive species, what good does it really do? Such a strategy is less than viable, biologically."

Low expectations produce mediocre results. Examples include the numerous failed Montana and Idaho bills which had a common theme: release of virtually all forested wilderness and limitations on judicial review. Rep. Pat Williams, D-Mont., has said that release language in a 1993 version of a Montana bill will be identical to past bills. Rep. Larry LaRocco, D-Idaho, has embarked on a similar effort to legislate logging of roadless areas throughout Idaho, totaling more than 9 million acres.

The best we can hope for with the state-by-state approach is a protracted defeat.

National Constituency a Must

The ecosystem approach can succeed where others have failed because there is a strong national constituency for the Northern Rockies. World-class treasures such as Yellowstone, Glacier, Hells Canyon and the Frank Church region have captured the imaginations of millions. It's difficult at best to rally national support for just one roadless area. However, when considering the last relatively intact forest ecosystems in the temperate zones of the earth, there is a real sense of national urgency and purpose. This constituency is being rapidly awakened by the Northern Rockies Ecosystem Protection Act effort. We outweigh the industry interests represented so ably by our regional senators and representatives the same way as before: with the sheer force of public opinion. It's *our* land. These same senators always line up against wilderness anyway, and must be overcome, no matter the scope of the legislation. Let's rephrase the debate in a way that maximizes our influences.

This approach allows us to defeat bad bills while we continue building the necessary support to pass a good one. After all, the timber industry can't by itself consummate wholesale deals that release millions of acres at once to the chainsaws. If they could, they would have already. Only with the acquiescence of conservationists do such deals become reality.

Thinking Big Enough to Save Ecosystems

Given the wealth of new biological and economic data, virtually no conservationist argues against the need to protect entire ecosystems and the essential linkages between them. Still, the fear of change is powerful, given the intransigence of Congress. But Congress works for the people, not the other way around. That's why the public must be rallied as never before. Alliance for the Wild Rockies and other grassroots groups have a strong program of town meetings, training workshops and other grass-roots outreach that are the backbone of ecosystem advocacy. Stressing empowerment of the people and lasting ecosystem protection, the results are showing: Forest Service surveys of citizens living near the national forests in Montana and Northern Idaho show overwhelming support for roadless area protection. At least 65 to 75 percent of the people are opposed to any roadless area development, and believe the national forests need to be managed more for wilderness and wildlife values, with less logging and motorized vehicle use.

Finally, effective ecosystem protection doesn't begin or end with legislation. It requires the endless coordination of programs, including appeals and litigation, research and education, outreach and organizing.

While the Northern Rockies Ecosystem Protection Act is based on science, economics and law, nobody should be fooled into thinking that this vision is devoid of a political strategy. Indeed, just getting the Northern Rockies Ecosystem Protection Act introduced, and later ensuring a House floor debate over ecosystems, took considerable political skill and maneuvering. Conservationists have the experience and advice of people like Stewart Brandborg, John Craighead and many others who helped shape and enact the seminal environmental laws of this nation, including the Wilderness Act, the Endangered Species Act and the Wild and Scenic Rivers Act. These visionaries ran into similar roadblocks from people saying they were naive and lacking in appreciation for "political reality." They recognized that realities change. We are changing the political reality of the '90s, and we will prevail.

President Clinton has charted a new course for our country, based on the belief that we must not be afraid of change. A new politics of hope and empowerment has taken hold, showing genuine promise that years of frustration and mediocrity can be reversed with a spirit of cooperation and success, and a wildlands legacy in the Northern Rockies that can make Aldo Leopold and all of us proud.

APRIL 26, 1999

Visionaries or Dreamers?

BY GREG HANSCOM

The bottle of tequila circling the campfire wasn't doing much for the border country silence. Laughter and off-color jokes drifted up from the ring of wilderness hounds, over the Chisos Mountains in Big Bend National Park to where a full moon burned a perfect hole in the sky.

Above the din rose the drawl of Dave Foreman, the leader of Earth First!—a group of die-hard environmentalists determined to wage war against industrial society in the name of Mother Earth. It was 1984, and the group was headed for its heyday. Before the decade was out, activists would don spotted owl suits to protest logging, lock themselves to bulldozers, and unfurl a black plastic "crack" down the face of Glen Canyon Dam to lament the drowning of a redrock canyon. Around the West, monkey wrenchers pounded trees with spikes to keep them standing and toppled billboards in their stead.

"It was the only time I ever heard Foreman sing," recalls Barbara Dugelby, at the time a leader of the Texas Earth First! chapter. Her collection of hippie university students and biologists had trekked across the desert from Austin to meet Foreman and his Tucson, Ariz., clan.

Then, late in the evening, Foreman performed a miracle. He downed the last of the tequila, worm and all; with a great whoop, he heaved the bottle toward the heavens and toppled over backward in his lawn chair. A dozen pairs of eyes watched the bottle spin upward and disappear into the dark. They froze like a bunch of kids around a well waiting for the splash of a dropped rock. But they never heard the bottle shatter. The only

345

sound that cracked the air was the cackle of coyotes.

"We decided it never came down," says Dugelby.

"I had a two-week hangover," says Foreman, "and I haven't touched a bottle of tequila since."

But Foreman still fires things toward the sky. Seven years later, he joined a more sober gathering in San Francisco. At that 1991 meeting, an alliance of high-powered scientists and activists launched the "Wildlands Project." The project's goals were as ambitious and arrogant as its founders: to stitch together the roaded, subdivided landscape of North America and create a place where wolves, grizzly bears and other native wildlife could live as they had 500 years ago.

The Wildlands Project, which now has a staff of 10 based in Tucson, is a different beast than Earth First! Foreman left behind protests, blazing headlines and an arrest in favor of behind-the-scenes planning, lofty scientific ideals and a vision he says may take a century or more to realize. He said farewell to the hippie anarchists, and teamed up with conservation biologists and computer-mapping experts.

Foreman hasn't escaped his past altogether, however. Like the wolves and grizzlies he champions, Foreman is a lightning rod. To some, he is a visionary; to others, he is a threat. And like Earth First!, the Wildlands Project has the power to polarize as well as invigorate. While a new generation of activists is rallying around the project, critics say that they are aimed for a head-on collision with political leaders and rural people.

For nearly a decade, Wildlands Project supporters have batted their ideas around mapping tables, college classrooms and more than a few campfires. But the project has spun there, mid-air, with seemingly little relevance to what's happening in the real world.

This year, the project will finally hit the ground. Critics say it will shatter like so much junk glass. But a surprising group of proponents believes that the Wildlands Project has already percolated into the halls of environmental groups and federal agencies. They say it will revolutionize the way we look at the land.

An Earth First! Exodus

What happened between the launching of the tequila bottle and the launching of the Wildlands Project is a story of two paths— activism and science—that met over pancakes, eggs and a whole lot of coffee in a diner in Ann Arbor, Mich.

Barbara Dugelby spent the mid-1980s with Texas Earth First! doing street theater, direct action and going after the U.S. Forest Service to protect the endangered red-cockaded woodpecker. The group met with some success: It prodded the Texas attorney general to sue the Forest Service over its forest management plan and convinced the city of Austin to adopt an endangered species ordinance.

But Dugelby and her compatriots were frustrated at always being on the defensive, fighting over a timber sale here, an endangered species there, while developers and industry carved up the landscape.

"Earth First! had attracted a lot of intellectuals, people with academic backgrounds who started to wonder, 'What can I contribute here?'" says Kieran Suckling, who left Earth First! and helped found the media- and law-savvy Southwest Center for Biological Diversity in Tucson. "We realized there was this huge untapped world of litigation, scientific research and conservation planning that was stuck in these test tubes in universities and wasn't getting out into the world."

Then, on May 31, 1989, armed FBI agents stormed Foreman's Tucson apartment and arrested him.

The same day, agents arrested four other Earth First!ers, charging them with conspiracy and eco-sabotage. Four of them would do jail time. After a drawn-out trial, Foreman would plead guilty to felony conspiracy and agree not to speak out about monkey wrenching.

The arrest of the "Arizona Five" was a tough dose of reality for Foreman's academic-minded wilderness defenders. Over the next year, many split off from Earth First! and tried to put as much distance between themselves and their monkey-wrenching pasts as possible.

Earth First!ers like Suckling and Jasper Carlton, who had started the Earth First! Biodiversity Project a few years earlier, turned to "paper monkey wrenching" in the courtrooms. Wielding the National Forest Management Act, the National Environmental Policy Act and the Endangered Species Act like clubs, they halted logging on Southwest national forests for 10 months over the endangered Mexican spotted owl, kicked cows off streams, and put animals like the jaguar and Preble's meadow jumping mouse and plants like the lady's tresses orchid on the endangered species list.

Others, like Barbara Dugelby and Reed Noss, threw all their energy into science to achieve their conservation goals. Like Foreman, they were convinced that in order to stop the nation's wildlife from spiraling into oblivion, they would have to come up with a vision for North America based on the best science available.

"I came to science from extreme activism," says Dugelby. "I wanted to do visionary conservation activism."

Activism and Science Intersect

The man who could teach her more about the subject than anyone was Michael Soulé, a slight, goateed scientist in his 60s, known in academic circles as the father of conservation biology. Soulé, who had studied under ecologist Paul Ehrlich, author of the 1968 book, *The Population Bomb*, concluded that he could not sit back and be an "objective" scientist while the natural world went to hell.

The human race was driving the sixth great extinction crisis, Soulé believed, on a par with the disappearance of the dinosaurs and of Pleistocene creatures like the woolly mammoth and the saber-toothed tiger. It was only natural, he thought, to search for ways to protect life, and his profession. Taking the cue from Aldo

Leopold and others, he added conscience to science. Soulé's conservation biology has been likened to medicine; it's science aimed at healing the land.

Conservation biology grew largely out of a school of thought called island biogeography. The theory was pioneered by such notable naturalists as Charles Darwin, and captured in the 1967 book, *The Theory of Island Biogeography*, by ecologist Robert MacArthur and biologist Edward O. Wilson. Its basic principle is that large islands close to the mainland can support more types of plants and animals than smaller, more isolated islands. As islands shrink, species fall prey to inbreeding and accidents, and start dying off.

The principle applies to the mainland as well. In 1984, Michigan graduate student Bill Newmark traveled around the West, visiting national parks and setting up camp in their libraries. In the records of wildlife sightings, he found an unsettling picture: National parks had become islands in a sea of development. Large parks such as Banff and Jasper in Alberta, Canada, still held all the creatures that were seen 100 years ago. But smaller parks were losing residents.

Yosemite had lost the mink and the black-tailed jackrabbit. The white-tailed jackrabbit, red fox and spotted skunk had disappeared from Bryce Canyon in Utah. Most startling was Lassen Volcanic National Park in Northern California—a mountain park surrounded by the heavily logged and roaded Lassen National Forest. Since its establishment in 1907, the tiny park had lost six animal species: the Nuttall's cottontail, fisher, river otter, striped skunk, ringtail and pronghorn.

Newmark's conclusion, published in the journal *Nature* in 1987, was that virtually none of the national parks in the West were large enough to provide a long-term home for the animals that lived there.

If we were serious about saving the West's wildlife, argued Michael Soulé, we would have to protect larger wilderness areas, buffer them from development and connect them with migration corridors to allow isolated animal populations to reach one another. Where there were islands of wilderness surrounded by a sea of humanity, he wanted to see human islands in a sea of wilderness.

So where do the pancakes and eggs come into the picture? By the late 1980s, Soulé and Foreman knew each other's work— Soulé had been publishing papers in the scientific journals, and Foreman and his cronies had followed conservation biology in the *Earth First! Journal*. But the two had never met.

In 1988, Barbara Dugelby, who had come to the University of Michigan in Ann Arbor to study with Soulé, arranged to have Dave Foreman and Sierra Club "archdruid" David Brower speak at the university. The next morning, she took Foreman, Brower and Soulé out to a local diner for breakfast. Brower shoveled his eggs onto his pancakes and coffee flowed like the Colorado River in spring.

The talk revolved around the fate of the conservation movement and the need for a broader, science-based vision, recalls Dugelby. Soulé expressed his support for radical conservation that set the standards much higher than standards set by the big greens like the Sierra Club and The Wilderness Society. He also emphasized that, for the first time, science could demonstrate the need for a system of large-scale, interconnected nature reserves.

In Foreman, Soulé saw the passion and the drive to take his science to the people. And in Soulé's science, Foreman saw the foundation for his vision. The wilderness preacher had found his new gospel.

The Cover of the Puzzle Box

The diner breakfast led to a larger gathering of scientists and activists in 1991 in San Francisco. About a dozen wilderness activists from around the country spent two-and-a-half intense days on Russian Hill at the house of Doug Tompkins, who had used his Esprit clothing fortune to start the Foundation for Deep

Ecology. It was there, in a green oasis in the middle of the city, that Foreman, Soulé and 11 others launched the Wildlands Project. "Our vision is simple," they wrote later. "We live for the day when grizzlies in Chihuahua have an unbroken connection to grizzlies in Alaska; when gray wolf populations are continuous from New Mexico to Greenland; when vast unbroken forests and flowing plains again thrive and support pre-Columbian populations of plants and animals; when humans dwell with respect, harmony, and affection for the land; when we come to live no longer as strangers and aliens to this continent."

In more recent iterations of the mission statement, the word "simple" has been replaced with "ambitious." Still, some folks think a more fitting description would be "pie in the sky."

Maybe, but the project serves a purpose, says Soulé, who retired from the University of California at Santa Cruz three years ago and moved to rural western Colorado. "Our mission is to embolden the conservation movement to think much bigger and on a larger time scale," he says. He compares the Wildlands Project to building the great European cathedrals: Many of the workers died before the buildings were finished, but without the grand architectural plans, they never would have been built. "Without an inspiring vision," Soulé says, "nothing is going to happen on the ground."

The project is aloof by design. Its founders did not want to compete with existing conservation groups. They wanted to create a framework those groups could work within, and a clearinghouse for information and science. They modeled the group after the old Wilderness Society, where Foreman had worked as a lobbyist and organizer before starting Earth First! Foreman describes The Wilderness Society of the 1970s as "a great collection of old wilderness warriors working with local, independent groups."

Based in a nondescript Tucson, Ariz., office complex, the Wildlands Project now has 10 paid staff and no members. Its money comes entirely from donations and foundation grants. Its mouthpiece is *Wild Earth* magazine, based in Richmond, Vt., which is technically a separate organization, but is overseen by Foreman, as its publisher. Reading *Wild Earth* is a little like watching Christians debate the Bible. Wilderness is Truth in these pages, and Foreman is happy to take on any who question it.

The task of making wilderness real on the ground falls to regional groups that are busy remapping the continent. In the West, there are 10 affiliates. One, Yellowstone to Yukon, or "Y2Y," based in Canmore, Alberta, is trying to protect an 1,800-mile stretch of the Northern Rockies from Yellowstone National Park to Canada's Yukon Territory. In Bellingham, Wash., the Northwest Ecosystem Alliance is gearing up for an "R2R" (Rainforest to Rockies) campaign to reconnect the Cascades to the Rockies.

From Casper, Wyo., south through Colorado to northern New Mexico, the Southern Rockies Ecosystem Project is mapping territory for reintroducing wolves. And farther south, where the U.S. Fish and Wildlife Service has already returned wolves to the wild, the Sky Island Alliance is mapping habitat for grizzly bears from New Mexico's Gila Wilderness to the Sierra Madre in northern Mexico.

Wildlands mappers start with state and federal agencies that have information about the ranges of plants and animals, and the extent of human development. But agency data is often fragmented or out of date, says Bill Martin, mapping coordinator with the Southern Rockies Ecosystem Project in Boulder. The next step is to get people out on the ground, surveying roads and roadless areas, taking inventory of old-growth forest, counting trail users and looking for signs of important or rare wildlife.

All of this information is fed into a computer, which spits out a map of the world from wildlife's point of view. "After a while, you start to see how a landscape fits together," Martin says. "The Wildlands Project is big-time, big theory. This is a way to communicate that. People see things on a map that would take a 20-page paper to write."

Wildlands mappers provide the vision, explains Foreman, while grassroots groups will make it all happen. "It's like the picture on the cover of a jigsaw puzzle box," he says. "We don't know which group is going to put each piece down."

Big Cats and Blood

Bill Martin admits that some people look at his maps and see nothing but red. "Maps are dangerous," he says, and explains that many wildlands affiliates have become wary of releasing the maps to the public. He tells the story of a 1997 range tour in western Colorado, where one of his maps went off like a bomb. The tour was sponsored by the Delta-Montrose Public Lands Partnership, a group of environmentalists, ranchers and recreationists that was looking at the Forest Service's travel management plan for the Uncompahgre Plateau.

Martin's map showed "core" areas for wildlife, from which he thought motorized vehicles and cattle should be excluded. He hadn't intended to show it to the group, but someone got a copy and passed it around.

"That put me on one hell of a spot. I was completely blindsided," says Southern Rockies Ecosystem Project President Dennis Hall. "They jumped all over me. They were asking, 'What about the people who graze their cows out there?'"

Also sure to raise hackles is planned habitat for top-of-the-food-chain critters with big teeth.

Conservation biologists argue that if you protect large predators, you protect a host of other animals as well. Large predators need large areas of relatively unmolested country to survive. An adult male grizzly bear, for example, needs 300 to 500 square miles, so if you protect enough wilderness to support a population of grizzlies, you're bound to catch lots of smaller, less charismatic animals and plants.

Big predators need big wilderness, but does wilderness need predators? Absolutely, says Soulé. Remove predators, and the whole landscape suffers. In Yellowstone National Park, for example, wolves were wiped out in the 1920s. Without its main predator, the northern Yellowstone elk herd has grown so large that it has grazed the range down to tatters, say some scientists.

One of the best illustrations of the importance of predators to natural systems comes from Alaska's Aleutian Islands, where Russian fur hunters drove the sea otter almost to extinction in the late 1800s. Today, otters have returned to some islands but not to others, and the difference is striking. University of California Santa Cruz biologist Jim Estes found that the waters surrounding islands without otters are relatively barren; sea urchins have grazed plants down to the ocean floor.

But where otters have returned, they've eaten enough sea urchins to allow a rich kelp forest to grow, and along with the kelp come fish, bald eagles and sea ducks. Estes calls the otter a "keystone species" because it has an inordinate impact on the shape of the entire ecosystem.

The same goes for wolves, grizzly bears, mountain lions and an array of other animals that ranchers and the federal government have done their best to drive out of the West.

"If your goal is to protect biodiversity, we have to have large carnivores," says Soulé. "In order to save the wilderness in Colorado, we have to have the wolf and grizzly back."

Or as Dave Foreman put it at a conference last October, flashing a slide of an African lion making a gory meal of a gazelle: "This is what the Wildlands Project is all about: Big cats and blood."

Fear and Loathing

Talk of "rewilding" North America gives some people nightmares of wolves running through the streets of Chicago and of grizzlies in L.A. One critic has posted "simulated" wildlands reserve maps on the Internet, showing the entire Western United States as wilderness areas or "Buffer Zones—Highly Regulated Use." Similar maps have shown up in small towns around the West.

"Foreman's dream, known as the Wildlands Project, has transmuted to an Orwellian nightmare, supported by innumerable

U.N. agencies, embraced by the United Nations Environmental Programme, UNESCO, the Sierra Club, The Nature Conservancy, the U.S. Department of the Interior and the EPA," writes another alarmed onlooker. "It is being unleashed relentlessly across America."

The backlash is no surprise to some observers, who say the Wildlands Project is ivory-tower conservation at its worst. In their excitement about creating a new wild America, Wildlands backers have forgotten about people, they say. And without concern for people, the project will be about as welcome as a rattlesnake in a sleeping bag.

Supporters within the environmental community also have reservations. "You want to talk about island biogeography—let's talk about island political geography," says Steve Hinchman, director of the Western Slope Environmental Resource Council in Paonia, Colo., a rural coal-mining and fruit-growing community that is also the home of *High Country News*. "Their supporters live in Boulder, Salt Lake and Santa Fe. They're like isolated gene pools that have been inbreeding too long."

Hinchman's group sponsored a talk by Dave Foreman at a local meeting hall two years ago, where the eco-preacher gave his stock Wildlands sermon and finished by telling the story of Aldo Leopold killing a wolf and realizing the error of his ways. The finale, as always, was a cathartic howl by the group.

Hinchman had been attracted to the Wildlands Project by its fresh vision—one that took conservation beyond beautiful mountains for backpackers, to healthy landscapes and wildlife. But what struck Hinchman at the talk was not the excitement Foreman's vision generated, but the fierce antagonism it sparked.

"The wise-users came armed for bear and just attacked Foreman," says Hinchman. While he still thinks the project's vision is inspiring and its science is invaluable, his group voted to disassociate itself with the Southern Rockies Ecosystem Project, the local Wildlands affiliate. "They're branded as the ludicrous fringe. We can't possibly adopt this strategy and survive—not in our community," he says. "Unless it makes sense to any person who grew up here, who lives out here and who's going to die out here, it's not going to work."

Hinchman's prediction played out in the Southwest last year, where the U.S. Fish and Wildlife Service reintroduced Mexican gray wolves on the Arizona-New Mexico border. Before the year was out, five of 11 wolves had been shot. A sixth wolf was found dead in March, just six days after officials released it into the wild.

Says Hinchman, "You can't change the rural West from the outside."

It's a lesson Northwest Ecosystem Alliance Director Mitch Friedman learned the hard way in the early 1990s, when he aired a plan to protect the Columbia Mountains in British Columbia, Canada. The proposal met widespread opposition, even from some environmental groups that felt overlooked. The project "withered on the vine," says Friedman, a former Earth First!er and one of the founding members of the Wildlands Project.

A second proposal, this one for an international park on the U.S.-Canada border, was shot full of holes by Gingrich Republicans and United Nations-fearing conspiracy theorists. "The lesson there," Friedman says, "was that simply putting out the best science-based land proposal isn't going to make it happen."

"No one is going to implement this plan because it's a good idea," agrees Kieran Suckling, whose Southwest Center started as a Wildlands Project affiliate but moved on. "You've got this big vision and this big visionary (Foreman). The big question is, how are they ever going to get it implemented? How do you get it off the paper?"

A Roadmap for Conservation

Despite their vague strategy for making the Wildlands Project happen on the ground, Soulé's science is compelling and Foreman's preaching has a way of getting people starry-eyed. Together, they've managed to enlist a surprising troop of supporters.

"I am aware of the debate between vision and pragmatism," says Wilderness Society President Bill Meadows, who recently joined the Wildlands Project board. "But if we don't have a vision, we won't get the practical results we deserve. They have a vision that inspires all of us—the grassroots groups and the big national groups like The Wilderness Society."

Other groups, such as the Sierra Club, have come up with their own maps, dividing the country into "eco-regions."

It's not just the big greens who have jumped on the bandwagon. Take, for example, Jim Winder, 38, who grazes about 1,000 cows on mostly public land in south central New Mexico. "When I first heard about Wildlands, I was just like any rancher. I wasn't real thrilled with it," he says. "But they're the only people in the environmental community who are doing things in a scientific manner.

"They're developing a roadmap for conservation," he adds, and that saves ranchers a lot of guesswork. "You never know when an environmental group is going to protest something."

But then, Winder is no ordinary rancher. He supported reintroducing wolves in the Southwest, and now sells "Wolf Country Beef" for a premium in specialty stores. Now, he's reintroducing endangered fish in a stream on one of his ranches, and he's started a small eco-tourism business. It's all in the name of survival, he says, in a time when ranchers are selling out and hanging up the saddle for good.

"I've gotta be out there kicking some ass," he says. "I want to see ranchers get rich as hell off of healing the land. We got rich screwing it up."

There are also signs that Wildlands Project thinking has permeated the thick walls of land management agencies. The Yellowstone to Yukon initiative, for example, has garnered the support of both the U.S. and Canadian national park services.

Even some skeptics admit that the science behind the Wildlands Project is making waves in the agencies. "The Wildlands Project is a little beyond political and social reality. It can't deal with the tide of humanity," says Hal Salwasser, director of the Forest Service's Pacific Southwest Research Station in Berkeley, Calif. "But conservation biology is not a pipe dream. We use the concepts and tools that came out of conservation biology pretty regularly. They're in the regular toolbox."

In the Northern Rockies, for example, the U.S. Fish and Wildlife Service has been working to connect grizzly bear habitat in Yellowstone, Idaho and Montana, according to agency bear biologist Chris Servheen. Montana's Swan Valley is an important passageway for grizzly bears traveling between the Bob Marshall Wilderness Area and the Mission Mountains. Servheen's agency has helped show that bears will steer clear of residents' homes as long as they don't grow apple trees, raise chickens or keep dog food outside.

"The local people live in these areas because they have space; there're no streetlights, barking dogs or cars racing around," he says. "Bears need the same things."

But Servheen is quick to draw a line between the kind of conservation biology he practices and the kind that appears in the academic journals. "Who reads Soulé's books? Is it the people who live in these areas? Absolutely not," he says. "The future of these animals rides on public support, not on these grand concepts."

Unless conservation biologists can find a way to convince common people that their ideas are legitimate, adds Servheen, they will only make battles over public lands and private property worse. "We (agency officials) end up picking up the pieces of poorly sold ideas," he says. "And the ones that really suffer are the animals."

Here Comes the Wildlands Project

Wildlands proponents understand that they'll never get a second chance with a first impression. If they blow it, it could take a long time to recover.

They're gearing up for the big debut, which should hit the

pages of *The New York Times* this fall in the form of a two-page ad with maps. By the end of the year, they expect to release a string of reserve maps, including plans for the Sky Island region of Arizona and New Mexico, the Southern Rockies, the Klamath Siskiyou region of Oregon, the central coast of British Columbia and the Northern Yukon territory.

"We're looking very hard at how to make the Wildlands Project immediately relevant and how to make it have an impact right now," says Foreman. "Otherwise, it's not worth the paper it's printed on. It'll do nothing but collect dust."

Making the project relevant, he says, starts with the grassroots wilderness proposals that are popping up like wildflowers around the West. Many are modeled after the Utah Wilderness Coalition's proposal that seems to be making some headway in Congress, thanks to a national constituency.

The New Mexico Wilderness Alliance wants to protect 2.5 million acres of Bureau of Land Management land as wilderness. A similar proposal for Arizona is in the works. Colorado Rep. Diana DeGette has introduced a bill in Congress that would designate 1.5 million acres of wilderness in her state. California activists are pushing for up to 6 million acres of new wilderness. Nevada environmentalists want approximately 16 million acres. In Oregon, it's 4.5 million acres. And in Washington, conservationists are asking for 3.1 million acres.

Some activists contemplate a national or West-wide wilderness bill, according to Jack Humphrey of the Sky Island Alliance. "The national wilderness movement is really kicking in," he says. "A national bill would take it out of the hands of Western senators and make it a national debate."

Also in the works on the national level is a "Native Ecosystem Protection Act," sort of an Endangered Species Act for whole landscapes. This "new NEPA" would outlaw the "taking" or destruction of protected ecosystems on public lands, says Reed Noss, a former Earth First!er who is now the president of the Society for Conservation Biology. The act, which has not yet been written up as legislation, would also set up a fund to buy wildlife habitat on private land.

"Instead of addressing species one by one, we need to focus on ecosystems and slow down the cascade of species warranting listing under the Endangered Species Act," says Noss. "The idea is not to wait until things are virtually impossible to fix."

He admits that a national law is not a panacea, and that conservation plans will vary from place to place. "It's a little foggy. No one knows what's going to work."

To make the Wildlands Project work, Foreman admits he needs to step out of the wilderness and into the messy private lands and human communities in between. He has taken the lead in presenting the new Sky Island-Greater Gila reserve design in the Southwest. Once the environmental movement's chief agitator, he now finds himself struggling to become its head peacemaker.

"In the past, the conservation movement's greatest weakness has been that private-lands conservation has been divorced from public-lands conservation, wilderness protection has been divorced from endangered species protection, economic practices have been divorced from ecosystem recovery," says Foreman. "What we're saying is, let's look at all of it and see how it fits together."

Foreman has also been meeting with sympathetic ranchers like Jim Winder and Drum Hadley, who runs the Gray Ranch in the New Mexico boot heel. "Big private ranches that are managed for their ecological values are in many ways the best places to restore sensitive species," he says.

Land trusts, conservation easements and raising money to simply buy up land are all part of the picture, he says. He also supports efforts to make conservation make sense to people's pocketbooks. In the Southwest, for example, environmentalists are working to convince ranchers to sell predator-friendly meat and retire grazing allotments on public lands in exchange for trophy elk-hunting permits.

Barbara Dugelby, now the Wildlands Project's ecologist, says she's seen Foreman change his tack in recent years. "He's become a little softer, more focused and analytical," she says.

Still, the old eco-warrior acknowledges that he's walking into a fight with many rural Westerners. "We're not going to throw all economic uses off the land. That's realism," he says. "On the same token, we're going to have wolves back throughout the West. That's a reality they're going to have to live with."

"It's like the Manhattan Project..."

INTERVIEW BY GREG HANSCOM

From an interview with Michael Soulé, one of the founders of conservation biology, and a founder of the Wildlands Project.

Michael Soulé: "We live in an extraordinarily bleak period for nature. Things are going to get worse before they get better. We'll lose, I would guess, half of the world's species in the next 50 years. It's quite tragic—and preventable. The degree to which we have to manage nature now precludes speciation from occurring—no other species of bears or dogs will be able to evolve. It's not possible under the current hegemony of humans on the planet.

"It's our responsibility if we're biologists to dedicate a certain portion of our professional lives to protecting nature. It's like the Manhattan Project during World War II. Physicists were called together to address a threat to world civilization. So it is now with biologists and ecologists. The problem is slower—it's not as acute as Hitler and fascism. But if you love nature, it's just as dire.

"I think a lot of scientists come to conservation biology because they're compelled to. They can't stand aside and be an objective observer of the death of nature. I think many scientists in my generation have had a sad epiphany when they saw a place where they had grown up, or a field site they had gotten attached to, trashed by development. Conservation biology is very popular for many bright young people. It's the idealism factor. Young people want to make a difference.

"Most people don't make the distinction between conservation biologists and conservationists. Whenever you step over the line (between science and activism) you get criticized on both sides. You have to be a better scientist in a way. You learn that that's the cost of being a popularizer, a translator, a hybrid.

"We'd like to restore as much true wilderness to North America as we possibly can. It's out there—relatively undeveloped land. But it's being multiple-used to death. Our job is to minimize the damage, to hold onto as much nature as possible so that future people and organisms can persist on the planet. It's kind of like passing the fire.

"Enemies of conservation say we're 'locking away' wildlands. They'd like to have people believe that their rights are being taken away. A better metaphor would be that we're making a deposit in the bank for the future.

"The conservation movement in the past has been looking for special places, places with beauty, aesthetic and political values. Other (environmental) groups focus on jewels in the crown. We really focus on connectivity.

"It's not yet clear whether it is possible to implement conservation on the scale we're talking about. In some places it will be possible, in other areas it won't even be conceivable—like in Denver and Chicago. (Up until recently,) we hadn't understood the complexity of the problems, the difficulty of the problems and the obstacles. There will be resistance.

"The myth of the working landscape we find repugnant. The idea of a working landscape as a (wilderness) core just won't work.

"The economy of the West is rapidly changing. Natural resource extraction and cattle are diminishing rapidly in importance. The future of the West's economy is going to be much more diverse, with a great emphasis on tourism and recreation. If people are really concerned about western Colorado, they should support setting aside as much of it as possible as wilderness. That's going to be the major source of wealth in the next century. Our congresspeople haven't figured out that the real economy is not what they think it is. They're 20 years behind."

Can Science Heal the Land?

BY GREG HANSCOM

From the air, west-central New Mexico is a sea of brown, lined here and there with a dry riverbed or peppered with juniper and mesquite. In places, the vegetation is so sparse that from 3,000 feet up, you can make out the pockmarks of kangaroo rat colonies. "They look like smallpox vaccinations," says Merry Schroeder, a former nurse and a pilot for LightHawk, a troop of flyers who volunteer their time for environmental causes. Schroeder flies a little Cessna 210 single prop out of Santa Fe, and has offered to be my tour guide to the Sky Island region of southwest New Mexico and southeast Arizona.

The land looks barren from up here, but the region is one of the most biologically colorful in the West. It's the collision point of four major biological provinces: the Rocky Mountains from the north, the Sierra Madre from the south, the Sonoran Desert from the west and the Chihuahuan Desert from the east.

Here you'll find such incongruities as black bears and Gila monsters, tropical hummingbirds and northern goshawks. The Coronado National Forest in southeastern Arizona harbors more plant species than the entire Northeastern United States. According to biologist Peter Warshall, the region hosts more kinds of ants, mammals and reptiles than anyplace else in the country. And thanks to a U.S. Fish and Wildlife Service reintroduction effort, Mexican wolves are running here for the first time in two decades.

"All the (national) attention is focused on beautiful but biologically depressed country, like Utah's redrock country," says Jack Humphrey, director of the Sky Island Alliance, who has joined the air tour. "But we've got beautiful places and some of the greatest biodiversity in the nation."

Humphrey's leather jacket, black beard and American Spirit cigarettes give him the air of a preppy Hell's Angel. Also along is Martin Heinrich, a longtime wolf advocate with the New Mexico Wilderness Alliance, whose long hair hangs from under a warped cowboy hat.

Humphrey and Heinrich have big plans for this land. Heinrich's group is pushing Congress to protect 2.5 million acres of Bureau of Land Management land as wilderness. And Humphrey, working side by side with Dave Foreman and the Wildlands Project, would like to protect enough public and private land in between to create a web of wild country stretching from the Gila Wilderness southwest of Albuquerque to Mexico's Sierra Madre.

"We still have big open areas," Humphrey's voice sputters in my earphones over the buzz of the plane's engine. "We still have stuff to save here."

Sky Islands in Exile

The term "sky islands" describes the region's mountain ranges that jut 3,000 to 5,000 feet from the surrounding desert. Their slopes are thick with piñon and juniper trees and topped with ponderosa pine and spruce-fir forests. Some sky islands, such as South Baldy lurking on the southern horizon, are capped with alpine tundra.

The mountain ranges are home to endemic species of animals and plants that exist no place else in the world, such as the Mount Graham red squirrel, talus snails and fleabane plants. But many sky islands are too small to support populations of larger animals like jaguars and wolves, which must travel from one range to the next to find territory, food or a mate.

"Biologists say that if a mountain lion or wolf can see from the top of one sky island to the next, they'll travel," says Humphrey, pointing to Ladrone Peak, which stands shin-deep in desert. Then, with characteristic sarcasm: "Of course, they can't see major roads, or ranchers with guns that'll shoot anything they see." Ranchers with guns are just the tip of the iceberg. Roads, cotton fields, copper mines, cattle grazing, logging, predator control, weeds and urban development are turning the Southwest's desert seas into seas of development.

For wildlife, this isolation means a life of exile. Desert bighorn sheep in the Santa Catalina mountains north of Tucson are a sad example. Early in this century, more than 200 desert bighorns lived in the mountains, but as human activity and development swelled, the sheep population receded.

In 1978, Congress created the Pusch Ridge Wilderness Area to protect bighorn habitat. But University of Arizona biologist Paul Krausman says the wilderness designation was "too little, too late." Suburbs hemmed in the sheep and the remaining habitat suffered as Forest Service firefighters squelched the flames that once kept glades open for the sheep. At the same time, recreationists rolled in, bringing more than 1,500 unleashed dogs each year, according to Krausman.

Today, only a handful of bighorns remain in the Catalinas. "The increasing human population in Tucson has literally pushed bighorn sheep over the brink," Krausman wrote in a 1994 report.

A Prescription for Healthy Land

The people who manage and care about the land are just as isolated as the wildlife, according to Jack Humphrey. "We need one management plan for the entire region," he says. "Right now, one Forest Service district doesn't talk to another." The same is true for conservation groups, he says, to say nothing of agencies or the state and federal governments. "They're isolated in their little islands."

By the end of the year, Humphrey, Dave Foreman and the Sky Island Alliance plan to release the "Sky Island/Greater Gila Nature Reserve Network," a conservation blueprint they hope will bring the land managers and conservationists, and eventually the landscape, together.

The alliance's plan is based on protecting enough land to save, over the long run, a collection of carefully chosen "focal species." The list includes Mexican wolves, black bears and jaguars, which all need large, wild territories. These "umbrella species" should help protect a host of other animals and plants. Also listed are bighorn sheep, elk and Coues deer, which will provide prey for the meat-eaters and help garner public support.

Others, like prairie dogs and beavers, are called "keystone species" because of their critical effects on the landscape. "Beavers create whole ecosystems," by damming streams and creating ponds and wetlands, says Humphrey. "They're one of the most godlike creatures on the planet."

Finally, the group chose critters like the Gila and Apache trout, the Chiricahua leopard frog and the endangered Southwest willow flycatcher that serve as indicators of healthy rivers and streamside habitat—crucial havens for wildlife in this dry region.

The Sky Island Alliance has also hired bear biologist David Mattson to determine whether there is enough habitat in the region to support a population of grizzly bears. "It's basically for human population control. They eat babies. It's well-documented," Humphrey jokes. "I wouldn't be so brash as to call it a harvest or anything."

In truth, grizzly bears are both a symbol of wilderness and a biological necessity, he says. A growing field of scientific research points to predators like the grizzly as the driving force that shape entire ecosystems. "Predators are the only thing that can control prey populations," says Humphrey. "Hunters are taking all the trophies and leaving the diseased and retarded elk. They're genetically watered-down because there's nothing out there nipping at their heels."

Wildfires and native forests must also be restored, according to the alliance, while exotic species such as tamarisk, bullfrogs and rainbow trout need to be controlled. What is the group's vision for human communities? Here, Humphrey is a little foggy, but he says he foresees a shift away from cattle-ranching and other industries toward wilderness-guiding and ecotourism. "Let's make a big deal out of fishing, hiking, horse-packing and all that," he says. "We've gotten everything we can out of the land. Grazing in the Southwest is dying, and not even the Cattlegrowers Association would argue with that."

Building and urbanization should follow ranchers out the door, he says. "We're going to rage against development everywhere."

Rural Green: A New Shade of Activism

INTERVIEW BY ED MARSTON

While the Wildlands Project incorporates wilderness as one element in a broader mosaic of wildlife habitat, some environmentalists are beginning to question just how much of an ecological function wilderness really serves.

Steve Hinchman came to Paonia, Colo., in 1986 as a *High Country News* intern and stayed on as a staff member until 1994. In 1995, he went to work as director of the small Western Slope Environmental Resource Council (WSERC). *High Country News* publisher Ed Marston interviewed Steve Hinchman this June.

Marston: What's the difference between what you're seeking locally and the national agenda?

Hinchman: WSERC is too maverick, too local, too willing to compromise the national platform for the sake of local success. Local success is evolutionary and gradual. National success is measured by how much new wilderness you convince Congress to designate.

Marston: Are you against the current push to create more wilderness in Colorado?

Hinchman: I'm not against it. I just think it's irrelevant. And that's where I start to get into trouble. The foundations and big environmental groups are pouring almost all their resources into the wilderness fight, at least here in Colorado. I think that's a mistake, both ecologically and politically.

Marston: But wilderness now protects some of the most beautiful places in Colorado and the West: magnificent peaks, high mountain valleys, extensive forests...

Hinchman: Most of it is rocks and ice, or high-elevation summer range. I'm glad that land is protected, but that is not where the biological need is today. What we're doing now is nostalgia. The wilderness tool won't work at the low elevations—below 9,000 feet—where the land has already been massively changed, where people aren't just visitors, and where most of the critical wildlife habitat is, or at least used to be.

Marston: Used to be?

Hinchman: Yeah, ask an anti-wilderness coal-mining hunter or construction worker. They know the big-game habitat—deer, elk, bear, lion—is trashed. It's full of roads, people, ATVs, and now, 35-acre ranchettes. The conditions on the ground are so bad that even the wise-users can see that environmental integrity and the quality of life are going down the tubes together.

Marston: What do they see?

Hinchman: Mostly that they can't go hunting anymore—not the way they used to. Their hunting camps, the ones they've used for generations, are overrun by people from Arkansas and Missouri, and their hunting areas are crisscrossed by people on ATVs. Most of all, there isn't much game.

Environmentalists miss what the locals see because the locals go different places at different times. We go to the high country, or we kayak the river canyons, or float the rivers—all in the summer. But most locals go into the piñon-juniper or scrub oak, ponderosa pine and aspen—the drier middle-elevation country—during hunting season.

Locals also want solitude and quiet, but in our county the number of hunter-visitor days in the fall is now three times our county population. Locals are being driven out of places they have enjoyed all their lives.

Marston: So why isn't there a natural alliance?

Hinchman: There could be. But they don't trust us, and we don't even bother to talk to them. Local people are angry about wilderness because they know it doesn't create pristine ecological reserves, nor does it necessarily protect the game herds. Wilderness is just a recreation designation. All you're doing is favoring backpackers and horse people over ATVs and snowmobiles.

Marston: Doesn't wilderness help?

Hinchman: To the southeast of us is the West Elk Wilderness, one of the biggest in the state, and just to our north is Grand Mesa, with all its roads and cabins. Both are the same size, and both are prime big game habitat. Compare those places using the locals' viewpoint: the number of bucks per 100 breeding does. In both areas, the mule deer herds are averaging a pitiful four bucks for 100 does, and the bucks are just little 2-year-old spikes. Meanwhile, in Montana and Idaho, they have 25 bucks per hundred does, including 4- and 5-year-olds.

If wilderness meant anything, the West Elk would have healthier herds than the Grand Mesa, with its roads and cabins. But both areas suffer from the same problems: too many hunters, an unreasonably long hunting season, high road densities along the buffer zones and exponential growth and development along the valley bottoms, where the herds try to winter. The only difference is, in the West Elks the hunters are on foot or horseback, and on

Grand Mesa they come in with recreational vehicles and ATVs.

Marston: Some would say good riddance to the hunters and their ATVs.

Hinchman: They would be wrong, because the vanishing of the mule deer is a sign of what's going wrong out here. It's the result of Colorado Division of Wildlife's "cash-register" approach to big game management, of 100 years of fire suppression and improper grazing, of ranches converted to suburban sprawl, of more hunters and backpackers and of lots of elk in the high country pushing deer down into sterile old-growth piñon-juniper, where they starve. These are things new wilderness can't fix.

Marston: Why is the herd crashing now? These conditions have been around for a long time.

Hinchman: Not as intensively as now. There's much more development and sprawl. Ed Abbey's prediction of industrial recreation has come true in ways perhaps he didn't even imagine. Add hunting to that, too—there's more than double the hunters, and they're mechanized. And there are no more bulldozers pulling anchor chains through the brush and piñon-juniper to create grass and browse. That can't be done politically anymore, and there aren't enough controlled burns to replace them. Chaining was big through the 1960s, and now the areas they opened up to grass are being taken over fast by brush.

Marston: If the local people are so smart, and the wilderness movement is ecologically irrelevant, why aren't the local people doing something about the problem?

Hinchman: They are, at least here. The example I know best is the local Delta-Montrose Public Land Partnership. It was initially a group with wise-use motives. But they invited agency representatives and environmentalists like me in for political cover. They spent two years learning the Forest Service budget process, trying to find a way to smuggle in money for logging and grazing. I'm grateful that the national environmentalists beat them back in the Congress.

Meanwhile, we were meeting once a month religiously, and it turned into the most fantastic book club I've ever been part of, even if we didn't read any books. They taught us, and we taught them. We were also all being polite and respectful to each other, even as we pursued our own agendas. For a long time, it seemed interesting but pointless. Then, driven by the crashing of the mule deer herd in the Partnership's back yard, on the Uncompahgre National Forest, came the Uncompahgre Restoration Project.

Marston: You mean this consensus group came up with a restoration project?

Hinchman: The group didn't conceive it. The BLM, the Forest Service and the Colorado Division of Wildlife came to the Partnership with the project. But the Partnership recast it into a plan that could be implemented by the community, and they went to the Ford Foundation and got a $750,000 grant over five years.

Marston: Why isn't this just another way to do more grazing and logging—except now the money comes from Ford?

Hinchman: It is going to be used mostly to burn, if we are ever allowed to burn again. I've sat with those people for five years now, and I'm convinced their goal is to restore biological integrity necessary to keep their rural economies alive. They understand what's been done to the land, and I don't think they are going to let more damage be done. They're going to want the timber sales to improve the land, and to help the industry transition to sustainable logging methods and small-timber marketing. The best thing is, these concepts are going mainstream.

Marston: How do you restore that mess up on the Uncompahgre National Forest: small trees, roads as thick as in subdivisions, motorized recreation everywhere?

Hinchman: Some of the solution will come from understanding what drives the Forest Service. It always wants to log in roadless areas because there are the fewest people there. Most people recreate where the roads are. It's how the agency minimizes political opposition to logging.

If we as a community decide to use logging for ecological restoration, we could cooperate with the Forest Service. There is little roadless (area) left anyway. We will have to do most of the work in the roaded areas. If we put timber sales, fires and roto-chopping in roaded areas, then we could level the forest and start from scratch. I know this sounds horrible, but it would help obliterate existing roads and trails, and they could be replaced with a planned system. Then, over the years, as the forest came back, we would be re-creating species and age-class diversity in the vegetation. The ORVers and jeepers might oppose it at first. But people who care about the long-term restoration of the middle level elevation lands should support it.

Marston: But in the end, you'd still have some roads. It wouldn't be roadless.

Hinchman: Insistence on complete roadlessness or wilderness is dogmatic and needlessly antagonizes potential allies. And without those allies you won't get all the other pieces needed to complete the puzzle: reform of the Colorado Division of Wildlife, improving grazing management, protecting migration corridors, restricting growth through (the creation of) more private conservation easements, creating a local land ethic and so on.

Marston: Aren't you asking environmentalists to give up just as the movement is on the brink of victory?

Hinchman: I'm not saying give up; I'm saying think about what we're after. We should become more like what Dave Foreman and Michael Soulé are advocating with their Wildlands Project—biological integrity. To truly achieve that, we have to add local people and economies to their strategy.

But you're right: We are getting close to where recreation-based environmentalism can roll the opposition. The commodity-based Western senators like Ben Nighthorse Campbell and others are anachronisms, and once they go, it's all over for the old West. But the current single-strategy wilderness effort will just substitute a kayaking and peak-bagging myth for the ranching and prospector-with-a-mule myth. Let's face it: The wilderness myth is walking hand-in-hand with the real estate developer reality.

Marston: Aren't you trying to have it both ways: biological integrity and economic activity in the forests and grasslands?

Hinchman: No. Economic activity in the woods has changed. Logging and grazing, done right, can be compatible with improved habitat. Wilderness was the right strategy when the enemy was a destructive extractive industry. Now the enemy is us—people, backpackers, anglers, hunters, new houses and resorts. From what I have seen, wilderness exacerbates the problem, draws in more people, more development at the edges.

Let's go back to roads. The problem is not the roads and trails, but people traveling them. Remember that a low density of roads is compatible with biological integrity in the Central Rockies. Some in the environmental movement think the problem is forest fragmentation. But at a conference at Colorado State University a few years ago, the scholars said that the Central Rockies are different from the Pacific Northwest. This area is naturally fragmented by canyons and avalanches and the like. You

never had unbroken forest. So the species here are generalists—
they've adapted to mixed habitat. A few roads and logging cuts—
and I emphasize few—mimic what's already here. And they can
be used to speed restoration.

The problem is too many people on those roads and trails. It
doesn't matter if they are on foot or on an ATV. In other words, it
doesn't matter if it's a wilderness or not.

Marston: For better or for worse, you've come a long way from
1986, when you arrived in Paonia as a hippie with long hair and
all the answers.

Hinchman: That was eco-rhetoric. The truth is, you get co-opted
when you live in these small, rural towns and see the incompatibility of a one-size-fits-all wilderness strategy with needs on the
ground. That's when you move to talking about a more integrated
approach: loggers doing restoration, the BLM and Forest Service
setting big fires, hunters working on habitat restoration, and putting private-land winter range into protection.

A lot of my friends and compatriots will be very angry at me
for saying this. And I know the penalty for traitors. But the
wilderness movement has almost gotten intoxicated with the
amount of money and power they are bringing in, so much so
that they are willing to fight a scorched-earth political campaign
in the rural West.

No modern society has ever managed to simultaneously
inhabit and preserve fully working ecosystems. The wilderness
movement is a great and noble experiment, but it ignores the
inhabit part and therefore it will fail, at least ecologically.

Marston: Did this come on you bit by bit, or as an epiphany?

Hinchman: It was an epiphany because of someone else's
epiphany. Jeepers I know fought to open some roads earlier in the
year. They won, and the first time they used the reopened road

they drove upon an elk calving. They were horrified. They told me: "We had no right being there." In a way they were apologizing, because I'd been on the other side of that fight.

It made me realize we had the same values. We just had to figure out how to work together.

EDITORIAL

Do You Want More Wilderness? Good Luck

BY JON MARGOLIS

In 1999, political commentator Jon Margolis, who had just finished writing The Last Innocent Year: America in 1964, *wrote this column marking the 35th anniversary of the Wilderness Act. Just as Steve Hinchman was wondering whether wilderness had failed ecologically, Margolis contemplated whether it had failed politically as well, and pondered the opportunities that might lie in private lands conservation.*

WASHINGTON, D.C.—Poor W. Howard Gray didn't know what hit him.

Just a few years before, in the early 1960s, the head of the American Mining Congress seemed justified in confidently predicting oblivion for this absurd proposal to set aside millions of acres of land for…well, for doing nothing with it. All that would do, he sneered, would "provide a very limited number of individuals with wilderness pleasures."

But Gray had greatly underestimated that number. The appeal was much greater than the miner had dreamt. And so it was that exactly 35 years ago this month, President Lyndon Johnson signed into law the Wilderness Bill, declaring that 9.14 million acres of the American earth should remain "untrammeled by man."

Of all the laws passed that year, only the legislation he'd signed two months earlier, the one outlawing racial discrimination, had greater consequences.

There are now 104 million acres in the National Wilderness Preservation System. That's a lot of land, but it's only 4.6 percent of the country, and because more than half is in Alaska, only 1.8 percent of the Lower 48 states is official wilderness.

Led, logically, by The Wilderness Society, environmentalists would like to double or even triple the size of the system, adding perhaps 100 million acres in Alaska and up to another 100 million elsewhere in the West.

Lots of luck. At the age of 35, the wilderness system appears to be in the early stages of premature political arteriosclerosis. Some of its most celebrated areas are so crowded that a "wilderness experience" feels more like a trip to Shea Stadium than a commune with nature. Organized and well-financed lobbies of motorized recreationists are mobilizing to get permission to zoom their vehicles along wilderness trails. Without waiting for the laws to change, individual riders increasingly ignore wilderness boundaries.

As for additions to the system, well, that's been stymied for most of the 1990s. At the tail end of the Democratic congressional majority in 1994, the Clinton administration managed to eke out passage of the California Desert Protection Act, adding 7.58 million acres to the system. Since then, there have been but two small additions, one in Oregon and one in New Mexico.

From their rhetoric, it seems that some leaders of the Republican majority in Congress would like to repeal the 1964 law. They won't do that, but they have tried to weaken some protections, and they are hardly likely to add to the system any time soon.

Just Try Defining "Wilderness"

As if these were not troubles enough, now come attacks from the political left. Well, actually, they're from the post-modernists, which is not the same thing. It's not that these critics are against wilderness, exactly; they're just disturbed by the idea of wilderness.

The problem, according to a 1995 essay by William Cronon, is not "the things we label as wilderness…but rather what we ourselves mean when we use that label." The novelist Marilynne Robinson dismissed wilderness because "we are desperately in need of a new, chastened, self-distrusting vision of the world, an austere vision that can postpone the outdoor pleasures of cherishing exotica…"

No, I don't know what it means, either.

Central to the postmodern critique is the conviction that the concepts of "wilderness" and of "nature" are merely cultural constructs.

But these attacks have not been without some benefit to wilderness advocates, for whom the current news is not all bad. First of all, some of the criticism, such as Cronon's warning that wilderness worship can blind people to the wonders of nature in their own backyards, makes sense. Besides, the minds of wilderness supporters were probably atrophying from the debate with the other side, which is still mumbling the rhetoric of W. Howard Gray. Having to respond to a more complex critique has forced pro-wilderness troops to sharpen their scientific, cultural and political case.

But this is not the main thing the pro-wilderness guys have going for them. No, the main thing is what they had going for them 35 years ago. There's a reason wilderness areas are so crowded: People love them. If I may quote from a recently published book about the events of 1964 (and I may because I wrote it), this was a "country that was now rich enough, educated enough and sufficiently at leisure (so that) for the first time in the nation's history, there were more people who wanted to enjoy the public land than to make money off it."

If that was true then, think how much truer it is in this richer, more educated, and, yes, more self-centered society. As several polls show, most people, including affluent people who vote

Republican, favor putting more land into wilderness.

On this issue, the congressional majority and the popular majority are out of sync.

From which it does not follow that the second majority will erase the first. Conservationists and their political allies have not figured out a way to transform this popular sentiment into a voting sentiment.

However, the people in their adroitness have figured out that there is more than one way to keep land in its natural state, or something close to it. It's called "the private sector."

Wilderness advocates regard this as a mixed blessing, because it might divert attention from the goal of adding to the system, but the fact is that instead of waiting for an out-of-touch Congress to act, a growing number of people have proven that the private sector can do part of the job.

It's Not Chopped Liver

Between them, The Nature Conservancy and the Conservation Fund, both based just across the Potomac in Arlington, Va., have bought millions of acres of land outright and acquired conservation easements on millions more. The San Francisco-based Trust For Public Land has bought more than a million acres and turned it over to state and federal agencies. In addition, according to the Land Trust Alliance, more than 2.2 million acres of open space around the country is being conserved by more than 1,200 land trusts.

True, the level of protection granted to most of this land falls well short of what many would consider wilderness. On the 330,000 acres the Conservation Fund recently bought and resold in the Northeastern forests, for instance, logging and snowmobiling will continue.

So it isn't wilderness. But it ain't chopped liver, either. These acres will remain forested and open to the public, with easements ensuring responsible logging methods.

The same is true of much of the privately preserved land in the West. In southwestern New Mexico, The Nature Conservancy bought and re-sold to a private foundation the 321,000-acre Gray Ranch. The land is still being grazed, as is a great deal of the wilderness system, often less responsibly, but under deed restrictions requiring the ranchers to maintain biodiversity.

In southwestern Montana, part of the Lee Metcalf Wilderness is buffered by 66,000 acres of ranchland and timberland managed according to conservation easements worked out with the Montana Land Alliance.

"There's less human impact on some of these ranches than on the Bob Marshall Wilderness," says Rock Ringling of the Alliance.

None of this means the government is not an important factor in preserving land. Even these private actions are possible only because of tax laws and other public policies. Besides, no institution can protect wild land as simply, as sweepingly, or as strongly as the Congress. Only the Congress has power over the public land, where its power is "total," as the Supreme Court put it, and where most of the wilderness-eligible land is situated.

If such huge swaths of public land as Alaska's Gates of the Arctic are going to be protected as wilderness, only the Congress can do it.

Eventually, it may, even if the Republicans stay in charge, because all that private activity is evidence of public sentiment.

After 35 years, the lesson is sinking in that miner Howard Gray had it half right: Wilderness areas do "provide...individuals with wilderness pleasures." What he missed was that the number of people seeking such pleasures becomes less limited every day.

Road Warriors
Back on the Offensive

BY MICHELLE NIJHUIS

The press release couldn't have been blander. The "Final Rule on Conveyances, Disclaimers, and Correction Documents," announced by the Bureau of Land Management on Christmas Eve, sounded like little more than regulatory housekeeping. The rule, said the agency, was simply designed to "remove clouds of title to the lands in which the BLM no longer holds interest."

So why had the proposed rule received more than 17,000 public comments, most of them negative? Why did press releases from environmental groups use the words "bulldozers" and "national parks" in such uncomfortably quick succession?

The newly minted rule continues an old, ugly argument over roads on public lands. The tussle has already spawned a string of lawsuits, at least one arrest, and countless hours of overblown rhetoric. These days, a lot rides on its resolution.

The state of Utah has claimed rights-of-way for about 10,000 routes across federal lands, some within Grand Staircase-Escalante National Monument. Southeastern California's San Bernardino County has claimed about 5,000 miles of desert trails and roads, about half of them in the Mojave National Preserve.

On Jan. 10, just days after the Bush administration's final rule was officially adopted, commissioners in northwestern Colorado's Moffat County also took action: They adopted a resolution that claims rights-of-way for hundreds of miles of routes on public lands, including Dinosaur National

Monument and areas proposed for wilderness designation by environmental groups.

Former Moffat County commissioner T. Wright Dickinson, who stepped down from his post in January, says his county's position is simple. "These are valid existing rights that were granted by Congress," he says. "They're based on the most common-sense law that Congress ever passed."

New Life for an Old Law

That "common-sense law" dates back to 1866, when Congress passed the Lode Mining Act. Buried in the act was a single sentence known as Revised Statute 2477, or "RS 2477" for short: "(T)he right of way for the construction of highways over public lands, not reserved for public uses, is hereby granted."

In those days, the acres "reserved for public uses," such as parks, were almost nonexistent, so local governments had more or less blanket permission to build and maintain roads on public land.

More than a century later, the 1976 Federal Land Policy and Management Act repealed RS 2477 and established more stringent restrictions. The new law contained a catch, however: If states, counties or even individuals could prove that a road had been in continuous use since before 1976—or before the land was reserved for a park or other protected area—they could still claim it under RS 2477.

This caveat remained relatively obscure until 1988, when President Reagan's Interior secretary, Donald Hodel, issued a new official policy on RS 2477. His loose interpretation of the statute said even the most primitive paths could be claimed as rights-of-way.

The Hodel policy was welcome news in southern Utah, where county governments were fighting their state's growing wilderness movement. Since wilderness areas must be roadless, county commissioners began using RS 2477 claims to literally tear holes in proposed wilderness areas, as well as existing wilderness areas and parks.

The tactic proved popular throughout the West. Some counties even sent bulldozers and road crews to widen and pave routes on public land.

In the mid-1990s, Interior Secretary Bruce Babbitt attempted to tighten the federal road policy, but the Utah congressional delegation successfully pushed for a moratorium on all RS 2477 policy changes. Babbitt responded with a moratorium of his own, blocking his department from processing nearly all RS 2477 claims.

"A One-Two Punch"

That's how things stood on Christmas Eve, when the bland BLM press release appeared on the Internet. Under the new final rule, counties and other "entities" are eligible to apply to the agency for a "disclaimer of interest" on a piece of disputed property, such as a road. The BLM will then decide if the federal government is willing to give up its claim to the property.

Environmentalists fear the rule will make it quicker and easier for counties to get federal support for their RS 2477 road claims—and make it tougher to fight the claims in court.

BLM spokesman Jeff Holdren says the rule does provide "another option" for these RS 2477 claimants. But is it a way around the existing Babbitt moratorium? "I just don't know that yet."

It may be a moot point, as the moratorium's days are likely numbered. In a speech to the Alaska Resources Development Council in late November, Deputy Secretary of the Interior J. Steven Griles promised that his department would issue a new policy on RS 2477. Though Interior Secretary Gale Norton isn't likely to return to the Hodel era, her policy will surely be more relaxed than the thwarted Babbitt proposal.

"We're going to see a one-two punch here," says Ted Zukoski, an attorney for Earthjustice in Denver. The combined effect of the final rule and the new policy, he says, could be enormous. "We're going to see thousands of proposals, and we're going to have to fight them route by route."

Wilderness Takes a Massive Hit

The Door Closes on New BLM Wilderness Proposals

BY MATT JENKINS

For years, wilderness groups have been hounding the Bureau of Land Management (BLM) to continue to identify lands worthy of formal protection as wilderness. An initial round of wilderness inventories, completed in 1991, led to protection of 6.5 million acres of BLM wilderness. But citizens' wilderness groups argued that substantial areas of potential wilderness were overlooked. In Utah, for instance, the original BLM inventory identified 3.2 million acres which met Wilderness Act criteria—areas larger than 5,000 acres with "outstanding opportunities for solitude or a primitive and unconfined type of recreation." The Utah Wilderness Coalition argued that the true number was closer to 9 million acres and—under the direction of Clinton-era Secretary of the Interior Bruce Babbitt—the BLM re-inventoried its Utah lands, ultimately identifying an additional 2.6 million acres eligible for protection.

But on April 11, the BLM stepped back in time. The Department of the Interior settled a lawsuit with the state of Utah, eliminating the 2.6 million acres of potential wilderness identified during the 1990s. Not only that, but Interior also agreed to prohibit the BLM from conducting further wilderness inventories or designating new "wilderness study areas" without explicit congressional direction—a policy the Interior Department intends to extend across the West.

Interior Secretary Gale Norton outlined the new policy in letters sent the same day to Sen. Pete Domenici, R-N.M., and Sen.

Bob Bennett, R-Utah. It effectively knocks tens of millions of acres out of the running for wilderness protection—and it will likely open up wildlands to development just as the BLM implements a new industry-friendly policy for oil and gas drilling on its lands.

"You have to understand just how radical a proposition this is," says Jim Angell, an attorney for Earthjustice, the nonprofit law firm that represents several wilderness groups. "What they're saying is: Those wilderness inventories that got done, for the most part, under Reagan—and were deeply flawed and highly political back then—are what we're stuck with. BLM can't even re-inventory its own lands to see if they're eligible for wilderness. They have to turn a blind eye to those lands and continue to develop them."

A Long Battle

The 1964 Wilderness Act directed the U.S. Forest Service to identify forestlands that might qualify for protection as wilderness. But it wasn't until 1976, with the passage of the Federal Land Policy and Management Act (FLPMA), that the same mandate was extended to the BLM. FLPMA required BLM to complete a one-shot, nationwide inventory of eligible wilderness by 1991. As a result, Congress formally protected 6.5 million acres of BLM land as wilderness, while another 14.4 million acres were protected as wilderness study areas for future consideration.

But the BLM's responsibility didn't end there. Federal law requires the agency to maintain an ongoing inventory of potential wilderness. That opened a window of opportunity to wilderness groups, which argued the agency's initial surveys were far from complete. After years of on-the-ground surveys by citizens, the groups took their findings to the BLM and urged the agency to consider more areas for protection.

"It's been very common practice for the BLM to recognize that the first inventories that were done in the mid- to late-'80s were not entirely accurate," says Heidi McIntosh of the Southern Utah

Wilderness Alliance. Interior Secretary Babbitt recognized this and, in 1996, he called for the re-inventory of BLM land in Utah, which ultimately identified 2.6 million more acres of potential wilderness.

The agency did a similar thing in Colorado. In 1996, the Colorado Environmental Coalition pushed the BLM to re-evaluate the Vermillion Basin, an oil-and-gas hotspot in the far northwest corner of the state that was being eyed for development by the Marathon Oil Company.

"We were making the case that BLM shouldn't allow any wilderness-damaging activities until (it) has a chance to take a second look," says Jeff Widen of the Colorado Environmental Coalition. And the BLM agreed, identifying some 600,000 acres of land—not only in the Vermillion Basin, but around the state—to protect as citizens' wilderness proposal areas until Congress could consider them for formal wilderness designation.

These re-evaluations were not without controversy. In 1996, the state of Utah sued Interior to invalidate Babbitt's new survey. The state abandoned the suit after an appeals court upheld the BLM's authority to re-inventory wilderness. But this March, Utah refiled, and just two weeks later—on April 11—the state and the Interior Department announced that they had reached a settlement.

"The timing of the suit is incredible," says Widen. "A number of state-based wilderness groups tried to intervene, and before the judge ever even ruled, Interior just came out of the blue and settled this thing." The settlement follows a Bush administration pattern of inviting lawsuits that could weaken environmental protection and then settling them out of court.

The End of Wilderness?

The new policy could demolish efforts for more wilderness protection—and it is likely to spread quickly region-wide.

The Utah settlement came on the heels of two March letters to

Norton from Republican senators and congressmen in Utah, Colorado, Idaho, New Mexico, Nevada, Arizona, California and Montana, asking that "the Bureau of Land Management immediately suspend any new wilderness reviews of public lands other than reviews specifically directed by an Act of Congress." In her April 11 letters to Senators Bennett and Domenici, Secretary Norton made it clear that the invalidation of wilderness proposed after 1991 would extend across the West.

"It's pretty clear that what we're going to see BLM start doing pretty quick is start leasing lands (for oil and gas development) that are in citizens' wilderness inventories," says Ken Rait of the Campaign for America's Wilderness. In Colorado, the first land on the block could be the Vermillion Basin and the energy-rich Roan Plateau near Rifle. In Utah, it's the area around Moab as well as the Book Cliffs outside of Green River, which have long been eyed by oil and gas companies.

The Arizona Wilderness Coalition's just-released, million-acre wilderness proposal for the remote Arizona Strip, north of the Grand Canyon, is also on the rocks, and the new policy affects wilderness efforts in California, New Mexico, Nevada, Oregon and Idaho as well.

Wilderness groups are still pondering their response to the move, but a lawsuit seems likely. Says Widen, "BLM didn't say to the oil and gas industry, 'You applied for drilling permits back in 1980-whatever, so you had your chance.'"

"This is a major issue for the future of the BLM and how it will manage its lands in the 21st century," says The Wilderness Society's Dave Alberswerth. "It's wrong for the administration to say, 'We're never going to do wilderness again.'"

Backcountry Road Deal Runs over Wilderness

BY TIM WESTBY

A nearly three-decade-long fight over who controls backcountry roads crossing federal land in Utah may soon come to an end—and the resolution casts a huge cloud over the future of wilderness protection. In 2000, the state threatened to sue the federal government, claiming ownership of the roads under RS 2477. On April 9, Utah Gov. Mike Leavitt, R, dropped the threat, signing an agreement with Interior Secretary Gale Norton.

Under the agreement, Utah will stop seeking ownership of unimproved dirt roads in areas such as national parks, national wildlife refuges and wilderness areas. But roads on other federal lands—such as the 2.6 million acres stripped of interim wilderness protection by an April 11 settlement between the federal government and the state—are fair game. If those roads are recognized, surrounding lands will be disqualified for protection as wilderness, which must be roadless.

While state and federal officials say they will include an opportunity for "full public participation" in deciding which roads belong to the state, no mention of public comment is made in the agreement itself. "The doors still haven't been opened," says Heidi McIntosh of the Southern Utah Wilderness Alliance (SUWA). "From what we know of the closed-door sessions, the major decisions have already been made."

Maps obtained by SUWA under the Freedom of Information Act show the state was preparing to sue for upwards of 100,000 miles of roads, according to McIntosh. Gov. Leavitt won't say how many roads the agreement could cover, but Utah has spent $4.2 million on a database of roads that it could try to claim. The state will begin submitting claims to the federal government early this summer.

JANUARY 19, 2004

Two Decades of Hard Work, Plowed Under

The Bush Administration Gives Oil and Gas Drillers First Crack at the West's Last Wild Lands

BY MATT JENKINS

BIG RIDGE, Colo.—Not far from the northwest Colorado oil and gas outpost of Rangely, benches of shattered sandstone rise to a seven-mile-long, piñon-and-juniper-mottled landmark called Big Ridge. A herd of wild horses ranges across the land here, and the draws that run down from the 7,500-foot-high ridge shelter Fremont Indian pictographs, petroglyphs and archaeological sites that date from around 600 to 1300 A.D. On a bitterly cold December day, the flat winter haze has given way to a deep cerulean blue. Time seems to be marked only by the lazy pass of an eagle overhead.

In its own modest way, Big Ridge stands where two worlds collide. It is one small chunk of the Piceance Basin, a gigantic oil and gas field that has lured energy companies for decades. But it is also still a relatively untouched island, and conservationists have tried to protect it as wilderness.

In 1997, Amoco drilled a well here, but came up dry. The company plugged the well and moved on, leaving behind a half-mile of road and a barren well pad. At about the same time, the Colorado Environmental Coalition (which would later team with several other groups to form the Colorado Wilderness Network) discovered that Big Ridge still qualified as wilderness, as defined in the 1964 Wilderness Act: "an area of undeveloped Federal land retaining its primeval character and influence...with the imprint of man's work substantially unnoticeable."

In July 2001, the Wilderness Network nominated the area to the federal Bureau of Land Management (BLM) for protection as wilderness. That nomination was a gamble: Just eight months earlier, another oil and gas company had leased several parcels of the area. And oil and gas leases generally trump a wilderness designation, even if they haven't been developed yet.

"Even though the area was leased, the larger landscape was getting hammered," says CEC's Kurt Kunkle, who helped identify the area as potential wilderness. "Protecting a little part of that seemed important, so we were willing to take the risks."

At first, the gamble seemed to pay off. Under a Clinton-era directive, the BLM agreed to include Big Ridge in its roster of places that might be eligible for wilderness protection, and to take a "second look" at any proposal—such as oil and gas drilling—that might disqualify it from protection. As a result, in 2002, when El Paso Corporation applied to the BLM for permission to drill an exploratory well on its lease in the proposed wilderness, the BLM thought twice about allowing it. The agency gave El Paso permission, but only after it determined that the well would affect just .01 percent of the proposed wilderness. The company promptly drilled another "duster," a dry hole.

It looked, for a moment, as if Big Ridge might escape with only a few scars. Then, last April, wilderness activists across the nation were rocked to their core. Interior Secretary Gale Norton and then-Utah Governor Mike Leavitt settled a wilderness lawsuit that blew the doors wide open for drilling in Big Ridge and many of the hundreds of other areas in the West proposed for wilderness protection.

Just over a month later, El Paso applied for—and quickly won—permits to drill five more wells in the proposed Big Ridge wilderness. Last November, the company tried a second well about 200 feet from Amoco's dry hole. That, too, proved dry. Late in the month, El Paso plugged the well and abandoned it; the company has momentarily pulled out and is deciding whether to drill the other four wells.

A few days after El Paso moved out, I arrive with Jennifer Seidenberg and Reed Morris from the Colorado Environmental Coalition. We park our cars at the bottom of the hill and hike the half-mile up to the abandoned drill pad. The sign from the earlier Amoco lease has been knocked to the ground, and silence reigns over the site. In the middle of the 1.3-acre pad bulldozed out of the side of a ridge, the well—a capped pipe—sticks out of what looks like a bomb crater of oozing muck.

On the edge of the pad, a rented trailer sits empty, its TV satellite dish pointed at the sky. The door is unlocked. Inside, mud is caked on the thin carpet, and the just-departed drillers have left a note on the counter: "Sorry to leave a mess."

The Making—and the Undoing—of
the Citizens' Wilderness Movement

Welcome to the world of citizen-led wilderness protection. Behind the big official wilderness areas—celebrated places like the John Muir Wilderness in California and the Frank Church-River of No Return Wilderness in Idaho—a gritty, on-the-ground fight is on to protect the West's last remaining wild places. These are areas that citizens' groups believe should be protected from harm until Congress can decide whether to formally recognize them as wilderness areas.

Many of the proposals have been around for years. But they may not survive much longer, because the Bush administration has made energy development the first priority on public lands. Big Ridge is an emblem of what could happen to the several hundred proposed wilderness areas throughout the West. This fall, the BLM began offering a new wave of oil and gas leases that could set the stage for intensive development on lands that, only eight months ago, the agency considered candidates for wilderness.

Understanding the recent controversy requires going back to

1964, when Congress passed the Wilderness Act, laying the foundation for subsequent bills that protected over 400 wilderness areas on the national forests. In 1976, Congress passed the Federal Land Policy and Management Act (FLPMA), which expanded the Wilderness Act to cover lands run by the Bureau of Land Management. It gave the BLM 15 years—until 1991—to recommend wilderness areas to Congress. As a result, the 1990s saw several large BLM wilderness bills, including the 1990 Arizona Desert Wilderness Act and the 1994 California Desert Protection Act.

FLPMA did something else significant: It opened the door for continuing, citizen-initiated efforts to protect more BLM wilderness. The law required the BLM to continuously inventory "resource and other values" on public lands, and to protect those values. That allowed citizens' groups to find lands that met the BLM's own criteria for wilderness—areas larger than 5,000 acres that were roadless and free from human disturbance—and to ask the agency to protect those lands until Congress could decide.

These are not "wilderness study areas," which, for the most part, the BLM itself identified and must manage as wilderness until Congress has the opportunity to grant—or deny—them formal protection. Instead, they're more like proposed wilderness study areas: wilderness-quality lands that the agency missed during its own inventories.

During the Clinton administration, the BLM agreed to take another look before permitting potentially damaging activities on these lands. According to Dave Alberswerth, who served as a special assistant to the Interior Department's head of land and mineral management during the Clinton administration, and now works for The Wilderness Society, "The idea was to try to protect—within the secretary of the Interior's discretion—the wilderness, roadless, undeveloped character of lands proposed for wilderness designation. For a while, it became known as the 'take-care' policy."

The BLM wasn't required to protect these areas as wilderness, but it could impose stipulations on development projects to minimize their impacts on wilderness character, or recommend postponing such projects. And in practice, the BLM frequently denied mineral leases on these lands.

Clinton's secretary of the Interior, Bruce Babbitt, gave citizens' wilderness proposals their most explicit recognition in Utah. In its initial inventory in the 1980s, the Utah BLM identified only 3.2 million acres—which remain protected as wilderness study areas, because Congress has yet to pass a BLM wilderness bill for the state. Not satisfied with this, activists did their own inventory, spurring the agency to designate an additional 2.6 million acres as "wilderness inventory areas," bringing interim protection to a total of about 5.7 million acres.

Wilderness advocates scored a similar victory in Colorado, where in 1997, the BLM agreed to take a "second look" at a total of 600,000 acres proposed for wilderness protection by the Colorado Environmental Coalition.

In both Colorado and Utah, the BLM began to consider giving citizen-proposed wilderness more formal protection. In January 2001, Babbitt issued the *BLM Wilderness Handbook*, which laid out a standardized, nationwide procedure for determining which lands were eligible for "upgrading" from citizen-proposed inventory areas to official wilderness study areas.

But the *Handbook* was issued without an opportunity for public comment, in a wave of controversial last-minute directives just 10 days before President Clinton left office. The Utah government, and the oil and gas companies, saw the *Handbook* as a circumvention of public process.

"There is a big difference between BLM giving essentially policy effect to environmental groups drawing their private line on the map, and the public process of oil and gas leasing," says John Andrews, associate director and general counsel of Utah's School and Institutional Trust Lands Administration, who fought the rule.

And the *Handbook* played straight into an intensifying debate over FLPMA. Wilderness foes contend that the BLM had a one-shot opportunity to recommend potential wilderness to Congress—and that the opportunity ended with FLPMA's 1991 deadline. By their reckoning, the citizens' wilderness proposals were moot; they'd come in too late.

Again, the locus of that fight has been Utah. In 1996, the state sued the U.S. Department of the Interior, arguing that the BLM didn't have the authority to add areas it missed the first time around. But two years later, the 10th Circuit Court of Appeals rebuffed the state when it ruled that the "plain language" of FLPMA required the BLM to continue to inventory potential wilderness.

The ruling only fueled frustration among oil and gas companies. "People had a horrible time getting (drilling permits) through. It was this endless cycle of review," says Connie Brooks, a Denver lawyer who represented Utah in the wilderness case. The citizen-proposed wilderness in Utah, she says, "was the land in between. It was basically off-limits for oil and gas leasing. (BLM) would actually use pages from *Wilderness at the Edge*"—a compendium of citizen-proposed wilderness put together by the Utah Wilderness Coalition—"and they'd redraw the boundaries (of leases offered for sale). We had them cold on it."

According to the Utah BLM, between November 1999 and April 2003, energy companies sought leases on 214,170 acres of wilderness inventory areas and citizen-proposed wilderness. The BLM turned down all of them.

But last March, Gov. Leavitt resurrected Utah's legal challenge—and got a very different reaction from the Bush-appointed leaders in the Interior Department. Late in the day on Friday, April 11—just two weeks after Utah refiled the lawsuit—Secretary Norton signed the settlement agreement that stripped interim protection from Utah's 2.6 million acres of wilderness inventory areas and invalidated Babbitt's *Wilderness Handbook*.

"We looked at the concerns Utah was raising, and took a close look at the law," says Lynn Scarlett, the Interior Department's assistant secretary of Policy, Management and Budget. "People might have hoped it said something different, but our read is that Congress said, 'There's the process, and it's 15 years, and that's the end of that.'"

On Sept. 29, BLM Director Kathleen Clarke officially rescinded the interim-protection policy nationwide, removing protection from millions of acres and dealing a serious blow to two decades of citizens' effort to save the West's last wild places.

All of the citizens' wilderness proposals that fell under the old policy "had a chance to be protected as wilderness," says Ted Zukoski, a lawyer for Earthjustice, a nonprofit environmental law firm. "Now, BLM is saying, 'We can't and we won't plan to protect that character in terms of creating (wilderness study areas).' BLM is making those decisions now that will make it impossible for those areas to be protected in the future. That's what we're losing."

Now, as at Big Ridge, the oil and gas industry is beginning to move drill rigs onto lands it already has leased. And it's looking to lease more: One series of proposed wilderness lands has already hit the auction block, and a second is coming in a matter of days.

Legal Settlement Blows Away a Homespun Wilderness Proposal

Thirty miles west of Big Ridge, just south of Vernal, Utah, lies another area that's long been torn between wilderness and energy development. Here, the White River cuts through the Uinta Formation on its way to the Green River, creating towering turrets and battlements. On the benchlands above the river, golden eagles roost atop old sheepherders' cairns on sandstone outcrops.

Back in 1871, explorer Frederick Dellenbaugh, who was part of John Wesley Powell's expedition, wrote of the area: "Beautiful is the wilderness at all times, at all times lovely, but under the spell of twilight it seems to enfold one in a tender embrace, pushing back the sordid, the commonplace, and obliterating those magnified nothings that form the weary burden of civilised man."

Starting in the 1950s, the Vernal area was largely overrun by oil and gas development. But the area around the White River came to stand at the center of a truly homegrown wilderness proposal. In 1985, a doctor named Will Durant and an oil and gas driller named Doug Hatch ran the river with Clay Johnson, a local machinist—who found the spot Dellenbaugh described, with the help of a postage stamp-sized sketch in the fold of another explorer's journal.

The following winter, says Durant, "We sat down at Doug Hatch's kitchen table, and pulled out the topo maps and started drawing lines. We shrunk it as much as we could to avoid anything that would interfere with the proposal."

On paper, they came up with about 9,000 acres, which they then checked on the ground to be sure that no roads or wells would disqualify them from protection. "We'd go out and get lost and wander around, and then we'd try to figure out where we went. We were pretty satisfied that everything was copacetic," Durant says.

As it turned out, their proposal wasn't perfect: An oil company held a lease within the area. But they were able to stave off development of the lease in an exhausting fight that went all the way to an Interior appeals board in Washington, D.C. Later, Durant's Uintah Mountain Club teamed up with the Salt Lake City-based Southern Utah Wilderness Alliance, which expanded the club's proposal to about 19,000 acres, and incorporated it into what is now a 9.1 million-acre statewide wilderness proposal. In 1999, the BLM designated 15,800 acres of land around the White River as a wilderness inventory area.

In the 3.3 million acres of land that the BLM's Vernal field office administers, a 15,800-acre wilderness inventory area was a small but important contrast to the rest of the well-dotted landscape. Many in the agency realized its significance. While the BLM couldn't deny a company's "valid existing right" to drill, which comes with a lease, it could refrain from issuing new leases, and it could quietly allow existing ones to expire. And that's what it did.

"I think the BLM realized how important it was to us," says Durant, "and I think there were some people in the BLM who wanted to see more balance."

But the expanded 15,800-acre area brought more trouble, because some of the newly incorporated land was already leased for oil and gas development. And in 1997, the consortium that owned those leases, the Resource Development Group, started pushing to drill.

The Uintah Mountain Club may have felt it had BLM support in the earlier fight, but all that changed following the Norton-Leavitt settlement. Last summer, three months after the settlement, the BLM released a draft environmental impact statement that would allow 423 wells south of Vernal, including 15 wells in the White River wilderness inventory area, and 35 more in the citizen-proposed areas nearby. A final environmental impact statement should be completed before this summer, and drilling could start any time after that.

"Up until recently," says one agency insider, "it looked like, of any place in the state, (White River) was going to be wilderness."

Now, that looks unlikely.

Oil and Gas Companies Rush Onto Wild Lands

Last October, Pete Kolbenschlag of the Colorado Environmental Coalition (CEC) wrangled a spot in an oil and gas leasing course put on by the Rocky Mountain Mineral Law Foundation. Kolbenschlag found himself filling out a worksheet on how to bid for an oil and gas lease in an area proposed by his group for wilderness protection.

The exercise, written by Craig Carver, a Denver lawyer who represented Marathon Oil in a mid-'90s wilderness battle against CEC, reads: "The current Secretary of the Interior has determined to turn over management of the surface and subsurface resources of the CEC lands to those friends of the Vice-President who served on his energy advisory board. You can't find out who those folks are, but they tell us to lease the CEC tracts come hell or high water."

As industry dives in, BLM offices have clear direction from Washington, D.C., to make oil and gas their first priority. Four months after taking office, President Bush issued two back-to-back executive orders, directing government agencies to expedite energy projects, and ordering agency managers to produce extensive documentation any time they deny a project. At the same time, Vice President Dick Cheney's energy task force called for expediting development in the Rocky Mountain states. This summer, the Bush administration established the Rocky Mountain Energy Council to fast-track oil and gas projects.

Not all of this started with Bush. In November 2000, President Clinton signed the Energy Policy and Conservation Act Amendments (EPCA), which required the Departments of Interior, Agriculture and Energy to study oil and gas reserves on federal lands, and "restrictions or impediments" to their development. That report was released last January, and the April wilderness settlement knocked a lot of "impediments" out of the way. In August, BLM Director Kathleen Clarke issued a memo to agency managers, requiring them to re-evaluate restrictions "in areas where access to public lands and energy minerals is severely restricted."

Washington is also taking a much more hands-on approach. "People at the very local level are getting phone calls from these political people within the (Interior) department, saying what to do," says Martha Hahn, the former BLM state director in Idaho. "(As) a state director, you constantly try to buffer everything that's being shot at you and your employees (from Washington, D.C.) and keep your employees on task. The political types in the department are going around that buffer. It's driving the state directors crazy."

Hahn was pushed out of her position with the BLM in 2002 under pressure from Idaho Republican Sen. Larry Craig. She later lost a job at the Argonne National Laboratory, after she was quoted in a *Vanity Fair* article critical of J. Steven Griles, the former oil and gas industry lawyer who is now second-in-command of the Interior Department.

The political types have made it clear that dissent will not be tolerated. In an appearance before the Interstate Oil and Gas Compact Commission in Reno, Nev., last October, BLM Director Clarke said land managers in her agency had "lost some discipline, lost some accountability, did a lot of freelancing." According to The Associated Press, Clarke vowed to send a "team to look at some of our more problematic field offices."

It's almost impossible to get BLM staffers to talk about life inside the agency these days. Two current BLM state directors contacted for this story declined interviews, and only a handful of BLM employees would comment on the record.

"The pressure, in terms of them not saying anything, is so huge it's obvious," says Hahn. "People are just terrified right now." But the shift within the agencies is clear: In the wake of the April wilderness settlement, the BLM has been moving to get citizens' wilderness lands back into the leasing line-up—first and foremost in Utah. A July 2003 briefing for BLM Director Clarke noted that Washington sees Utah as "leading the way" in leasing such areas. The memo proposed establishing a "SWAT team" to conduct the environmental analysis for leasing "backlogged" wilderness inventory and citizen-proposed wilderness areas.

This November, the first of the Utah wilderness inventory areas hit the auction block in the BLM's quarterly oil and gas lease sale. Several found no buyers. But several parcels in a former wilderness inventory area in Desolation Canyon on the Green River—best-known as a boaters' paradise, but also on the edge of a large oil and gas field—were actually purchased. (The BLM did defer five parcels for further analysis of their "wilderness characteristics.")

"A lot of the areas that are moving forward with potential leasing activity are adjacent to long-standing oil and gas activity," says Interior's Lynn Scarlett. "In many instances, the leases are smack-dab next to (existing) oil and gas activity."

A much bigger round of parcels will be leased from late January to mid-February, including parts of citizen-proposed wilderness in Utah, Colorado, New Mexico and Wyoming.

In Vernal, the first rumblings of change came last year, with a massive seismic exploration project that, in part, targeted two wilderness inventory areas and four citizen-proposed wildernesses. "I think (that) was just an eye-opener for what was getting ready to happen," says Mary Hammer, a former Vernal BLM wildlife biologist. "As soon as that (Norton-Leavitt) settlement was reached, it was like, 'Bingo! We're gonna go in.'"

One BLM employee says that in areas like Vernal, "Up until recently, industry was pretty cooperative. Even if they had a lease in one of these areas, they wouldn't exercise it. But right now, because they're being politically pushed, they're coming in right and left."

John Andrews, of Utah's School and Institutional Trust Lands Administration, downplays the leases. "Don't buy into the concept that, if lands are leased, ruin and destruction are actually happening. From leasing to any sort of significant development involves a lot of what-ifs, and the percentage of leases that ultimately have much activity on them is very, very limited."

Nonetheless, these new energy leases are the biggest threat to the future of wilderness. "Undoing" leases is next to impossible, buying them out is extremely expensive, and they give companies a right to drill. They lay a nearly bomb-proof foundation for future development.

And if there's a sense of urgency in the rush to drill, it may be because the Norton-Leavitt settlement has not gone unchallenged. A coalition of environmental groups, represented by Earthjustice and including The Wilderness Society, SUWA, the Colorado Environmental Coalition and several other state wilderness groups, has asked the federal courts to overturn the settlement. The challenge is now before the 10th Circuit Court of Appeals in Denver—the same court that shot down the state's anti-wilderness lawsuit in 1998.

The industry is pushing hard to buy leases before that challenge gets heard by a judge, says CEC's Kolbenschlag. "They want their drilling permits approved, they want to get those leases in— they want to have all that stuff ready to go, because they know they can get it in now."

The Battle Rages on in the Courts

To some extent, however, the legal challenge to the Leavitt-Norton settlement may be tempering the rush into wild areas.

"I think it's a very great disincentive," says Craig Carver, the Denver lawyer who wrote the exercise teaching companies to lease proposed wilderness areas. "Industry doesn't like controversy; it's not a good place to invest money."

Now, conservation groups are engaged in the legal equivalent of hand-to-hand combat, challenging every lease and drilling permit application. The Colorado Environmental Coalition has appealed El Paso's wells on Big Ridge to the Interior Department's Board of Land Appeals. The Resource Development Group's proposal to drill in the White River area will almost certainly be challenged. And the November lease sales in Utah are under litigation by SUWA.

Earthjustice and The Wilderness Society have also sued to gain access to the records of the negotiations between the Department of the Interior and Utah that resulted in the Norton-Leavitt wilderness settlement. But challenging even one specific project requires tremendous resources. And for some spots, such as Colorado's Big Ridge, it may already be too late.

Back at Big Ridge, Seidenberg, Morris and I walk up to the first well El Paso drilled and abandoned. We're in no hurry: Occasionally, we step off the road to weave through old-growth piñon, the ground beneath the trees dappled with snow and rich moss. When we finally reach the well, we find that the pad is in the first stages of a long recovery. Shredded piñon and junipers have been raked across the ground, but the scar is unmistakable.

As the sun begins to dip and the cold sets in, we linger a while. We take in Big Ridge itself, rising to the east. And we talk about that question of balance that follows the wilderness movement, always.

In the Rocky Mountain states, about 2.5 percent of the land is protected as wilderness. Roughly 64 percent of the public land is open to leasing. "Look at what we're trying to save vs. what oil and gas companies have access to," says Morris. "Oil and gas wants all of it. We want to protect 5 percent."

Big Ridge is by no means the last chance for the gas companies—there's plenty more land, even around here, for them to take a stab at. But here in the Piceance Basin, Big Ridge may be the last chance for wilderness. And for now, it looks as if that chance has been lost.

Interior's Lynn Scarlett points out that, in oil and gas leasing and development, "there's a lot of points of public engagement as you march along in the process"—points where concerned citizens can intervene to shape the fate of wild places. But while the public still has a voice with the BLM on how those areas will be developed, protecting them as wilderness is no longer an option.

In the painfully delicate public-lands balancing act called multiple use, wilderness—and its citizen supporters—have been cut out of the picture. "Why is it that you can keep leasing forever?" Seidenberg asks as we begin to trudge back through the snow and mud. "You can keep finding oil. But you can't find any more wilderness."

The 2003 Utah wilderness settlement reopened BLM lands for development. Not much later, something similar happened on Forest Service lands.

In 1999, during the Clinton presidency, Forest Service Chief Mike Dombeck had announced an 18-month moratorium on road-building in national forest roadless areas. The administration attempted to make the moratorium permanent with the Roadless Area Conservation Rule, which prohibited logging, mining and oil and gas drilling on 58.5 million acres of forest. The Forest Service issued the "roadless rule" on Jan. 12, 2001—eight days before President Bush took office.

Soon after taking office, the Bush administration put the rule on hold—during which time the roadless areas were still effectively closed to development. But on July 12, 2004, Secretary of Agriculture Ann Veneman announced that the Forest Service would only protect roadless areas in states whose governors explicitly requested such protection—and only if they completed extremely expensive environmental analysis and public comment processes.

As this book goes to press, it is unclear how many governors will ask the Forest Service to uphold roadless protections in their states.

MANAGING THE WILD

Motors in Wilderness

The Wilderness Act prohibits the use of motor vehicles and motorized equipment in wilderness— with certain exceptions. Aircraft can continue to land in wilderness areas where they did so before wilderness designation, such as the backcountry airstrips in the Frank Church-River of No Return Wilderness. Aircraft can also be used "as necessary to meet the minimum requirements for the administration of the area," including rescue and firefighting.

In general, land managers are required to identify and use the "minimum tool" necessary to accomplish a specific project. But it is not always a clear-cut decision, as the first story in this subsection, about the use of helicopters in wilderness for scientific research shows.

In other instances, the use of motorized vehicles such as snowmobiles is outright illegal but continues nonetheless—an issue addressed in the second story.

Should the EPA's Acid Rain Researchers Be Allowed to Helicopter into Wilderness?

BY BETSY MARSTON

Two federal agencies went head to head this spring over the issue of using helicopters in wilderness areas to reach high-altitude lakes for an acid-rain study.

The issue also split conservationists. Some said because acid rain might threaten the survival of wilderness lakes, the need for research justified "mechanized transport" banned by the Wilderness Act. Others argued for a case-by-case decision for each lake.

The agencies in the dispute were the U.S. Environmental Protection Agency, which released its draft environmental analysis for a Western wilderness lake study in March, and the Forest Service, which balked at the preferred alternative. The EPA's first choice was to fly helicopters into 425 designated wilderness areas to test lakes. A total of 888 lakes have been selected for testing in nine Western states. More than a thousand lakes have already been studied in the East.

What seemed to rankle the Forest Service most was EPA's preparation of its draft analysis in a vacuum. "We knew there was something going on for a year and a half," says Dennis Haddow, air quality specialist for the Forest Service in Denver, "but there wasn't coordination with us. The draft turned out to be a justification document."

The EPA based its case for using helicopters on the Wilderness

Act itself, which reads: The areas are to be devoted to "public purposes of recreational, scenic, scientific, educational, conservation and historical use." And since helicopters were used to touch down and gather water samples from eastern lakes, said the EPA, methods and results would only be consistent if helicopters were used in the West. Speed was also crucial, the EPA said, as samples deteriorate over time. The EPA added that the only wilderness values affected would be "experiential and mental and moral."

For the Forest Service, which received mixed signals from conservationists, the EPA's draft oversimplified wilderness management.

Jim Byrne, head of the Forest Service's air quality program in Washington, D.C., asks, "Should you give up what's fairly explicit in the Wilderness Act because somebody wants to do some research?" Another tricky problem, he says, is precedent. There are so many requests for vehicles in wilderness, he points out, that they're "queued up like a breadline in the Depression."

Haddow says where the EPA failed was in its premise that the study's requirements were paramount and could only be met one way—by using helicopters. The result is that the "study was not designed to protect wilderness. We would have done it differently."

Alternatives not selected by the EPA in its draft are horse access, helicopters combined with horse access, and no study at all. Haddow said 70 percent of the wilderness lakes could be reached by horseback within the EPA's 24-hour time limit for obtaining and analyzing lake samples.

Haddow said the EPA, which has been "bruised" by the controversy, also failed to include the second and third phases of its acid-rain research in the environmental analysis. Those phases require more detailed studies of lakes inside wilderness as well as analyses of lakes just outside wilderness boundaries.

Most conservation groups welcomed the acid-rain study on the grounds that the more known about acid-rain damage the better wilderness will be protected. Supporters included the Environmental Defense Fund, Wyoming Outdoor Council and the Colorado Mountain Club. The Wilderness Society, National Audubon and Sierra Club expressed reservations to the Forest Service, some after vigorous internal debate over the issue.

For Larry Mehlhaff, regional staffer for the Sierra Club, the issue was one of precedent and adherence to the Wilderness Act. Even though some wilderness areas allow some form of mechanized access through prior use, "does that mean we compromise the rest?" Ranchers are always requesting motorized access in wilderness, he says: "That's why case-by-case approval is needed."

After the draft was released, the EPA and Forest Service began to negotiate. The process was not smooth, and Forest Service Chief Max Peterson twice delayed his announcement of the Forest Service's response to the EA.

On May 20, 1985, as *High Country News* went to press, an announcement was delayed again. A Forest Service spokesman would only say that it appeared EPA's helicopter use would be limited. EPA hopes to begin its survey immediately.

The EPA's acid-rain study proceeded, but only some of the sites were sampled using helicopters, while others were sampled by foot and horseback. Acid rain samples from the Mount Zirkel Wilderness in northwest Colorado provided key evidence in a push for major pollution-control improvements in nearby coal-burning power plants during the 1990s.

MARCH 3, 1997

Wilderness Has a New Foe: Snowmobiles

BY GREG HANSCOM

SEELEY LAKE, Mont.—The February drizzle has done little to dampen the spirits of the crowd here for the Snowmoblivious festival. Snowmobile aficionados from as far away as Washington and Colorado bounce along the shoulders of the main street and buzz through the woods on groomed trails.

"We're out with the whole family," says one rider. "Seeley Lake is one of our favorite sledding spots—even with a little rain."

Locals in this west-central Montana town, pop. 2,000, will tell you that timber is still king in this country, but they've found a new, often noisy queen—tourism. In the summer, the lake hums with the sound of Jet Skis. Winter recreation keeps the town buzzing in the off-months too, says Curtis Friede, who owns a snowmobile shop in town.

More visitors mean more pressure on limited space. Increasingly, snowmobilers are leaving the groomed trails in search of powder in the high country. The catch is that much of the high country here is federal or tribal wilderness, off limits to motorized users.

Although snowmobilers have been illegally riding in the Mission Mountains Wilderness near Seeley Lake for more than 20 years, trespass problems get worse every year, according to Frank Gillin, fish and game chief on the Flathead Indian Reservation. Foothills around Seeley Lake provide easy access, and logging roads and state-funded snowmobile trails lead right up to the wilderness boundary. As faster, more reliable snowmobiles allow people to ride deeper into the wilderness, those routes multiply and tempt trespassers.

Snowmobile trespass is a Montana-wide problem, not just limited to Seeley Lake, says John Gatchell of the Montana Wilderness Association. One Forest Service report, says Gatchell, cited 472 confirmed violations of the Absaroka-Beartooth Wilderness boundary by snowmobilers during the 1995–96 season. Those 472 violations resulted in just seven tickets issued by the Forest Service.

The laws are there: A snowmobiler caught in a wilderness area can face a stiff penalty—up to a $5,000 fine and six months in jail. A second-time offender could lose his sled. Yet chances of being caught are slim to none.

The problem, says Swan Lake forester Remy Pochelon, is that busting a snowmobiler is next to impossible. "Everybody has a black suit and a black helmet and they're on a red or yellow snowmobile doing about 80 miles per hour in a plume of snow." And unlike cars, snowmobiles have no visible license numbers. "I'd have to put on glasses and get down on my knees to read one of those (registration) stickers," says Pochelon.

In Pochelon's eight-year stint on the Swan Lake District, snowmobilers have been prosecuted for trespassing in the Mission on only two occasions. Ironically, the prosecutions stemmed from two sledding accidents. In 1995, Leo Sudan of Bigfork died when he fell from his snowmobile and slid down an embankment into a tree. Less than a year later, Ron Martin, a Swan Lake peat-moss salesman, fell 1,100 feet to his death when the cornice he was riding on broke. Both men died deep inside wilderness boundaries.

Snowmobile trespass is creating "a drive-through wilderness," says Gatchell. "If we don't get a handle on this now, we might as well accept that there is no more wilderness left."

There is hope of a solution for some of Montana's backcountry. In Seeley Lake and other communities around the Mission Mountains, agencies, activists and snowmobilers may have found a way to keep the wilderness quiet.

Their effort stems from frustration. Kari Gunderson, a Forest Service contracted manager of the Mission Wilderness, says in 17 years she and her partner, Joe Flood, have only caught a few trespassers. But then the judge threw out the cases, she adds.

Gunderson and Flood decided it was time for a new approach. This winter, they joined with Jill Duryee of the Montana Wilderness Association to create a coalition of federal, state and tribal officials, law enforcement officers, environmentalists and snowmobilers dedicated to keeping snowmobilers out of the Mission.

The Forest Service and tribal Fish and Game have posted more signs at access points and stepped up patrols of popular inroads and aerial surveys of the wilderness boundary. Local sheriffs' offices have also joined the effort.

In Seeley Lake, the Driftriders Snowmobile Club has pitched in by posting maps in shops around town with warnings: "Tribal Land! Wilderness! Stay Out! No-No Land!" Their trail grooming report in the local paper includes reminders that wilderness is off limits.

Snowmobilers have good reason to police themselves. Montana Fish, Wildlife and Parks, the agency responsible for doling out state gas-tax dollars for trail grooming, has given the Driftriders an ultimatum: Stop trespassing in the Mission or lose your trails near the wilderness boundary. "Our goal is not to get thrown out of the Forest Service Land," says club member Jim Weatherly. "If we police our own people, we won't get thrown out."

Meanwhile, the Montana Wilderness Association has created a form to help backcountry users report trespassers, and volunteers have been patrolling the wilderness boundary on weekends.

So far, the new approach seems to work, as no trespasses have been reported in the Mission Wilderness this season. "This couldn't happen without the help of all of the people involved," says Duryee. But the snowmobiling season is far from over, and long spring days may tempt sledders to head for the mountain meadows and bowls.

Still, Forest Service recreation manager Woody Baxter says prevention is the best hope. "Let's educate them with a big sign. Let's give them a warning," he says. "Then, if they go into a wilderness—nail their ass."

Finding a Path to the Future

The Stratosphere Casino in Las Vegas, Nevada, set
against the backdrop of the La Madre Mountain
Wilderness, designated in 2002.

—PHOTO BY R. MARSH STARKS, *LAS VEGAS SUN*

The Bush administration's wilderness and roadless reversals of 2003 and 2004 blew apart the Clinton-era policies of interim protection for lands in citizens' wilderness proposals. Now, the political realities of the day are forcing wilderness organizers to reconsider how they approach wilderness protection. Activists have been forging innovative deals to keep wilderness moving forward, some of which even predate the wilderness rollbacks. In 2002, Nevada activists shepherded 17 new wilderness areas surrounding Las Vegas into reality, by piggybacking them onto a bill that sold off federal land to fuel the city's white-hot growth boom. In Idaho, the decline of traditional Western economies such as grazing, logging and mining has created the opportunity to cut a similar wilderness deal. There, a Republican-sponsored bill inspired by Nevada's experience could create a quarter-million acres of new wilderness in the Boulder and White Cloud mountains—and at the same time provide money for a two-year college that would offer local residents educational opportunities for a place in the New West's economy.

But protecting new wilderness sometimes takes a little downright orneriness. In Idaho's Owyhee Canyonlands, for example, environmentalists have used court challenges to force ranchers to the negotiating table—and offered wilderness as a way to end bitter disputes about grazing.

And there's still hope in the old tried-and-true stand-alone wilderness bill. Some groups are moving smaller, locally focused bills, such as the Tumacacori Highlands proposal in Arizona and the bipartisan bill to designate the Ojito Wilderness in New Mexico.

In the absence of federal leadership on wilderness protection, one state government is seizing the initiative to fend off development in potential wilderness areas. New Mexico Gov. Bill Richardson has issued orders to prevent oil and gas companies from drilling Otero Mesa—the last remaining tract of Chihuahuan Desert grassland in the United States, and an area that the New Mexico Wilderness Alliance has proposed for wilderness.

There are as many tactics to designate wilderness as there are potential wilderness areas. But it is clear that the future of wilderness lies in a renewed commitment to creating — or recreating — a local politics that can take wilderness proposals forward.

The Wild Card

As the Wilderness Act Nears its 40th Anniversary, Protecting Wild Lands Requires a New Kind of Deal-Making

BY MATT JENKINS

LAS VEGAS, Nev.—Walking through the gaming floor of the Stratosphere casino is like navigating the inside of a pinball machine. The clang-clang-clang of slot jackpots rings in the air as grandmothers pump video poker machines full of quarters; cocktail waitresses bounce between blackjack tables with trays of Budweiser and gin and tonics. Jeremy Garncarz and I weave through the crowd and cram into an elevator full of tourists for the ride to the top of the 1,149-foot-tall Stratosphere tower.

On the way up, two coiffured women chatter about their plans for the evening: a trip to the all-male Australian strip show over at the Excalibur called "Thunder from Down Under." One of the women cracks a joke about "southern exposure" that makes her husband turn crimson.

When we pile out onto the observation deck, we're hit with the harsh glare of the January sun and the hum of air-tour helicopters wheeling past the tower. Below us, the city spreads wide. The palm-lined Strip and its powerhouse casinos shimmer in the sun: Treasure Island, the Mirage, Caesars Palace, Bellagio, the Excalibur, the Luxor and Mandalay Bay. Beyond them, the city reaches all the way to the desert mountains that edge the Las Vegas Valley.

This has to be the most optimistic place in the nation. Vegas is a city that beats the odds: Its boosters have taken a patch of desert and built a sprawling, decadent paradise. Today, the city announces its triumph with neon casino marquees and opulent water fountains.

And it seems like the last place a public-lands wilderness advocate would make camp. But Garncarz, who wears a week's worth of stubble and is an organizer for Friends of Nevada Wilderness, has brought me here because this is where conservationists ground out a gutsy wilderness victory last year. The day after the 2002 elections gave Republicans control over Congress, President George W. Bush signed a bill into law protecting 452,000 acres of roadless land, much of it ringing Las Vegas like numbers on a roulette wheel.

The victory has taken on symbolic overtones for the long-suffering wilderness movement. As the Wilderness Act nears its 40th anniversary, the movement to protect the nation's last wild lands seems to have stalled out, and the results of last November's elections read to some like a death notice. Yet, Nevada's wilderness gain points out that even in a political desert, the heart of the wilderness movement still beats, although with a different cadence than in the glory days of the past.

I've come with a lot of questions. And as Garncarz begins walking me around this perch, high over the fastest-growing city in the nation, I begin to get some answers.

A People's Movement Lands on the Rocks

For conservationists, wilderness is the holy grail of public-lands protection. Ask one, and she'll probably rattle off a few lines from the 1964 Wilderness Act—lines about places "where the earth and its community of life are untrammeled by man, where man himself is a visitor who does not remain," places where you'll find "outstanding opportunities for solitude."

Of course, one person's holy grail is another's holy hell, and this is as true for wilderness areas as anyplace; there are no roads allowed in wilderness areas, or cars or four-wheelers or other forms of "mechanical transport." This makes the timber and mining industries, the off-road crowd, and even some mountain bikers a little uncomfortable.

But like it or not, the push to protect wilderness is a people's movement. Today, there are 662 wilderness areas in the U.S., encompassing more than 106 million acres. How it came to be that way is a story of visionary Americans, hard work and thousands of unsung citizen activists in every corner of the country.

"The Wilderness Act is a real example of democracy at work. It is a citizens' law," says Bart Koehler, a graying, robust 54-year old wilderness veteran who stands with a logger's pitched-forward stance. "People can come together, draw up proposals to protect their public lands and petition their members of Congress. And they, in a very real sense, shape the future of their country."

A few weeks before my trip to Vegas, I visited Koehler at The Wilderness Society's Wilderness Support Center in Durango, Colo. The Center, incongruously located on the fourth floor of the only high-rise in town, serves as a logistical home base for numerous local groups around the country. Maps were tacked up all over the walls, and stacks of paper overflowed from Koehler's desk onto the floor and even his chair. It hinted at the work it takes to transform a wilderness vision into a political strategy.

Koehler worked as a field organizer for The Wilderness Society in Wyoming during the 1970s, helping to form local groups and build the confidence and skills of local leaders, and making trips to Washington, D.C., to testify in front of Congress. It was tough, on-the-ground work.

"We all took perverse pride in how many miles we put on our beat-up cars," he said, "driving VW bugs with nothing but cheeseburger wrappers and empty beer cans in the back."

In 1972, the Lincoln-Scapegoat Wilderness in Montana became the first citizen-proposed wilderness to be officially protected. The late '70s brought others, like Gospel Hump in Idaho and Sandia Peak outside Albuquerque. And later, the Forest Service and BLM included innumerable other citizen-proposed wilderness areas in their recommendations to Congress.

In 1994, Congress passed the California Desert Protection Act, protecting nearly 3.5 million acres of land as wilderness. It was the largest wilderness bill in the Lower 48 ever, but it was also the last major wilderness bill to see a president's desk. Later that same year, elections brought the "Gingrich Revolution," when Republicans, led by Georgia Rep. Newt Gingrich, ended the Democrats' 40-year domination of the House and took control of the Senate. The wilderness push hit a rock wall.

"When Gingrich came in, it was a rude awakening," said Koehler. "We had to devote more attention to playing hard-core defense."

Wilderness activists dug in, fighting timber, mining and energy companies that wanted to cut into roadless areas. Some groups, such as the Southern Utah Wilderness Alliance—which had crafted a proposal to protect 9.1 million acres statewide—held their ground, trying to keep their grassroots energized and a national constituency informed, until that magical day in Congress arrived when they could actually pass a bill. Others, like The Wilderness Society, put more energy and funding into helping grassroots groups, knowing that local support was crucial in passing wilderness bills in a Republican-dominated Congress. In 1999, the society set up the Wilderness Support Center, with offices in Durango and Washington, D.C., and staffed it with Koehler and other wilderness warhorses.

By 2001, the political outlook seemed to improve slightly. Bush was in the White House, but Democrats held a slim majority in the Senate and seemed to be gaining ground in the House. Even some Republican congressmen, such as Rep. Scott McInnis of Colorado, were willing to consider small wilderness bills.

In a focused push, the Pew Charitable Trusts spent more than a million dollars a year on public opinion surveys and national media campaigns to build support for wilderness. There was more money, more dedicated organizers, and even a lot of ballyhoo about a "wilderness renaissance"—but the bald fact was that, although a few small bills squeaked through Congress, no major wilderness legislation passed.

Then came the election of 2002, which solidified Republican control of Congress just as the Bush administration stormed into the third year of an aggressive offensive against the environment. A huge cloud rolled over the prospects for more wilderness, and I rolled into Durango with a stack of questions. After I talked with Koehler, I headed down the hill to the Durango office of Campaign for America's Wilderness. There, I found executive director Mike Matz, the intense former director of the Southern Utah Wilderness Alliance. Last summer, the group, primarily funded by Pew, announced a crusade to get 50 million acres of wilderness designated over the next 10 years, focusing primarily on Alaska, California, Idaho, Nevada and Utah.

But two weeks after the election, an obviously dispirited Matz sat in a nearly empty room with a TV propped up in one corner, keeping a desultory eye on C-SPAN the entire time I was there. Talking to him felt like poking a dead cat with a stick.

"When we initially designed the list of (wilderness protection) priorities, it was under a much different set of assumptions," he said, explaining that he'd hoped the Democrats would hold onto the Senate and gain ground in the House. "We thought, if anything, the (political) lay of the land would get better. Now, everything's on the table."

Compromise Ties Wilderness to Its Antithesis

On the national level, things have rarely looked so grim for wilderness, but on the ground, people are getting creative. And that's why Jeremy Garncarz, the Friends of Nevada Wilderness organizer, has brought me to the top of the Stratosphere.

Garncarz walks me around the observation platform, past vacationing twenty-something couples posing for snapshots, and points beyond the city skyline to the new Rainbow Mountain Wilderness, the La Madre, the Muddies, the North and South McCulloughs and the Mount Charleston wilderness expansion.

"The majority of people (who come to Vegas) put their quarters in the slot machines and stick to the city," says Garncarz, a compact 32-year-old who seems to be fueled solely by coffee. "But now, with places like the Muddy Mountains Wilderness, you can point to them and say, 'That's what we're talking about.'" The new areas are puny compared to giants such as the million-acre Bob Marshall Wilderness in Montana and the 558,000-acre Gila in New Mexico, but they're a symbolic advance in a city—and state—where wilderness has long been something of a pariah. Nevada—which has more federally managed land than any other state except Alaska—ranks ninth of the 11 Western states in percentage of designated wilderness, with only about 3 percent, compared to California's 13.3 percent.

These new wilderness areas are even more remarkable, because Nevada has the fastest-growing population in the nation. In 2000–2001, the state grew by 5.4 percent; Clark County, home of Las Vegas, grew by 6.6 percent. The demographics are incredibly unstable: For every three people who move to Las Vegas each month, one moves out. "Most of the folks who live here don't get involved (in environmental issues)," laughs Garncarz. "It's Las Vegas: They have a lot of other things on their minds."

So how, in this atmosphere, did Nevada wilderness groups get a bill passed? In many ways, the story followed the traditional trajectory of many other citizens' wilderness proposals. Formed in 1999, the grassroots Nevada Wilderness Project began scouring the Mojave Desert of southern Nevada, using volunteers and paid field teams to identify 4.1 million acres of roadless land. Then, the Project and the Friends of Nevada Wilderness banded with five other conservation groups to form the Nevada Wilderness Coalition, and set out to build support for wilderness protection.

Most of the support came from urban areas such as Las Vegas and Reno. They also found some unlikely allies, such as the last public-lands rancher in Clark County, a straight-talking guy named Cal Baird, who wears a black hat and runs 150 head of Mexican corriente roping cattle about 30 miles south of Las Vegas.

The support of locals like Baird helped the cause, but they still needed political help from on high. "And in Nevada," says John Wallin, a former Patagonia mail-order manager who directs the nonprofit Wilderness Project, "it begins and ends with Sen. (Harry) Reid."

Reid, the second-highest ranking Democrat in the Senate and the anchor of the Nevada delegation, is a staunch wilderness supporter. But he understood better than anyone that in wilderness, as in Nevada, you can't win big without some wheeling and dealing. Getting the proposal through Congress would require a tactical departure from the classic wilderness formula. It would require tying wilderness protection to its antithesis: urban growth.

When Reid first proposed this, conservationists balked. In 2000, Congress was considering a bill that transferred 6,500 acres of BLM land to Clark County for the planned Ivanpah Airport, about 30 miles south of the city. Reid approached the Wilderness Coalition about using the airport bill as a vehicle for a wilderness designation for the North and South McCullough mountains. They turned up their noses, saying they didn't want wilderness tied to the massive airport bill.

A year later, however, Vegas was running up against the public lands surrounding the city. The BLM had been steadily auctioning off land to accommodate spreading suburbs, but the city was fast approaching a congressionally established growth boundary. So the Nevada delegation drew up the Clark County Conservation of Public Land and Natural Resources Act, which, among other things, would expand the BLM "disposal boundary," allowing Vegas to sprawl across another 22,000 acres.

Once again, Reid made it known to wilderness activists that he could get something done for them — if they were willing to cut a deal. And this time, wilderness activists saw the writing on the wall. "We have to be realistic and admit that a lot of these (development bills) are inevitable," says Brian O'Donnell, one of Koehler's compatriots at the Wilderness Support Center, who worked closely with the Nevada wilderness activists. "Can we (take advantage of them to) make protections for threatened land, or do we say 'no' and get rolled?"

The Nevada Wilderness Coalition pared down its 4.1 million-acre proposal to just over a tenth of its original size and polished it up, proposing 17 new BLM, Forest Service and Park Service wilderness areas, and one wilderness expansion, totaling 452,000 acres. Through 2002, the coalition took its message to farmers' markets, the University of Nevada Las Vegas campus, and music and beer festivals, ultimately generating 5,000 letters to Nevada's congressmen. Garncarz and Wallin even made a tongue-in-cheek attempt to get the local brothels to sign on.

The Campaign for America's Wilderness helped with organizing and public outreach, and the Wilderness Support Center's O'Donnell and Koehler shuttled back and forth between Durango and Vegas to offer guidance through legislative tangles, crashing out at night at Garncarz's apartment.

"The all-time record was 13 people," says Wallin. "The last person was sleeping on the kitchen floor with his head against the stove."

But even with this relatively small proposal, getting the cooperation of Nevada's congressional delegation required compromise. As a concession to the hunting community, the bill included a condition allowing the Nevada Division of Wildlife to use trucks and helicopters in the wilderness to survey and capture wildlife and to maintain "guzzlers"—artificial watering holes.

The state's other senator, Republican John Ensign, co-sponsored Reid's bill, but Republican Rep. Jim Gibbons added language to his House version that would have "hard released" 180,000 acres of roadless land not included in the wilderness areas—making them permanently ineligible for subsequent consideration as wilderness.

It would have been the first wilderness bill ever passed with hard-release language, and that, says O'Donnell, "is not something that we would have compromised on."

Gibbons finally dumped the hard-release provision, but insisted that the bill not assign the new wilderness areas a federal water right. The bill passed the House on Oct. 17 and was approved by the Senate the following day. And on the day after the November elections, President Bush signed it into law.

"If I were the king, I would have lots of wilderness," says Reid. "(But) I had to compromise."

"Galactic" Differences Within the Movement

The Nevada wilderness bill was a hard-won bargain that tempered idealism with realism—and it's a sign of the times for the wilderness movement, which can either move forward incrementally, or risk grinding to a complete standstill. Among the groups that have been successful in getting wilderness passed recently, there's been a return to the movement's local, democratic roots. There is also a growing skepticism of the huge wilderness proposals, which some critics believe have seen their day. Wallin says there's a "galactic" difference between the mega-wilderness approach and the go-local style that ultimately worked in Nevada.

Jeff Widen, the associate director of the Colorado Environmental Coalition, who worked on the massive 1994 California Desert Protection Act, says big-ticket bills are good "because (they) hold out the bigger vision of things. But the political realities dictate that the packages we're going to move are going to be smaller ones.

"We can pass wilderness bills forever, as long as we talk about places and not acres," says Widen. "If you have a whole bunch of areas together, it makes it harder to talk about the specifics of individual areas and work out compromises."

But any talk of compromise bothers some wilderness advocates. "We're glad that the wilderness system is growing and that people are able to get new areas added," says George Nickas, the head of the Missoula, Mont.-based Wilderness Watch. "The concern is that there were also a lot of special provisions added to the bill that make it so (the new areas in Nevada) are managed as something less than wilderness as it's defined under the Wilderness Act."

Nickas fears that concessions in the Clark County bill—such as those made for hunters—are the small end of a wedge: "Every time we make another (exception to the rules), we diminish what wilderness is."

Nickas' broader agenda is to push wilderness to its purest ideal. Wilderness Watch fights to remove cabins and airstrips grandfathered into wilderness areas around the West—and to generally undo many of the concessions made in the process of designating wilderness.

But Widen says that compromise has been a constant theme in the wilderness movement: "It's always been about really working with people and coming up with something that is less than perfect, but is awfully damn good."

Idaho's River of No Return Wilderness and Montana's Great Bear, for example, have active backcountry airstrips, while other wilderness areas hold installations such as microwave towers. The boundaries of the proposed Wild Sky Wilderness in Washington State have been adjusted to allow snowmobiles in some areas, and the proposal would allow float-plane landings, as well. Concessions like these have long been used to get locals to back wilderness protection, and some activists argue that Nickas' hard-line approach could undermine the chance to protect areas in the future. Right now, for example, Wilderness Watch is trying to force the BLM to crack down on ranchers who run cattle in the Steens Mountain Wilderness in Oregon, designated in 2000. In return for supporting wilderness protection, ranchers were permitted to graze cattle in parts of the wilderness, and they're allowed to drive into the area to check fences and stock tanks. Wilderness Watch forced the BLM to conduct an environmental assessment on the impacts of the occasional trips.

"Wilderness Watch wants to formalize what's always been done on a handshake," says Andy Wiessner, a Vail, Colo., attorney—and member of the *HCN* board of directors—who has helped

Steens ranchers swap land inside the wilderness for BLM land outside. "Some compromise has to be made with ranchers so their life isn't going to be micro-managed."

Bart Koehler agrees that, occasionally, concessions have to be made to protect wild places. He rings a theme of considered pragmatism. "The way we approach this stuff is what I half-jokingly call 'coyote planning.' You're on the ridgeline looking at the big picture, but you've got your eyes and ears open looking for opportunities—and if a rabbit runs in front of you, you pounce on it."

The Spirit Lives

And even in these dark political days, opportunities do come along. Last year, Coloradans got the James Peak Wilderness near Rocky Mountain National Park, Californians got 56,880 acres of wilderness expansion along the Pacific Coast at Big Sur, and South Dakotans saw the Black Elk Wilderness expanded. The common theme: Each of these areas was small, and came with strong local support.

And as the new Congress gets to work, there are prospects for moving forward. Sen. Patty Murray, D-Wash., has reintroduced her bill for the 106,000-acre Wild Sky Wilderness. The bill passed the Senate last year, but the clock ran out on it in the House. An hour's drive east of Seattle, the proposed wilderness is notable for including lowland forest as well as the traditional high-elevation terrain.

Another bill with some legs is the California Wild Heritage Act, sponsored by Sen. Barbara Boxer, D-Calif., which proposes 2.5 million acres of new wilderness. Boxer will introduce it for the second time this year, but she still has yet to pass a crucial hurdle: getting support from fellow California Sen. Dianne Feinstein, who sponsored the 1994 California Desert Protection Act. Feinstein is still gathering feedback from locals who could be affected by the wide-ranging bill.

And around the West, grassroots activists continue to scour

the landscape. In Nevada, the wilderness movement's old VW-driving esprit lives on. Last year, Jeremy Garncarz put 30,000 miles on his Toyota 4Runner—mapping potential wilderness, attending meetings, delivering slide shows at local garden clubs—and occasionally, even getting out to enjoy the fruits of his labor.

While I'm in Vegas, Garncarz and John Wallin take me out for a night at the new Lime Canyon Wilderness north of Lake Mead. On the way out of town, we stop for food, two cases of beer and a bottle of gin. As we wait in the checkout line, Garncarz quips over his shoulder about "keeping Nevada wild."

The new wilderness is spectacular. Beyond the smog-tinged city, the Mojave Desert is a sensuous landscape of rocky desert ranges tipped toward the sky and sweeping bajadas dotted with Joshua trees, yucca and creosote bush. The sun hangs high over the rugged desert terrain.

"Jeremy and I take a weird delight that it's fuckin' Sodom and Gomorrah surrounded by all these beautiful places," says Wallin.

As we pass the bottle that night, the two wilderness warriors tell me their next focus is eastern Nevada, where they hope to finish an inventory of potential wilderness later this spring.

Sen. Reid's office has made it clear that there's plenty of potential for more wilderness in Nevada—but its protection will be inextricably linked to development. In February, the state's congressional delegation held field hearings in rural Lincoln and White Pine counties to assess the potential for development bills similar to last year's Clark County bill.

"Eastern Nevada will be tougher," says Wallin. But he says the group's success rests with "our willingness to do things incrementally. There are so many public-lands issues here, and we see each one as an opportunity (to include) wilderness."

As an endless stream of jetliners sail overhead on their final approach to the Las Vegas airport, I ask Garncarz and Wallin if, even in the new wilderness areas, they feel like they can really ever escape the presence of Las Vegas. Garncarz thinks for a minute and says, "Yeah, sure. But no matter where you are, you can always see the light from the Luxor." Sure enough, the southern sky is shot through with a brilliant bluish beam from the 40-billion candlepower spotlight atop the pyramid-shaped, Egyptian-themed Luxor casino.

There's an old maxim in the wilderness movement that argues for a sense of balance: For every acre that's sold off and developed, or opened up for oil and gas drilling, some wilderness should be protected to compensate. Now, it seems that precept has been turned on its head: Protecting an acre of wilderness means surrendering another acre — or five acres, or 10 — to development. I can't help but wonder about this wilderness on the ragged urban fringe, hemmed in by ATV tracks and the nighttime glitter of growth pressing into the desert. It seems a world away from the classic wilderness of John Muir's High Sierra where, he wrote, "everything in it seems equally divine — one smooth, pure, wild glow of Heaven's love."

And a question lingers, one which hangs behind the entire wilderness movement as it pushes into the 21st century: Is this fringe wilderness really wild? An answer, of sorts, comes two nights later, back in a motel room in Las Vegas. I'm jolted awake by sudden shouting in the street outside my motel room window and a flurry of sirens screaming down Flamingo Road. Within minutes, a police helicopter takes up a tight orbit over the motel.

When the sun comes up, hours later, Vegas is sleeping off another long night. And as I drive out of town in the morning light, past the advancing edge of the city and into the wide desert, I realize that this wilderness is more important than ever. And more than ever, the movement to protect our last wild places demands the same brand of boundless optimism that lies at the heart of Vegas' strike-it-rich allure.

I can't help but think about what Bart Koehler had told me when I visited him in Durango. "If you're a pessimist, you shouldn't be working on this," he said. "You have to be a die-hard optimist."

Riding the Middle Path

In Idaho's Owyhee Region, an Effort to
Protect Wilderness and Keep Ranchers in Business
Threatens to Crack under Pressure

BY ROBYN MORRISON

BRUNEAU, Idaho—Rancher Chris Black pulls his pickup off the Shoofly Cutoff Road, concerned that a stranger may need help. There's a young man in a baseball cap, standing by a truck, who explains that he has just shot a rattlesnake. He wants the rattles for a trophy, but is too squeamish to finish the job. In neighborly fashion, Black climbs from his truck and, with a swift jab of his shovel, chops the rattles from the lifeless snake. He picks up the severed tail and tosses it at the young man's feet.

"Scared of snakes," muses Black, as he rattles on down the road, baby-blue rosary beads jiggling from the rearview mirror.

Around him spreads the rugged Owyhee, 9 million acres of sagebrush steppe, canyons, plateaus and mountains, covering southwest Idaho and spilling into Oregon and Nevada. Only a few thousand people live in the whole region, but it's home to one of the nation's largest populations of California bighorn sheep and the world's largest population of nesting raptors, as well as pronghorn, mule deer, sage grouse, redband trout and a host of rare and endangered plants found nowhere else in the world.

Black drives an hour on the washboard road to a sage-and-juniper plateau where he has a cabin, a hired hand, and cattle he needs to move. On this blistering-hot day in August, Black and his ranch hand move several hundred head through a gate and begin separating the yearlings from the adult cows. It's gritty work, and anything but simple. As yearlings bolt into the wrong pasture, Black wheels his horse around and, with the help of two dusty-tongued white-and-black dogs, drives them back to the herd.

Beyond the fences lies some of the land that Black leases for grazing from the federal Bureau of Land Management— 87,000 acres of unfenced sage, bunchgrass and canyons of lichen-splattered rhyolite rolling to the south. It's such rough country that it takes less time to trot a horse the 20 miles to the far end than it does to drive the rock-strewn and rutted roads.

Black's family has been ranching in the Owyhee since the 1870s, and for all useful purposes, he's king of this country. But he's recently offered to give up 20,000 acres of the backcountry kingdom he leases, in return for what will likely be a tidy sum from the federal government— and also for the sake of bringing some peace to this fiercely contested landscape.

For the last 30 years, this has been the site of some of the West's toughest battles over cattle grazing, as environmentalists have fought to protect public rangelands, while ranchers have struggled to retain control over land that has been in their care for generations. Land managers, meanwhile, have swung back and forth with changing political winds. But for more than two years, a group of ranchers, environmentalists, local officials, off-road vehicle riders and others—who call their group the Owyhee Initiative—has worked to reach consensus on a new way to manage these BLM lands.

In the give-and-take, Idaho's environmentalists could win a sizable wilderness designation—possibly 500,000 acres—the kind of victory they haven't tasted in nearly a quarter-century. In return, locals would get more control over these federal lands.

Black believes the Owyhee Initiative could bring needed stability to ranchers and the community. "It could temper the political see-saw," he says.

It's a remarkable situation: Idaho is one of the West's most politically conservative states, and battles have raged here for decades over just about every environmental issue. Yet the state is poised to pull off not just one, but two major consensus deals—the Owyhee Initiative and another to the north, in the Boulder and White Cloud mountains.

Consensus never comes easy, though, and both deals are under attack from the right and the left—and also creating friction within the environmental and ranching circles. Will the Owyhee Initiative write a new chapter on what it takes to find the middle ground and win wilderness in the Bush era? Or, like so many other collaborative efforts, is it doomed to lose momentum and stagger into oblivion?

Forced to the Table

In the Owyhee, ranchers and environmentalists haven't sat down at the bargaining table out of the goodness of their hearts. Metaphorically speaking, more guns have been pointed at more heads around here than you'll find in a Quentin Tarantino movie.

The conflict has centered on 4.9 million-acre Owyhee County, whose 11,000 residents are outnumbered by cattle nearly four-to-one. Uncompromising environmentalists in the Committee for the High Desert and the Western Watersheds Project believe the arid land can't support cattle at all, and they have evidence. The BLM, which manages nearly 70 percent of the land in the county, admitted that throughout the 1980s and 1990s, almost all the rangeland was in poor or only fair condition, and almost all the riparian areas along streams and rivers—crucial for wildlife—were in unsatisfactory condition, with eroded banks, battered vegetation and reduced and warmed water flows.

The BLM had been lax in its management, and clumsy with its rare crackdowns on overgrazing. So environmentalists took to the courts: In one case in 1997, they sued the BLM, arguing that 68 grazing permits stretching across 1 million acres had been issued without adequate environmental analysis. They won a ruling, finalized in 2002, that forced the BLM to begin cutting back grazing by 30 percent or more. In the melee, the BLM's state directory, Martha Hahn, quit, reportedly in response to pressure from the Bush administration, Idaho's congressmen and ranchers.

But environmentalists drew their biggest gun during Bill Clinton's final year in the White House, when groups, including the Committee for the High Desert, put together a proposal for a 2.7 million-acre Owyhee-Bruneau Canyonlands National Monument. It would have prevented any new development and limited motorized recreation. The groups pushed hard in the final days of 2000, filling Boise mailboxes with color brochures and buying full-page ads in East Coast newspapers, trying to generate public support. Although Clinton declared a series of new monuments, the Owyhee stalled on his desk, probably because environmentalists never got the locals on board.

"At the time, I didn't think (a monument) was a possibility," says Black, "but since then, I've realized that we came really close to getting a monument out here."

Early on, local officials had countered the environmentalists by trying to assert county supremacy, in the style of other Sagebrush Rebellion hotspots, such as New Mexico's Catron County and Nevada's Nye County. But many locals saw this as a losing battle, when the courts seemed to side with the environmentalists.

"The ranchers and the county were spending an enormous amount of money on lawyer and court fees," says Owyhee County Commissioner Chris Salove, creating a considerable burden in a poor county, where the median household income is only 60 percent of the national average. So the county and the ranchers began exploring other options. "We had to take a proactive stand that suited us," says Salove.

County officials turned to Fred Grant, a well-respected attorney who had worked with the county on natural resource issues for a decade. Grant, who was born in nearby Nampa and holds a law degree from the University of Chicago, had fought for property rights with Stewards of the Range, a group whose founders include the original sagebrush rebel, Wayne Hage.

Grant started by suggesting that the commissioners send a letter to Idaho's congressional representatives to see if they could help end the grazing fight. Just a few days after the letter went out, Republican Sen. Mike Crapo called. "He explained the climate in Washington, D.C., and let us know that we weren't going to get any big breaks from environmental laws," says Grant. But Crapo agreed to support anything that a broad-based consensus group worked out.

"The best way to make decisions about our environment and land is to let the people who live there make those decisions," says Crapo, who isn't known for commitment to the environment: As a first-term congressman, Crapo scored a mere 6 percent on the latest League of Conservation Voters scorecard.

Grant soon built a bridge to the middle ground of the environmental movement, with the help of The Nature Conservancy. He sat down with representatives of the Idaho Conservation League and The Wilderness Society over coffee and bagels, and he convinced them to help put together a proposal for Sen. Crapo. Both groups were known in the Owyhee community, since in the 1980s and '90s both had worked with locals to limit low-altitude flights from nearby Mountain Home Air Force Base.

The Owyhee Initiative's official meetings began in the fall of 2001. For the first year and a half, the work group gathered monthly. Lately, it has picked up the pace, and subcommittees meet several times a month at various ranch offices and the headquarters of Stewards of the Range and the Idaho Conservation League.

Ten people have voting rights—four representatives of environmental groups, four ranchers, one for outfitters and guides and one for off-road vehicle drivers. In any given meeting, others, including officials from the Air Force and the BLM, might be present, offering their opinions at times. From the first meeting onward, everyone has agreed to two basic goals, says Grant: They want to maintain a viable ranching economy, and they want to protect some wilderness.

Wilderness, Cows and Then Some

So far, it's been a tedious, and at times tenuous, two years of negotiations, centering on 22 "wilderness study areas" that cover nearly 700,000 acres. Cows are allowed in these areas, as they are in official wilderness areas. According to the BLM, the lands have "wilderness characteristics," and are managed with tight restrictions until Congress decides whether to give them official wilderness protection.

To keep their cattle out of streams—and lawsuits—the ranchers say they need to build new fences and stock tanks, but BLM regulations in the study areas make that difficult to impossible. Ironically, official wilderness designation might make it easier for the ranchers: While the 1964 Wilderness Act banned mechanized vehicles from wilderness areas, agency regulations have long allowed occasional use of backhoes and pickup trucks to maintain stock ponds and fences—regulations that Congress has affirmed in subsequent wilderness laws.

Nonetheless, says Black, "There's always been a mistrust of wilderness on the part of ranchers."

Meanwhile, environmentalists feel a desperation of their own. Last April, the Interior Department eliminated protection for many proposed wilderness areas in Utah, a policy that has since been extended to other states. "Our expectation is that (many Owyhee study areas) will lose protection under the current administration," says Craig Gehrke, Idaho's regional director for The Wilderness Society, and a voting member of the Initiative.

The consensus among Owyhee negotiators is that study-area limbo isn't good for anyone. Therefore, they're seeking to have some of the areas designated as wilderness, and the remaining study areas eliminated altogether. The BLM has recommended 390,000 acres for wilderness. At first, the ranchers suggested a smaller, rim-to-rim proposal that included only the canyon bottoms. "That was a nonstarter for us," says the Idaho Conservation League's John McCarthy, another voting member. "We told them that we'd only accept at least what the BLM has recommended."

It took a reserved, unassuming range management consultant to overcome the ranchers' suspicions. At the Owyhee table, Chad Gibson represents the powerful Owyhee Cattlemen's Association, Idaho's oldest grazing organization. Unlike many of his peers, he understands that the Wilderness Act and other laws prevent land managers from using wilderness as an excuse to kick cows off the land. And with a Ph.D. in range science and 31 years with the University of Idaho's Cooperative Extension Agency, Gibson, now retired, carries a lot of clout. "He was our 'in' with the ranchers," says McCarthy.

In early 2002, Gibson started traveling around the Owyhee, meeting ranchers at rural schoolhouses and libraries, and in their homes, often with McCarthy and Gehrke in tow. "We sit down at kitchen tables," says McCarthy, "roll out the maps, talk about what we're trying to do, mark up the maps with existing fences and structures, where they think they need new fences and which roads they use."

With Gibson backing the idea, members of the Owyhee Cattlemen's Association voted unanimously in 2002 to support at least a rim-to-rim wilderness proposal, plus anything additional agreed to by the individual ranchers who hold permits in wilderness study areas. "Cattlemen not involved with (wilderness study areas) are still philosophically opposed to wilderness designation," says Gibson, "but they aren't opposed to their neighbor working out a deal that keeps him in business."

All the face-to-face talks have led to an unprecedented level of trust among the Owyhee stakeholders. "There's no brow-beating, no stand-offishness," McCarthy says. "I'm more familiar (with timber-issue meetings) out in the forest, where you meet with people and there's a lot of positioning, pissing on stumps, sniffing around and people being huffy and angry. (In the Owyhee) it's not that way at all. These people realize that some kind of change needs to happen."

Hard-Liners Feel Burned

The deal-making in the Owyhee involves much more than deciding which land will be designated wilderness.

The county and ranchers insist on setting up an independent scientific review panel, because they're suspicious of the BLM's science. Ranchers are angry because the judge who ruled against the 68 grazing permits refused to allow them to submit their own scientific data, which, they say, showed that the range was improving. The 10-person science panel would likely be selected from the University of Idaho. For it to fly, says Gehrke, the panel will need to include not just range specialists, but also biologists, plant and fire ecologists and wildlife specialists.

The Initiative would also call for a new 10-person, county-appointed board of directors that would advise the BLM on grazing and road management, and act as a mediator between land users and land managers. The board slots would be filled by those currently at the table. Anyone who disagrees with a BLM decision could take it to the board of directors, where eight out of 10 votes would be needed to engage the panel scientists to review the data used in the decision. The BLM would not have a seat on the board—but neither would it be obligated to follow the board's advice.

"Initially, we felt a little left out of the process, but that's not the case anymore, because we're more directly involved," says BLM spokesman Barry Rose. "If we can help people achieve consensus over something that works for the ranchers and environmentalists and others involved, whether we're a voting member or not isn't important."

The Initiative group is also negotiating with individual ranchers to purchase access easements over private land, to acquire scattered private inholdings, and to buy out some of Chris Black's grazing permits. The sale could lead to 20,000 acres of cow-free wilderness.

But the groups that take a hard line against grazing—and that originally helped force the ranchers to the table—feel burned. They are barred from participating in the negotiations because they're seen as uncompromising. Yet the cattlemen have their own hard-liner at the table—Grant, who worked for Stewards of the Range.

"(The Initiative's plan) would be a disaster," says Jon Marvel, head of the Western Watersheds Project, which is leading a national campaign to get cattle off public land. He's suspicious that the group's wilderness bill would allow more fences, water lines and motorized use. "I'd rather deal with (grazing) under current conditions than give up (wilderness study areas) and capitulate to a county review board and science review board."

Katie Fite, former director of the Committee for the High Desert, who now works for Marvel, says she's been allowed to attend Owyhee Initiative subcommittee meetings, but hasn't been allowed to speak. Like Marvel, she opposes the idea of giving the locals—and the middle-ground environmentalists—more say over public land. "It interjects this whole elitist layer of established ranching families and large conservation organizations," she says.

It's a concern resonating around the West. In July, more than 30 environmental groups from New Mexico, Oregon, Montana, Utah and other states joined High Desert and Western Watersheds in sending a five-page letter of criticism to the leaders of the three main environmental groups that support the Initiative. In September, Fite and two others launched a Web site detailing their concerns.

The Owyhee Initiative's environmentalists acknowledge that barring the hard-liners could be a mistake, but they show little remorse for the decision. "They've been players in the Owyhee for a long time, and no one could expect that the locals would want to sit down and talk with them," says Gehrke. "They've made their own bed and now they can lie in it."

Consensus Could Crumble

For now, at least, the large, national environmental groups are on board this collaborative effort. But it will be hard-pressed to survive without support from Washington, D.C. Unlike its predecessor, however, the Bush administration has shown outright disregard for collaborative solutions.

In 2000, the administration killed a plan by local timber interests and environmentalists to reintroduce grizzly bears to central Idaho and western Montana. This year, pressured by the administration to fast-track energy development, the BLM nixed a gas-drilling proposal that emphasized land conservation on Colorado's Roan Plateau, even though the proposal was backed by local ranchers, hunters, environmentalists, county commissioners and five town councils.

"It's really negative and discouraging when people work so hard on something and get shot right out of the saddle," says Patrick Heffernan, director of the Red Lodge Clearinghouse, a Montana-based nonprofit that supports consensus efforts around the West. "The general trend (with consensus efforts) is that a lot of them are waiting, in a holding pattern right now, to see whether they're going to be listened to and heard" by the federal agencies and the Bush administration.

Sen. Crapo says he expects the administration to support the Owyhee Initiative. But that's part of the problem, some wilderness advocates warn. This deal has so many trade-offs, says Fite, "Why not save wilderness for a different day?"

But the environmentalists in the Owyhee Initiative aren't willing to pass up the opportunity to get some wilderness locked in. Idaho no longer has a champion like the late Democratic Sen. Frank Church, who backed the 1964 Wilderness Act and the 1980 creation of the 2.3 million-acre Frank Church-River of No Return Wilderness. "Another Frank Church isn't on the horizon, and the politics in Idaho aren't going to change," Gehrke says.

Actually, even the 1980 wilderness bill that created the Frank

Church-River of No Return was a compromise: It grandfathered in airplane-landing strips and jet boats along the Salmon River. "For those of us who have been stalled out for a generation trying to get wilderness in Idaho," McCarthy says, "we know there has to be a variation on this cooperative theme."

It's a delicate truce that is holding together the Owyhee Initiative, and it's not just hard-line environmentalists who are threatening the balance. Irrigators on the Snake River recently held the Initiative hostage — along with a similar effort under way in the Boulder-White Cloud mountain ranges — in a fight over salmon and dams. [In August 2002, four pro-salmon groups, including the Idaho Conservation League, threatened to sue the federal government to force it to release water from Snake River dams for endangered salmon. In retaliation, a group of water users called the Coalition for Idaho Water convinced irrigators participating in the Owyhee wilderness talks to walk out until the Idaho Conservation League dropped out of the threatened suit.] Off-road vehicle enthusiasts are also putting a lot of pressure on both collaboration efforts, especially the Owyhee.

Few people feel that pressure as strongly as Inez Jaca, who represents the county at the Owyhee Initiative table. Jaca has a ranch south of Nampa that sits just beyond the sparsely vegetated buttes of the Owyhee Front. These buttes have become Boise's off-road playground, and now are crisscrossed by a maze of ever-widening and rutted roads. "They're just trashing the place," she says.

The off-roaders have a representative at the table, but they haven't been easy to please. Most members of the Initiative want those wilderness study areas that are not designated as wilderness to be released to multiple use, so fences, water developments, new roads and motorized recreation could be allowed. So far, all but the motorized-recreation representative have agreed that any legislation would "soft release" that land — meaning it could still be considered for wilderness designation in the future. "We absolutely won't accept hard-release language" that wouldn't allow future wilderness protection, says Roger Singer, director of the Sierra Club's Idaho chapter, and an Initiative voting member. But so far, the off-road crowd has said it will only accept the BLM's recommended wilderness acreage, and only if the remaining study areas are "hard released," or permanently removed from wilderness consideration. "The (off-road) community has said all along that our bottom line is that this would be the first and last dance for wilderness within the Owyhees," says Sandra Mitchell, the motorized-users representative.

There have also been some murmurings about distrust and dissatisfaction within the ranching community. And without the ranchers, the Initiative is lost.

A Moment of Truth

The ranchers' resolve is put to the test later in August, at the Owyhee Cattleman's Association's 125th annual summer meeting in the old mining town of Silver City. Up a twisting dirt road, the town clings to the steep hillsides of Owyhee County's forested uplands. Straw-hatted and jeans-clad ranchers sit on benches and metal folding chairs in the Masonic Temple.

Chris Black is here in the crowd of 80 or so people, as are Chad Gibson, the wilderness-peddling range management consultant, Chris Salove with Owyhee County and several representatives of the BLM. Also here are the National Beef Association's head, himself an Owyhee County rancher, Sen. Crapo and former Idaho Rep. Helen Chenoweth-Hage, R. The meeting's attendance list speaks to the influences in this county.

The cattlemen are slated to vote again on whether to continue supporting the Owyhee Initiative, and rumors are floating around that the debate could get nasty.

As rain sprinkles outside, Fred Grant, the aging attorney who got the Owyhee Initiative started, takes the podium. He is clearly ailing, suffering from a faulty hip and a heart problem. His physical difficulties seem to symbolize the fragility of the Owyhee Initiative. Yet his delivery to the crowd is robust.

Grant tells the ranchers that he's not surprised at the bitterness that's evolved over the long and tedious process, and he chides the "deceit and deception" that's boiled up from the various camps. "My only interest," he says, "has been to protect the Owyhee Cattlemen."

Grant steps down from the podium. When the moderator calls for the vote, asking if anyone in this room opposes the Initiative, there is only dead silence.

Since the August meeting, Grant has been admitted to a Boise hospital, and undergone two heart surgeries. Members of the Owyhee Initiative have stuck it out, however. They say they expect to announce their proposal to the public sometime in December. In January, they hope to take the proposal to Sen. Crapo, who will formalize it into a bill to take before Congress.

DECEMBER 8, 2003

In Boulder-White Cloud Mountains, Another Wilderness Compromise

BY ROCKY BARKER

A hundred miles north of the Owyhee Canyonlands, another bold wilderness deal is brewing in Idaho, and the brewmaster is another conservative Republican congressman.

"We have a rare opportunity to control our own destiny, by crafting our own legislation that fits our needs, without staring down the barrel of (any future Clintonesque actions in Washington, D.C.)," says Rep. Mike Simpson.

Simpson is close to announcing the terms of a bill that would designate about 250,000 acres of wilderness in the Boulder Mountains and the White Cloud Peaks, between the booming resort of Sun Valley and the small, remote town of Challis on the Salmon River. The bill is the culmination of two years of talks with environmentalists and locals in Custer County, where Challis is the county seat. The trade-offs built into it are advertised in its title: The Central Idaho Economic Development and Recreation Act.

If the deal holds, it will hand the county several thousand acres of federal land—isolated tracts not considered important for wildlife—which could then be sold for homesites and other economic development. Simpson wants the sale proceeds, along with additional money from the federal government, to be used to create a new Central Idaho Education Center, which would stimulate the local economy by offering a suite of higher-education services from Idaho's universities, and perhaps from a vocational college.

The Idaho Conservation League—the lead negotiators for the environmentalists' side—and the BlueRibbon Coalition, which represents off-road vehicle users, both see benefits in the deal. It would end a stalemate on a wilderness study area that was established nearly 30 years ago, on land that is a haven for many sensitive species, including wolves, lynx, wolverines, fishers, bighorn sheep, mountain goats, bull trout and rare plants.

And in sprawling, Connecticut-sized Custer County, the deal couldn't too come soon. Like many rural Idahoans, the county's 4,300 residents struggle to get by. Mines that once provided jobs have closed, or are winding down. Net income from farming and ranching has plummeted 80 percent since 1970, according to the Sonoran Institute think tank. The tax base is also choked off, with 95 percent of the land in the county owned by the federal government. The nearest post-high-school classes are a couple of hours' drive away.

"For us, education is the key to economic development," says Gynii Gilliam, a local economic development official.

The education center could host conventions and serve as a base for wildland scientists, Gilliam says. And the new wilderness area could bring more visitors to the rest of Custer County; nearby Sawtooth National Recreation Area now attracts 1.5 million tourists each summer.

Simpson's bill would protect only half of the total 500,000 roadless acres in the area, which is said to be the largest roadless area in the Lower 48. Snowmobilers and ATVs would have increased access to the unprotected land. The bill would authorize land trades and buyouts to reduce conflicts over grazing. But some of the most controversial wildland—prized, for different reasons, by both sides—has been left out of it altogether.

"I have mixed feelings about the bill. I want to see wilderness there, but don't want to pay too high a price for it," says Jerry Jayne, a director of the Idaho Environmental Council. Jayne doesn't like giving away federal land and increasing ATV access, and says more of the roadless land needs to protected.

But Bart Koehler, director of The Wilderness Society's Wilderness Support Center in Durango, Colo., says, "This is Idaho's time in the sun. You can't be afraid of your shadow. You can't be reckless, but you should do everything possible to strive for a workable resolution."

In New Mexico, a Homegrown Wilderness Bill Makes Headway

BY JOSH GARRETT-DAVIS

In the face of the Interior Department's top-down decision to stop looking for new wilderness areas on federal land, some communities are working to protect wilderness from the bottom up. Sidestepping White House-appointed bureaucrats, wilderness advocates are working with their elected representatives in Congress.

Last June, the Coalition for New Mexico Wilderness — a group of over 375 businesses and local environmental organizations — along with Zia Pueblo, gave the New Mexico congressional delegation a proposal to preserve a rugged patch of northwest New Mexico, called Ojito, as wilderness. The proposed bill would also sell federal land surrounding Ojito to Zia, whose people have lived nearby for almost 800 years.

In September, four of the state's five legislators — New Mexico Reps. Tom Udall, D, and Heather Wilson, R, and Sens. Jeff Bingaman, D, and Pete Domenici, R — sponsored the Ojito Wilderness Bill in Congress. The bill would protect almost 25,000 acres, half of it as wilderness. Congress has yet to take action on the bill, but proponents are optimistic that it will pass in 2004.

"We're going back to the basics: Build strong public support (for wilderness designations)," says Jim Scarantino, executive director of the New Mexico Wilderness Alliance. "We don't rely on some bureaucrat to give us wilderness or take it away."

Give and Take

A land of curvy hoodoos and badlands, Ojito has been a wilderness study area since 1991. At that time, Manuel Luján Jr., Interior secretary under George H.W. Bush and a veteran Republican congressman from New Mexico, recommended it for wilderness protection. He sent a proposal to Congress, but lawmakers never got around to passing the bill. For the past 12 years, the rough terrain has been in limbo, with temporary protection as a study area.

Ojito might have remained in limbo if not for the 807-member Zia Pueblo, the source of the New Mexican flag's red-on-yellow sun. For over a decade, Zia Pueblo has been trying to bridge two sections of its reservation with a parcel of Bureau of Land Management land that includes the proposed wilderness. The area contains pottery made by the pueblo's ancestors, as well as places to dig clay to make new pottery.

The BLM and at least one environmental group, the New Mexico Native Plant Society, had opposed Zia's effort, fearing that the pueblo might lock the public out. A December 2002 letter from the BLM expressed the agency's "long-standing position" against transferring federal land to the pueblo, saying the action would not serve the "national interest" as required by the Federal Land Policy and Management Act.

But about three years ago, the pueblo reached out to wilderness advocates to fashion a compromise, which has won over at least one critic — the Native Plant Society. "I think that many people within the federal government were surprised that the environmental groups and the pueblo were able to work this out," says Peter Pino, an administrator for Zia. "They thought we would butt heads and never come together."

A BLM spokesperson declined to comment on the legislation, but at a county commission meeting last year, an agency employee sounded the only objection to the Ojito bill — specifically to the sale of public land to the pueblo. More recently, the Albuquerque Wildlife Federation, a hunting and conservation group, has also opposed that provision. The group's president, Richard Becker, says he's concerned the bill will "take that (land) out of the public domain and the potential use for hunters."

The bill would allow Zia to buy about 12,500 acres for the land's market price, in return for the pueblo's promise to leave it undeveloped and open to the public. To guarantee those restrictions, Zia agreed to waive its sovereign immunity from lawsuits. Some pueblo members initially opposed the provisions, Pino says, "but they realized that if this is going to happen, they're going to have to make that concession."

The agreement has won support not only from the congressional delegation, but also from Gov. Bill Richardson, the county commissions of Sandoval County and neighboring Bernalillo County, the New Mexico commissioner of Public Lands, and a legion of American Indian and environmental groups. Sandoval County Commissioner Daymon Ely says, "From a local point of view, (in a county) where you have lots of controversy over wilderness issues, this was an exception to the rule."

Supporters hope the bill's bipartisan support will carry it through a congressional committee hearing early this year, and on to a vote. "The neat thing about Ojito," says NMWA's Scarantino, "is that here, in the face of a White House that is not pro-wilderness, the citizens of New Mexico made the system work for them. That's the genius of the Wilderness Act."

Small Steps for Wilderness

Arizona Activists Shop for Wilderness by Congressional District

BY JODI PETERSON

America's wilderness movement has had a lot of the wind knocked out of its sails lately. But an Arizona grassroots group and a Latino congressman are making headway with a small-scale proposal: wilderness designation for 84,000 acres of the Tumacacori Highlands in southern Arizona, 7,500 of them tacked onto the existing Pajarita Wilderness.

"We want to make this a model for how to operate in the future," says Don Hoffman, executive director of the Arizona Wilderness Coalition, "looking at small, individual opportunities rather than huge, statewide bills."

Rep. Raúl Grijalva, the Democratic freshman congressman of Arizona's 7th District, proposed the Tumacacori Wilderness in January; it would be the state's first new wilderness area in nearly 15 years. "Some of my colleagues have never seen a place they wouldn't drill," says Grijalva, the son of a Mexican cowboy, whose environmental voting record last year earned him a 100 percent rating from the League of Conservation Voters.

A rugged land of lichen-draped cliffs and grassy oak-dotted hills, the Tumacacori Highlands sit in the Coronado National Forest along the Mexican border. The closest settlements are Tubac and Arivaca, high-desert towns sustained largely by tourism and retirees. Nine ranchers graze cows in the Tumacacori, and the endangered jaguar occasionally haunts these arid canyons.

The Friends of the Tumacacori, part of the Tucson-based Sky Island Alliance, had bided its time for years, waiting for the right moment to seek permanent protection for the Highlands, says Matt Skroch, field program director for Sky Island Alliance. That moment arrived in 2003, when both the Forest Service and the Bureau of Land Management in Arizona updated their land-use plans, providing an opportunity to examine lands for formal wilderness designation. Seeing its chance, the Arizona Wilderness Coalition, an umbrella group that includes the Sky Island Alliance, went looking for areas that were not only scenic and roadless but that were also in the turf of wilderness-friendly politicians.

"We took the wilderness inventory and displayed it by congressional district instead of by eco-region," says Hoffman. The district around the Tumacacori Highlands, the largest unprotected roadless area in the state, happened to be Grijalva's.

A Long Road Ahead

Once they'd gotten political backing, the Tumacacori's boosters moved on to the public. They built support by presenting the proposal to "everyone from the Lions Club to the Rotary Club," says Skroch. He notes that ranchers, hikers and hunters have all had their say about the proposed wilderness boundaries, drawing them so that 20 existing dirt access roads would remain open.

But some local miners and ranchers still disagree with the proposal. "It would make our already-hard job as ranchers much harder. Instead of one day in a pickup, it'll take us five days of horse-packing to haul in fence materials and salt," says rancher Edith Lowell.

Also, the Tucson Electric Power Company wants to build a $70 million, 345-kilovolt transmission line across almost 30 miles of the Tumacacori Highlands, to improve reliability for the Nogales area and connect the U.S. and Mexican grids. While critics claim that a smaller, cheaper 115-kilovolt line would be more than enough to serve Nogales' needs, the Arizona Corporation Commission, which regulates public utilities, recommended the larger line to allow for future growth.

"We'll take whatever action is necessary to get that line built," says Joe Salkowski, spokesman for Tucson Electric Power. Wilderness supporters oppose the power line, but say that if it does garner the necessary federal and state permits—which seems likely—they'll adjust the wilderness boundaries accordingly.

There's still some hard work ahead: Grijalva has delayed introducing the Tumacacori bill until this fall to drum up more support, starting with Democratic Gov. Janet Napolitano and local governments. He's also hoping to enlist Rep. Jim Kolbe, R-Ariz., whose district encompasses the southeast corner of the state, and other congressmen as co-sponsors, and to get support from Arizona's senators.

Arizona wilderness activists think the chances of the bill passing Congress are good—and they're already setting their sights on more like it. "We'll look for more opportunities where we have local and political support," says Hoffman. In Grijalva's district alone, he adds, his group has identified 680,000 acres of potential wilderness.

Mountain Bikes in Wilderness

The Wilderness Act itself is silent on the subject of mountain bikes, but subsequent regulations have prohibited them in wilderness areas. In recent years, however, many new citizens' wilderness proposals have overlapped with popular mountain bike trails, touching off a renewed debate over the place of mountain bikes in wilderness. The following editorials present two sides of that debate.

EDITORIAL

Let Bikers in, and We'll Stand behind Wilderness

BY JIM HASENAUER

I'm a mountain bicyclist. The pleasure of my life is pedaling through wild places, experiencing the views, the changing colors and textures of the plant life, the occasional animal sightings. On the trail, I'm renewed, and my commitment to public-land preservation is strengthened. I think that's the way most mountain bikers feel, and historically, we've been eager to back conservation efforts.

We're troubled, though, that designated wilderness, the highest level of protection, is encumbered with regulations that ban bicycling. Across the country, wilderness advocates are advancing new proposals while mountain bicyclists struggle to find a meaningful place at the table. It's a wedge issue with a capital W.

The Wilderness Act is a remarkable tool. Once Congress acts, wilderness areas are protected in perpetuity for their own sake and for the recreational and spiritual sustenance they provide visitors. Wilderness recreation offers adventure, discovery, solitude and awe — exactly the kinds of experiences most valued by bicyclists like me.

But wilderness advocates, like kids with a jackknife, are inclined to use the tool at hand. They mark their accomplishments in acres designated and their losses as anything less than wilderness as proposed. Though bicyclists should be natural allies of the wilderness movement, because of the bike ban we're understandably reluctant to embrace proposals that would kick us off cherished trails.

It would certainly be easier for cyclists to oppose wilderness outright, but that's not who we are. We value wild places. We've endorsed preservation of all roadless areas as the foundation of real resource protection.

We try to support wilderness where possible, and when proposals include significant bicycle trails, we work to find ways to protect the land and still preserve the riding. These tools include boundary adjustments, cherry-stem trails and land designations that provide wilderness-like protection from roads, motors and extraction, but still allow bikes.

Unfortunately, many wilderness advocates see these measures as losses, discounting alternatives as "wilderness-lite." They characterize bicyclists as selfish and uncooperative. The cost of this infighting has been acrimony, poisoned relationships and lost time, energy and trust. Meanwhile, the BlueRibbon Coalition and other anti-wilderness groups court cyclists.

The 46 million U.S. mountain bicyclists are a giant constituency of public-land enthusiasts. They're increasingly committed to wildland protection, but they're understandably wary of wilderness designations. That's why it's clear to me that there ought to be a way to work for wilderness protection that doesn't ban bicycles. If the regulation were changed, and bikes were allowed on some trails in some wilderness, the entire nature of this debate would shift.

Most wilderness advocates are astonished to learn that the Wilderness Act did not ban bicycles. It banned "mechanized transport," which was defined in Forest Service regulation as "powered by a nonliving power source." Bicycles were allowed and ridden in some wilderness until 1984, when a ban first introduced in 1977 was made final. This is significant because it means the bike ban is regulatory, not statutory. It was imposed 20 years after the Wilderness Act by folks who mistook mountain bikes for motorcycles.

It's time to get past this. Bikes are muscle-powered, human-scale, quiet and nonpolluting. The tradition and history of bicycle use on the wild lands of the West goes back to the 1880s. Bicycling is trail-based recreation. We may range as far as horses and runners, but our impacts on the trails and on plants and animals have been shown to be similar to those of hikers. Yes, bikes do provide a mechanical advantage, but it's only a degree of difference from oarlocks, suspension poles, skis and the high-tech alloys and composites associated with other outdoor equipment.

I believe that if mountain bikers were allowed on some wilderness trails, cyclists would overwhelmingly endorse new wilderness. Rest assured: Trails would never swarm with bikes; most would still be earmarked for hikers. Yet in the same way that backpackers cherish wilderness regardless of whether they ever visit it, mountain bikers would support more wilderness, both in principle and at the ballot box.

It's time to make a niche for mountain biking in the push to preserve wild places. Cyclists, with their commitment, passion and numbers, could swell the ranks of a new, more inclusive movement. The only difference between wilderness now and wilderness future would be the presence of bicycles on some trails — and much, much more wilderness.

EDITORIAL

Get off and Walk—
Wilderness Is for Wildlife

BY MICHAEL CARROLL

Like many mountain bikers, I'm happiest when I'm charging up and down hills through the West's spectacular public lands. I live in Durango, Colo., arguably the mountain bike capital of the world, and I ride every day. While I've spent most of my cycling years on roads, in the last five years I've been spending more time on trails.

But I believe there are places my bike doesn't belong, and ranking first is wilderness. I have thought about this a lot lately, because some of my fellow cyclists think mountain biking should be legalized within our federal system of protected wilderness.

I am against this, because it would violate the letter and spirit of the Wilderness Act of 1964, whose section 4(c) says: "...there shall be no temporary road, no use of motor vehicles, motorized equipment or motorboats, no landing of aircraft, no other form of mechanical transport..." Under any reasonable definition, mountain bicycles are a form of mechanical transport.

In defining wilderness, even before mentioning the word recreation, the law mentions "earth and its community of life" and "outstanding opportunities for solitude." It refers to primitive recreation, not just recreation. That was no accident. There's a line between activities that belong legally in wilderness and those that don't. The Wilderness Act drew that line clearly.

Wilderness areas were always meant to be more than playgrounds. They not only protect nature, they also provide us with the opportunity to connect with nature at a basic level. I take my bicycle almost everywhere I go, but I am not wedded to it. I enjoy trails by foot just as much.

We are spoiled here in Colorado, which recently won the International Mountain Bicycling Association's highest rating for riding opportunities. But we can easily lose these opportunities. The threats we face are oil and gas development, sprawl, logging and mining, which lock us out of areas and close trails. These are the threats we should focus on, rather than squabbling over access. This is especially true now that the Bush administration is charging ahead with its drill-log-and-mine agenda.

Once wilderness areas are designated, the Wilderness Act requires that they be managed in a manner that "will leave them unimpaired for future use" and ensure the "preservation of their wilderness character." Sure, all-terrain vehicles are more damaging than bikes, but we're kidding ourselves if we claim that we don't also take a toll on the places we ride through.

What's more, since mountain bikes were developed some 15 years ago, our impact has magnified. Bikes can go places that were all but inaccessible before, thanks to advances that have led to lighter and stronger materials, suspension systems similar to those on off-road vehicles and gearing that enables riders to conquer steep slopes.

While most mountain bicyclists have continued to ride on dirt roads and well-established, multiple-use trails, these changes have enabled some to venture farther and blaze new trails—just like some dirt bikers and off-road vehicle users. The result is a dramatic cultural shift in the bicycling community toward extreme aspects of the sport, including "downhilling" and "freeriding."

There are plenty of places outside the wilderness system to ride, and we should work together to protect both those areas and our remaining wild places. Aldo Leopold, in *A Sand County Almanac*, wrote, "Mechanized recreation already has seized nine-tenths of the woods and mountains; a decent respect for minorities should dedicate the other tenth to wilderness."

Forested mountains dotted with lush meadows may be great places to ride mountain bikes, but these are also the places that make ideal summer range for elk, where even the presence of people causes elk to flee to areas where they have less access to nutrient-rich meadows. Many wilderness areas are already under stress from a variety of sources, and adding mountain bicycles to this list will only continue to degrade the land. Though only 2 percent of the land in the Lower 48 is part of the wilderness system, I think we all know that this 2 percent is under increasing pressure as our population booms.

I believe that most mountain bikers are conservationists who want to join me in the fight for the trails and areas we love. We can and should work together to protect these special places, without endangering what few safeguards we have in place.

Return to the White River

The White River proposed wilderness in northeast Utah.
—PHOTO BY STEVE MULLIGAN, COURTESY SOUTHERN UTAH WILDERNESS ALLIANCE

In January 2004, a month after my trip to the White River proposed wilderness area in Utah, I started delving into *High Country News*' archives to gather material for this anthology. I found a photo of the White River in the Nov. 9, 1973, issue— back when wilderness and energy first dominated *HCN*'s pages. At that time, the area was the site of a proposed dam that would have stored water for a nearby oil shale development.

Thirty years later, it seems that not much has changed. Though the threat it faces is slightly different, the White River is no closer to being protected as wilderness. Citizen-proposed wilderness areas enjoyed a brief period of interim protection during the Clinton administration, but after the 2003 wilderness settlement between Secretary of the Interior Gale Norton and then-Utah Gov. Mike Leavitt, the drill rigs have begun to move closer than ever.

In the wake of the settlement, the White River's plight became a minor cause célèbre. The Outdoor Industry Association threatened to move its massive, $24 million, twice-yearly Outdoor Retailer trade show out of Utah to protest both the settlement and the 15 wells proposed for the White River, and the controversy received almost daily coverage in the *Salt Lake Tribune* and *Deseret News*.

But something was wrong. People were talking about keeping 15 wells out of a *proposed* wilderness area, but they weren't talk- ing—and hadn't been in years—about making that area official, honest-to-god wilderness.

The idea of "vision" comes up a lot in discussions of wilderness. Forty years on, however, it is clear that vision isn't enough. More than 14 million acres of land that the BLM itself recommended for wilderness designation are still in limbo, without formal protection—to say nothing of millions of acres of additional lands proposed for wilderness designation by citizens' groups. Places like the White River have disappeared inside gigantic schemes for wilderness that exist only in ringbound, three-inch-thick, four-and-a-half-pound citizens' proposals. And while they wait, they're being gnawed away at until they're not even wilderness anymore.

As I write this, the BLM has begun its third round of auctions of citizen-proposed wilderness lands around the West, transforming wilderness proposals into lease-sale parcels, and determining their market value on the auction block.

We've been here before. Beginning in 1929—35 years *before* the Wilderness Act—the Forest Service created a series of regulations to designate "primitive" and then "wilderness" areas on the national forests. But because the designations were—like the Clinton-era interim-protection policy—merely administrative, they could easily be reversed by succeeding presidential administrations. In 1950, for example, the Forest Service carved off a part of New Mexico's Gila Wilderness—Aldo Leopold's visionary contribution to the wilderness system—for logging.

That was exactly the scenario that led early wilderness champions such as Bob Marshall and Howard Zahniser to campaign for the Wilderness Act, to ensure that Congress, rather than the land-management agencies, would have the sole authority to designate wilderness. In the years since the Wilderness Act, Congress has never de-designated a single wilderness area. There is no substitute for real, capital "W" wilderness.

It is time to draw lines around wilderness again, to transform it back into a real issue, like water conservation, or urban planning, or mining reform, and to treat each place as a real problem to be solved, rather than an abstract vision.

Many agency wilderness proposals, particularly those from the BLM, stalled out not because the agency itself was hostile, but because the people who cared most about them—the wilderness advocates—failed to make a case that mattered. Moving the process forward again is a task of intimidating magnitude. But if the effort to protect more wilderness is going to make any progress, we need to move away from a focus on wilderness packages, and start talking about protecting individual places that people know intimately.

Compromise has always been an inherent part of wilderness protection, and continued progress will require some places to be traded away. Some acreage in specific proposals may be opened to off-road vehicles, or oil and gas drilling. There are obviously limits to compromise: The hard-won tenet of soft-release language, which ensures that lands that aren't designated as wilderness can be reconsidered for protection in the future, should never be given up.

Working piece-by-piece doesn't mean abandoning the larger ecoregional wilderness visions that emerged during the 1990s. It simply means working toward them incrementally, and making as strong a case as possible for every piece of land that has real significance for wildlife, or watershed health, or human solitude. That is being done now by the Arizona Wilderness Coalition with the Tumacacori Highlands wilderness proposal, which would protect a key piece of the proposed Sky Island Wildlands Network. That and other efforts to create smaller, stand-alone wilderness proposals—such as Idaho's Boulder-White Clouds, New Mexico's Ojito and Washington's Wild Sky—are all local attempts to rebuild the wilderness protection process and begin gaining political traction again.

There is no reason why other places, such as the White River, can't join that list. Making the White River real again will mean taking a hard look at what the proposal has become, and adapting it to the realities of the day. The 15 wells now being proposed are in the expanded wilderness proposal developed when the Southern Utah Wilderness Alliance took the White River under its wing in the late 1990s. The original, 9,700-acre wilderness proposal put together by Will Durant, Doug Hatch and Clay Johnson is still untouched—at least for now. Why not break that out of SUWA's 9.1-million acre statewide megaproposal, use it as the basis to begin building support, and turn it into a truly local proposal to take to Rep. Jim Matheson, D, the congressional representative for the area? It would be one way to see if, after all the years of entrenched bitterness, real wilderness can still have a place in Utah.

This could be the last chance to negotiate back to a reasonable middle ground, and finally protect a tiny, still-wild place in the middle of a pumped-out landscape. Doing that would accomplish nothing less than exactly what Durant, Hatch and Johnson dreamt up around the kitchen table in 1985.

—Matt Jenkins

Contributor Profiles

MARJANE AMBLER is a former managing editor of *High Country News.*

MIKE BADER is co-founder and former executive director of the Alliance for the Wild Rockies. He is a natural resource consultant and blues musician in Missoula, Montana.

JILL BAMBURG is a former director of *High Country News.*

ROCKY BARKER is environmental reporter for the *Idaho Statesman* based in Boise, Idaho, and author of the book *Saving All the Parts: Reconciling Economics and the Endangered Species Act.*

CARL BROWN is a former Idaho smokejumper who, thirty years later, continues to work on natural and cultural conservation issues (and mentor young writers). He has worked with salmon restoration in the Northwest, tropical forest and marine issues in the Caribbean, and is now helping preserve Tibetan healthcare practices. He lives in Georgia.

LOUISE BRUCE manages the University of Montana-Western's Birch Creek Center for Environmental Education. She lives in Dillon, Montana.

MICHAEL CARROLL is an avid cyclist, a former Idaho and Colorado state champion. When he isn't on his bike, he works passionately to protect wilderness. He lives in Durango, Colorado.

JON CHRISTENSEN is at Stanford University on a History Department Fellowship pursuing a Ph.D. in American History with Western historian Richard White. A freelance science writer and environmental journalist, Christensen has written for *The New York Times, High Country News, Outside, Nature,* and many other newspapers and magazines.

TONY DAVIS, a reporter for the *Arizona Daily Star* in Tucson, has written about Southwestern environmental issues for *High Country News* since 1985.

BRUCE FARLING is a former *High Country News* intern. He is executive director of Montana Trout Unlimited, in Missoula.

PHILIP L. FRADKIN is a former environmental writer for the *Los Angeles Times,* Western editor of *Audubon* magazine, and author of nine books on the American West and Alaska. He lives in Point Reyes, California.

JOSH GARRETT-DAVIS is a former *High Country News* intern. He lives in Brooklyn, New York.

GREG HANSCOM is editor of *High Country News.*

JIM HASENAUER is a professor of communication studies at California State University Northridge and a former president and board member of the International Mountain Bicycling Association. He lives in Northridge, California.

NOLAN HESTER is a freelance writer and editor. He lives west of the West in Los Angeles.

JOHN HORNING is a former *High Country News* intern. He is executive director of Forest Guardians in Santa Fe, New Mexico.

CAROL JONES is a former associate editor of *High Country News.*

LISA JONES is a former staff writer of *High Country News.* She is a freelance writer based in Paonia, Colorado.

PAUL LARMER is publisher of *High Country News.*

ELIZABETH MANNING is a former *High Country News* assistant editor. She is a reporter for the *Anchorage Daily News* in Alaska.

JON MARGOLIS is a freelance writer who covers Washington, D.C., for *High Country News* out of his home in Barton, Vermont.

BETSY MARSTON was the editor of *High Country News* from 1983 until May 2001, when she became editor of Writers on the Range, *HCN*'s syndicated essay service.

ED MARSTON is publisher emeritus of *High Country News*.

MIKE MEDBERRY lives in Salt Lake City, Utah, and is working to protect wilderness in the West Desert.

MICHAEL MILSTEIN covered Wyoming for *The Billings Gazette* from 1989 to 2000. He now lives in Portland, Oregon, and writes for *The Oregonian*.

ROBYN MORRISON cut her teeth on Western environmental issues washing oil-soaked ducks on Wyoming's North Platte River and penning indignant letters to then-Interior Secretary James Watt. Twenty-five years later, she is still as passionate about the West. She lives in Paonia, Colorado.

JOAN NICE, now JOAN HAMILTON, is a former editor of *High Country News*. She is currently editor-in-chief of *Sierra* magazine.

MICHELLE NIJHUIS is contributing editor of *High Country News*.

GEOFFREY O'GARA was editor of *High Country News*. He is now an author and video producer based in Lander, Wyoming.

JODI PETERSON is a former *High Country News* intern. She is a freelance writer in Fort Collins, Colorado.

TOM PRICE, who spent years as a full-time wilderness advocate in Washington, D.C., now works as a freelance journalist covering conservation issues from his home in Salt Lake City, Utah.

C.L. "CHIP" RAWLINS was formerly *High Country News*' poetry editor. He is the author of a collection of poetry called *In Gravity National Park* (University of Nevada, 1998), and the nonfiction books *Sky's Witness: A Year in the Wind River Range* (Henry Holt, 1993), *Broken Country: Mountains & Memory* (Henry Holt, 1996), and *The Complete Walker IV*, with Colin Fletcher (Alfred A. Knopf, 2002).

CRAIG RAYLE lives a more domestic life now as a father and special education teacher in Missoula, Montana. He still dreams only in the colors found in sedimentary rocks and hunts elk in a secret spot each fall.

TOM RIBE is a writer and professional tourist who lives in the fire zone outside Santa Fe, New Mexico.

RAY RING, *High Country News'* editor in the field, has been doing Western journalism for more than 20 years, based in Arizona, Colorado and Montana.

BECKY RUMSEY lives near Boulder, Colorado, and visits wilderness whenever possible.

DUSTIN SOLBERG is a former assistant editor of *High Country News.*

TRACY STONE-MANNING left a freelancing career—during which she founded headwatersnews.org—to direct the Clark Fork Coalition, a group working to protect and restore the Clark Fork River Basin in western Montana and northern Idaho. She lives in Missoula, Montana.

STEPHEN STUEBNER'S latest book is *Salmon River Country* (The Caxton Press, 2004). He lives in Boise, Idaho.

ROBIN TAWNEY is the author of many books, including *Family Fun in Yellowstone National Park* (Falcon/Globe Pequot Press, 2001). A former contributing editor to *High Country News,* her articles have appeared in many regional and national publications. She serves on the boards of the Cinnabar Foundation and the Phil Tawney Hunters Conservation Endowment of the Montana Wildlife Foundation. Robin lives in a forested canyon on the outskirts of Missoula, Montana.

JERRY THULL now lives and works in Flagstaff, Arizona.

JAMES MORTON TURNER has recently completed a dissertation at Princeton University on the history of the American wilderness movement. He lives in Princeton, New Jersey.

TIM VITALE lives in Logan, Utah.

TIM WESTBY is a freelance writer in Salt Lake City, Utah.

RAY WHEELER is a journalist, photographer, and activist with a passion for expedition-scale backcountry exploration in the West. He lives in Salt Lake City, Utah.

DAN WHIPPLE is an author and former editor of *High Country News*.

PETER WILD, a professor of English at the University of Arizona, is one of the foremost poets of the American West. He lives in Tucson, Arizona.

LOUISA WILLCOX is the Natural Resources Defense Council's Wild Bears Project Director based in Livingston, Montana. She has an M.S. from the School of Forestry at Yale University and a B.A. from Williams College in Williamstown, Massachusetts.

FLORENCE WILLIAMS is a former staff writer of *High Country News*. She is now a freelance writer based in Helena, Montana.

Index

FEED A FRIEND!

Receive two *FREE* issues of *High Country News*

Covering 11 western states, from the Great Plains to the Northwest, and from the Northern Rockies to the desert Southwest, *High Country News* is an award-winning source for environmental news, analysis and commentary on water, logging, wildlife, grazing, wilderness, growth and other issues changing the face of the West.

To receive one free issue of *High Country News* and one for a friend, send your name and mailing address to:

HIGH COUNTRY NEWS
PO Box 1090
Paonia, CO 81428
1-800-905-1155 (phone)
970/527-4897 (fax)
circulation@hcn.org
www.hcn.org

THEN AGAIN, WHY WAIT?

If you don't want to wait to begin receiving the best reporting on the issues that most affect the American West, contact us using the information above to start your subscription immediately. And we have good news for your friend: Ask for our "Friend Subscription" and we'll discount your second subscription.